JUDICIAL INDIVIDUALITY ON THE UK SUPREME COURT

This book presents an empirical analysis of the UK Supreme Court's output over its first ten years, with a specific focus on each individual judge's contribution to each case. It shows that judges, like all of us, are human; it would be difficult to imagine that any of us, even in our most professional capacity, could act completely independently of our predilections, motivations and biases. The same is true for the judges sitting on the UK's highest court.

Drawing on insights from a bespoke dataset of judgments, this work discerns trends and tendencies across each judge's voting patterns and the reasoning they adopt when disposing of cases. It not only highlights areas of divergence, but also shows how each of the judges tended to vote in different contexts, including which were more likely to overturn appeals from lower courts, side with certain parties such as the state or underdogs, and find liability in various areas (tort, contract, criminal, EU, immigration and tax law, with a special focus on human rights cases). Another section illustrates the differences between the judges when it comes to judicial reasoning, such as their approach to precedent and preferred methods of statutory interpretation.

This work shows that different judges exercise their power in different ways. Some are more comfortable with pushing boundaries whilst others are more restrained. Some grant the state a lot of leeway whilst others apply heavy scrutiny. Some are, as Lord Denning suggested, 'bold spirits' whilst others are 'timorous souls'. It shows, at least when it comes to the Supreme Court, that it matters who our judges are.

Hart Studies on Judging and the Courts: Volume 3

Hart Studies on Judging and the Courts

Series editors: Erin F Delaney, James Lee & Andrew Lynch

Hart Studies on Judging and the Courts aims to publish exceptional scholarship examining judges, the judiciary and the courts, from a range of doctrinal and theoretical perspectives. The primary focus is on appellate courts in the common law world, but we welcome submissions beyond this, including those offering a comparative angle, such as from civilian jurisdictions, or jurisdictions in developing nations. The series supports innovative work by emerging and established scholars in the field.

Volume 1: Values in the Supreme Court: Decisions, Division and Diversity
Rachel J Cahill O'Callaghan

Volume 2: Foreign Judges in the Pacific
Anna Dziedzic

Volume 3: Judicial Individuality on the UK Supreme Court
Lewis Graham

Judicial Individuality on the UK Supreme Court

Lewis Graham

• HART •
OXFORD • LONDON • NEW YORK • NEW DELHI • SYDNEY

HART PUBLISHING

Bloomsbury Publishing Plc

Kemp House, Chawley Park, Cumnor Hill, Oxford, OX2 9PH, UK

1385 Broadway, New York, NY 10018, USA

29 Earlsfort Terrace, Dublin 2, Ireland

First published in Great Britain 2025

A catalogue record for this book is available from the British Library.

A catalogue record for this book is available from the Library of Congress.

Library of Congress Control Number: 2024946864

ISBN: HB: 978-1-50997-110-7
ePDF: 978-1-50997-112-1
ePub: 978-1-50997-111-4

Typeset by Compuscript Ltd, Shannon

For Pat and Ron

ACKNOWLEDGEMENTS

My work on the Supreme Court began with my doctorate at the University of Cambridge, which was generously funded by the AHRC. There, my supervisors Mark Elliott and David Erdos helped ensure that I produced a defensible thesis within three years. That thesis became the basis for the present work. I am immensely grateful to them both.

This book took a long time, and there are too many people to acknowledge who have helped me on my way. They include Steven Vaughan, who supported this project from the start, and Akis Psygkas, who encouraged me to think about this kind of research back at my undergraduate degree at the University of Bristol. Special thanks should go to Lindsey Bell, Steven Greer, Jo Hynes, Elise Maes, Jennifer Russell, Alex Sinclair, Joe Tomlinson, my colleagues at Wadham College and my colleagues at Public Law Project for help, support and encouragement at various points over the last few years.

Thank you also to the team at Hart, especially Kate Whetter, for their invaluable assistance throughout the whole publication process. It has been a very smooth ride and I have felt incredibly privileged to be working with such a kind team, especially considering some serious road bumps we encountered along the way.

As ever, the biggest thanks go to my wife Sophie, who has supported me in every way throughout this process.

CONTENTS

TABLE OF CASES

ECHR Case Law

EU Case Law

US Case Law

Domestic Case Law

1

Introduction: The Court and its Judges

This is a book about the UK Supreme Court (UKSC) and its judges. It discusses the paradoxical position of those judges, who act simultaneously in an individual and collective capacity. Individual judges are appointed; individual judges sit; individual judges write opinions. Individual judges discuss cases with other individual judges, and might dissent or disagree with other individual judges too. But the Court also operates as an institution. Judgments are attributable to the Court as a whole. Individual disagreements fall away once a majority emerges. The Court's authority is understood to be singular. The collective Court is in one sense *far more than* and in another sense *no more than*, the individual judges who comprise it. The Court *is* its judges; its judges *are* the Court.

Twenty-seven judges were appointed to the Court's permanent roster during its first decade. This already places significant power in the hands of a small number of individuals. But the Court sits with a maximum of twelve members at any given time. A smaller number of judges – ordinarily just five – will sit and hear any given case. Even then, the bench in a given case might be split, where as few as three judges may carry the day. These majority judges will not necessarily contribute to the judgment equally; typically only some judges will write, with one judge usually authoring a lead judgment setting out the Court's most authoritative position. In such a case, it might be said that one single judge is speaking for – or perhaps speaking as? – the UKSC. The individual judges sitting on the Court therefore do not just wield collective power, but hold a lot of individual influence, too. It therefore matters a great deal who our judges are, and it matters a great deal how they think, because it matters a great deal what they do. The link between all three is a major theme in this book.

This work focuses on the *individual dimension* to judicial decision-making on the UKSC, and thus how the Court's output is shaped by the work of the *individual judges* within it. Those judges are 'human like everyone else'.[1] The central question in this study is therefore: how is the work of the Court affected by the 'humanity' of its judges?[2]

[1] S Sotomayor, Talk at University of Houston, 26 January 2018. See also Lord Dyson, 'The Shifting Sands of Statutory Interpretation, (Statute Law Society, 9 October 2010) 3: 'It may be surprising, but occasionally we need to remind ourselves that judges are human beings. They respond to problems in different ways.'

[2] To borrow a term used in A Paterson, *Final Judgment: The Last Law Lords and the Supreme Court* (Hart Publishing, 2013) 315.

Many further issues immediately arise for consideration: does it matter who our judges are? Does it matter which judge decides a case? How accurate is our current perception of the judicial role? The contours of these questions will be unpacked and examined fully in the following chapters. At the outset, however, this introductory chapter will set up some of the relevant background issues to these questions, including the ever-present caricature of judicial neutrality, and will lay out the specific lines of enquiry which this work will later explore.

I. The Humanity of the Judiciary

The humanity of the judges is bound up with their role. This requires some examination of what that role is, or what it ought to be. Whilst it would be too audacious to set out some absolute definition here, it is apt to begin with one common and straightforward understanding, which is that the courts simply apply the laws drawn up by the legislature. To do this, the judges apply objective, wholly detached reasoning, and do not, or at least should not, draw upon their own values, policies or preferences. If this is how the judicial function operates, the composition of the judiciary, and the personal values and preferences of the individual judges, would be totally irrelevant to the outcome of cases so long as the judges were doing their job 'correctly'.[3] It would be 'largely immaterial'[4] which judge from an available pool were to sit on a particular case. The humanity of the individual judge would – or at least *should* – be forsaken in the pursuance of the Court's collective objectives.

This crude understanding of how our courts work, although superficially attractive, is clearly false. Although the 'pure' declaratory theory of law has long since become moribund, its essence, that the law and its application (and therefore who the judge is and what they do), are not just separable but must *necessarily be separate*, continues to stick around. This is the case, regardless of whether the judge's job is conceived of as applying the written law, some breed of natural or objective rights, or some patchwork of Dworkinian principles. There is, in each case, an impermissible barrier between the act of judging *and the one doing the judging*. This, to anyone with even a basic understanding of how human decision-making processes work, is surely very odd. And yet the idea is not just popular, but attractive, too: it is easier to justify the constitutional position of the judges if they are taken to be absolutely neutral and perfectly objective. This kind of unreal detachment is sometimes framed as something which is essential to the very idea of justice, fairness and authority in the judicial context.

[3] That is not to deny that the composition of the judiciary may be important for reasons beyond case outcomes: JUSTICE, 'Increasing Judicial Diversity' (April 2017) at justice.org.uk/increasing-judicial-diversity/#:~:text=In%20April%202017%2C%20JUSTICE%20published,backgrounds%20in%20reaching%20the%20bench.

[4] This was the view of Atiyah: P Atiyah, 'Judicial-Legislative Relations in Britain' in RA Katzmann (ed), *Judges and Legislators: Towards Institutional Comity* (Brookings, 1988) 137.

This standard of neutrality is humanly impossible. And yet our judges are human. They *will* hold values, preferences, ideologies, ideas and biases. They *will* be sympathetic to certain groups, and care less about others. They *will* have ideas about the role courts should play in the constitutional framework. It is impossible to imagine that judges, with their own 'experience of life',[5] would not bring all of this to the Court with them. It would be strange if judges were different from the rest of us in this respect. Lord Justice Balcombe has stated that judges 'cannot, even if they might prefer otherwise, refrain from taking a view on social and moral issues'.[6] As Michael Kirby, former Justice of the High Court of Australia, put it, 'if judges say that they have no sin of personal inclinations … they deceive themselves'.[7] Lord Hoffmann seemed relatively confident that different judges assumed their own 'doctrinal disposition[s]'[8] and Lord Sumption has admitted that UKSC judges 'have differences of outlook, as one would expect of any twelve intelligent, articulated and opinionated people'.[9]

The more important question is whether these predilections, held by virtue not of being judges but of being human, filter through the conscious adherence to judicial neutrality and affect judicial performance. Intuitive though an affirmative answer to this question may seem, judges are often framed as 'cognitively exceptional'[10] in this regard. For example, it is sometimes suggested that judges can, either naturally or through training, leave their preferences aside and conduct their work without being influenced by their own ideals. As Linda Mulcahy put it: 'Judges are expected to rise above personal politics, to resist and transcend their personal, instinctive and intuitive sympathies and submit to something beyond them.'[11] Some judges see this as a reasonable, and achievable, possibility.[12] Certainly

[5] BBC Law in Action, 'The Supreme Court' (BBC Radio 4, 26 February 2019) per Lady Hale. Elsewhere, Hale has said that 'everyone brings their own inarticulate premises to the business of making the difficult choices inevitably involved in judging': Lady Hale, 'Women in the Judiciary' (The Law Society, 27 June 2014) 22.

[6] J Balcombe, 'Judicial Decisions and Social Attitudes' (1993) 84 *Proceedings of the British Academy* 209, 233.

[7] M Kirby, 'A Darwinian Reflection on Judicial Values' in J Lee (ed), *From House of Lords to Supreme Court: Judges, Jurists and the Process of Judging* (Hart Publishing, 2011) 18. See also J Bell, *Policy Arguments in Judicial Decisions* (OUP, 1983) 247: 'a judge does not come to a case neutral'.

[8] *Lewis v AG of Jamaica* [2001] 2 AC 50 at [90].

[9] Paterson (n 2) 272.

[10] G Edmond and K Martire, 'Just Cognition: Scientific Research on Bias and some Implications for Legal Procedure and Decision-Making' (2019) 82(4) *MLR* 633, 664.

[11] L Mulcahy, 'The Possibilities and Desirability of Mediator Neutrality: Towards an Ethic of Partiality' (2001) 10(4) *Social & Legal Studies* 506. See also B Barry, *How Judges Judge: Empirical Insights into Judicial Decision-Making* (Routledge, 2021) 1: 'Often, judges admirably resist, or at least strive to resist, some of the insidious consequences of [factors beyond the law]. Mindful of the lofty standards expected of them, judges aspire to perform the task of judging solely within the four corners of applicable law.' And see more generally, L Barmes and K Malleson, 'Lifting the Judicial Identity Blackout' (2018) 38(2) *Legal Studies* 357, 367–68.

[12] See eg Lord Bingham (judges are 'the product of their upbringing, experience and background' but they can 'alert themselves to, and … neutralize, any extraneous considerations which might bias their judgments': *The Rule of Law* (Penguin, 2011) 93). Interestingly, whilst the European Convention

Lord Neuberger has made statements suggesting that personal preferences can be, if not eliminated, at least restrained: 'all good judges have learnt to keep their prejudices and hobby-horses under control when sitting on the bench'.[13] For others, this is seen as an impossibility: Terence Etherton has stated that it is 'impossible to exclude' all personal preferences from case consideration[14] and Lord Phillips has mused that such a proposition is 'perhaps mischievous to wonder' about.[15] Indeed, it seems almost impossible, even with significant training and diligence, to eliminate all personal aspects of decision-making altogether.[16] Benjamin Cardozo once declared that 'there is in each of us a stream of tendency, whether you choose to call it philosophy or not, which gives coherence and direction to thought and action. Judges cannot escape that any more than other mortals'.[17] As long ago as 1943, Lord Wright opined that 'the judge does not approach the case with a blank mind. Subconsciously or consciously, trained mental processes are involved, rules learned in the past function in his mind, his own past experience and his past reading of other cases all combine to lead to a judgment'.[18] This conclusion seems inescapable. Judging involves the 'authoritative allocation of values',[19] And as one senior Law Lord once remarked, such values are allocated on a basis 'upon which reasonable people may differ'.[20] This includes judges.

All of this is fairly anodyne. More interesting is whether judges have the *opportunity* to bring these preferences to fruition, and implement them in practice, during their work on the court. The answer is: they *very clearly* do. It is acknowledged, of course, that judges on UK courts are not totally free to do as they please, and there are many significant constraints on judicial creativity. Some trite examples include the fact that judges are bound by precedent, must adhere to the terms of legislation, must not 'legislate from the bench', and cannot question the validity of primary legislation. Indeed, some commentators have considered that these constraints are so significant that their existence provides a conclusive rebuttal to the idea that a judge's personal preferences might influence their role: however

of Human Rights includes, unsurprisingly, a notion of judicial neutrality within its 'right to a fair trial' under Article 6, in its case law, the Court has accepted that judges holding and even expressing political views is not problematic in and of itself, because they can be discarded when performing the judicial role: *Pitkevich v Russia*, Application 47936/99 (8 February 2001) *Previti v Italy* Application 45291/06 (8 December 2009).

[13] Lord Neuberger, 'Tweaking the Curial Veil' (Blackstone Lecture 2014, 15 November 2014) para 48.

[14] T Etherton, 'Liberty, the archetype and diversity: a philosophy of judging' [2010] *PL* 727, 743. See also Lady Hale, 'Principle and pragmatism in developing private law' (Cambridge Freshfields Lecture, 7 March 2019).

[15] Lord Phillips, 'Terrorism and Human Rights' (2006) 2(2) *High Court Quarterly Review* 61, 71.

[16] R West, R Meserve and K Stanovich, 'Cognitive sophistication does not attenuate the bias blind spot' (2012) 103 *Journal of Personality and Social Psychology* 506.

[17] B Cardozo, *The Nature of the Judicial* Process (Yale University Press, 1921) 12.

[18] Lord Wright, 'Precedents' (1943) 8(2) *CLJ* 118, 138. In doing so, he cited, seemingly approvingly, the work of Karl Llewellyn, one of the most famous writers of the American realist tradition.

[19] R Hodder-Williams, 'Six Notions of "Political" and the United States Supreme Court' (1992) 22 *British Journal of Political Science* 1, 2–3.

[20] *Piglowska v Piglowski* [1999] All ER 632. He went on to say that '[s]ince judges are also people, that means that some degree of diversity in their application is inevitable'.

radical a judge may be, there would be no space in our legal system for their influence to materialise in practice.[21]

With respect, this view is misconceived. Legal rules do not necessarily stand in opposition to, and prevent the seepage of, personal values. First, in the context of the UK's unwritten constitution, the contours of these aforementioned judicial limits are often determined, at least in part, by the judges themselves. They are bound by precedent, but determine what the relevant authorities stand for. They must apply the terms of primary legislation, but determine the meaning of that legislation. They must not legislate from the bench, but determine what judicial law-making constitutes in practice.[22] They must respect the sovereignty of Parliament, but have mused that even this cardinal rule may contain exceptions and conditions.[23] As such, the fact that the judges influence the contours of their own limitations means that the existence of these limitations cannot constitute some hard limit upon the influence of internal factors and personal preferences on judging.

A further point is that even if it is accepted that judges are significantly constrained in some areas, there remains a significant number of cases in which this is not the case. The common law is entirely judge-made and is 'awash in the rolling and mucky waters of political power'.[24] Judges can determine the validity of secondary legislation and the legality of actions taken by the government and other public bodies, free from the dampener of sovereignty (although Parliament is in theory free to overturn any judicial decision it pleases, the 'Hobbesian Sovereign … only most infrequently bothers to interfere' with judicial decisions in practice).[25] Many laws invite judges to apply their own discretion[26] or otherwise to *exercise their own judgment*,[27] and to engage with public policy in

[21] E Thomas, *The Judicial Process* (CUP, 2005) 86; F Morrison, *Courts and the Political Process in England* (Sage, 1973) 174, 224; J Waltman and K Holland, *The Political Role of Law Courts in Modern Democracies* (Palgrave Macmillan, 1988) 118 and S Lee, *Judging Judges* (Faber & Faber, 1988) 96, 155.

[22] Lord Hodge has noted that 'judges recognise that there is a boundary to judicial law-making but there is no consensus as to where it is': Lord Hodge, 'The scope of judicial decision-making in the common law tradition' (Max Planck Institute for Comparative and International Private Law, 28 October 2019).

[23] See eg *R (Privacy International) v Investigatory Powers* Tribunal [2019] UKSC 22; [2019] 4 All ER 1.

[24] A Hutchinson, 'Judges and Politics: An Essay from Canada' (2004) 24 *Legal Studies* 275, 284.

[25] D Robertson, *Judicial Discretion in the House of Lords* (Clarendon, 1998) 4. See also Lord Dyson, 'Are the Judges Too Powerful?' in *Justice: Continuity and Change* (Hart Publishing, 2018) 56 and R Stevens, *The English Judges: Their Role in the Changing Constitution* (Hart Publishing, 2002) 36–37, 45, 141.

[26] Stephen Sedley has noted that in the judicial behaviour literature the idea of 'discretion' is sometimes used to mean 'the entire process of choosing between or among available outcomes': see (1999) 58(3) *CLJ* 627.

[27] At this stage no distinction is made between so-called 'hard' and 'easy' cases, on which see J Crowe, 'Not-So-Easy Cases' (2019) 40(1) *Statute Law Review* 75; L Moran, 'In Conversation with Lord Justice Etherton: judicial legitimacy, diversity and the representation of judicial authority' [2010] *PL* 662, 663–65. Even if it is accepted that 'hard' cases can be meaningfully distinguished from 'easy' ones, the following analysis remains valid so long as a significant number of UKSC cases can be categorised as 'hard'.

one way or another.[28] It has been argued that the level of discretion available to judges is particularly heightened in public law and human rights cases[29] which have become an increasingly prominent feature of the modern judicial docket.[30]

Therefore in spite of, and in some ways because of, the nature of the UK constitution, there seems to be ample room for personal preferences and individual values held by judges to influence the law. Judging, like all decision-making, is a messy exercise, influenced by innumerable internal and external factors. To suggest that personal preferences, ideas and values would not form at least *part of* this array of influences is to deny the nature of human decision-making. Meanwhile, to suggest that there is no sufficient opportunity for a judge's internal world to affect their work is to deny the nature of judicial decision-making under the UK constitution.

This work seeks to try and make sense of the relationship between a judge's internal systems – their views, their values, their preferences – and their external work – their judgments. It asks: which internal factors are relevant and influential? How might their influence be measured? How do those preferences seem to influence judgments? How far do judges differ from one another in terms of the preferences they hold, and the strength with which they hold them? Can we make sense of these preferences by using political or other labels?

It goes without saying that I am not the first to ask these questions. Examining judicial behaviour is now an established field of study in its own right, with mountains of research, published and unpublished, seeking to understand how judges operate all over the world.[31] Some works have investigated these kinds of questions within the context of the UK judiciary, as I note below. But it would be fair to say that the most famous work in this field remains that emanating from the USA. As such, what follows is a quick primer on the so-called 'behavioural model' which has become so prominent in that jurisdiction.

II. The Behavioural Model

The 'behavioural model', simply put, suggests that judicial behaviour can be explained, and in some cases predicted, by looking at who the judges responsible

[28] T Koopmans, *Courts and Political Institutions: A Comparative View* (CUP, 2003) 282; Balcombe (n 6), 209–10; S Shetreet and W McCormack, *The Culture of Judicial Independence in a Globalised World* (Brill, 2016), 58; *cf* Waltman and Holland (n 21) 116–17: 'neither law nor its practice regularly confronts the major questions of public policy'.

[29] TT Arvind and L Stirton, 'Legal ideology, legal doctrine and the UK's top judges' [2016] *PL* 418, 434; Stevens (n 25) 138, 180–81. But the influence of judicial preferences cannot be said to be limited to public law or human rights cases: see eg Etherton (n 14) 742; L Whitehouse, S Bright and M Dhami, 'Improving procedural fairness in housing possession cases' (2019) 38(3) *CJQ* 351, 353–56.

[30] Morrison (n 21) suggests that in the 1970s, the UK court was not political, partially because it mainly dealt with 'private and criminal cases': 101, 115–8. This is no longer the case: Lord Neuberger, 'Judge not, that ye be not judged': Judging Judicial Decision-Making' (2016) 6 *UK Supreme Court Yearbook* 13, 16; K Malleson, *The New Judiciary: The Effects of Activism and Expansion* (Routledge, 1999) 7–35.

[31] For an extremely useful exploration of studies, past and present, into different aspects of judicial decision-making around the world, see Barry (n 11).

are and what they have done in the past. Generally, this work focuses on identifying the 'attitudes' of individual judges (a term wide enough to encompass almost any internal motivating behaviour, but is generally expressed in terms of ideology, values and goals),[32] usually (although often not exclusively) through examination of their past voting records. Put simply, if particularly noteworthy voting histories are uncovered, this may justify some inference about the attitude of the judges responsible for them: it is not a leap to suggest that a judge who consistently sides with the state holds a pro-state *attitude*.

Of course, the literature is more complex than this, with researchers differing sharply on questions relating to the means by which judicial behaviour should be measured, the strength of inferences which can be made from past behaviour, the appropriate methods and standards for analysis and computation, the appropriate labels to be applied, and so on. Studies have also differed in their treatment of the role played by other external[33] and internal[34] influences upon judicial behaviour. Despite these differences, the behavioural research as a whole has been extremely successful in demonstrating the attitudinal differences between individual judges in the US context. For example, studies have demonstrated ideological variance between judges at the federal[35] as well as state level,[36] and in relation to specific issues and categories of case.[37] The work does not always invoke political language when describing individual judicial behaviour, although many of the most

[32] For a good overview, see A Dyevre 'Unifying the Field of Comparative Judicial Politics: Towards a General Theory of Judicial Behaviour' (2010) 2(2) *European Political Science* Review 297. The most prominent work in this field remains E Segal and H Spaeth, *The Supreme Court and the Attitudinal Model Revisited* (CUP, 2002). Note also the so-called 'attribute model', which focuses on judicial characteristics rather than attitudes per se: Barry (n 11) 112–45; N Tate and R Handberg, 'Time Binding Theory and Theory Building in Personal Attribute Models of Supreme Court Voting Behaviour 1916–1988' (1991) 35 *American Journal of Political Science* 460; S Ulmer, 'Dissent Behaviour and the Social Background of Supreme Court Judges' (1970) 32 *Journal of Politics* 580; S Nagel, 'Testing Relationships between Judicial Characteristics and Judicial Decision-Making' (1962) 15(3) *Western Political Quarterly* 425.

[33] L Strother, 'Case Salience and the Influence of External Constraints on the Supreme Court' (2019) 7(1) *Journal of Law and Courts* 129; L Epstein, W Landes and R Posner, T*he Behavior of Federal Judges: A Theoretical and Empirical Study of Rational Choice* (Harvard, 2013) 116–20; M Bailey and F Maltzman, *The Constrained Court: Law, Politics, and the Decisions Justices Make* (Princeton, 2011); T Johnson, P Wahlbeck and J Spriggs, 'The Influence of Oral Arguments on the US Supreme Court' (2006) 100 *American Political Science Review* 99; H Gillman, 'What's law got to do with it? Judicial behaviouralists test the legal model of judicial decision making' (2001) 26 *Law and Social Inquiry* 465; D Songer and S Lindquist, 'Not the Whole Story: The Impact of Justices' Values on Supreme Court Decision Making' (1996) 40(4) *American Journal of Political Science* 1049; L Epstein, 'Courts and Interest Groups' in J Gates and C Johnson, *The American Courts: A Critical Assessment* (CQ Press, 1991).

[34] Ditto the above with regards to internal factors. See eg B Alaire and A Green, *Commitment and Cooperation on High Courts* (OUP, 2017) 39–40, 136–40; L Baum, 'Motivation and Judicial Behaviour: Expanding the Scope of Enquiry' in D Klein and G Mitchell (eds), *The Psychology of Judicial Decision Making* (OUP, 2010); L Epstein and J Knight, *The Choices Judges Make* (CQ Press, 1998); T Hagle, 'Freshman Effects for Supreme Court Justices' (1993) *American Journal of Political Science* 1142.

[35] See eg Segal and Spaeth (n 32); Epstein Landes and Posner (n 33).

[36] See eg A Segal, D Songer and M Cameron, 'Decision Making on the US Courts of Appeals' in L Epstein, *Contemplating Courts* (CQ Press, 1995); *cf* E Posner, *How Judges Think* (Harvard, 2008) 311–12; 370.

[37] See eg C Pritchett, *Civil Liberties and the Vinson Court* (Chicago, 1954) (on civil liberties); L Epstein, C Parker and J Segal, 'Do Justices Defend the Speech They Hate? An Analysis of In-Group

high-profile studies have placed judges on a liberal-conservative scale.[38] Indeed, the evidence demonstrating ideological differences between the US Supreme Court Justices has been so convincing that the idea of a political, partisan Court is now well-accepted, and is common in mainstream news reporting. The influence of the behavioural model is significant, and has influenced studies examining judicial behaviour across the world, for example (the following is necessarily a very partial and truncated list) in relation to judges and courts in Canada,[39] Australia,[40] South Africa,[41] India,[42] Israel,[43] Brazil,[44] Chile,[45] Ireland,[46] Spain,[47]

Bias on the US Supreme Court' (2018) 6(2) *Journal of Law and Courts* 237 (on free expression); T George and L Epstein, 'On the Nature of Supreme Court Decision Making' (1992) 86(2) *American Political Science Review* 323 (on capital punishment).

[38] See eg Segal and Spaeth (n 32) and S Segal, A Cover and D Albert, 'Ideological Values and the Votes of U.S. Supreme Court Justices' (1989) 83(2) *American Political Science Review* 557.

[39] D Songer et al, 'Law, Ideology and Collegiality: Judicial Behaviour in the Supreme Court of Canada' (McGill-Queens University Press, 2012); C Ostberg and M Wetstein, *Attitudinal Decision-Making in the Supreme Court of Canada* (UBC Press, 2007); C Ostberg, E Wetstein and C Ducat, 'Attitudinal Dimensions of Supreme Court Decision Making in Canada: The Lamer Court, 1991–1995' (2002) 55(1) *Political Research Quarterly* 235; N Tate and P Sittiwong, 'Decision Making in the Canadian Supreme Court: Extending the Personal Attributes Model Across Nations' (1989) 51(4) *The Journal of Politics* 900; S Peck, 'A Behavioural Approach to the Judicial Process: Scalogram Analysis' (1967) 5(1) *Osgoode Hall Law Journal* 1.

[40] G Appleby and A Lynch (eds), *The Judge, the Judiciary and the Court: Individual, Collegial and Institutional Judicial Dynamics in Australia* (CUP, 2021); R Smyth, 'Empirical Studies of Judicial Behavior and Decision-Making in Australian and New Zealand Courts' in N Garoupa, R Gill and B Tiede (eds), *High Courts in Global Perspective: Evidence, Methodologies, and Findings* (UVA Press, 2021); R Smyth, 'Explaining Voting Patterns on the Latham High Court 1935–50' (2002) 26 *Melbourne University Law Review* 8; G Schubert, 'Political Ideology on the High Court' (1968) 3(1) *Politics* 21; G Schubert, 'Opinion Agreement Among High Court Justices in Australia' (1968) 4 *Australia and New Zealand Journal of Sociology* 2.

[41] T Roux, *The Politics of Principle: the First South African Constitutional Court, 1995–2005* (CUP, 2013); S Haynie, 'Judicial decision-making and the use of panels in the South African Appellate Division, 1950–1990' (2002) 29 *South African Journal of Political Studies* 147.

[42] S Parikh, 'Empirical Studies of Judicial Behavior and Decision-Making on Indian Courts' in N Garoupa, R Gill and B Tiede (eds), *High Courts in Global Perspective: Evidence, Methodologies, and Findings* (UVA Press, 2021); A Chandrachud, 'An Empirical Study of the Supreme Court's Composition' (2011) 46 *Economic and Political Weekly* 71.

[43] T Eisenberg et al, 'Does the Judge Matter? Exploiting Random Assignment on a Court of Last Resort to Assess Judge and Case Selection Effects' (2012) 9 *Journal of Empirical Legal Studies* 246; T Eisenberg, T Fisher and I Rosen-Zvi, 'Israel's Supreme Court Appellate Jurisdiction: An Empirical Study' (2011) 96 *Cornell Law Review* 693.

[44] D Arguelhes and I Hartmann, 'Timing Control without Docket Control: How Individual Justices Shape the Brazilian Supreme Court's Agenda' (2017) 5(1) *Journal of Law and Courts* 105; S Desposato, M Ingram and O Lannes, 'Power, Composition, and Decision Making: The Behavioral Consequences of Institutional Reform on Brazil's Supremo Tribunal Federal' (2014) 31 *Journal of Law, Economics and Organization* 534.

[45] A Mediano and D Carrasco, 'Ideology beyond Partisanship: The Behavior of Judges on Freedom of Information Cases in Chile' (2019) 36 *Government Information Quarterly* 614; R Carroll and L Tiede, 'Judicial Behaviour on the Chilean Constitutional Court' (2011) 8 *Journal of Empirical Legal Studies* 856.

[46] R Elgie, A McAuley and E O'Malley, 'The (Not-so-Surprising) Non-Partisanship of the Irish Supreme Court' (2018) 33 *Irish Political Studies* 88.

[47] N Garoupa et al, 'Political Influence and Career Judges: An Empirical Analysis of Administrative Review by the Spanish Supreme Court' (2012) 9 *Empirical Legal Studies* 795; C Hanretty, 'Dissent in

Portugal,[48] France,[49] Germany,[50] Norway,[51] Bosnia,[52] the Philippines,[53] China[54] and Japan,[55] and more generally in jurisdictions covering Eastern Europe,[56] Asia,[57] Africa[58] and the Middle East.[59] That is to say, the scholarship on strategic judicial behaviour of judges is varied and plentiful.

Despite the distinctions between the various proposed models and the complexities of their results, there is more which unites these theories than divides them; they all have in common, at their core, the idea that judicial behaviour can be explained, at least partially, by something relating to the judges themselves: *who* they are, *how* they are, or *what they want*: (largely) *internal* factors as opposed to *external* factors such as the legal sources in play. The behavioural model makes a modest claim: judges are human, and in performing their job it is likely that the

Iberia: the Ideal Points of Justices on the Spanish and Portuguese Constitutional Tribunals' (2012) 51(5) *European Journal of Political Research*, 671.

[48] Hanretty, ibid.

[49] C Hönnige, 'The Electoral Connection: How the Pivotal Judge Affects Oppositional Success at European Constitutional Courts' (2009) 32(5) *West European Politics*, 963.

[50] ibid; G Vanberg, *Politics of Constitutional Review in Germany* (CUP, 2004).

[51] J Skiple et al, 'Supreme Court Justices' Economic Behaviour: A Multilevel Model Analysis' (2016) 13(1) *Scandinavian Political Studies* 73.

[52] A Schwartz, 'International Judges on Constitutional Courts: Cautionary Evidence from Post-Conflict Bosnia' (2019) 44(1) *and Social Enquiry* 1.

[53] B Dressel, T Inoue and C Bonoan, Justices and Political Loyalties: An Empirical Investigation of the Supreme Court of the Philippines, 1987–2020' (2023) *forthcoming*, Law and Social Inquiry; B Dressel and T Inoue, 'Informal networks and judicial decisions: Insights from the Supreme Court of the Philippines, 1986–2015' (2018) 39(5) *International Political Science Review* 616; D Gatmayan and C Magno, 'A review of appointments and nominations to the Philippine supreme court' (2018) *Asian Journal of Comparative Law* 61; D Pellegrina, L Escresa and N Garoupa, 'Measuring Judicial Ideal Points in New Democracies: the case of the Philippines (2014) 1(1) *Asian Journal of Law and Society* 125; S Haynie, 'Paradise Lost: Politicisation of the Philippines supreme court in the post Marcos era'(1998) 22(4) *Asian Studies Review* 459; N Tate and S Haynie, 'Authoritarianism and Functions of Courts: A time series analysis of the Philippine supreme court' (1993) 27(4) *Law and Society Review* 707.

[54] H Xin and Y Su, 'Do the Haves Come Out Ahead in Shanghai Courts?' (2013) 10(1) *Journal of Empirical Legal Studies* 120.

[55] J Ramseyer and E Rasmusen, 'Why are Japanese judges so conservative in politically charged cases?' (2001) 95 *American Political Science Review* 331.

[56] K Pócza (ed), *Constitutional Review in Central and Eastern Europe* (Routledge, 2024); K Pócza (ed), *Constitutional Politics and the Judiciary: Decision-making in Central and Eastern Europe* (Routledge, 2019).

[57] B Dressel, 'The Politics of Judicial Review in Asia' in D Law, H Lau and A Schwartz (eds), *The Oxford Handbook of Asian Constitutional Law* (OUP, 2023); C Lin and T Ginsburg, 'Judicial Behavior Research in East Asia' in N Garoupa, R Gill and B Tiede (eds), *High Courts in Global Perspective: Evidence, Methodologies, and Findings* (UVA Press, 2021); B Dressel, 'Courts and Constitutional Politics in Southeast Asia 'in M Bünte and B Dressel (eds), *Constitutions and Politics in Southeast Asia* (Routledge, 2017).

[58] D Lewis, 'Empirical Studies of African High Courts: An Overview' in N Garoupa, R Gill and B Tiede (eds), *High Courts in Global Perspective: Evidence, Methodologies, and Findings* (UVA Press, 2021); S Ryan, 'The Challenges of Researching African High Court Opinions' 32(4) *Legal References Services Quarterly* 294.

[59] C Aydin-Cakir, 'What do we know about the Middle Eastern Constitutional Courts?' in N Garoupa, R Gill and B Tiede (eds), *High Courts in Global Perspective: Evidence, Methodologies, and Findings* (UVA Press, 2021).

personal, internal dimension to decision-making plays at least *some* role, and that constraints do not completely eliminate the space for individual preferences and values to seep through into their judgments.

III. Judicial Behaviour and the UK Supreme Court

Despite its prominence in other jurisdictions, the 'behavioural model' feels somewhat alien to the UK academic landscape, where there are 'relatively few works that address the politics of judging'.[60] As scholars, we are seemingly 'far less attentive' to quantitative study of the judicial process compared to our US and international counterparts.[61] The existing scholarship tends to examine the judiciary as an institution, rather than the individual judges which comprise it.[62]

I will not spend too much time pontificating on the potential reasons for this lack of enthusiasm for examining individual judicial behaviour in the UK. The close association between the behavioural model and the US judiciary, one very different from our own, probably does not help matters. Certainly, the idiosyncrasies of the US system make it an ideal candidate for studies of judicial behaviour. The process of appointing appellate judges in that jurisdiction, for example, is more overtly ideologically-driven than that of most other jurisdictions.[63] But it is difficult to see why the admittedly very different process of appointment for senior judges in the UK[64] would foreclose the possibility of judges acting on their own preferences (ideological or otherwise). It may be true that political appointment processes encourage ideological behaviour, but they do not *cause* it; therefore, it is not the case that an apolitical appointment process prevents ideological behaviour from occurring. Studies looking at other jurisdictions convincingly point to the appointment process as just one of many factors which influence legal decision-making.[65]

[60] Arvind and Stirton (n 29) 424.

[61] J Skiple et al, 'Supreme Court Justices' Economic Behaviour: A Multilevel Model Analysis' (2016) 13(1) *Scandinavian Political Studies* 73, 74.

[62] Stevens (n 25); R Stevens, *Law and Politics: The House of Lords as a Judicial Body 1800–1976* (Weidenfeld and Nicolson, 1979); L Blom-Cooper and G Drewry, *Final Appeal: A Study of the House of Lords in its Judicial Capacity* (OUP, 1972).

[63] By contrast, in the UK, studies have shown no link between the behaviour of a judge and the party in power at the time of appointment in the UK context: E Salzberger and F Fenn, 'Judicial Independence: Some Evidence from the English Court of Appeal' (1999) 42(2) *Journal of Law and Economics* 831.

[64] Most judicial appointments are handled by the Judicial Appointments Commission:. The process for appointing Supreme Court judges is different, and involves an ad hoc independent commission: www.supremecourt.uk/about/appointments-of-justices.html. The old 'tap on the shoulder' approach inevitably involved a consideration of the ideological mettle of appointees: J Griffith, *Politics of the Judiciary*, 5th edn (Fontana Press, 1997) 14, 17.

[65] E McFarlane, 'Consensus and Unanimity at the Supreme Court of Canada' (2010) 52 *Supreme Court Law Review* 379; D Weiden, 'Judicial Politicization, Ideology, and Activism at the High Courts of the United States, Canada, and Australia' (2011) 64(2) *Political Research Quarterly* 335.

An examination into individual judicial values requires, for a start, at least an open mind about its realist underpinnings, and at least a partial abandonment of the purely formalist model outlined at the beginning of this chapter. In the UK, there has been a stubborn adherence, in classrooms as well as courtrooms,[66] to the long-outdated conceptions of judging sketched out at the beginning of this chapter, whereby judges are framed as absolutely neutral arbiters, impervious to external (or internal) influence.[67] Of course, there may be good reasons for portraying judges this way.[68] But this does not mean that this is necessarily the truth of the matter – official judicial performance might not match with empirical reality. In any case, the fact that this view is widely held should not in itself present a barrier to academic study into the reality of that view.

However, lying just beneath this superficial acceptance of the impenetrable, impossibly neutral judge is an important vein of scholarship which has been deeply sceptical of this idea.[69] In his influential work *The Politics of the Judiciary* Griffith lambasted, with characteristic aplomb, the British judges as being conservative, elitist and out of touch[70] (although paradoxically, as Lord Dyson has pointed out, those same judges have been described in the tabloid press as liberal, bleeding-heart 'do-gooders').[71] Feminist and critical scholars working in the UK have criticised the power dynamics disguised and legitimated by the idea of absolute judicial neutrality.[72] The influence of American critical scholarship has cropped up in numerous, sometimes quite surprising, places.[73] Certain commentators have

[66] A number of judges seem to adhere to this view: see P Darbyshire, *Sitting in* Judgment (Hart Publishing, 2011) 401.

[67] S Bandes, 'Empathetic Judging and the Rule of Law' (2009) *Cardozo Law Review De Novo* 133; R Moorhead, 'The Passive Arbiter: Litigants in Person and the Challenge to Neutrality' (2007) 16(3) *Social and Legal Studies* 405. There is, according to Stevens, an 'old English intellectual chestnut [that] if the judges do something, it is, by definition, non-political': R Stevens, 'Unpacking the Judges' (1993) 46 *CLP* 1, 19.

[68] As well as making the judiciary seem more legitimate, repeated 'official' perceptions of judges as neutral arbiters might, in a roundabout way, discourage explicitly ideological behaviour: A Paterson, *The Law Lords* (Palgrave Macmillan, 1982) 102–09, 132–46, 170–76; Thomas (n 21) 244, 246–48, 250–51; Morrison (n 21) 28–29.

[69] This judge has been described as a 'deeply entrenched myth' (G Drewry, 'Judges and Political Inquiries: Harnessing a Myth' (1975) 23 *Political Studies* 49, 49), an 'illusion', 'myth' or 'misunderstanding' (Moran (n 27) 664); a 'myth' which is 'unlikely to last much longer' (Kirby (n 7) 12); a 'fig leaf' (Stevens (n 25) 180).

[70] Griffith (n 64).

[71] Lord Dyson, 'Criticising Judges: Fair Game or Off-Limits?' (Third Annual Bailii Lecture, 27 November 2014) 19.

[72] Barmes and Malleson (n 11); U Schulz and G Shaw (eds), *Gender and Judging* (Hart Publishing, 2013); R Hunter, C McGlynn and E Rackley (eds), *Feminist Judgments: From Theory to Practice* (Hart Publishing, 2010); Moran (n 27) 666–71.

[73] In writing *Judicial Discretion in the House of Lords*, for example, David Robertson admitted that he 'perhaps unconsciously' became a 'convert … to judicial realism' (n 25, vi). Senior judges have occasionally cited 'realist' passages with apparent approval: see eg Lady Hale, 'Appointments to the Supreme Court' (University of Birmingham, 6 November 2015), citing B Cardozo, *The Nature of the Judicial Process* (Yale University Press, 1921) 177. For a more historic example, see Lord Wright's invocation of the wisdom of Karl Llewellyn (n 18).

long accepted that judges are not 'ideologically homogenous' and have argued that it is improper to treat them as such,[74] and the idea that it is worth investigating whether the identity of the judge(s) deciding a case might make a difference is far from a novel one.[75] It is this counter-strand of academic thought, sceptical of the fig-leaf of absolute neutrality, to which this book is heavily indebted.

It is worth noting that these ideas are not limited to cynical academics. Some very senior judges have made comments which, perhaps surprisingly, suggest at least an openness to the behaviouralist endeavour.[76] Lady Hale seems to have acknowledged that some judges are inherently more likely to be sympathetic to certain claims compared to others.[77] Lord Reed was able to identify judges who are guided by a 'strong and instinctive sense of justice' above all else as well as those who apply 'a more legalistic approach'.[78] Lord Neuberger suggested that he was particularly proud of convincing Lords Reed and Kerr to agree to his lead judgment in the *Evans* case, because they are at the 'opposite ends of the spectrum'.[79] In fact, Lord Neuberger has made a number of fascinating statements in public lectures and speeches. Writing in 2022, he 'challenge[d] anyone to identify an experienced judge who has not on occasion let their feelings cloud their judgment'[80] (a challenge I am very happy to take up in this work), whilst in a speech from November 2014 he said:

> It is of course inevitable that there are differences in outlook and variations in temperament between the Justices, and it is, I believe, inevitable that a judge's particular outlook and temperament will sometimes play a part in his or her decision making.[81]

In a later speech, he suggested that '[w]e are all subject to conscious and unconscious biases … one cannot be a functional human being without having preconceived ideas and notions'[82] and elsewhere that judges would be

[74] D Robertson, 'Judicial Ideology in the House of Lords: A Jurimetric Analysis' (1982) 12(1) *British Journal of Political Science* 1, 2.

[75] See eg in relation to administrative law: V Bondy and M Sunkin, 'Accessing Judicial Review' [2008] *Public Law* 647; L Bridges, G Meszaros and M Sunkin, *Judicial Review in Perspective*, 2nd edn (Cavendish, 1995) 164–90.

[76] See, in addition to sources below, references at n 14 and n 15.

[77] She suggested that some judges prefer 'pragmatism' whilst others prefer to start with 'principle', and some are 'greater believers in freedom of contract' than others: Lady Hale (n 14). She also admitted that during her time working in personal injury law, it was known that some judges were 'instinctively in favour of claimants' and others 'instinctively in favour of defendants' and that some judges were more likely to be in favour of mothers and wives, and others for fathers and husbands: see B Hale, 'Safeguarding London's Standing in International Dispute Resolution' (Prospect Webinars, 6 October 2020).

[78] Lord Reed, 'Tribute for Lord Kerr' (UK Supreme Court, 30 September 2020).

[79] A Paterson, 'Presidency and the Supreme Court: Lord Neuberger's Legacy' (UCL Judicial Institute, 2 December 2019) 48.

[80] D Neuberger, 'On the Bench with Brenda' in R Hunter and E Rackley (eds), *Justice for Everyone: the Jurisprudence and Legal Lives of Brenda Hale* (CUP, 2022) 18.

[81] Lord Neuberger (n 13).

[82] Lord Neuberger, 'The Role of the Judge: Umpire in a Contest, Seeker of the Truth or Something in Between?' (Singapore Panel on Judicial Ethics and Dilemmas on the Bench, 19 August 2016).

'superhuman' if they could cast such convictions completely aside.[83] In March 2018, he delivered a lecture featuring a surprisingly stark insider view of the judicial role, acknowledging the reality of individual judicial approaches.[84] He said that 'judicial temperaments vary', and that since judicial pronouncements ultimately amount to 'no more than matters of opinion', it would be unsurprising that 'different judges might come to different conclusions' on a range of issues. He suggested that when it came to statutory interpretation, he and his colleagues would fall 'on a spectrum' and that he would have a 'pretty clear idea' of the sort of approach they would take. He even admitted that as President, when involved in panel selection for a controversial case, he would take care to ensure that there was 'ideological balance' on the Court, viewing some judges as 'progressives' in a given area and others as 'conservatives'. If these astonishing comments are at all accurate, they give strong weight to the idea that the behavioural model of judging might be applicable in the UK context.

A. The UK Supreme Court

Why, then, does this work focus on the Supreme Court? In one sense, the answer is obvious: it is the UK's most senior court, holds the most power, and deals with the most interesting and difficult cases. Its judgments are public and easily accessible. It mostly deals with questions of law rather than disputes of fact, and is a generalist court which considers a wide array of cases. Importantly, it operates in something of a sweet spot for empirical judicial studies: its judicial roster and case output is small enough for examination to be manageable, but significant enough for the results to be meaningful.

This might be especially significant given the UKSC's use of judicial panels. The Court (usually) maintains a roster of twelve judges, but judges sit in smaller panels, usually five at a time. The exact criteria for panel formulation remains somewhat vague, but it seems to be the case that panel selection involves consideration of each judge's availability, their personal expertise (the so-called 'horses for courses' approach), their interest in the case, and their general case load. There is also an attempt to align the judges hailing from devolved institutions with cases emanating from their respective jurisdictions.[85] Any ideological considerations, or any consideration of allocating judges to cases in order to influence its outcome are, at least officially, completely excluded. But if our judges *do* hold preferences and these preferences might affect their behaviour in a given case, the composition of a judicial panel might, in fact, be very important. Could it be said that one panel of judges might be more favourable to a case than a differently composed one?

[83] Lord Neuberger (BBC World News, HardTALK, 30 January 2018).

[84] Lord Neuberger, 'Judicial Impartiality: Essential or Impossible?' (Clare College Cambridge, 12 March 2018). Some of the surrounding quotes are direct quotes from the oral lecture, whilst others are taken from a response to a question posed by the author.

[85] See ch 4.

Those who have sought to understand judicial behaviour in the past have also tended to focus on the UKSC and its predecessor, the Judicial Committee of the House of Lords (HoL). Alan Paterson's two masterworks *The Law Lords*[86] and *Final Judgment*,[87] comprehensively detail the 'inner workings' of the House of Lords and UKSC. Both are cited heavily in the present work, but as Paterson himself accepts, they focus on the social processes of appellate decision-making rather than the impact of decision-making or the temperance of individual judges.[88] David Robertson's *Judicial Discretion in the House of Lords*[89] is now over 20 years old but for a long time was the most significant work on individual and collective aspects of judicial decision-making in the UK. Whilst he embarked upon '[n]o extensive attempt … to predict the behaviour of individual judges', his data did show some trends which allowed for a 'high level of prediction' in some instances.[90] Robertson's work undoubtedly remains the touchstone of this sort of empirical work, but since he stops short of offering a wholesale account of judicial approaches, and the data is now outdated, there is definite scope to go beyond his work.

More recently, some specific studies have been published, each examining certain kinds of judicial behaviour on the UKSC across a certain period.[91] Each study employed different methods, and sought to measure different things (Dickson, for example, has investigated the extent to which both the Court as a whole and its individual judges employ judicial activism,[92] Arvind and Stirton have looked at how individual judges approach the powers of public authorities,[93] and others have focused on human rights cases).[94] Each is important, and all are interesting in their own right. They set the scene for a more integrated approach examining multiple different facets of judicial behaviour.

The two most impressive works undertaking general, holistic assessments of individual judicial behaviour on the UKSC were published in 2020. The first is *Values in the Supreme Court*[95] by Rachel Cahill-O'Callaghan, which is a fascinating

[86] Paterson (n 68).

[87] Paterson (n 2).

[88] ibid 2.

[89] Robertson (n 25).

[90] ibid 40, 50–53. Another study has found (very moderate) differences between judges in this same era: M Iaryczower and G Katz, 'More than Politics: Ability and Ideology in the British Appellate Committee' (2016) 32(1) *Journal of Law, Economics and Organizations* 61.

[91] In addition to those noted below, see R Hunter and E Rackley, 'Judicial Leadership on the UK Supreme Court' 38(2) *Legal Studies* 191; H Tyrrell, *Human Rights in the UK and the Influence of Foreign Jurisprudence* (Hart Publishing, 2018).

[92] B Dickson, 'Activism and Restraint within the UK Supreme Court' (2015) 21(1) *European Journal of Current Legal Issues.*

[93] Arvind and Stirton (n 29).

[94] T Poole and S Shah, 'The Law Lords and Human Rights' (2011) 74 *MLR* 79; B Dickson, 'UK Supreme Court Justices and Human Rights in the 2015–16 Legal Year' (2016) 7 *UK Supreme Court Yearbook* 214; M Blackwell, 'Indeterminacy, Disagreement and the Human Rights Act: An Empirical Study of Litigation in the UK House of Lords and Supreme Court 1997–2017' (2020) 83(2) *Modern Law Review* 285.

[95] R Cahill-O'Callaghan, *Values in the Supreme Court* (Hart Publishing, 2020).

account of how psychological values affect decision-making, including in the judicial context.[96] Not only does it show that judges draw upon values in the decision-making process, but that individual judges are guided by different values; in doing so, it succeeds in uncovering 'the myth of objectivity and impartiality'[97] of which this thesis also seeks to scrutinise. The work is not only novel in terms of the perspective offered, but is perhaps the most significant work to analyse the behaviour of individual judges to date. The work differs from the present due to its unique use of psychological values to construct judicial profiles, the pursuit of slightly different goals and the use of significantly different methods.

The second, Chris Hanretty's *A Court of Specialists*[98] is the most well-developed empirical analysis of the UKSC and its judgments published so far. It seeks to uncover influences on UKSC decision-making, including at various points the various influences on individual judges. In a particularly illuminating chapter,[99] Hanretty uses a particular model[100] to interrogate the inter-agreement and dissent rates of judges, finding patterns that are interpreted upon an ideological dimension. Although it varies in many respects from the present work, it is a sophisticated example of the sort of insight that empirical analysis can generate, and is the most thorough empirical treatment of (certain aspects of) the UKSC's work to date. At the same time, most of Hanretty's analysis concerns the output of the Court in its collective dimension, and even in this respect the present work differs, including applying a different methodology and drawing insights from a legal content.[101]

The breadth and depth of these works is impressive. Whilst for the most part, I did not have the benefit of consulting and learning from those works directly during the time of writing, this work owes a great debt to both. Hanretty and Cahill-O'Callaghan have produced thorough and sophisticated works which take judicial behaviour on the UK Supreme Court seriously. Their models and methods are distinct from (and in many ways more sophisticated than) those employed here, and we each have different subjects and particular goals. But it is encouraging to see the emergence – and success – of empirical legal work which focuses on the UK Supreme Court. I hope that this work can contribute something positive to this blossoming space.

It is clear, then, that there exists some theoretical support for the idea that in the UK, individual judges might engage their personal preferences when doing their job, and that this might affect the judgments they produce. There is also some limited but important empirical support for the idea. This work seeks to go

[96] For a review, see (2020) 47(3) *Journal of Law and Society* 526.
[97] Cahill-O'Callaghan (n 95) Prologue.
[98] C Hanretty, *A Court of Specialists* (OUP, 2020).
[99] ibid ch 8.
[100] A variant of an item-response model, outlined in ch 2 of this work and explained further in Hanretty's book.
[101] Hanretty himself suggests that the work is not 'a book about law', although it certainly does reveal a lot more about how law operates compared to many more 'legal' texts.

further and test empirically the extent of individual judicial approaches across the output of the UKSC. It is, importantly, designed as a wide and general study, focusing on all cases which reach the Court rather than a study of a specific field of law. The full scope and methods of the project are set out in chapter two, but my goal boils down to this: can we understand something about the preferences held by the judges on the Court, exclusively from looking at their judgments (which includes considering both outcomes and reasoning)? If it is true that judges with a progressive disposition decide cases differently from their more conservative-minded colleagues, we *should* start to see some evidence of this, one way or another, in the Court's output. And if this is the case, we may be able to identify *which* judges influence which kinds of output, and impute something about the preferences and values they hold. This has been done successfully in certain jurisdictions. Could this be true with respect to the UK's Supreme Court too? Could we have our own judicial *types* on the Court?

This work will begin (chapter two) with a brief overview of the methods adopted and employed in order to investigate these questions, and provides an explanation of the dataset which was used to conduct the quantitative analysis presented later in the work. The bulk of the book considers, explores and explains the trends which emerge from that dataset. First, chapter three looks at the nature and extent of each judge's overall contributions to the Court, including how involved each was with the Court's work, the frequency and length of their judgments, and the propensity of each to lead, concur and dissent. Chapters four to eight look at the substantive content of the Court's decisions, both in terms of what was actually decided and the reasoning adopted. Separate chapters consider the judges' approach to the court subject to appeal (chapter four); the parties involved (chapter five); the subject of the case at hand (chapter six, with chapter seven focusing exclusively on cases involving human rights issues), and the available legal tools and techniques available (chapter eight). Chapter nine looks at the political dimension(s) of judicial decision-making and presents individual judicial profiles of the Court's members. Chapter ten considers the changes which have occurred on the Court since the period at which the dataset cuts off, as well as possible future developments. Chapter eleven brings the book to a close by offering some conclusions and considering the implications of the work.

IV. Conclusions

In the UK, we have largely resisted the idea that our judges channel their own preferences and values into their job; perhaps this is understandable to some extent, and there are certainly benefits to adopting our traditional 'ostrich posture'.[102]

[102] Segal and Spaeth (n 32) 26.

But doing so is at odds with both common sense and what is now a vast corpus of scholarship, looking at judiciaries across various jurisdictions, which suggests that Herculean detachment is impossible.

Judges are human. They are bound to have preferences and values. The domestic system allows these to come to the fore – as long ago as 1972, commentators were able to declare that '[i]ndividuality remains the essential characteristic of the English judicial function'.[103] Indeed, judges display their individual personalities, preferences and ideals when performing other roles, such as conducting inquiries and delivering public speeches.[104] Would it be such a stretch to suggest that they play a role in decision-making, too? And if so, how much do individual preferences seep through and affect the output of the Court? How different are the preferences of our judges? Does it matter which judges decide cases and does it matter who sits on a given panel?

The Supreme Court officially opened its doors in October 2009, its creation in part spurred on by a desire for greater transparency and independence than its previous incarnation as the Appellate Committee of the House of Lords. The Court celebrated its tenth anniversary in 2019, leaving a decade's worth of judgments to examine. Much has changed in that time, including the public interest in the judges sitting in our highest court. The political response to the Brexit litigation, and particularly the media's obsession with 'spider-woman' Lady Hale,[105] showed how, perhaps aided by the rise of social media, discussions – and grievances – about UKSC judges are becoming more common. Taking all of this into account, it is apt to note that at the advent the Supreme Court's opening, Terence Etherton remarked that '[t]here can be no better time to understand, and be honest about, the true nature of how [judges] do and should make decisions'.[106] This work seeks, at least in some small way, to do just that.

[103] Blom-Cooper and Drewry (n 62) 79.

[104] Griffith (n 64) 25–38; 42–46; Darbyshire (n 66) 139–40; Stevens (n 25) 51–53, 59–61, 92.

[105] A moniker which she has seemingly since reclaimed for herself: Lady Hale, *Spider Woman: A Life* (Vintage, 2021).

[106] Etherton (n 14) 746.

2

Measuring Judicial Behaviour

This chapter will set out the scope of the remainder of the work and will describe the methods employed to generate the data and tables which appear in the following chapters. To reiterate, I am trying to see whether, by looking at what different judges on the Supreme Court said and did in their judgments, and looking for distinctive features, patterns or trends which may arise, we can learn something about the individual judges on the Court. As was noted in the previous chapter, this book is far from the first to attempt quantification of judicial outputs. However, the methods employed in other studies cannot be straightforwardly imported into the present context without discrimination. Any good quantitative study of a particular jurisdiction must take into consideration the specific characteristics of that jurisdiction.[1] This is especially important considering that many of the most important works in this area, for better or worse, focus on the USA and the quite particular – and in many ways fairly unusual – legal system there. As judges on both sides of the Atlantic will attest, their respective Supreme Courts may share a name, but they are otherwise very different indeed.

This chapter, therefore, will set out, first, *what* I have measured (and why), and second, *how* I measured it. Naturally, these two questions are not distinct: questions relating to what counts as a good indicator of judicial behaviour, or which variables are to be measured will, to a significant degree, depend on how the methodology adopted for measuring that behaviour works. Nevertheless, the two are tackled separately here, for ease of explanation.

I. Study Parameters

A. What is Being Measured?

Many accounts of judicial behaviour understandably seek to employ political terms, where judges are described as liberals, conservatives and centrists. However

[1] See R Smyth, 'Explaining Voting Patterns on the Latham High Court 1935–50' (2002) 26 *Melbourne University Law Review* 8, 107–108; C Ostberg, E Wetstein and C Ducat, 'Attitudinal Dimensions of Supreme Court Decision Making in Canada: The Lamer Court, 1991–1995' (2002) 55(1) *Political Research Quarterly* 235, 237–39.

attractive such a prospect may be, political terms such as 'left', 'right', 'liberal' and 'conservative' are slippery and ambiguous.[2] They are difficult to define and even more difficult to apply.[3] Anyone employing them in the context of judicial behaviour should proceed very cautiously.[4] I am not totally against these labels (in any case, it would be unrealistic to disavow them completely, given that it is doubtful that we can really treat 'preferences', 'values', 'ideologies' and 'political positions' as distinct things, as it is not at all clear where each properly begins and ends) but I suggest that they are better used as part of a second-stage evaluation, employed to describe the results of the dataset analysis, rather than being part of the primary coding exercise. Chapter ten features an attempt, even if it is somewhat crude, to do this.

Therefore, in this work, we will save the 'politics' of judicial behaviour for later. The present study is engaged with the question of *general* judicial behaviour. This means that the measured variables should, so far as possible, be applicable across the range of cases Supreme Court judges might hear. Nonetheless, because the Supreme Court decides upon a huge range of issues, it needs to be acknowledged that judicial behaviour might not be uniform across all areas.[5] For this reason, rather than focusing on one particular, contestable measure of 'judicial behaviour', the dataset sought to capture a number of different measures, some relating to general issues (do judges tend to agree with the judges in the courts below?),[6] with others relating to certain specific areas of law (do judges tend to uphold contracts?).[7] A full explanation of each of the measured dimensions, and detail as to how each is measured, can be found in the following chapters.

[2] As Epstein, Landes and Posner put it plainly, '[i]t is unclear what standard liberal or, especially, conservative, ideology is': L Epstein, W Landes and R Posner, *The Behavior of Federal Judges: A Theoretical and Empirical Study of Rational Choice* (Harvard, 2013) 46.

[3] G White, 'Unpacking the Idea of the Judicial Center' (2004–05) 83 *North Carolina Law Review* 1089, 1172; E Posner, *How Judges Think* (Harvard, 2008) 93; J Gerring, 'Ideology: A Definitional Analysis' (1997) 50(4) *Political Research Quarterly* 957, 957.

[4] See eg the warnings in M Iaryczower and G Katz, 'More than Politics: Ability and ideology in the British Appellate Committee' (2016) 32(1) *Journal of Law, Economics, and Organization* 61, 63: judges have 'general attitudinal differences that cannot be easily ordered along a conservative-liberal dimension'. See also B Dickson, 'Close Calls in the House of Lords' in J Lee (ed), *From House of Lords to Supreme Court: Judges, Jurists and the Process of Judging* (Hart Publishing, 2011) 302; S Lee, *Judging Judges* (Faber & Faber, 1988) 36. For a good example of the left-right dimension used appropriately see C Hanretty, *A Court of Specialists* (OUP, 2020).

[5] The US literature is inconclusive on this issue; some find that judges behave differently across subject areas: Posner (n 3) 93–94; W Eskridge and L Baer, 'The continuum of deference: Supreme Court treatment of agency statutory interpretations from Chevron to Hamdan' (2008) 96(4) *Georgetown Law Journal* 1083, 1137–47; whereas some find a relative consistency: G Nelson, *Pathways to the US Supreme Court* (Macmillan, 2013) 197; J Jost, C Federico and J Napier, 'Political Ideology: Its Structure, Functions and Elective Affinities' (2009) 60 *Annual Review of Psychology* 307, 313. Some find that some judges are more consistent than others in this respect: Epstein, Landes and Posner (n 2) 112; G Schubert, *The Judicial Mind: Attitudes and Ideologies of Supreme Court Justices* (Northwestern, 1965) 99.

[6] For example whether the judge disagrees with the court below, or whether the judge applies the statute narrowly.

[7] For example whether the judge found criminal or tortious liability, or whether the judge found that a statute had been breached.

Further, most studies on UK courts have focused solely on case outcomes. This is, in many respects, a useful measure, as it provides the most obvious example of divergences in judicial approaches, but it is certainly not the only way to identify judicial behaviour. It is not uncommon in the UKSC for the judges in a given case to be unanimous as to their preferred outcome, but to differ, sometimes quite significantly, between one another as to the reasoning supporting that conclusion.[8] For this reason, the dataset sought to capture both outcome-based differences and reasoning-based differences, as both can indicate something useful about individual judicial behaviour.

B. The Supreme Court

The study focuses on the UK Supreme Court.[9] As was noted in the previous chapter, this is because the Court, at least in theory, is the most powerful court in the UK, deals with most controversial cases, and tends to focus on the pronouncement of broad principles rather than the determination of facts. On a practical level, and unlike some other UK courts, it produces a manageable amount of judgments which can be subject to analysis and quantification.[10]

Ten years was chosen as the relevant time period of study. Thus, all UKSC judgments from October 2009 (the date of incarnation of the modern Court) to the end of the Summer 2019 term fall within the dataset. This period was chosen for a number of reasons. The number of judgments handed down during this period, 682, creates a manageable amount of data whilst being robust enough to show stronger trends and changes over time. A number of judges also retired in the period before October 2009 (and to a lesser extent, in the period after October 2019) marking useful cut-off points for the sake of continuity.[11] Ten years is also a notably longer time period than that adopted in other studies of the Supreme Court.

This brings the total number of full-time judges included in the dataset to 27. For the parts of this work which compare the approaches of individual judges, a small number of judges are generally excluded from analysis due to the low number of contributions they made within the time-frame. This means generally excluding newer appointments Lord Kitchin (who sat on 18 cases), Lady

[8] See eg *Patel v Mirza* [2016] UKSC 42; [2017] AC 467.

[9] The vast majority of existing empirical research dealing with judicial behaviour focuses on apex courts. It also seems to be the case that, at least in the US context, 'attitudinal' effects are more pronounced at higher levels: D Pinelo, 'Linking Party to Judicial Ideology in American Courts: A Meta-Analysis' (1999) 20 *Justice System Journal* 219.

[10] In the period surveyed, the Supreme Court handed down an average of 68 cases in each judicial year.

[11] Lords Scott and Neuberger both sat on the House of Lords until its dissolution but did not join the Supreme Court (at least initially); Lords Hoffmann and Carswell each retired from the House of Lords earlier in 2009. Lords Collins, Kerr, Clarke and (in April 2010) Dyson took their place.

Arden (11) and Lord Sales (7) but generally including, where relevant, Lady Black (49 cases), Lord Lloyd-Jones (45) and Lord Briggs (41).[12] Also excluded from consideration is Lord Saville, who sat on the Court during its first year but was involved in just 16 judgments. A number of supplementary judges also made appearances on the Court from time to time, but each sat too infrequently for anything meaningful to be said about their individual records and profiles.

C. Judgments

The dataset exclusively relied on UKSC judgments for its data sources. Some scholarship has relied on some further sources which modify or augment their case law analysis, such as extrajudicial speeches,[13] newspaper reports[14] and interview materials.[15] However, it is arguably even more difficult to 'quantify' this kind of material compared to ordinary judgments. Also, importantly, there may exist a potential disconnect between the way judges behave in the courtroom and the way judges present themselves in other contexts. This study primarily focuses on judges in the courtroom, not in the lecture hall. For this reason, the dataset focused exclusively on the *judgments* produced by the Supreme Court.

D. All Cases or Select Cases?

The next question was whether to measure judicial behaviour using all available cases or a more limited set of cases of particular utility. Some studies have refined or filtered their target court's jurisprudence and have sought to focus only on interesting, difficult sensitive, or politically-charged cases.[16] to refine the corpus of analysis to create a more fertile site for measuring meaningful differences between judges. Whilst there is a certain attraction to these arguments – it is of course true that the influence of judicial values is more in some cases compared to others – this

[12] However, in some cases, some of these judges are included – where this is the case, this is noted at the outset.

[13] J Griffith, 'The Brave New World of Sir John Laws' (2000) 63(2) *MLR* 159, 159–60; J Lee, 'The Judicial Individuality of Lord Sumption' 31 *UNSW Law Journal* 862; R Cahill-O'Callaghan, *Values in the Supreme Court* (Hart Publishing, 2020) 127, 129.

[14] S Segal, A Cover and D Albert, 'Ideological Values and the Votes of US Supreme Court Justices' (1989) 83(2) *American Political Science Review* 557; E Segal and H Spaeth, *The Supreme Court and the Attitudinal Model Revisited* (CUP, 2002) 321–23.

[15] H Tyrrell, *Human Rights in the UK and the Influence of Foreign Jurisprudence* (Hart Publishing, 2018); Cahill-O'Callaghan (n 13).

[16] For example, C Sunstein et al, *Are Judges Political?* (Brookings, 2006) deals only with affirmative action, obscenity and certain constitutional issues, whilst TT Arvind and L Stirton, 'Legal ideology, legal doctrine and the UK's top judges' [2016] *PL* 418 concerns only cases involving the state. In other studies (eg Hanretty (n 4) and L Blom-Cooper and G Drewry, *Final Appeal: A Study of the House of Lords in its Judicial Capacity* (OUP, 1972)), authors considered how frequently certain cases were reported in official reports as a rough proxy for importance or significance.

methodological choice was rejected for this dataset. Aside from the problem of identification (which cases are the sensitive, political or difficult ones?)[17] a robust study should surely include as many cases as possible and the simplest way to do this is to include all UKSC cases in the dataset (even if some turn out to be more useful than others). If the behavioural thesis is true, *all* judgments have the potential to involve 'authoritative allocation of values' which, to some degree, reflect individual predilections.[18] As Moran has noted, if a search for a generally applicable thesis of judicial behaviour focuses only on exceptional cases, it fails to be convincing as this adopts too narrow a conception of judicial power and discretion.[19] Individual judicial approaches should be noticeable across the board, and if they are not, that will be an interesting finding in and of itself.

E. Salient Cases

An additional option is to follow in the footsteps of other empirical researchers[20] and consider only 'split' cases – that is, those in which one or more judges sitting on a case disagree in some way, usually as regards to the outcome. This can serve as a proxy for sensitive cases or 'hard' cases, or as a distinguishing category of its own. There is an attraction to this approach, too – split judgments allow direct comparison of the views of different judges to the same legal questions. However, not all judges sitting on the dissenting 'wing' of a case will necessarily disagree with all aspects of a majority decision.[21] Equally, not all judges sitting in the majority will necessarily speak with one voice, especially as to the reasoning to be adopted. Therefore, rather than focusing on *split* cases, this book instead employs the concept of 'salient cases' instead – cases in which different judges on the panel disagree on the subject of the variable being examined. A judgment can be a 'salient case' in one context and not another. For example, suppose Judgment X finds the Court agreeing, unanimously, that a defendant has committed some crime. However, three of the judges form a majority and choose to depart from one of the Court's previous cases, whereas two of the judges would be content to uphold that

[17] For a masterful argument demonstrating the lack of a clear distinction between 'easy' and 'hard' cases see J Crowe, 'Not-So-Easy Cases' (2019) 40(1) *Statute Law Review* 75.

[18] R Hodder-Williams, 'Six Notions of "Political" and the United States Supreme Court' (1992) 22 *British Journal of Political Science* 1, 2–3. See also L Epstein, W Landes and R Posner, 'Are Even Unanimous Decisions in the United States Supreme Court Ideological?' (2012) 106(2) *Northwestern University Law Review* 699.

[19] L Moran, 'In Conversation with Lord Justice Etherton: judicial legitimacy, diversity and the representation of judicial authority' [2010] *PL* 662, 664. Moran argues that 'if the category "hard cases" seeks to separate out and confine the political nature of judgment to "exceptional cases", or to place politics only at the penumbra of meaning, it fails.'

[20] See eg Cahill-O'Callaghan (n 13), Hanretty (n 4) ch 8; Arvind and Stirton (n 16) 426; W Farnsworth, Signatures and Ideology: The Case of the Supreme Court's Criminal Docket' (2005) 104 *Michigan Law Review* 67, 69.

[21] See Epstein, Landes and Posner (n 2) 255–303.

old law. This would be identified as a 'salient case' when it comes to the operation of precedent (examined in chapter eight) because the judges sitting on the case were not in agreement, but it would *not* be considered a 'salient case' with respect to criminal liability (examined in chapter six) because the court was unanimous on this issue.

In practice, most salient cases are also split cases, but focusing on whether judges differ between themselves in relation to *the specific factor examined* proved to be a more helpful and somewhat more sophisticated measure for measuring judicial disagreement rather than simply looking at whether a dissenting judgment was technically issued in a case. Whilst this study does not rely *exclusively* on salient cases, the wider dataset is occasionally filtered to show results for salient cases, at least where doing so may provide some further insight or interest. When this is the case, it will be stated clearly.

Overall, then, the parameters of the dataset relied upon in this work can be described as follows: it focuses on the individual judges, rather than the trends of the Court as a whole. It tracks range of behavioural indicators rather than one general measure, and will not, at the outset, use political labels. It focuses on the UK Supreme Court, and the judgments it delivered, over a ten-year period from 2009 to 2019. Rather than focusing on split decisions or controversial judgments, all judgments handed down in this period are assessed and quantified; sometimes, salient cases are examined separately where it is appropriate to do so.

I hope the above section makes it reasonably clear as to *what* was measured when compiling the dataset. The next section sets out *how* it was measured.

II. Data Collection and Analysis Methods

Lawyers and political scientists are spoiled for choice when it comes to the methods available for measuring judicial behaviour, and the existing research on courts around the world employs a good range of them. Some more esoteric research, for example, features such unusual methods as 'scalograms'[22] and even game theory.[23] As interesting as they may be, the reader need not worry too much about those. The author certainly has not. Rather, I have opted for a much more straightforward method, which essentially boils down to a manual coding and counting exercise.

Political scientists may be aggrieved at this point to find that my method of choice was not factor analysis. For the uninitiated, the term 'factor analysis' is a

[22] For a good explanation of scalogram methodology, see J Holmes and E Rovet, 'The Ontario Court of Appeal: Some Observations on Judicial Behaviour' (1969) 7(1) *Osgoode Hall Law Journal* 31, 32. For an example, see G Schubert, *Quantitative Analysis of Judicial Behaviour* (The Free Press, 1959). For criticism, see SR Peck, 'A Behavioural Approach to the Judicial Process: Scalogram Analysis' (1967) 5(1) *Osgoode Hall Law Journal* 21 and A Tyree, 'The Geometry of Law' (1975) 8 *Victoria University of Wellington Law Review* 403, 419–20.

[23] W Berns, 'Law and Behavioral Science' in HW Baade, *Jurimetrics* (Basic Book, 1963) 187–95.

general one, which in the very broadest terms, seeks to take one particular feature (factor) of a dataset and identify its relationship with other aspects of that dataset. Thus, in judicial behaviour work, factor analysis generally attempts to identify the relationship between the judge's contribution to a case (typically the outcome they prefer) and the other aspects of the same case including the identity of the judges involved.[24] Through analysing a large number of cases, the relative strength of each of these relationships can be compared and tested, leading, if successful, to the identification of different groupings and types.[25] Broadly, factor analysis, if successful, identifies which factors are relevant to the identified target (eg case outcomes). A particular brand of factor analysis, the item-response theory (IRT) model,[26] is particularly well-suited to untangling the influences of multi-factorial decision-making and it has been employed successfully in a number of recent quantitative studies looking at judicial behaviour in the UK.[27]

However, factor analysis is limited in a number of respects. First, most conventional factor analysis can only link judicial appearances with case outcomes. It is less adept at identifying differences in, for example, the reasoning adopted by judges. Further, for various reasons, factor analysis works better when it comes to uncovering the disagreements between judges rather than identifying trends in the whole corpus of judgments produced by a court. Only a portion of cases handed down by the UKSC are split, limiting its particular utility here. Further, factor analysis is particularly useful when considering a whole set (here, of judges), and has to be adapted or modified in order to accommodate the use of judicial panels, as employed by the UKSC.

The most attractive aspect of factor analysis is that it is more 'objective' than other methods, as it identifies trends that are not, in theory, hampered by the subjective evaluation of the researcher. In a sense, factor analysis produces trends and results that are designed to be content-neutral. However, even if this recovered dimension *can* be easily identified, there is a real risk in an analysis program picking up patterns which are merely incidental. There are few ways to identify and correct these problems apart from including manual checks by the researcher, which again detracts from the allure of the method's objectivity. Factor analysis is very good at drawing out the relationship between fairly objective measures (who sat, who won, etc). But it is, I suggest, less adept when it comes to identifying certain features of a case, such as its legal content, its subject-matter, and the reasoning which features. Factor analysis eschews the need for human evaluation.

[24] A succinct and straightforward definition in the judicial behaviour context can be found in S Ulmer, 'The Analysis of Behavior Patterns on the United States Supreme Court' (1960) 22 *Journal of Politics* 629, 634–36.

[25] Ulmer, ibid, describes this as 'a typal structure which identifies types, whereby every member of the type is more like other members than non-members': 633–34.

[26] Unlike general probabilistic and statistical models, this model was developed specifically to interpret spatial voting by multiple actors (originally in the legislative, rather than judicial context).

[27] For good examples, see Hanretty (n 4) ch 8 and Arvind and Stirton (n 16). Neither author explicitly endorses the IRT model, but both accept that they employ something *very close to it*.

In some contexts, this is a strength. But in this work, I suggest, a degree of human evaluation is *required*, and is indeed *beneficial*, for the purposes of properly understanding judicial behaviour in practice.

The methods employed in this work do not focus, as factor analysis would demand, upon judicial formation patterns and inferences from inter-agreement, but on the direct contributions of the judges, both in terms of outcome and reasoning, measured according to different variables. Factor analysis could be said to work from the 'outside in' – working with certain known information to create a space in which the desired dimension can be implied. By contrast, the methods applied in this work (in truth a fairly crude application of 'frequentist' modelling) could instead be said to work from the 'inside out', directly measuring the desired dimension in the context of other known information, without the need for too much additional imputation. This method is sometimes termed 'content analysis',[28] and involves analysing the text and language of judgments (this is either performed manually or done by using machine technology).[29] The text can be searched according to some pre-existing metric,[30] or evaluated using an inductively generated schema.

Whilst factor analysis is useful for identifying which variable(s) best explain(s) the Court's output as a whole,[31] I suggest that a frequentist approach like the one applied in the current work is more useful for identifying how, and to what extent, preferences differ between judges in certain categories. Differences between attitudes towards the state, for example, can be measured straightforwardly by simply measuring how frequently each judge tends to side with the state. Unlike factor analysis, the present method facilitates direct measurement of the desired dimension.

As such, at the risk of oversimplification, the frequentist approach adopted here involved taking each case in the dataset in turn, recording which of the relevant variables are present in each one, and determining which approach that judge adopted in relation to each of the examined questions. Broadly, the finished dataset should (and did) make it clear how many times Judge A adopted approach X (where X could be almost any aspect of judicial behaviour – siding with the state, developing the common law, departing from precedent, etc) across their entire tenure on the court. More detail on the scope of the dataset, the relevant variables

[28] R Kirkham and E O'Loughlin, 'A Content Analysis of Judicial Decision-Making' in N Creutzfeldt, M Mason and K McConnachie, *Routledge Handbook of Socio-Legal Methods* (Routledge, 2020).

[29] T George and T Weaver, 'The Role of Personal Attributes and Social Backgrounds on Judging' in L Epstein and S Lindquist, *The Oxford Handbook of US Judicial Behaviour* (OUP, 2017) 297; N Aletras et al, 'Predicting judicial decisions of the European Court of Human Rights: a Natural Language Processing perspective' (2016) *PeerJ Computer Science* 2:e93; R Black et al, 'Emotions, Oral Arguments and Supreme Court Decision Making' (2011) 73(2) *The Journal of Politics* 572.

[30] Cahill-O'Callaghan, for example, uses the pre-existing measure of the typology of values developed by Salom Schwartz: see n 13.

[31] For example, Hanretty found that, more than anything else, a judge's personal expertise and subject specialism tends to play a greater role than any other factor in terms of behaviour on the UKSC: see n 4.

and criteria involved, and the coding method employed are all set out below. Readers may be reassured, or horrified, if I summarise these methods as more or less an exercise in *sophisticated counting*.

There are two significant pitfalls when it comes to this method: subjectivity and exclusivity. First, at least in the present context, it necessitates a level of manual coding and *human* assessment.[32] The translation of essentially qualitative data into 'abstract numerical dimensions'[33] is not always self-evident. Whilst 'marking' a case according to how many judges sat in the case, or whether the case was unanimous is a (fairly)[34] objective task, the same may not be true when seeking to identify whether the outcome of a given case reflects a 'pro-contract' position or which sort of approach to statutory interpretation was adopted by a given judge.

This is not some trifling concern. Too much subjectivity on the part of the coder risks undermining the legitimacy of the entire dataset and any conclusions which might be drawn from it. However, since *some* risk of subjectivity is, I concede, inevitable (if judges are human, so are coders), I submit that if the evaluation applied in each is robust, convincing and consistent, arbitrariness and subjectivity is significantly reduced. In compiling the dataset, coding decisions were not made haphazardly. Coding and reviewing was carried out, in each case, according to the terms of a robust coding table, and in line with detailed guidance as to how each category should be evaluated and recorded. Whether a given judgment reflects a 'contract law win' or a 'pro-government position' might be hopelessly contestable in the abstract, but where, in each instance, it was marked according to the specific parameters adopted in the relevant part of the codebook (which contained the same criteria and definitions set out in this work, in the relevant later chapters) the task becomes much more logical and objective. The coding exercise also complied with applicable rules of good practice,[35] which involved recording all decisions, with supporting justificatory reasoning provided for cases which gave rise to any real difficulty. A representative sample of coding decisions was then blindly cross-checked by outside markers, and particularly contestable cases were additionally cross-checked by multiple parties. All of this, I hope, reduced the level of errant subjectivity involved. Given that almost all modes of will involve *some* degree of subjective evaluation,[36] adopting a controlled definition with appropriate safeguards appeared to be a workable and practical compromise which paid off in practice.

[32] Whether 'machine' coding is any less error-prone, however, is another matter.

[33] D Robertson, 'Judicial Ideology in the House of Lords: A Jurimetric Analysis' (1982) 12(1) *British Journal of Political Science* 1, 4.

[34] A Paterson, *The Law Lords* (Macmillan, 1982) 111. See ch 3 on identifying unanimous and dissenting cases.

[35] See Cahill-O'Callaghan (n 13) 39–41.

[36] For example, even if factor analysis is 'successful' and shows, for example, three separate 'flanks' in the dataset, it is up to the researcher to identify what each signifies: the 'recovered dimension' (see Hanretty (n 4) ch 8) must therefore be imposed from the outside: see V Flango and C Ducat, 'Toward an Integration of Public Law and Judicial Behavior' (1977) 39(1) *The Journal of Politics* 41, 43.

The second concern is that whilst factor analysis does a very good job at taking into account the various factors which influence a judge's decision-making, the sort of frequentist analysis deployed in the present work can only, by its very nature, identify the single influence being measured. There is no way to guarantee that the dimension sought is affected by the measured variable more than any other (unmeasured) variable. For example, suppose a judge decides 50 cases, and 40 of them are against the state. This suggests (but, crucially, does not prove) that that judge holds some sort of 'anti-state' preference. But supposing that all 40 of those cases were appeals against judgments of the Scottish courts, it becomes unclear whether that judge should be best described as 'anti-state' or 'anti-Scot'. Of course, judicial influences are rarely so stark. But it remains the case that simply asking how frequently a judge finds for a certain party, or adopts a certain sort of reasoning, does not 'explain' judicial behaviour.

Judicial reasoning is a very specialist and particular sort of deliberation.[37] The process of judging self-evidently involves much more than acting on personal predilections. A whole host of factors will influence a given legal decision, legal and otherwise.[38] The answer to this concern – admittedly not a particularly satisfying one – must be simply to admit that this kind of study is affected by limitations, and to accept that correlation and implication does not equal causation or proof. However, it remains the case that correlation *can* be very significant – if a judge decides almost every case before them over a ten-year period in favour of the state, and their colleagues are much more balanced, the implications of this are obvious, and correlation can carry a lot of weight. This is especially so if multiple competing influences are measured and compared, and where a qualitative assessment of the case law, which I have sought to employ where possible, supports the implications drawn.

As such, whilst the tools used in frequentist analysis are necessarily limited, so long as the inferences and interpretations which follow are informed by good sense (and certain statistical checks are employed) they are, I submit, well suited for assessing differences in judicial behaviour between individual judges.

III. Dataset and Coding

As explained above, the dataset included information about cases handed down by the UKSC during its first ten years (682 distinct cases in total), including any

[37] D Hutt, 'Measuring judicial and popular deliberation: a critical comparison' (2018) 16(4) *IJCL* 1121.

[38] See ch 1. Works exploring judicial influences more generally include L Baum, 'Motivation and Judicial Behaviour: Expanding the Scope of Enquiry' in D Klein and G Mitchell, *The Psychology of Judicial Decision Making* (OUP, 2010); D Ho and M Morse, 'New Measurement Technologies: A Review and Application to Nuremberg and Justice Jackson' in L Epstein and S Lindquist, *The Oxford Handbook of US Judicial Behaviour* (OUP, 2017) 515–18 and B Alaire and A Green, *Commitment and Cooperation on High Courts* (OUP, 2017) 38–43. The most accomplished text in this field remains N Duxbury, *Jurists and Judges: An Essay on Influence* (Bloomsbury, 2001).

basic information about the case, for example: its name, the date it was heard, the date of hand-down, the judicial term it was handed down in, the number of judges sitting in it, the names of judges sitting, whether the case was an appeal and if so, the identity of the court below, the names of the parties involved, whether the case featured certain kinds of parties, whether the outcome was unanimous and whether the outcome featured a single judgment or not. This was recorded and reviewed manually by the author.

More importantly, the dataset recorded featured information about each sitting judge's contribution to each case, even if they did not make a contribution of their own.[39] Many of the relevant categories examined are detailed fully in later chapters, but broadly involved recording, for each judge taking part in each case: whether they sat on the case; whether they contributed something of their own; whether they issued a lead judgment, concurrence or dissent; how many paragraphs they contributed, if any (on all of these, see chapter four); whether they sided with a number of different parties (on which see chapter five); whether they adopted a certain kind of outcome and whether their outcome reflects a certain approach to a given subject area (on both, see chapters six and seven); whether they employed certain reasoning or used certain legal tools in a particular way (see chapter eight) and any other relevant information. Ultimately, the coding of each factor for each case was conducted manually by the researcher, through individual case-by-case evaluation.[40] In each case, basic information about the way each sitting judge voted was recorded, even if they did not make a contribution of their own (of course, where a judge *did* contribute something of their own, the length, nature and detail of that contribution was recorded).

A simple binary scale was used when it came to 'marking' each variable. A more granulated scale would be difficult to apply consistently (how could it be known whether a particular approach to statutory interpretation should merit a score of 7 out of 10 or a slightly more generous 8 out of 10?) – a more straightforward mark (1 for positive, 0 for negative, 0.5 for a mixed or inconclusive position) seems to reduce arbitrariness and works well for the vast majority of cases.[41] The simple scale provides a clear metric of comparison across categories. Finally, but importantly, presenting data upon such a simple coding scale will likely be more digestible to the reader.

Each case was marked separately. All individual judgments were equally weighted. Distinct appeals within a case were treated as part of one judgment (and

[39] A 'contribution' must be something which goes beyond simple agreement – a judge who makes their own speech but simply says 'I agree with Lord X' would not count, but even a short concurrence which set out some reasoning, even if that reasoning is identical to that of another judge, would be deemed to be a 'contribution'. This is in line with the approach adopted by other scholars such as T Poole and S Shah, 'The Law Lords and Human Rights' (2011) 74(1) *MLR* 79 and Tyrrell (n 15) 28.

[40] Whilst imperfect, this avoids the downsides of DBM methods, which require some sort of universal keywords to 'anchor' AI searches.

[41] See similarly A Martin, K Quinn and L Epstein, 'The Median Justice on the United States Supreme Court' (2004–05) 83 *North Carolina Law Review* 1275, 1297–98; H Spaeth, 'The Attitudinal Model' in L Epstein, *Contemplating Courts* (CQ Press, 1995) 296–314.

did not form a distinct unit of measurement taken on their own)[42] although where a case involves multiple claimants, or multiple distinct issues, this was reflected in the coding where appropriate.[43] Each judgment with a different neutral citation counted as a separate 'case',[44] therefore, for example, *Willers v Joyce (No 1)*[45] and *Willers v Joyce (No 2)*[46] were treated as separate cases warranting separate marking despite technically stemming from the same appeal; by contrast, *EV (A Child); EV (A Child) (No 2)*[47] was reported as one single case using one neutral citation so all issues in those appeals were marked together as part of one case.

A. Presenting Data

The majority of the figures and graphs presented in the following chapters should be self-explanatory and relatively easy to interpret; any necessary information is provided in-text. Beyond the reference to *salient cases*, which are described and defined above, the only other language to note at this stage is the reference which will be made to 'more significant', 'less significant' or 'insignificant' data. These terms are vague, but here is what I mean by their use: judges sit on different numbers of cases from one another, which may affect the reliability of conclusions drawn from their behaviour in those cases. Suppose two judges side with the state in each and every case in which they sat. But if one of them only sat on three cases, and the other sat on 300 cases, it is obvious which judge we would consider more *reliably* pro-state. As such, where appropriate, judges with 'more significant' data (ie those involved in more relevant cases) are distinguished from those with 'less significant' data (ie those involved in fewer relevant cases).[48] The former would be considered to have sat on enough cases for the figures drawn to be considered robust (enough) and representative (enough) to be particularly insightful, whereas the judges with 'less significant' records may provide data which is less reliable (judges were considered to have 'insignificant' records if they sat on too few cases to be worth considering at all). However, 'less significant' records may usefully

[42] This is line with A Paterson, *Final Judgment: The Law Lords and the Supreme Court* (Hart Publishing, 2013) who notes the 'distorting effect' multiple appeals might have (14) *cf* S Benesh, 'The Use of Observational Data to Study Law and the Judiciary' in L Epstein and S Lindquist, *The Oxford Handbook of US Judicial Behavior* (OUP, 2017) 546–47.

[43] For example, if two claimants succeed against the state and one loses, this would be marked as 0.33 in the 'state win' category.

[44] Again, this is in line with the approach adopted by Tyrrell (n 15).

[45] *Willers v Joyce (No 1)* [2016] UKSC 43; [2016] 3 WLR 477.

[46] *Willers v Joyce (No 2)* [2016] UKSC 44; [2015] 3 WLR 534.

[47] *EV (A Child) (Nos 1 and 2)* [2017] UKSC 15; 2017 SLT 319.

[48] The exact parameters distinguishing the two categories depend on the data being examined; judges were generally considered to hold 'less significant' records in a given area if they sat on a number of cases which is: (i) lower than 20% of the number sat on by the judge sitting on the greatest number of relevant cases; (ii) in any case, lower than 10. These rules were not adhered to strictly and were departed from where necessary to accommodate the nature of the variable being examined and the comparative sitting rates of others.

serve a purpose when considered alongside the more reliable data, and as such are sometimes presented in this work. Where this is the case, and 'less significant' data is presented alongside 'more significant' data, an asterisk (*) is appended and the data is coloured in grey.

IV. Conclusions and Going Forwards

The methodology employed herein can be summarised as follows. The primary method of analysis involved the manual coding of cases, tracking the individual contributions of judges across different variables. A dataset was created consisting of each judge's personal contribution to all cases handed down between the beginning of Michaelmas Term 2009 to the end of Trinity Term 2019 (682 cases). Details about each case as well as each judge's contribution (in whatever form) were recorded, and where applicable coded on a binary scale, from 1 to 0, with intermediate marking permitted for mixed approaches or those cases involving multiple claims or claimants. Each case, defined by reference to an individual citation number, is tracked and weighted equally. Analysis of that data will follow in each individual chapter of this book.

Whilst it is hoped that the methods outlined here are robust and sensible, and that the presentation and analysis of the data in subsequent chapters is both convincing and interesting, I do not wish to be cavalier about the limitations of this method. The exercise pursued here is necessarily limited to establishing *correlation*, rather than *causation*. Counting votes *proves* nothing. Strong correlation may, however, imply causation. Robertson reminds us that 'to demonstrate that certain sorts of cases are regularly decided in a specific way [by a specific judge] would go a long way to sowing the possibility of ideological seepage'.[49] Further, the insights which can be gained from analysing statistical voting patterns are necessarily limited in nature, especially when used to approximate the 'messy interiors'[50] of the senior judiciary. Yet, as I have noted, the restraints, safeguards and good practice methods adopted during the creation and use of the dataset should ensure that the dataset nonetheless reveals *something* useful.

I am aiming to show that different judges hold different personal preferences and positions, and that this might play a role in why judges decide cases. I am not trying to sketch out some wholesale account of judicial behaviour, or to deny the influence of legal and extra-legal factors on judicial decision-making.[51]

[49] D Robertson, *Judicial Discretion in the House of Lords* (Clarendon, 1998) 36.

[50] Farnsworth (n 20) 92.

[51] One limitation which I have not addressed at this stage is the fact that individual judicial opinions are often, in practice, influenced by multiple judges. Often, according to Lord Reed, individually authored judgments are in reality composite contributions; judgment-writing is 'an iterative process, within which every member of the Court participates': Lord Reed, 'Collective Judging in the UK Supreme Court' in B Häcker and W Ernst, *Collective Judging in Comparative Perspective* (Intersentia,

No scholar has seriously argued for a 'purely' ideological model of judging.[52] My argument is simply that the internal preferences and personal approaches of individual judges play a part – and, indeed, perhaps a *significant* part – in the judicial decision-making process. The current project seeks to map just one influence on judicial behaviour on the UKSC; it cannot wholly account for the myriad of other influences.

Finally, this project largely looks at *whether* personal preferences can be identified, and if so, what they might be. It is not directly concerned with the admittedly fascinating question of *why* those preferences might be held. Some inferences may naturally be made by the reader in this respect (and, if it can be forgiven, some will be tentatively suggested by the author throughout), but as Baum contends, '[f]ull explanation [of judicial behaviour] goes well beyond successful prediction'.[53] Here I am chiefly concerned with identifying what individual judges think and believe. I leave it to others to determine *why* they might do so.[54]

As such, I believe that we can deduce something about the preferences of the judges sitting on the Court by examining the content of their judgments over time. Given what we know about judicial (and human) behaviour, how could it be otherwise? I believe that the frequentist content-analysis methods I adopt here have something unique to offer, which cannot necessarily be captured by competing methods such as factor analysis. What I hope to show in the following chapters is that this method *works*: it produces interesting results which are both statistically robust and which fit with our wider understanding of the judges and their behaviour. It is important to be candid about the limits of this project. But an awareness of those limits allows the data to be examined properly, and its conclusions to be presented fairly. Quantitative analysis of judicial behaviour is always going to be a limited tool, but, I suggest, when it comes to examining individual judicial behaviour, it can be a very valuable one.

2020) 25. See also Lord Reed, 'The Supreme Court Ten Years On' (Bentham Association Lecture, 6 March 2019) 10–11.

[52] Even the ever-caricatured JAG Griffith does not argue that the judges' innate conservative preferences constitute the *only* reason for judicial action.

[53] L Baum, *The Puzzle of Judicial Behaviour* (Michigan, 1997) 3. See also Segal and Spaeth (n 14) 320–21 and J Fischman and D Law, 'What is judicial ideology and how should we measure it?' (2009) 29 *Washington University Journal of Law and Policy* 133, 158.

[54] Readers may want to consult eg J Griffith, *Politics of the Judiciary*, 5th edn (Fontana Press, 1997) and Cahill-O'Callaghan (n 13) for interesting answers in this respect.

3

The Nature of Individual Judicial Contributions

All judges on the UKSC have the same formal powers. No vote is weightier than any other. Judgments authored by the Court's President are as authoritative as those authored by a new appointment.[1] However, output varies considerably between judges. Some are fairly verbose, whilst others are more reserved. Some take the lead, while others are content with following. Some dissent readily, others rarely. As such, before turning to the *substance* of judicial contributions (chapters four to nine) this chapter will look at what might be called the *form* or *nature* of the judges' output: which judges contributed to the Court's judgments, and what kind of contributions did they bring? Although perhaps a comparatively uncontroversial aspect of judicial behaviour, the results can nonetheless certainly tell us something about the kinds of judges who sat on the Court during its first decade.

Section I sets out each judge's headline numbers: how many cases they decided, how often they were in the majority or dissented, and how often they wrote lead, concurring and dissenting judgments. Section II then looks at the length of each judge's output and considers their respective writing styles.

I. Judicial Contributions

This first section looks at the nature of each judge's contributions to the Court: in particular, how often they sat, how many lead judgments they authored, how often they concurred, and the number (and type) of dissents they wrote.

[1] That is not to say that, in practice, court presidents will have equal influence. Research shows that, in other jurisdictions, court leaders exercise distinct power compared to, and sometimes with respect to, their colleagues: A Blisa and D Kosar 'Court Presidents: The Missing Piece in the Puzzle of Judicial Governance' (2018) 19(7) *German Law Journal* 2031, 2047–49; F Cross and S Lindquist, 'The Decisional Significance of the Chief Justice' (2006) 154 *Pennsylvania Law Review* 1665. See, in relation to the UKSC, R Hunter and E Rackley, 'Judicial Leadership on the UK Supreme Court' (2018) *Legal Studies* 191, 204–205.

A. How Often did Judges Sit?

The first question concerns how many cases each judge was involved in. Given that the judges sit for different periods of time, and because the Court generally sits in panels of five (or sometimes more) judges at a time, this means that some judges will naturally sit on more cases than others.

Incidentally, the question of which judges sit in each case is largely decided by the Court registrar, subject to some tinkering by the President and Deputy President.[2] There are no set rules for making the decision and there is no requirement for all judges to sit on an equal number of cases (although there is an attempt to distribute their workload fairly). Judges with particular expertise or relevant experience in a given area might be asked to sit on a case related to that area, and judges hailing from one of the devolved institutions may be selected to sit on cases involving an appeal from that jurisdiction. Otherwise, the decision seems to be based on considerations of convenience, availability and fit.[3]

Figure 1 lists the total number of cases in which each judge sat. The total number of cases over the whole period is 682 (but of course, few judges sat for the whole ten-year period). Each of the 26 judges who held a permanent appointment during the ten-year period surveyed are listed.

Figure 1 Number of cases sat per judge

Judge	Number of cases sat
Hale	385
Kerr	268
Mance	261
Reed	260
Neuberger	258
Clarke	254
Sumption	219
Wilson	218
Carnwath	208
Hodge	184
Hughes	159

(continued)

[2] A Paterson, *Final Judgment* (Hart Publishing, 2013) 72–73. *cf* L Graham, 'Lessons from Lord Hope's Diaries', UK Administrative Law Association Blog, ukconstitutionallaw.org/2020/06/18/lewis-graham-lessons-from-lord-hopes-diaries-judicial-ideology-and-panel-selection/.

[3] Chris Hanretty has stipulated that the most important factors influencing whether a certain judge will sit on a particular panel include their specialisms and expertise, followed by whether they sat on the case's permission to appeal panel and the extent of their workload: C Hanretty, *A Court of Specialists* (OUP, 2020) ch 5.

Figure 1 ***(Continued)***

Judge	**Number of cases sat**
Hope	150
Toulson	130
Walker	112
Brown	97
Dyson	80
Phillips	80
Rodger	63
Collins	56
Black	51
Lloyd-Jones	44
Briggs	41
Kitchin	18
Saville	15
Arden	13
Sales	8

The table clearly shows that the judge who sat on the greatest number of cases was Lady Hale. In fact, she sat on 50 per cent more cases than Lord Kerr, the only other judge to have sat on the Court for the entirety of the Court's first decade. Of course, given that different judges sit for different periods of time, it should not be expected that all judges should have sat on a comparable number of cases. Therefore, Figure 2 estimates how many times each judge sat on a case in an average year. The estimation is a crude one; it is a simple total number of cases sat on by a judge divided by the number of months they sat on the Court. Given that caseload differs, sometimes significantly, between judicial years, this estimation is far from precise. Nonetheless, it shows that there is a clear difference between judges as to how 'busy' they were during their tenure. 'Newcomers' to the Court, who sat on the Court for less than one year before September 2019, are included here, but are placed in brackets.

Figure 2 still casts Lady Hale as *one of* the Court's busiest members, involved in around 39 cases per year. However, it was Lord Neuberger who sat on the greatest number of cases using this measure, at roughly 53 cases per year, a *significantly* higher figure than the next most frequent sitter, Lord Hope. Remarkably, despite sitting as a permanent member of the Court for less than five years in total, Lord Neuberger sat on the fifth-highest number of UKSC cases *of all judges overall during the ten-year period surveyed*, and just ten fewer cases than Lord Kerr, who sat as a member of the Court for more than double the time he did.

Figure 2 Number of cases per year

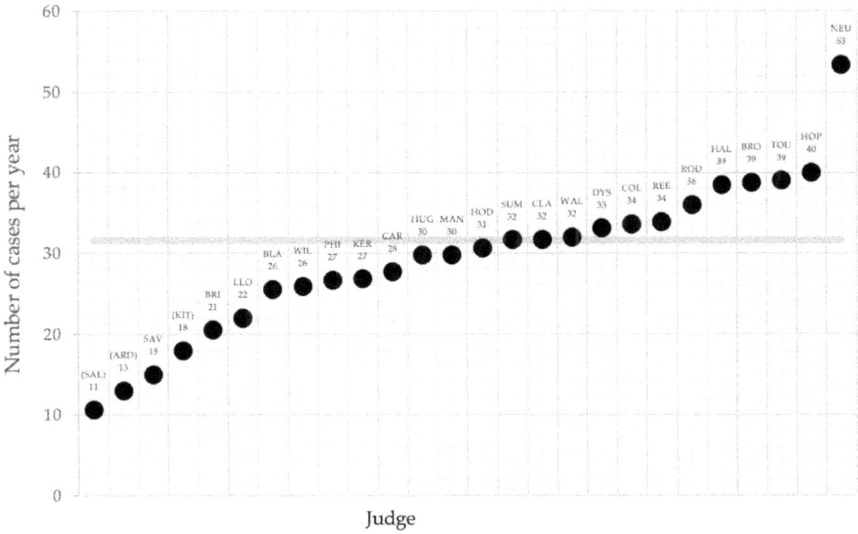

Some things should be noted about this data. First, many of the judges sitting at the lower end of the scale are relative 'newcomers' to the Court who joined relatively close to the cut-off point for the data (October 2019); these judges naturally underperform under the metric adopted here (because Figure 2 is based on the number of judgments handed down rather than the number of cases heard, more recently appointed judges will have spent a significant period hearing cases which were not handed down within the time period). Second, not all cases are equal: some are complicated and are argued over the course of many days, whilst some are comparatively simple and take half a day. Judges with lower output rates may simply have been involved in lengthier, more complex cases.[4] Third, not all judges had the same amount of time available to them; Lord Saville, for example, was engaged with the time-consuming Bloody Sunday enquiry during his time on the Court, leading to a low sitting rate.

It is interesting to note that Lady Hale and Lord Neuberger both sat on lots of cases as they both held the position of President of the Court.[5] Lord Hope, another

[4] Although this raises the interesting question of whether certain judges are more likely to be trusted with sitting on complicated cases involving multi-day hearings.

[5] The UKSC operates under a very rough hierarchy with a ranking consisting of the President and a Deputy President, followed by ten other judges of equal seniority. In practice, however, the difference between the two senior figures and the other judges is only very slight, with presidential duties mainly relating to representative functions and administrative leadership, although the difference is apparently more pronounced in the UKSC than was the case during the House of Lords era: G Gee et al, *The Politics of Judicial Independence in the UK's Changing Constitution* (CUP, 2015) 197–202. See also references to n 1.

frequent sitter, held the position of Deputy President. This might suggest that judges holding these leadership positions are expected to, and do, sit on more cases than other judges. However, this is not the case across the board. Lord Phillips, for example, only sat on around 27 cases per year as the Court's first President – a lower rate than most of his colleagues and almost half the rate of Lord Neuberger. Lord Mance, Deputy President between 2017 and 2018, sat on slightly more cases – around 30 per year – but this is not a particularly outstanding figure overall. As such, it is doubtful that taking on the role of President or Deputy President necessarily obliges the holder to sit on a greater number of cases[6] (although it may be the case that hard workers and frequent sitters were more likely to be appointed to leadership positions).

One explanation for the variance between judges in Figures 1 and 2 might simply be a difference in the kinds of judges sitting on the Court. Those at the higher end of the table with a prolific output may simply have more self-confidence, a distaste for boredom and a strong belief in their convictions. An alternative explanation, of course, is that judges at the lower end of the scale are more meticulous, and that their decision-making is more considered and reflective, and therefore more time-consuming. Perhaps all that can be really taken from this data is that Lord Neuberger was a remarkable judge with an astonishing work ethic. This should be attributed, I suggest, to Lord Neuberger as an individual, rather than to some kind of abstract duty attaching to the Presidency he was appointed to.

B. Lead Judgments

Obviously, each of the 682 cases in the dataset features at least one lead judgment. The vast majority (604) are lead judgments written by a single identifiable author; 40 cases featured a lead authored by multiple judges together,[7] and there were 25 cases where a lead judgment was not identifiable, either because they feature multiple substantive 'main' judgments, or because they are composite 'judgments of the court'.

As with much of the Court's output, there is no set formula to be applied when it comes to deciding which judge writes the lead. It is often decided by the presiding judge on a panel, and, per Lord Neuberger, 'should normally be a Justice who is aligned with the majority view on the answer and the reasoning'.[8] Beyond this, relevant considerations may include a judge's expertise – commercial experts will want to write the lead in commercial cases and so on – and workload.[9] These very

[6] Hanretty came to largely similar conclusions using slightly different methodological choices, see n 3, ch 5.

[7] Joint lead judgments became much more frequent in the period following the cut-off point for this dataset; for example, between October 2020 and October 2021, 33 cases featured a joint lead judgment (34% of all cases handed down).

[8] Lord Neuberger, 'Tweaking the Curial Veil' (Blackstone Lecture 2014, 15 November 2014) para 28.

[9] Hanretty found that this decision was most influenced by expertise: Hanretty (n 3) ch 6.

loose considerations mean that the number of lead judgments delivered by the judges in the dataset varied significantly. During their time on the Court, Lord Saville contributed to one joint lead judgment; Lady Arden one solo lead and Lord Kitchin just two leads (although each contributed to one collective judgment of the court once). Lady Hale, on the other hand, authored the greatest number of lead judgments: 88. After Hale, it is Lord Sumption who wrote the next greatest number of lead judgments (70), followed by Lord Neuberger (64). See Figure 3 below for more details. It is remarkable that these judges are the Court's second- and third- highest lead opinion writers overall, given that Sumption served for less than seven years and Neuberger less than five. Of course, these numbers do not take into account the time each judge served on the Court and the number of cases in which they sat, and the more important question is therefore how *likely* each judge was to deliver the lead judgment in *the cases in which they sat*. This is set out in Figure 3.

Figure 3 Cases in which lead judgment is authored, as a percentage of all cases sat

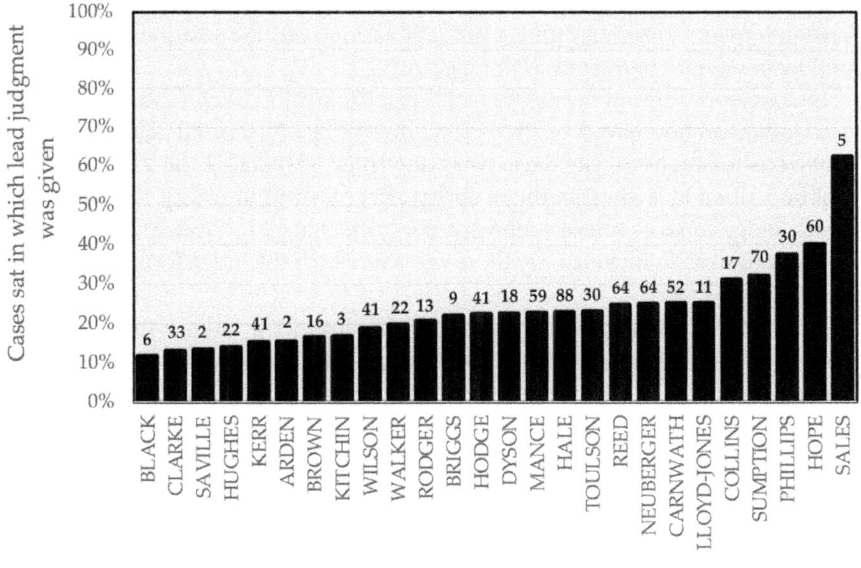

We see that although Lady Hale delivered more lead judgments than any other judge, the proportion of cases in which she delivered a lead judgment was lower than that of a number of her colleagues. At one end of the scale, Lords Sales, Hope, Phillips, Sumption and Collins each emerge as prolific lead judgment writers (Lord Sales' record should be read subject to the important qualification that he sat on just eight cases in the dataset). After that comes Lord Hope, who delivered the lead in 40 per cent of the cases in which he sat, and Lord Phillips, who did so in 37.5 per cent of cases; neither figure can be explained by low data numbers. Notably, Lord Phillips held the position of President, and Hope Deputy President, at the beginning of the Court's tenure. Their high lead judgment rate may reflect the specific role orientation they adopted as the new Court began its new era. Lord Neuberger was also quite likely to author a lead judgment, doing so in around one quarter of the cases in which he sat. Lord Mance and Lady Hale were a little less prolific, but both delivered more lead judgments than the average expected figure. It is therefore true to say that judges holding formal leadership positions tend to author lead judgments more frequently than other judges.

Judges appearing on the other end of the scale, and thus indicating a comparative reluctance to author a lead opinion, include Lady Black, Lord Saville, Lord Clarke and Lord Hughes, who each authored the lead judgment in less than 15 per cent of the cases in which they sat. Some of the judges appearing here sat on the Court for a relatively short amount of time, such as Lords Saville and Kitchin, although other judges sitting for a similarly short amount of time did author considerably more leads. However, there seems to be little evidence of the so-called 'freshman effect' whereby newly-appointed judges may take a while to ease into their work to find their voice, in play here. The judges appointed since 2017 are, as a whole, neither particularly likely nor particularly unlikely to author a lead judgment. 'Freshman' judges not only occupy various positions in Figure 3, but they bookmark both ends of the spectrum.

Interestingly, some of the judges with a particularly low likelihood of delivering a lead judgment also have a relatively high dissent rate (discussed below). There is an obvious reason as to why these two things may be linked – the lead judgment must be written by a judge in the majority, after all – but in reality, the likelihood of each judge to write a lead judgment does not change too much when adjusting the data so as to include only those cases in which the judge forms part of the majority.[10]

What might we attribute to a judge who authors a large number of lead opinions? Some judges may simply find the judgment-writing process an easier or more satisfying process than others; some may have particular skill or craftsmanship in terms of writing convincing leads. Alternatively, and more speculatively, judges who frequently author lead opinions may exhibit a certain type of judicial leadership, either through being particularly persuasive (convincing other judges to agree with their view) or compromising (being able to come to form a collaborative view in which all, or most, other judges agree).[11] One way of assessing this further is to look at how often judges were able to convince their colleagues to sign up to their lead opinion – in other words, what percentage of lead judgments were met with unanimous agreement?

[10] When adjusting for majority positions only in this way, each judge's likelihood to author the lead rises by 0–3%, with Lord Rodger's rate affected most significantly by this modification overall (3.01%).

[11] Some judges have been known to be particularly persuasive – Hunter and Rackley noted that Lady Hale was generally able to convince her colleagues to agree with her when she wrote the lead opinion in cases (n 1, 203–204), whereas Hale herself has identified Lord Sumption as a judge who was capable of convincing others to agree with him: Lady Hale, 'Valedictory for Lord Sumption' (UK Supreme Court, 12 December 2018).

Figure 4 Unanimous cases, as a percentage of all cases in which lead judgment is authored

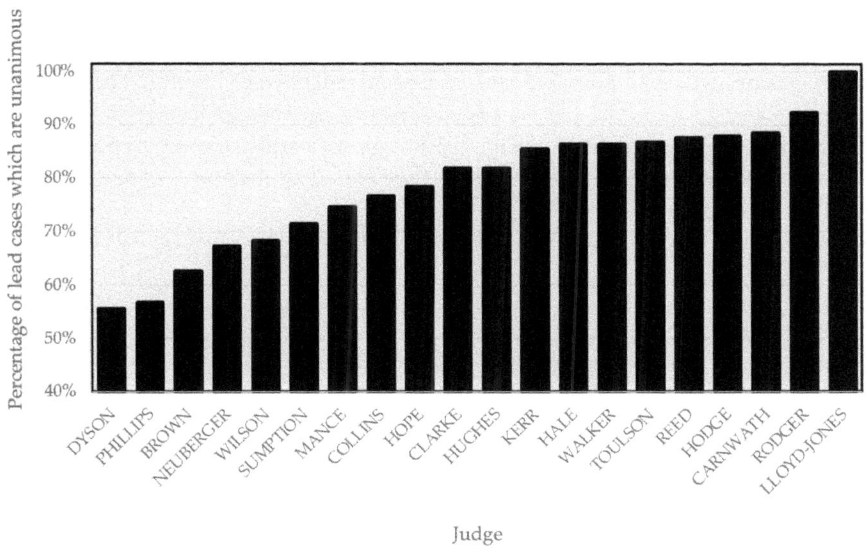

The data in Figure 4, which sets this out, is open to interpretation. Those judges who delivered a high number of lead opinions which garnered the unanimous support of their colleagues, such as Lords Lloyd-Jones and Rodger, could be seen as particularly persuasive judges, who were able to bring the divergent opinions of the Court together. They may be good at marshalling compromise, where the views of multiple colleagues could be synthesised into a position acceptable to all. Alternatively, these judges may simply have taken the lead in 'easy' cases in which divergence was less likely, leaving more confident figures or the Court President to take the lead in divisive cases. Indeed, around one-third of Lord Neuberger's lead opinions were issued in split cases, as were around 44 per cent of the leads delivered by Lord Phillips. As such, these judges, along with Lords Dyson and Brown, might be seen as more reliable and authoritative, taking up the task of writing the lead opinion in the Court's trickiest cases where the strength and confidence of the lead opinion matters most. Again, explanations by way of judicial personality should not be ruled out; as Lord Neuberger has stated, it is simply the case that 'some appellate judges are more prone than others to seeking to persuade their wavering or potentially wavering colleagues to agree with them'.[12]

[12] Lord Neuberger, 'Judgment and Judgments – the Art of Forming and Writing Judicial Decisions' (Denning Society Lecture, 30 November 2017) para 31.

C. Concurring Judgments

In this section, the likelihood of individual judges issuing a concurring opinion will be examined. A total of 545 spoken concurrences were identified across 289 cases, meaning around 42 per cent of all cases in the dataset feature at least one substantive spoken concurrence. Figure 5 straightforwardly sets out the percentage of cases in which each judge sat in which they issued a substantive concurrence.

Figure 5 Cases in which a (spoken) concurrence is authored, as a percentage of all cases sat

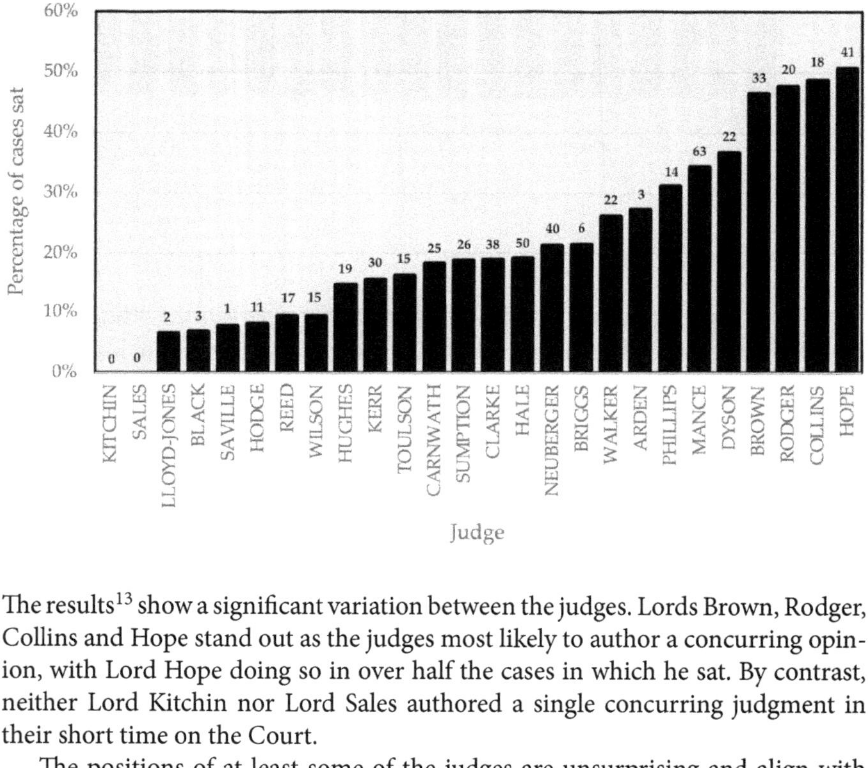

The results[13] show a significant variation between the judges. Lords Brown, Rodger, Collins and Hope stand out as the judges most likely to author a concurring opinion, with Lord Hope doing so in over half the cases in which he sat. By contrast, neither Lord Kitchin nor Lord Sales authored a single concurring judgment in their short time on the Court.

The positions of at least some of the judges are unsurprising and align with the views expressed in extrajudicial statements. Lord Rodger, for example, was known to his colleagues as a defender of multiple judgments and resisted the

[13] Which do not seem to support the conclusions in S Amaral-Garcia and N Garoupa, 'Judicial Behavior and Devolution at the Privy Council' (2017) 13(3) *Review of Law and Economics* [online, DOI: doi.org/10.1515/rle-2015-0013] which suggest that Scottish judges are less likely to write separate judgments; whilst Lords Hodge and Reed were relatively unlikely to author a concurrence, Lords Hope and Rodger were some of the Court's most frequent writers of them.

move towards single judgments.[14] Lords Hope, Collins and Walker have also made public comments in support of concurring judgments.[15] All appear at the 'top end' of Figure 5. On the other hand, Lord Clarke,[16] Lady Hale,[17] Lord Carnwath[18] and (especially) Lord Neuberger[19] have all been publicly sceptical of the utility of concurring opinions yet all four sit around the middle of Figure 5, each authoring a concurrence in about one-fifth of their cases.

The judges' individual positions reflect the wider trend of concurrences in the UKSC becoming much rarer occurrences over time.[20] Indeed, apart from Lord Dyson, who joined the Court full-time within the first year of its operation, Lady Arden is the judge with the highest concurrence rate who was not appointed to the Court as part of its initial judicial roster.[21] The likely reason for this is because during its first few years, the Court was still finding its feet and adopting its own distinct practices; the frequency of concurrences might be seen as something of an overhang from the way things worked in the House of Lords, where multiple speeches were the norm.

In addition, it is interesting to see which judges are keen to write lead judgments compared to those who write many concurrences. Some judges, such as Lords Hope and Collins, would frequently write when they were in the majority, whether in the form of a lead opinion or a concurring one. However, whilst judges such as Lords Lloyd-Jones, Reed and (to a degree) Sumption seem quite keen on writing lead judgments, they do not have a particular proclivity for writing concurrences. Lords Rodger and (especially) Brown show the opposite tendencies; they were relatively unlikely to produce a lead judgment but were considerably more comfortable with writing a concurring opinion, each contributing a concurrence in more than 45 per cent of cases in which they agreed with the majority. Some judges are great leaders, some, as noted below, are great dissenters; some, it seems, could be described as *great concurrers*.

[14] R Reed, 'The Form and Language of Lord Rodger's Judgments' in A Burrows, D Johnston and R Zimmerman, *Judge and Jurist: Essays in Memory of Lord Rodger of Earlsferry* (OUP, 2013) 130.

[15] D Hope, *UK Supreme Court 2009–2015: Lord Hope's Diaries* (Avizandum, 2019) 133–34; Paterson (n 2) 104–105.

[16] *Re Lehman Bros* [2012] UKSC 6; [2012] 3 All ER 1 at [109]. See also *R (E) v Governing Body of JFS* [2009] UKSC 15; [2010] 2 AC 728 at [125].

[17] *OBG Ltd v Allan* [2007] UKHL 21; [2008] 1 AC 1 at [303]; Lady Hale, 'Lessons from our first ten years' (UK Supreme Court Ten-Year Anniversary Lecture Series, 12 December 2019) 6–7 and Paterson (n 2) 104.

[18] *Doherty v Birmingham City Council* [2006] EWCA Civ 1739; [2007] HLR 32.

[19] See n 12 at paras 33–37 and further, Lord Neuberger, 'The Role of the Supreme Court Seven Years on: Lessons Learnt' (Bar Council Law Reform Lecture, 21 November 2016) at para 40; 'UK Supreme Court decisions on private and commercial law' (Centre for Commercial Law Studies Conference, 4 December 2015), paras 16–18; 'No judgment – no justice' (First Annual Bailii Lecture, 20 November 2012), paras 10–12.

[20] 70% of cases handed down in the 2010–11 legal year featured at least one substantive concurrence; just 31% of cases handed down in the 2018–19 legal year did.

[21] She has commented on the difficulty she feels with signing up to joint judgments: Counsel, 'Law Reformer', November 2020, 10.

D. Dissenting Judgments

Finally, this section turns to the likelihood of each judge to author a dissenting judgment. For context, of the 682 cases featured in the dataset, 140 of them were split judgments featuring at least one dissent. This puts the UKSC's unanimity rate at around 80 per cent.

However, there are internal mechanics governing the publication of dissenting judgments which muddy the purity of this conclusion. For example, according to Lord Neuberger, the judges themselves sometimes discuss whether a given judgment ought to be one in which they should put their differences aside for the sake of a clearer or more authoritative judgment (even if this cannot always be achieved in practice).[22] It has been suggested, for example, that certain types of case, such as criminal cases, should be unanimous where possible.[23] Unanimity may be preferred in cases dealing with highly-contestable political questions, to increase the authority of the Court's judgment and to alleviate potential charges of politically-motivated behaviour.[24] However, these considerations are very loose, and beyond these practical considerations, thresholds for dissenting are largely self-imposed.[25]

A judge's dissent propensity can be illuminating. But the veracity of the insights which can be drawn from it depends, to some extent, on what the function of the dissenting judgment is taken to be.[26] The most obvious reason for dissenting, and the reason why some judges might do so more frequently than others, is simply because they tend to disagree with their colleagues more often. This suggests that those judges might hold preferences or values which are different from the other judges on the court – they may hold unique values or act as ideological outsiders. But a judge's propensity to dissent may otherwise reveal something about their understanding of the judicial function and the Court's role: judges who see the UKSC's job as providing authoritative guidance to lower courts may be more likely to suppress their potential dissents, because pursuit of the right answer may be less important to them than producing a clear, straightforwardly applicable judgment.

[22] Lord Neuberger (n 8) para 28. Lord Neuberger was apparently very keen to ensure that the case of *HMRC v The Investment Trust Companies* [2017] UKSC 29 was unanimous, in order to ensure certainty in the law of unjust enrichment; whilst the previous cases on the issue had not been split, they featured multiple speeches by judges adopting significantly different reasoning between them: Lord Neuberger (n 12) at para 40.

[23] *R v Howe* [1987] AC 417 at 438; Lord Kerr, 'Dissenting judgments – self-indulgence or self-sacrifice?' (The Birkinhead Lecture, 8 October 2012) 10.

[24] The obvious example in this respect is the second *Miller* case, one of the very last cases in the dataset (*R (Miller) v Prime Minister* [2019] UKSC 41; [2020] AC 373). In that case, a panel of eleven judges unanimously held that Boris Johnson's prorogation of Parliament was unlawful.

[25] Judges have identified quite different 'thresholds' in this respect: Hunter and Rackley (n 1) 208–209; Paterson (n 2) 117.

[26] See L Epstein, W Landes and R Posner, *The Behavior of Federal Judges: A Theoretical and Empirical Study of Rational Choice* (Harvard, 2013) 255–303; L Epstein, W Landes and R Posner, 'Why (and when) Judges Dissent: A Theoretical and Empirical Analysis' (2011) 3(1) *Journal of Legal Analysis* 101; H Mistry, 'A Performative Theory of Judicial Dissent' (2023) 86(3) *MLR* 729.

Others may see the primary role of the Court as doing justice and getting the right answer, even at the cost of clarity, and may be more likely to publish their dissents as a result.[27] Dissent propensity might also be affected by personal and social factors such as a judge's self-confidence, openness to compromise, ability to influence, and relationship with their colleagues.[28] As such, the extent to which an individual judge dissents from their colleagues may not only indicate whether they hold particularly distinctive preferences and values, but also, perhaps, whether they see their role as a UKSC judge as primarily individual or collective in nature.[29]

It is unsurprising, then, to find that the 'dissent rate' of the judges in the dataset varies quite significantly. A total of 241 dissenting votes were identified and coded across 140 cases. Lady Hale authored the most dissents of any one judge (35), followed by Lord Kerr (33), Lord Clarke (20) and Lords Carnwath and Mance (19 each). As always, these numbers are not completely helpful given that each the judges sat on the Court for different periods of time (and, as was shown above, the number of cases in which they sat varied significantly). Figure 6 therefore sets out each judge's *likelihood* to dissent (dividing the number of cases in which they dissented out of the number of cases in which they sat, in order to account for length of sitting).

Figure 6 Dissents as a percentage of all cases sat

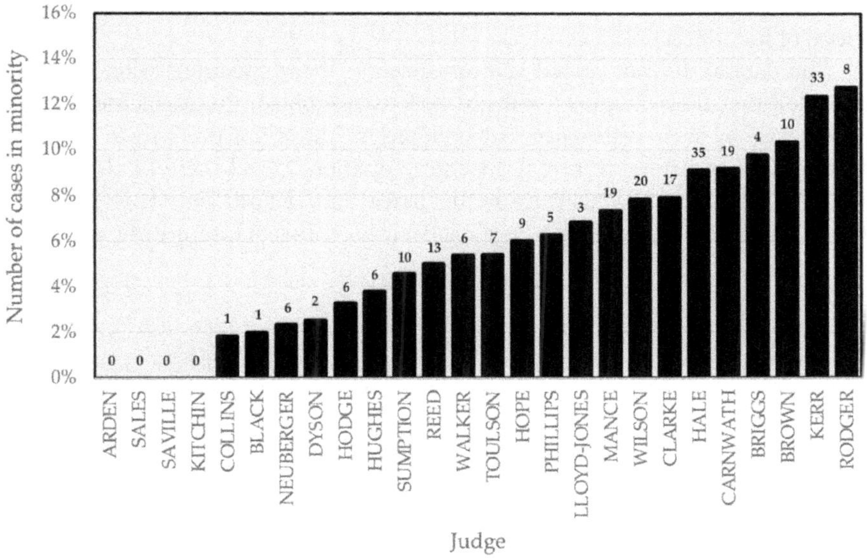

[27] Lord Kerr stated that the institutional effect of a dissenting judgment was generally irrelevant to him (n 23) 9.

[28] In some cases, judges may be less likely to issue a dissent where they greatly respect the expertise of their colleagues: see, in the context of the Court of Appeal, Etherton MR's comments in *Mirchandani v Lord Chancellor* [2020] EWCA Civ 1260; [2021] Lloyd's Rep FC 11 at [113].

[29] It is unsurprising that judges express different self-imposed 'thresholds' for dissenting: Lady Hale, The Emma Barnett Show, BBC Radio 5, 11 June 2019; Paterson (n 2) 131, 163.

As can be seen, three judges have a dissent rate of over 10 per cent (Lords Rodger, Kerr and Brown) whilst others score 0 per cent (admittedly most were judges with few cases in the dataset). Lord Rodger holds the position of the Court's 'greatest dissenter' (notably, his dissent rate may have been even higher had he not, apparently, held himself back in a number of cases[30] and Lord Brown has suggested that he may have dissented yet more times if the illness which he suffered towards the very end of his tenure had not prevented him from doing so)[31] although his relatively short tenure on the Court should be noted; he issued 8 dissents, whereas Lord Kerr dissented 33 times during his decade on the Court. Indeed, Lord Kerr's comparatively high dissent rate falls in line with his view, expressed in an extrajudicial lecture, that judges should readily dissent when they disagree with the majority view and that doing so contributes to the quality of the law overall.[32] There is no record of Lord Rodger's view on dissenting, but his tendency to dissent has been acknowledged by his colleagues.[33] Lord Brown, the third of only three judges to dissent more than 10 per cent of the time, has also publicly praised the utility of dissenting,[34] but his high dissent rate is particularly interesting in light of the fact that, according to both academics[35] and Lord Brown himself,[36] his propensity to dissent during his time in the House of Lords was much more modest. He explained that this was due to gaining confidence and 'courage' over time; once the House of Lords became the Supreme Court, he was more comfortable with questioning 'the likely correctness' of the views of his colleagues.[37]

The dataset did not record 'almost-dissents': those situations where a judge recorded that they disagreed with, or seriously doubted, the correctness of the view taken by their colleagues, but nonetheless chose not press their concerns to the point of issuing a formal dissenting opinion.[38] Had these kinds of cases been recorded, it would likely cause the dissent rate of both Lady Hale and Lord Carnwath to go up (who each have a relatively high dissent rate already, according

[30] W Swadling, 'Legislating in Vain' in A Burrows, D Johnston and R Zimmerman, *Judge and Jurist: Essays in Memory of Lord Rodger of Earlsferry* (OUP, 2013) 667. For example, Lord Rodger expressed frustration with the conclusion in cases such as *Cadder v HM Advocate* [2010] UKSC 43; [2010] WLR 2601 and the House of Lords case of *R (AF) v Secretary of State for the Home Department (No 3)* [2009] UKHL 28; [2009] 3 WLR 74 but signed up to the majority in both.

[31] Lord Brown, 'Dissenting Judgments' in A Burrows, D Johnston and R Zimmermann, *Judge and Jurist: Essays in Memory of Lord Rodger of Earlsferry* (OUP, 2013) 119.

[32] Lord Kerr (n 23). See also Paterson (n 2) 117.

[33] Lord Brown (n 31).

[34] Lord Brown, 'In praise of dissenting judgments' Prospect, 28 May 2020, although elsewhere he cautioned that 'a court which speaks with two voices risks bringing the law into disrepute': *R (Lumba) v Secretary of State for the Home Department* [2011] UKSC 12; [2012] 1 AC 245 at [345].

[35] T Poole and S Shah, 'The Law Lords and Human Rights' (2011) 74 *MLR* 79, 97; Paterson (n 2) 118.

[36] Lord Brown, *Playing off the Roof* (Marble Hall, 2020) 189–90.

[37] ibid 190.

[38] See eg *Yemshaw v London Borough of Hounslow* [2011] UKSC 3; [2011] 1 All ER 912 at [60] (Lord Brown) and *FirstGroup Plc v Paulley* [2017] UKSC 4; [2017] 2 All ER 1 at [92] (Lord Sumption).

to Figure 6) as both issued these kinds of statements on multiple occasions.[39] It seems that Lord Rodger and Lord Kerr were less reluctant to push their opposition to the point of dissent compared to Lady Hale and Lord Carnwath: when they disagreed, they dissented.

Outside of recent appointments, Lord Collins had the lowest dissent propensity of any judge.[40] Lord Dyson dissented on two occasions, but both related to cases where he was drafted back into the Court's roster temporarily during his tenure as Master of the Rolls.[41] Lord Neuberger, Lord Hodge and Lord Hughes all had low dissent rates, and each served for over six years.[42] Despite a reputation which might suggest otherwise, Lord Sumption actually holds a relatively modest dissent rate overall and he was less likely to dissent than a number of his colleagues – his ten dissents represent only a very small percentage of his overall, quite substantial, judicial output. As noted above, the relatively low dissent propensity of these judges should not imply that they necessarily lack distinction or are in some way meek – some of these judges would certainly not be described as *shy* – a low dissent rate, in addition to reflecting a commitment to the Court's collective function, may also, as Paterson notes, mark a judge as being particularly adept at influencing their colleagues and changing the minds of other judges to form more majority coalitions.[43]

E. Solo Dissents

Extrajudicially, some judges have expressed comfort with the idea of dissenting on their own, without being joined by colleagues, whilst others confess to seeing little utility in doing so.[44] Figure 7, which sets out how many of each judge's dissents were *solo dissents* – that is, dissenting opinions which did not garner the support of any other colleagues – does indeed, as these remarks suggest, show a variance between the judges in this respect.[45]

[39] See eg *Re JR17* [2010] UKSC 27; [2010] HRLR 27 at [102] (Lady Hale); *Societe Generale v Geys* [2012] UKSC 63, [2013] 1 AC 523 at [107] (Lord Carnwath); *R (New London College) v Secretary of State for the Home Department* [2013] UKSC 51; [2013] 1 WLR 2358 at [41] (Lord Carnwath); *R (Faulkner) v Secretary of State for Justice* [2013] UKSC 23; [2013] 2 All ER 1013 at [127] (Lord Carnwath); *R (HS2 Action Alliance) v Secretary of State for Transport* [2014] UKSC 2 at [156] (Lady Hale).

[40] Although it seems that he almost dissented in further cases, such as *R (Coke-Wallis) v Institute of Chartered Accountants in England and Wales* [2011] UKSC 1; [2011] 2 AC 146 before changing his mind and voting with the majority: Paterson (n 2) 199.

[41] *cf* Paterson (n 2) 165.

[42] Interestingly, all of Lord Hodge's dissenting votes were cast over a relatively short period between Hilary Term 2014 and Trinity Term 2015.

[43] This is certainly how Paterson describes Lords Collins and Dyson, two of the Court's lowest dissenters: n 2, 164–65.

[44] Lady Hale (n 29) 11 June 2019; Paterson (n 2) 131, 163.

[45] Excluded from this table are those judges who authored fewer than five dissents overall.

Figure 7 Type of dissent (group or solo)

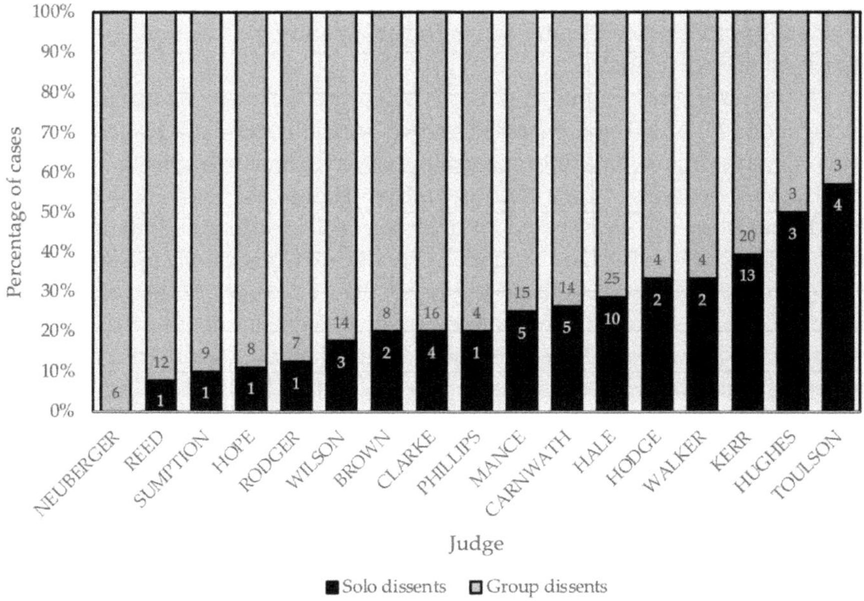

Most judges were more likely (often *much* more likely) to dissent alone than in a group. The only judge to reverse this trend, and to dissent alone more frequently than as part of a coalition was Lord Toulson, although it is notable that Lord Kerr authored the most solo dissents of all judges, doing so on 13 separate occasions (about 40 per cent of his dissents were individual dissents).[46] This is certainly in line with his general ethos of dissenting whenever he believes the majority arrive at the wrong answer, regardless of other factors.

On the other hand, Lord Neuberger *never* dissented alone at all; all six of his dissents were joined by at least one other judge. This means that he was able to agree with another judge (or convince another judge to agree with him) in all of the 258 cases he was involved in during his time on the Court. A total of five judges only dissented on their own in a single instance; Lord Reed, for example, dissented 13 times, but was joined by a colleague in 12 of them. The other one-time solo dissenters are Lord Phillips (four times with others); Lord Rodger (seven times with others) Lord Hope (eight times with others) and Lord Sumption (nine times with others).

[46] See generally R Cahill-O'Callaghan, 'Lord Kerr's Dissents: Jewels in the Crown of the Supreme Court' in B Dickson and C McCormick (eds), *The Judicial Mind: A Festschrift for Lord Kerr of Tonaghmore* (Hart Publishing, 2021) 75–80.

F. Speaking Dissents

Sometimes, when multiple judges form a dissenting wing, some judges will simply indicate their agreement with another dissenting judge, rather than writing a judgment of their own. Owing both to the existence of solo dissents (where, by definition, a dissenting judge would *have* to speak, having no other colleague to agree with) and the particular nature of dissenting opinions (judges would have to feel relatively strongly about the case to dissent in the first place, and at least one dissenter must write something), it should be expected that most dissenting votes would be 'spoken' dissents rather than mere agreements. This is explored in Figure 8.

Figure 8 Percentage of dissenting votes featuring a spoken contribution

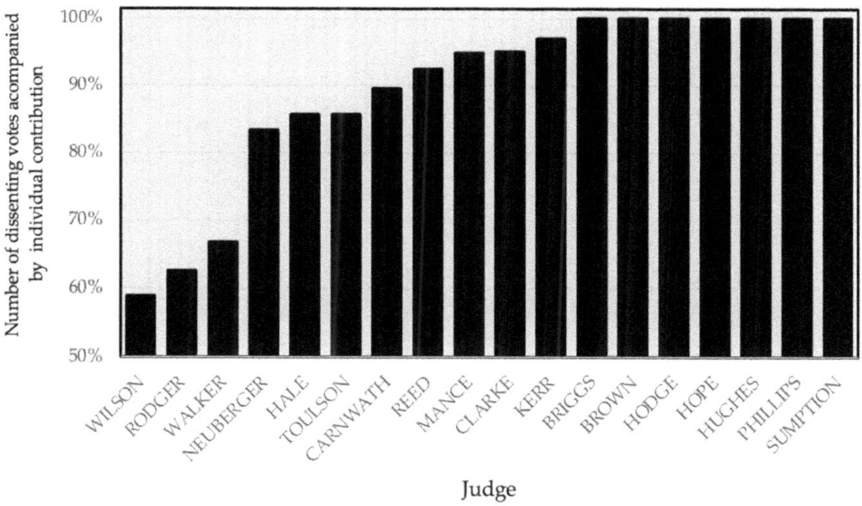

Spoken dissents are indeed far more popular than mere indications of agreement. This table only includes those judges who issued five or more dissents; most of the other judges' votes excluded here were also spoken contributions (although Lord Dyson spoke once and stayed quiet once, Lady Black's single dissenting vote in the dataset was a simple agreement with without any comment of her own, and only one of the dissenting votes cast by Lord Lloyd-Jones featured a contribution of his own). Eight judges spoke every time they dissented, including Lords Sumption and Brown who each dissented ten times. Lord Kerr's spoken output is remarkable; he added a speech of his own to all but one of his 33 dissents. By contrast, the 'quietest' dissenter was Lord Wilson; out of his 17 dissenting votes, he only spoke in ten of them; when considering only group dissents (where Lord Wilson would have had some *choice* as to whether to author his own dissent alongside that of a colleague), he spoke seven times and chose to indicate mere agreement seven times. Lord Wilson was therefore more concerned with voting for what he considered to be the right answer than authoring a unique contribution for the sake of it.

This section, then, has shown that judges offer different kinds of contributions to the Court's output, the most interesting of which may well be their propensity to dissent. Figure 9 brings this together, showing for each judge what proportion of their output ended up being lead, concurring or dissenting votes. As can be seen, some of the judges are already emerging as distinct figures, with records diverging from that which might be expected. The next section looks at whether the same can be said with regards to the length of the judge's contributions.

Figure 9 Types of vote (lead/concurrence/dissent)

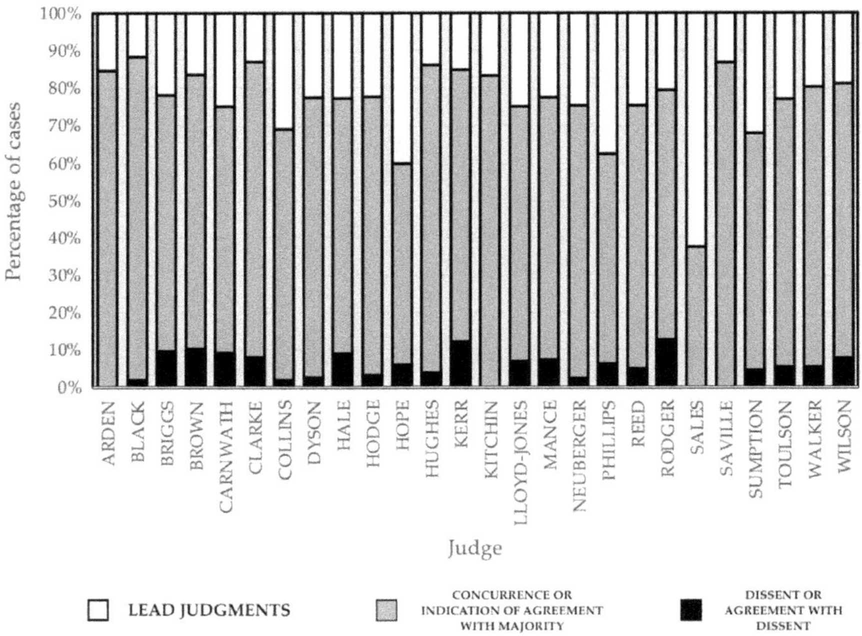

II. Contribution Length

A. Output Length

This section looks at the length of each individual judge's contribution to judgments. The length of an individual contribution was defined straightforwardly according to the total number of paragraphs each judge authored. Sometimes, judges wrote joint judgments together (usually, but not always, joint *lead* judgments); in such cases, the length of each individual judge's contribution was determined by dividing the whole contribution by the number of authors.[47] Unsurprisingly, those judges who sat on the Court for a longer period, and who sat on more cases overall, contributed more to the Court's overall output, as Figure 10 shows.

Figure 10 Total output in paragraphs

Judge	Paragraphs written	Judge	Paragraphs written
NEUBERGER	5225	WALKER	1515
MANCE	4942	DYSON	1513
REED	4740	HUGHES	1430
HALE	4709	COLLINS	1398
KERR	3999	BROWN	959
CARNWATH	3394	RODGER	916
SUMPTION	3282	BRIGGS	793
HOPE	3265	BLACK	586
CLARKE	2634	LLOYD-JONES	517
PHILLIPS	2376	SALES	191
WILSON	2358	KITCHIN	141
HODGE	2311	ARDEN	82
TOULSON	2047	SAVILLE	74

Lord Neuberger comes out top despite sitting on the Court for less than five years; he in fact produced significantly more paragraphs during this time than Lady Hale and Lord Kerr did over the full ten years of the dataset. Clearly, not only did Lord Neuberger sit on a lot of cases, as Figures 1 and 2 show, but he wrote a significant amount when sitting in those cases, too.

As each judge's total output was so deeply affected by the time they spent on the Court, Figure 11 instead sets out each judge's *average* contribution (total paragraphs contributed divided by number of cases in which a judge contributed). The data is separated to show each judge's average lead, concurrence and dissent lengths.

Some general trends regarding contribution length can be detected. Overall, lead judgments tended to be longer than dissenting judgments, which were themselves longer than concurring judgments. Whilst there is a fair degree of variance between the average length of each judge's lead judgments (and, at least to some extent, their dissents), the spread of average concurring judgment lengths was much less pronounced.[48] Incidentally, some judges authored *particularly* short concurrences; 31 of Lord Brown's 33 concurrences ran to less than 20 paragraphs

[47] For example in the case of a lead judgment of 100 paragraphs authored by two judges jointly, each judge is determined to have 'contributed' 50 paragraphs each.

[48] The range for each judge's lead is 59.95, the range for each judge's average dissent length is 50.6; the range for each judge's average concurrence is just 27.17.

long and 22 are shorter than ten paragraphs long. 34 of Lord Clarke's 38 concurrences were less than 20 paragraphs long and 24 were shorter than ten paragraphs. 42 of Lady Hale's 50 concurrences are less than 20 paragraphs; only one single concurrence runs to 30.

Figure 11 Average individual contribution length (lead, concurring, dissenting speeches)

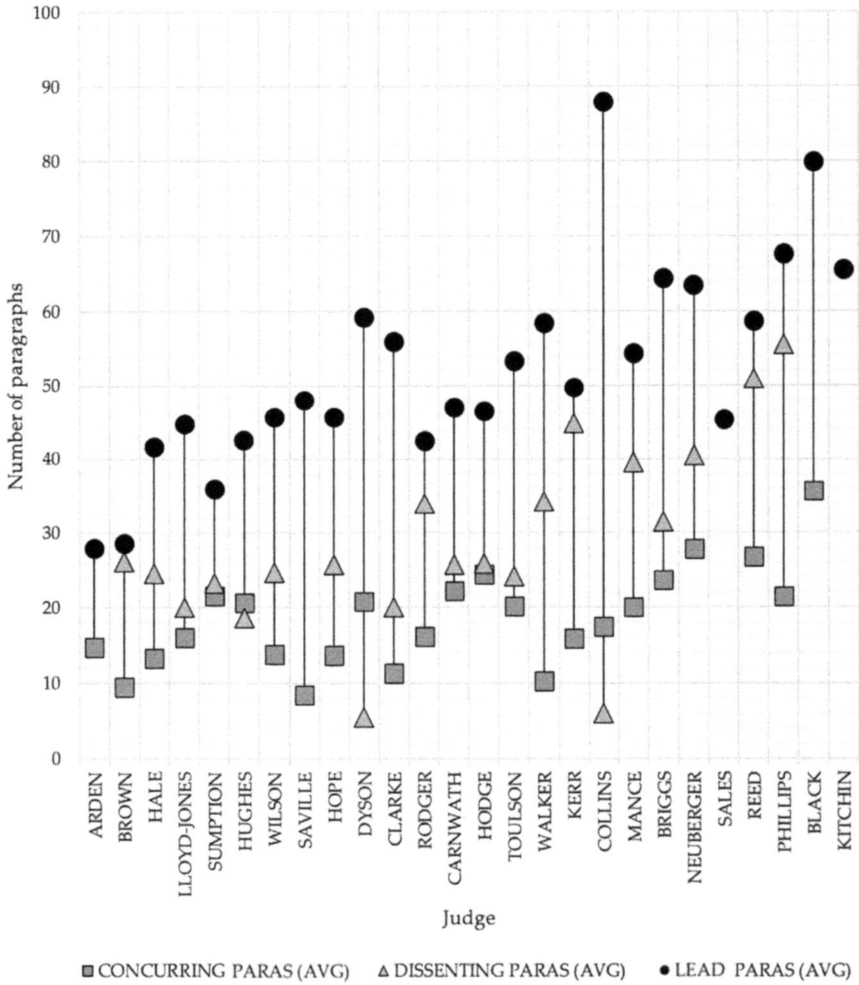

Generally, those judges who tended to write long lead judgments would also write long concurrences and dissents, although not this is not always so; Lord Collins, for example, wrote some of the Court's longest lead judgments but also some of its shortest dissents. Looking through the judges' records, we can note that in particular:

- Lord Collins wrote the longest leads, followed by Lady Black then Lord Phillips.
- Lady Arden wrote the shortest leads, followed by Lord Brown then Lord Sumption.

- Lady Black wrote the longest concurrences, followed by Lord Neuberger then Lord Reed.
- Lord Saville wrote the shortest concurrences, followed by Lord Brown then Lord Walker.
- Lord Phillips wrote the longest dissents, followed by Lord Reed then Lord Kerr.
- Lord Dyson wrote the shortest dissents, followed by Lord Collins then Lord Hughes.

Some of the positions of the judges in Figure 11 make sense, aligning with extrajudicial statements they have made previously; Lady Hale, for example, has suggested that judicial contributions should ordinarily be succinct,[49] and the above shows that she generally abides by this philosophy herself. On the other hand, both Lords Dyson[50] and Neuberger[51] have also criticised overly-long judgments, although neither appear to be particularly concise speakers themselves.

More generally, however, it is difficult to identify an obvious pattern when it comes to the writers of the Court's longer contributions. For example, whilst some are more recent appointees such as Lord Kitchin and Lady Black, some are much older, such as Lord Phillips. The same can be said of the judges occupying the lower end of the scale; Lady Arden, the judge with the shortest judgments on average, is a comparatively recent appointment who sat on the Court for just a few months during the ten-year period surveyed. Lady Hale, by contrast, was appointed to the Court at its point of creation, and served for the whole ten-year period. In addition, whilst Presidents and Deputy Presidents such as Lord Phillips, Lord Reed and Lord Neuberger appear at the 'top' end of Figure 11 as particularly verbose judges, Lady Hale appears at the other end of the table as a much more succinct speaker. A number of judges who tended to write quite short judgments such as Lady Hale and Lord Sumption also tended to sit on more cases and produce more judgments. Whilst these factors may well be related, the link is not absolute. For example, Lord Neuberger and Reed both produced lengthy judgments *and* sat on a high number of cases. A judge's free time and general workload does not explain this variance on its own. The best explanation for the variance in Figure 11 may therefore simply be individual judicial style.

Figure 11 recorded the length of each judge's *average* contribution. Taking a different perspective, Figure 12 instead looks at each judge's *longest* published leads, concurrences and dissents.

[49] Lady Hale, 'Judgment Writing in the Supreme Court' (UK Supreme Court First Anniversary Seminar, 30 September 2010) 5.

[50] Lord Dyson, *A Judge's Journey* (Hart Publishing, 2019) 199.

[51] Lord Neuberger, 'No Judgment – no justice' (n 19) paras 20–21.

Figure 12 Longest individual contribution length (lead, concurring, dissenting speeches)

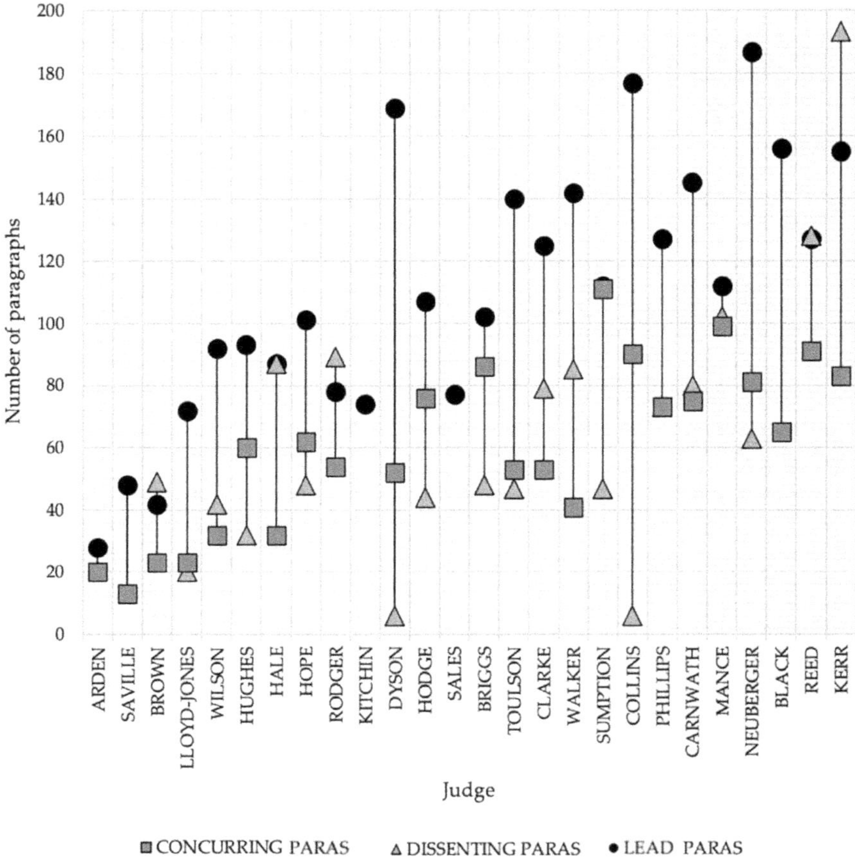

There is certainly a greater variance in the positions in Figure 12 compared to Figure 11. Generally, lead judgments still stand out; for the vast majority of judges, their longest contribution came in the form of a lead judgment. However, the longest contributions from Lords Brown, Rodger, Reed and Kerr were all dissents (unsurprisingly, but for Lord Reed, all are keen dissenters: see Figure 6). Lord Sumption's lengthiest concurrence was just one paragraph shorter than his lengthiest lead judgment. Lady Hale and Lord Mance both find themselves in the strange position whereby their longest lead and longest dissents are, in fact, found in the same case – this is because those contributions hail from two unusual cases where, in each, the lead judgment expresses a dissenting position.[52] Otherwise, there is

[52] In this case, *HH v Italy* [2012] UKSC 25; [2013] 1 AC 338 and R *(Kaiyam) v Secretary of State for Justice* [2014] UKSC 66 [2015] AC 1344 respectively.

less of an obvious 'gap' between concurrences and dissents compared to that in Figure 11; some judges' longest concurrences are longer than their longest dissents.

Figure 12 also reveals which judges have authored particularly long judgments during their time on the Court. Lords Dyson, Collins and Neuberger have each penned judgments of over 160 paragraphs in length. Lord Kerr authored the longest individual contribution of any judge in this period, and it is, characteristically, a dissenting judgment.[53] That dissent is, very notably, over 50 per cent longer than the next longest dissent in the dataset. By contrast, it seems that some judges have never authored a particularly long judgment during their time on the Court: ten judges have never written a judgment of more than 100 paragraphs; five have never written a judgment of more than 80 paragraphs; two have never written a judgment of more than 50 paragraphs.

As such, it seems that when it comes to the length of their judicial output, the judges do differ between one another to a fair extent, both in terms of looking at their average contribution, and looking at their longest contribution.

III. Conclusions

It has been shown that individual judges have different working patterns and behavioural tendencies. Some judges participated in more cases than others, even if accounting for duration of tenure. Lord Neuberger was a particularly 'busy' judge during his time on the Court in this respect.

In addition, certain judges were more comfortable than others with adding their own voice to a judgment. Judges such as Lords Hope and Collins quite frequently contributed something to a judgment, whereas judges such as Lord Kitchin, Lady Black and Lord Saville contributed much more rarely. In fact, outside of lead judgments, Lord Kitchin did not contribute a separate opinion of his own – whether concurrence or dissent – in a single case in the dataset. Remarkably, as of December 2022, Lord Kitchin authored just one separate concurrence, and has indicated agreement with (but did not himself write) just one dissenting judgment.[54] Lord Kitchin certainly cannot be accused of writing 'vanity judgments'.[55]

Further, it has been shown that judges contribute to judgments in different ways. Some issue concurrences and dissents readily, others much less so. Judges who were particularly likely to author a lead judgment include Lords Hope, Sumption and Phillips. Others were particularly likely to dissent, such as Lords Kerr, Rodger.

[53] The case is *Re Northern Ireland Human Rights Commission* [2018] UKSC 27; [2019] 1 All ER 173 where Lord Kerr's dissent runs to 197 paragraphs.

[54] He issued an 18-paragraph concurrence in *Royal Mencap Society v Tomlinson-Blake* [2021] UKSC 8; [2022] 1 All ER 497 and agreed with the dissenting judgment of Lord Sales in *Sevilleja v Marex* [2020] UKSC 31; [2020] 3 WLR 255.

[55] see Lord Neuberger (n 12) at para 35.

Here, too, Lord Kitchin emerges as a notable *non*-dissenter.[56] Concurrence rates differ across the judges, with more recent appointees tending to issue fewer *spoken* concurrences than their predecessors.

The extent and style of each judge's output also varies. The Court has some verbose members as well as much more succinct speakers. For some judges, the extent of their contributions depends on their nature and utility: there are, for example, loquacious dissenters and concise concurrers. The range of judicial outputs here is noteworthy: whilst some judges contribute fewer than 20 paragraphs to a case on average, others contribute more than 50 paragraphs per case. Overall, judges such as Lord Reed, Lady Black and Lord Neuberger tend to author substantial contributions, whereas Lord Brown and Lady Arden are amongst the most concise of the judges.

In sum, it is clear that even without looking at what their judgments say, it can be said that individual judges contribute to cases in different ways – some are enthusiastic participants, speaking frequently, and readily offering their own view. Others use their voice only when they consider it necessary to do so, or only when dissenting. There is no one established format for a 'judicial contribution' in the UKSC.

This chapter has shown that even at a fairly formal level, divergences between UKSC judges can be identified. Rather than suggesting that any of these models of judicial engagement are better than any other, this chapter simply shows that there is no one prevailing model of the judicial role (at least when the whole dataset is assessed in the round). In fact, it might be said that the Court benefits from different kinds of judges sitting together. The best judge to contribute to a niche case resting on a very technical, specialist point of law may be entirely different to the judge best-suited to author the lead judgment in a controversial case involving the invocation of grand principles. And neither of those judges may be best placed to contribute to a case raising sensitive, politically-charged matters. A mix of judicial types – loud and quiet, outspoken and reserved, leaders and followers – have now worked together remarkably well for over a decade. Indeed, to return to the central theme of this book, this chapter's findings could be expressed in the following way: judges, despite (or perhaps *because* of) divergent *individual* behaviour, were able to produce a *collective* output of remarkable frequency and quality.

[56] Although Lord Sales, Lord Saville and Lady Arden did not author a dissent in the dataset, they sat on far fewer cases than Lord Kitchin.

4

Appeals from Lower Courts

This chapter examines the approach of the UKSC and its judges when it comes to determining appeals from lower courts. It considers how likely an appeal is to be allowed, and whether appeals from certain courts are treated more favourably than others in this respect. Although it is suggested that the Court's approach to lower courts is fairly unremarkable, the records of individual judges, or certain groups of individual judges, are more noteworthy.

A quick note on the hierarchy of the UK court system may be useful for some readers. As the most senior court in the United Kingdom, the Supreme Court hears appeals from the courts beneath it in the judicial hierarchy.[1] As the most senior court *in all three UK legal systems*, it can hear cases from courts in all of them. This means that the judgment being appealed will usually come from the most senior court (bar the UKSC itself) in each jurisdiction (the Court of Appeal of England and Wales, the Inner House of Court of the Court of Session and the Court of Appeal of Northern Ireland) although the UKSC also hears 'leapfrog' appeals from courts further down the judicial hierarchy in certain circumstances.[2] Separately, the UKSC hears a comparatively small number of cases in which it holds an exclusive and original jurisdiction.

The UKSC can hear appeals on most matters arising in lower courts, although there are some areas in which it does not have jurisdiction (for example, there is only a very limited avenue for appeals involving criminal matters from Scotland to be appealed to the UKSC, most of which are generally dealt with by the High Court of Justiciary). Whilst there are certain kinds of issues which the Court has suggested are better determined by lower courts rather than the UKSC,[3] these

[1] HM Courts and Tribunals, 'The structure of the courts', available at: www.judiciary.uk/wp-content/uploads/2021/07/courts-structure-0715.pdf.

[2] See Administration of Justice Act 1969, ss 12–17; Criminal Justice and Courts Act 2015, ss 516–519.

[3] However, the Court has suggested that some decisions ought to be determined conclusively by lower courts, and that it will not intervene in such cases in the absence of exceptional circumstances: see eg *BPP Holdings v HMRC* [2017] UKSC 55; [2017] WLR 2945 at [26] (Upper Tribunal and Court of Appeal best placed for setting out guidance relating to tribunal practices); *Prince Abdulaziz v Apex Global Management Ltd* [2014] UKSC 64; [2014] 1 WLR 4495 at [39] (Court of Appeal best placed to deal with case management decisions); *R (Gourlay) v Parole Board* [2020] UKSC 50; [2020] 1 WLR 5344 at [24], [36], [49]; *CPRE Kent v Secretary of State for Communities and Local Government* [2021] UKSC 36; [2021] 1 WLR 4168 at [15]–[16] (Court of Appeal best placed to set out costs guidance).

limits are largely imposed by the Court itself for prudential reasons. The right to appeal a case to the UKSC from a lower court is not, however, automatic; permission must first be sought and granted, ether by the lower court or (more likely) the UKSC itself.[4] Permission is granted when judges think that the appeal 'raises an arguable point of law of general public importance'[5] and although this fairly opaque criteria is difficult to interpret on its face, Hanretty has found that a case is more likely to be granted permission if they involve issues relating to criminal or public law, or if the central government is a party to proceedings.[6]

Why, then, might it be interesting to consider appellate success rates? The UKSC has the power to overturn any lower court decision, in whole or in part. However, cases will typically have been argued fully, on multiple occasions, before experienced and often specialist judges, by the time they reach the Supreme Court. All UKSC judges naturally afford respect to the views of lower court judges and it seems to be commonly understood that their job is not necessarily to correct all errors made by the courts below.[7] But determining the level of scrutiny to be applied, and how much weight ought to be given to the views of lower court judges is not necessarily a straightforward question, and individual UKSC judges may take different positions as to exactly where the line is to be drawn. Further, whilst all judges may accept that a greater degree of intervention may be appropriate in certain cases but not others, they may disagree as to which kinds of cases warrant close scrutiny and which ones require a greater degree of deference.[8] The judges' attitude to appeals may therefore indicate something about their institutional understanding of the court system as a whole.

I. Operationalisation

This first section outlines some of the metrics which guided the *operationalisation* of the data. Many of the methods employed here are the same as those used in other chapters. Very briefly, an individual appeal was defined for the purposes of the dataset according to whether it was treated as a distinct case with unique citation *at the Supreme Court level*, regardless of the format of those cases in the courts below. This means, for example, that where two Court of Appeal cases which are

[4] Before 2015, it was much easier to get permission to appeal a decision from the Court of Session in Scotland; this has since been amended by the Courts Reform (Scotland) Act 2014. Although this means that specific procedural rules now apply to appeals from the Scottish courts, in practice these rules do not differ substantially from the practice of other jurisdictions.

[5] UK Supreme Court Practice Direction 3, 3.3.3.

[6] C Hanretty, *A Court of Specialists* (OUP, 2020) ch 3.

[7] Lord Reed, 'The Supreme Court Ten Years On' (Bentham Association Lecture, 6 March 2019) 2–4.

[8] See eg the degree of scrutiny required in appeals against the proportionality assessments of lower courts: see Lord Sales 'Proportionality and Appellate Courts' (ALBA Annual Lecture, 10 November 2020); P Daly, 'Appellate standard of review in public law cases' [2021] *PL* 334 and *Re Attorney-General's Reference (Safe Access Zones)* [2022] UKSC 32; [2023] AC 505 at [21]–[67].

joined and decided by the UKSC in one reported judgment, this constituted one singular appeal.

For the purposes of this chapter, only case outcomes were marked, and were usually recorded as simple 'wins' (appeal allowed, lower court overturned) or 'losses' (appeal dismissed, lower court decision affirmed). Because appeals frequently feature multiple challenges to lower court decisions, the database recorded any judgment in which the UKSC overturned a substantive conclusion of the judgment below as a successful appeal. Because appeal success was defined as relating exclusively to outcomes, those cases in which the UKSC agreed with the outcome of the court below, but arrived there via different reasoning, were not marked as successful appeals. However, where cases involved multiple claimants (either on the same 'side' or where each opposing party appeals aspects of the ruling below), and the UKSC allowed the appeals of some but not others, this was expressed as a partial 'mark' depending on the win/loss ratio.[9] Whilst the joining of appeals, appearance of multiple parties, and possibility of cross-appeals sometimes created a degree of artificiality when it came to coding appeals (eg in some cases the Court was recorded as considering as many as eight distinct appeals)[10] the vast majority of cases could be coded straightforwardly and raised few problems.[11] Those cases where no obvious lower court could be identified – including cases where the UKSC has original jurisdiction – were simply excluded from analysis.

II. Appeals Data

It may be useful, at the outset, to consider the Court's general tendencies when it comes to allowing appeals. Figure 1 shows how many cases were allowed compared to the number dismissed across the entire dataset. As can be seen, 282 cases were categorised as having been allowed by the UKSC, whereas 304 were categorised as being dismissed. 53 cases involved a mixed finding where one of the appeals was allowed and another was dismissed. A further 43 cases could not be straightforwardly coded as 'allow' or 'dismiss' (such cases included, for example, decisions which did not involve any appeal from a lower court, cases where

[9] For example, in *R (Faulkner) v Secretary of State for Justice* [2013] UKSC 23; [2013] 2 All ER 1013 the Court considered three distinct appeals: first, Faulkner's appeal against the Parole Board; second, the Parole Board's cross-appeal against Faulkner; third, the appeal of a second party, Sturnham, against the Parole Board. The first appeal was rejected; the second was allowed; the third was also allowed. Since two of three appeals in the case were successful, a partial mark of 0.67 was given.

[10] *R (Carmichael and Rourke) v Secretary of State for Work and Pensions* [2016] UKSC 58; [2016] WLR 4550. Since the majority dealt with each claimant separately (see especially [44]–[46]) and A's cross-appeal distinctly, the 8 live appeals were: (1) Carmichael's appeal against the state (2) Rourke's appeal against the state; (3) D's appeal against the state; (4) JD's appeal against the state; (5) Daly's appeal against the state; (6) the state's appeal against the Rutherford family; (7) the state's appeal against A; (8) A's appeal against the state.

[11] Not least because this information is almost always included in the judgment itself.

the Court solely decided upon issues relating to costs, and cases where the only outcome was to make a reference to the Court of Justice of the European Union). All in all, it seems that the UKSC was slightly more likely to dismiss appeals than it was to allow them, although the margin is only very slight when considering the overall numbers involved.

Figure 1 Number of appeals allowed (overall)

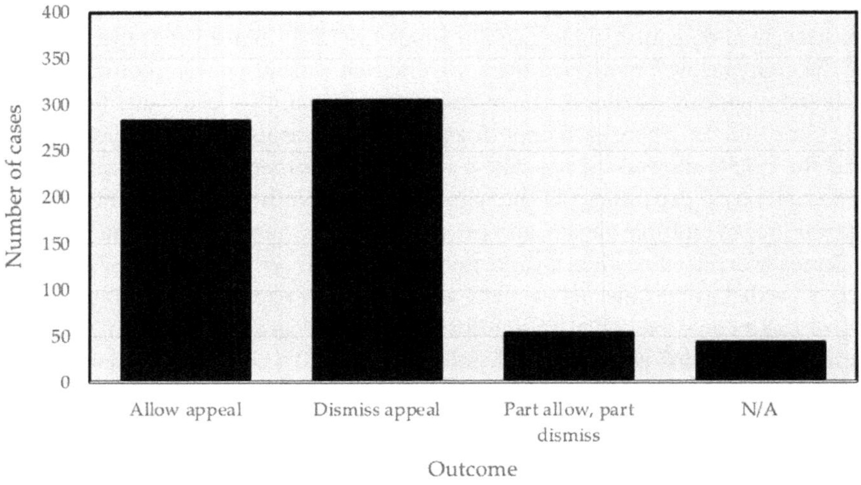

In one sense, the fact that the UKSC only agrees with the lower courts around half the time may be surprising. If the UKSC's own determinations are taken to be 'correct' and overturned decisions 'incorrect', this could be interpreted to mean that that some of the UK's most eminent and well-respected appellate judges were, according to the UKSC, no more likely to reach the correct answer than the wrong one. But three things should be borne in mind. First, lower courts are less powerful than the UKSC, and are bound by precedent in a way the senior court is not, meaning that in some cases the lower court was unable to reach the 'right answer' of its own accord. Second, sometimes the UKSC has before it certain material, such as a decision of the European Court of Human Rights, which was not available before the courts below, affecting the outcome. Third, and most importantly, the UKSC only reviews a tiny fraction of cases decided by lower courts. Most applications for permission to appeal to the Court are rejected, and a very high proportion of lower court decisions are not appealed in the first place. Seen from that perspective, notwithstanding the figures below, the vast majority of such lower court decisions can indeed be considered to have been decided correctly.

Further, the finding that the Court is (roughly) as likely to allow an appeal as it is to dismiss it remained relatively consistent over time, as Figure 2 illustrates. Based on these results, we can place the overall likelihood of a given appeal to be allowed by the UKSC at around 48 per cent.[12] This is a success rate broadly in line with that of the House of Lords.[13]

Figure 2 Percentage of appeals allowed (per legal year)

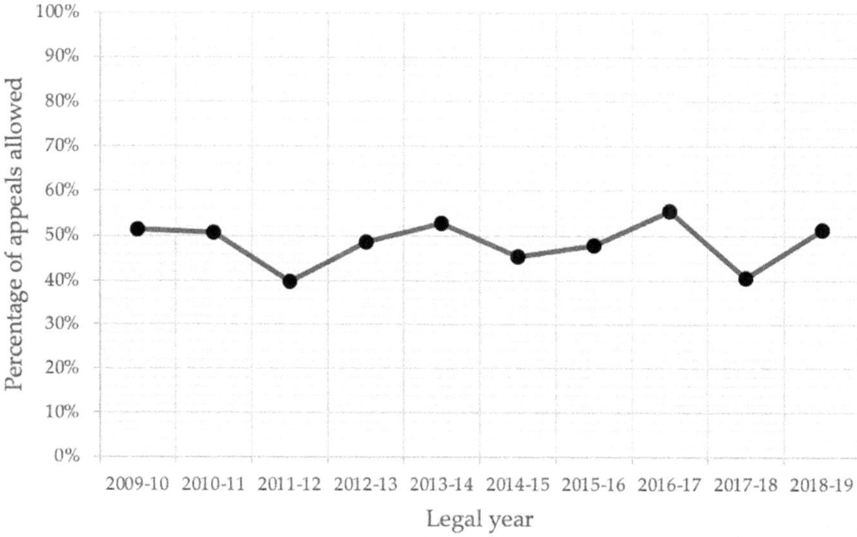

The data therefore suggests that there is no strong evidence to show that the UKSC leans towards either allowing or dismissing appeals, a finding which remains consistent across time periods. However, this may be true when considering the output of the Court as a whole, but what of the views of individual judges?

This is set out in Figure 3. If the Court's overall 'likelihood to allow an appeal' is taken to be 48 per cent, we can see that most judges do not deviate too far from this point: all but five judges have an 'allow rate' within around five percentage points of this average. However, there are some outliers. Lords Brown and Hope voted to allow the appeal from the court below in around 38 per cent and 39 per cent of the cases in which they sat, respectively, making them the judges most deferential to the view of the judges below them. By contrast, Lord Phillips and Lady Hale each has an 'allow rate' of just over 55 per cent, making them the judges most comfortable with overturning lower court rulings. It is worth noting that both Phillips and Hale sat as Court Presidents, which may have provided them with a degree of institutional bravery, their leadership positions

[12] This figure is the same whether calculated as the mean total of each yearly average 'allow' rate (essentially an average of each of the points in Figure 2) or as a figure based on the total number of cases allowed and dismissed (essentially the first two bars in Figure 1).

[13] A Paterson, *Final Judgment* (Hart Publishing, 2013) 236.

encouraging something of a less deferential approach in each instance. This is not a universal trait of the Court's leadership figures, however, as Lord Neuberger, the Court's second President, had a much lower 'allow rate'. At 45 per cent, this places him *below* the average.

Figure 3 Percentage of appeals allowed by each judge

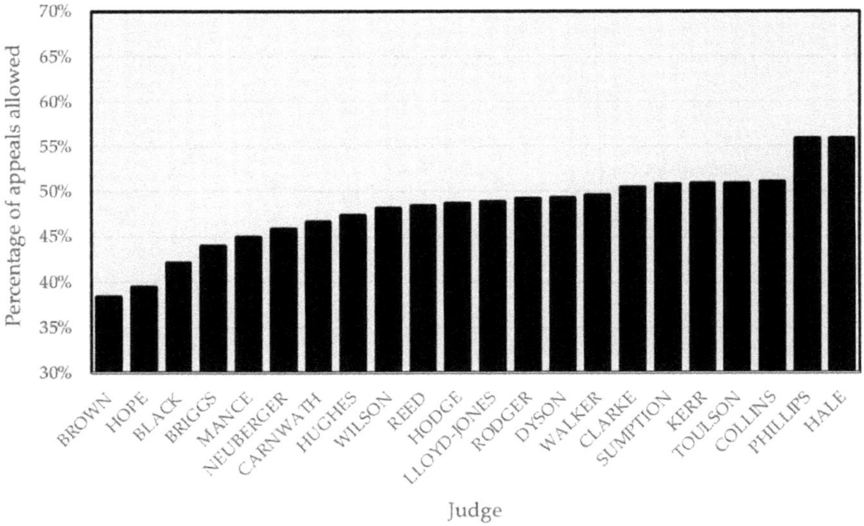

As such, there seems to be *some* variation between the judges when it comes to allowing appeals. Whether this indicates anything particularly significant about the respective judges is another question. As mentioned above, to some extent the 'allow rates' of individual judges might reflect judicial individualism or personal attitudes towards the judicial role; some scholars have attempted, although not altogether convincingly, to portray a judge's 'allow rate' as an expression of ideology.[14] In this vein, Lord Brown may hold a lot of respect for the views of other judges, over and above his own, whereas Lord Phillips may be more confident in insisting on putting forward his own views. However, whilst no individual statistic should be considered in isolation, the 'allow rates' of individual judges are likely to be affected by even more 'noise' than other trends. In particular, they are difficult to interpret without knowledge of the context of the judgment under appeal or the sort of behaviour (whether ideological or otherwise) exhibited by the judges of the lower courts. For example, given the fact that the vast majority of appeals came from the Court of Appeal of England and Wales, if that Court was made up of judges exhibiting liberal, activist, expansionist tendencies,

[14] M Iaryczower and G Katz, 'More than Politics: Ability and Ideology in the British Appellate Committee' (2016) 32(1) *Journal of Law, Economics and Organizations* 61.

high 'allow rates' at the UKSC level may reflect legal or ideological conservatism, rather than a lack of deference.[15]

Nevertheless, Figure 3 does suggest that there are at least some differences between the individual judges when it comes to allowing or dismissing appeals as a whole. It provides *some* evidence that individual judges are inclined to behave in different ways. The following section turns to how judges approach appeals from particular courts.

III. Scottish and Northern Irish Appeals

Out of a total of 682 cases, the UKSC heard a total of 97 appeals from Scottish courts over its first decade (henceforth 'Scottish appeals').[16] Nine appeals concerned exclusively Scottish matters (rather than general issues applicable to laws affecting other jurisdictions, but decided by Scottish courts).[17] During the same period it also heard 29 appeals from the courts of Northern Ireland ('Northern Irish appeals').[18] As such, over ten years, the Court heard over three times as many Scottish appeals as Northern Irish appeals.

Figure 4 looks at the success rate of appeals before the UKSC from courts of these different jurisdictions. The Court was about as likely to allow an appeal from a court in England and Wales as it was from a court in Northern Ireland (both have a 48 per cent success rate).[19] There is, however, a small drop in the success rate of appeals from Scottish courts, where only around 44 per cent of appeals succeed. Part of this may be due to the more generous (indeed, almost automatic) permission procedure which operated in respect to appeals from Scotland prior to 2015,[20] which would have seen weaker cases appear before the Court (and which may not have been granted permission under the more rigorous permission procedure applicable to other cases), resulting in a greater proportion of unsuccessful appeals. Otherwise, a fairly small divergence of just 4 per cent is unlikely to reveal anything too significant about the UKSC's treatment of Scottish court decisions.

[15] This will be explored more fully in ch 9.

[16] The list excludes the legal challenge to the validity of the 'Continuity Bill' passed by the Scottish Parliament (*Re Withdrawal from the European Union (Legal Continuity) Bill* [2018] UKSC 64; [2019] AC 1022) as it was a challenge lodged by the UK law officers under section 33 of the Scotland Act 1998.

[17] Lord Reed, 'The Supreme Court and Scotland: The First Ten Years' (UK Supreme Court Ten-Year Anniversary Lecture Series, 19 November 2019), 12, 15. Eight of these cases were unanimous; the exception is *David T Morrison v ICL Plastics* [2014] UKSC 48; 2014 SCLR 711 which divided the court 3–2.

[18] Excluded here is a direct reference to the UKSC by the AG for Northern Ireland: *Re Attorney-General's Reference (Northern Ireland)* [2019] UKSC 1; [2020] NI 793. Of the 29 Northern Irish cases heard by the UKSC, 6 were from the High Court, and 23 were from the Court of Appeal.

[19] Incidentally, the 'success rates' of appeals from the different courts in England and Wales were also very similar: 48.95% from the Court of Appeal and 48.9% from the High Court.

[20] See *Anderson v Shetland Islands Council* [2012] UKSC 7; [2012] 10 EG 89 (CS) at [7].

Figure 4 Percentage of appeals allowed (by court type)

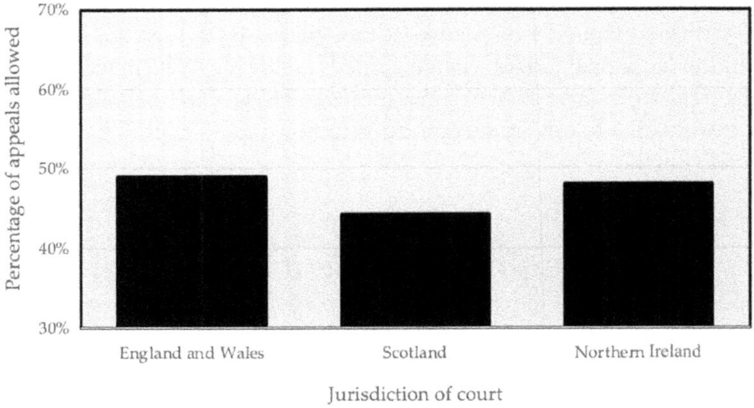

So much for the Court as a whole. However, at all points during the Court's first decade, the Court's roster featured at least one judge from Scotland and one from Northern Ireland. As such, it is fruitful to consider the different behaviour of other judges appointed from these jurisdictions when it comes to appeals from their respective jurisdiction. It may be the case, for example, that they are more likely than their colleagues to show deference to cases decided by judges in 'their' jurisdiction, or alternatively they may feel more confident in overturning the outcomes of cases coming from jurisdictions which they are more familiar with.

Unsurprisingly, Scottish judges were very likely to sit on Scottish appeals, and Northern Irish judges were very likely to sit on Northern Irish appeals.[21] Remarkably, of the 97 cases involving at least one appeal from a Scottish court, each featured at least one Scottish judge on the panel. Almost three-quarters of Scottish appeals featured not just one but two Scottish judges, and one case even featured three.[22] Lord Rodger sat on every Scottish appeal arising during his tenure. Lord Kerr, the only Northern Irish judge to sit as a permanent member of the Court during this time, sat on almost 90 per cent of Northern Irish appeals, leaving just three UKSC cases decided by a panel without the involvement of a sitting judge of the jurisdiction from which the appeal came. Of course, given that Lord Kerr was the single Northern Irish judge on the Court during its first decade, it is difficult to determine whether certain behaviour should be attributed to 'Northern Irish judges' as some collective group or simply Lord Kerr as an individual. Indeed, as the analysis in the rest of this book shows, Lord Kerr does not appear to be a very typical judge in many respects, necessitating even more circumspection when attributing his voting record to his Northern Irish nationality. Assessing the behaviour of Scottish judges presents a different challenge,

[21] This was also the case in the House of Lords: B Dickson, 'The processing of appeals in the House of Lords' (2007) 123 *LQR* 571, 590.
[22] This was more common in the House of Lords: see Paterson (n 13) 237.

because although the Court has featured a number of different Scottish judges, it tends to have two sitting at any given point. The behavioural preferences of a given Scottish judge must be assessed not only against those of non-Scottish judges but also against the other Scottish judge on the Court. In any case, it goes without saying that Scottish judges are not homogenous, nor will they necessarily agree on issues of Scots law – Lord Kerr once quipped 'we need two Justices from Scotland – the first to explain the impenetrability of Scots law and the second to correct the first'.[23]

A. Lead Judgments

As may be expected, Scottish judges were overwhelmingly likely to deliver the lead judgment in Scottish appeals. In fact, they delivered the lead (alone or with another judge) in 74 (76.29 per cent) of all Scottish appeals and authored a substantive contribution (whether as a lead, concurrence, or dissent) in 81.44 per cent of them. Each of the nine cases dealing exclusively with Scots law featured a lead judgment by a Scottish judge. Figure 5 shows how likely each judge was to author a lead judgment, if they found themselves sitting on a panel considering an appeal from a Scottish court (judges who sat on fewer than 10 Scottish appeals are excluded and Scottish judges are marked with an [S]).

Figure 5 Lead judgments in Scots appeals

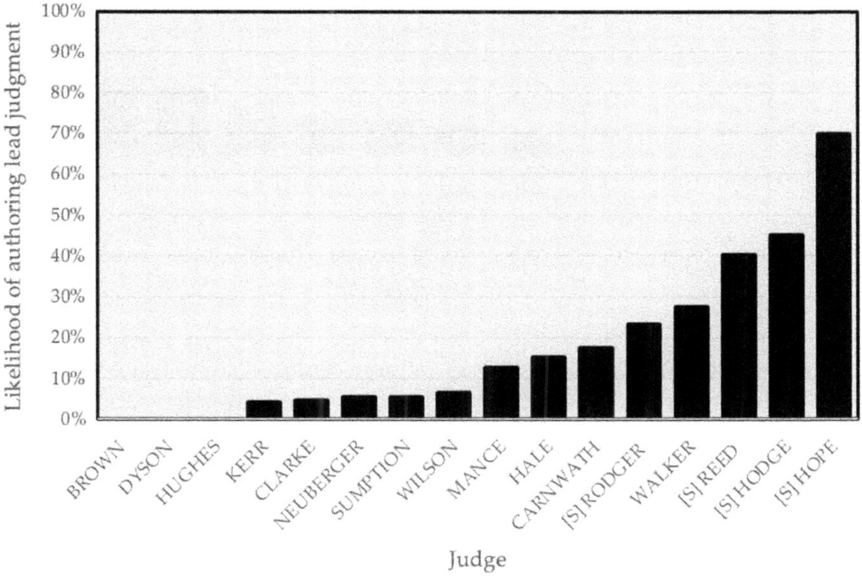

[23] Lord Reed's swearing-in ceremony, 13 January 2020.

Clearly, in Scottish cases, Scottish judges were much more likely to author the lead than their colleagues – and it should be remembered that in many of the cases in which a Scottish judge sits but does not deliver the lead judgment, that job would often fall to a different Scottish judge instead. Interestingly, Lord Rodger seems to buck the trend of Scottish judges writing more leads in Scottish appeals, delivering the lead judgment in just under a quarter of the Scottish appeals in which he sat. However, this may be attributable, at least in part, to the eagerness and confidence of fellow Scot Lord Hope (who sat alongside Rodger during his tenure at the Court) to write the lead judgment rather than any reticence on his own part. The fact that Lord Rodger was much more likely to dissent compared to other Scottish colleagues may also contribute.

A similar situation can be seen when turning to Northern Irish appeals, where, as Figure 6 shows, Lord Kerr delivered the lead judgment almost 58 per cent of the time (only those judges deciding five or more Northern Irish appeals are shown here). This made him more than twice as likely to author a lead in Northern Irish cases than the next most likely judge to do so.

Figure 6 Lead judgments in Northern Ireland appeals

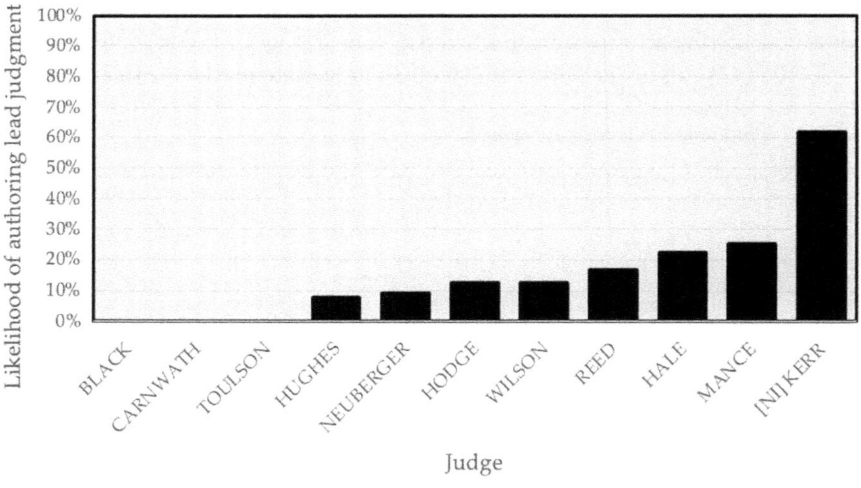

The high rate of lead judgment delivery in these contexts cannot be explained by each of the judges having a *general* tendency to issue lead judgments. In other words, it is the Scottish or Northern Irish context which made those judges more likely to issue a lead judgment. This is illustrated by Figure 7, which compares, for each of the judges hailing from Scotland Northern Ireland, their likelihood of authoring a lead judgment in an appeal from their own jurisdiction with the likelihood that they issue a lead judgment more generally. For example, Lords Hodge and Kerr were each more than twice as likely to deliver the lead judgment in a Scottish appeal compared to an average UKSC case, and Lord Kerr was over twice as likely to author a contribution. Lord Hope's already very high likelihood of delivering a lead judgment (see chapter three) jumps even further in the context of Scottish appeals, and remarkably, the data shows that he contributed to over 93 per cent of the cases in which he sat.

Figure 7 Likelihood to author lead judgment (Scots cases sat versus all cases sat)

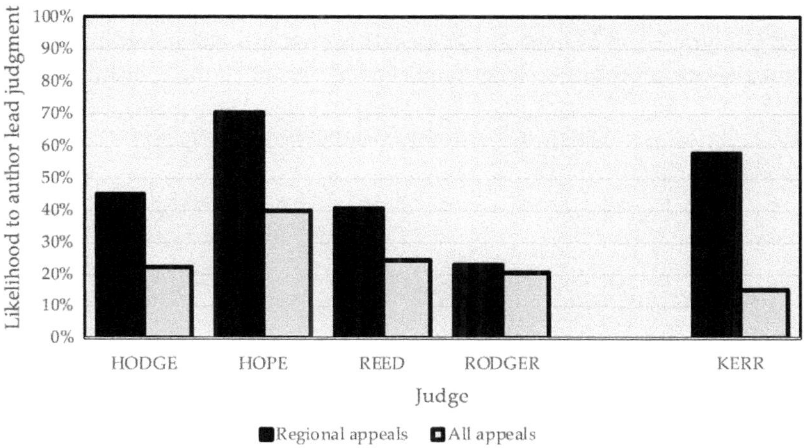

Figure 8 shows how likely each judge was to author a substantive contribution (regardless of whether this was as part of a lead judgment or not). This data confirms the impression given by the tables above. Scottish judges were more likely to contribute to Scottish appeals, and Lord Kerr was more likely to contribute to Northern Irish appeals. Lord Rodger again emerges as something of an outlier. It appears that any 'home turf' effect in play when it comes to contributing to appeals is much less pronounced for him compared to his colleagues.

Figure 8 Likelihood to contribute substantive judgment (regional appeals sat versus all cases sat)

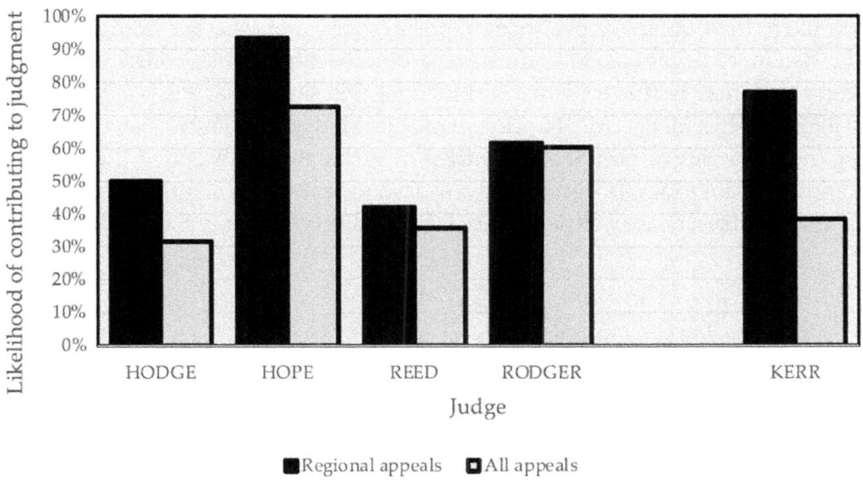

The *length* of each judge's average contribution is shown in Figure 9. This shows that most of the judges considered here tend not only to contribute more frequently to Scottish and Northern Irish cases, but that their contributions tend to be longer too. Lord Kerr's contributions to Northern Irish cases were, as a whole, over 50 per cent longer than his overall contribution length.[24] The exception this time is Lord Reed, whose average contribution sits at 51 paragraphs in Scottish cases, but 52 paragraphs on average in all cases. However, this still leaves him with the longest average contribution length in Scottish cases of all the Scottish judges.

Figure 9 Average contribution in length (regional appeals sat versus all cases sat)

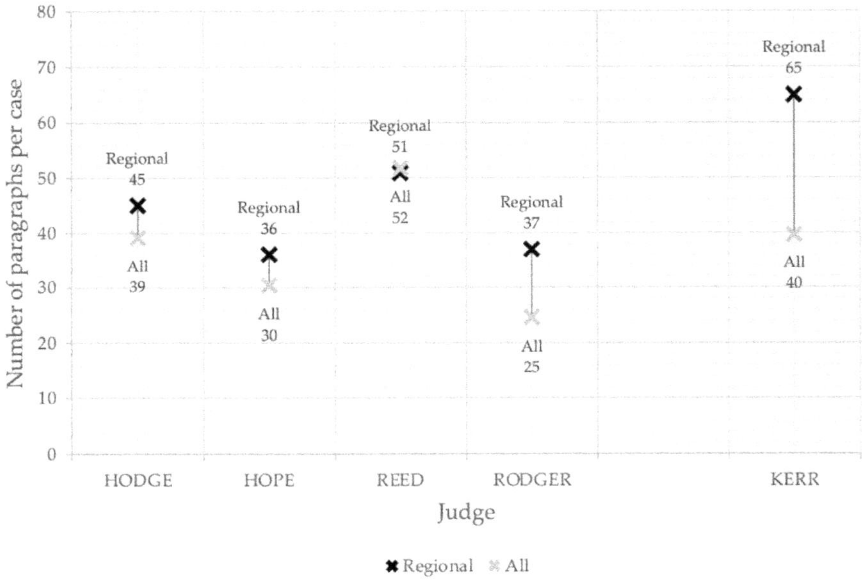

Perhaps the most intriguing question is whether Scottish judges were more or less likely than others to overturn Scottish courts, and whether Lord Kerr was likewise more or less likely to do so regarding Northern Irish courts. In fact, it seems that there is little evidence of this either way. Overall, Scottish judges voted to allow appeals in just over 44 per cent of Scottish appeals, almost exactly matching the allow rate of non-Scottish judges in such cases.[25] Tweaking the relevant comparator, for example to consider only lead judgments in Scottish cases, seems to change matters very little.[26] This lack of divergence is unsurprising when

[24] Affected, no doubt, by his mammoth dissent in *Re Northern Ireland Human Rights Commission* [2018] UKSC 27; [2019] 1 All ER 173.

[25] Scottish judges have a collective 'allow rate' of 44.09% whereas non-Scots have a rate of 44.3%.

[26] In Scottish cases, 48.38% of Scottish lead judgments include a vote to allow the appeal, compared to exactly 50% of non-Scottish lead judgments.

considering how frequently the lead judgment in a Scottish appeal was delivered by a Scottish judge (see Figure 5); a judge delivering a lead judgment must necessarily vote in the same way as (at least) two other (likely non-Scottish) judges on the panel, in order to find themselves in the majority wing and thus able to author a lead judgment. Perhaps paradoxically, Scottish distinctiveness in one sense (a disproportionate likelihood to issue lead judgments in Scottish cases) decreases the likelihood of Scottish distinctiveness in a different sense (the likelihood to vote in a different way to their colleagues). Whether the non-Scottish judges sitting on panels led by their Scottish colleagues would nevertheless have reached the same outcome independently remains an open question.

Turning to Northern Irish appeals, Lord Kerr voted to allow just 39 per cent of cases from Northern Ireland, whereas his colleagues voted, on average, to do so 48.61 per cent of the time. This difference is more significant than the Scottish gap in this respect, and the comparatively low likelihood of Lord Kerr allowing appeals from Northern Irish courts does seem to run contrary to his more *general* tendency to be more likely to allow appeals from lower courts than his colleagues (see Figure 3 above). However, with Lord Kerr being the only Northern Irish judge under examination, it is impossible to say how much of this divergence falls to some kind of national or institutional loyalty rather than Lord Kerr's own fairly distinctive judicial behaviour profile. For a thorough, qualitative assessment of the relationship between Lord Kerr's tenure on the Court and the Northern Irish dimension to his work, Brice Dickson and Conor McCormick's excellent study on these matters is highly recommended.[27]

As such, there seems to be little evidence that the jurisdictional background of a given judge makes a big difference as to whether they are likely to allow an appeal from that jurisdiction.[28] Scottish and Northern Irish judges may speak more frequently in 'their own' cases, but the outcome of their decisions does not seem to differ as a result of this loyalty.

IV. Conclusions

The analysis in this chapter allows for a number of conclusions to be drawn about the UKSC's approach to appeals, both in general and with respect to appeals from specific jurisdictions.

The vast majority of the Court's docket consists of appeals from lower courts, and when it comes to such cases, the Court is very slightly more likely to dismiss appeals than it is to allow them. The data indicates, at least to some extent, a degree

[27] B Dickson and C McCormick, 'Northern Ireland Dimensions to the First Decade of the United Kingdom Supreme Court' (2020) 83 *MLR* 1133.

[28] This is different from measuring a case's *success rate* (a party may be successful at both the Court of Session *and* the Supreme Court): on which see Dickson and McCormick, ibid.

of divergence between the 'allow rates' of individual judges. In other words, past voting patterns suggest that some judges may be more likely than others to allow appeals from lower courts, although what this might mean, or how this divergence should be interpreted, is not obvious.

Regarding jurisdiction, the vast majority of appeals come from the courts of England and Wales, and as such, the Court's general position with regard to appeals as a whole tends to reflect its approach to appeals from this jurisdiction. When it comes to Scottish and Northern Irish appeals, it is clearly the case that judges appointed to the Court from a given jurisdiction are disproportionately likely to participate in, and contribute to, appeals from the courts of that same jurisdiction. Whilst there is little evidence that Scottish judges are any more or less likely to allow cases coming from Scotland compared to other jurisdictions, there are indications that Lord Kerr was more comfortable overturning the decisions of Northern Irish courts compared to other courts. However, with no other Northern Irish judges sitting on the Court during the relevant period to dissect, whether this might reveal something about the behaviour of judges in relation to particular jurisdictions, or about Lord Kerr alone, is impossible to determine.

In short, it appears that looking at appeals from lower courts tells us some interesting things about which judges lead, speak, and make their voices heard. In this sense, the findings here compliment those of the previous chapter. There was, however, less evidence of a substantive difference between the judges in the appeals context when it comes to casting votes and deciding cases. The next few chapters look at whether this might instead be found in other ways, first by looking at whether different judges were each more or less likely to side with certain parties.

5

Party Sympathy

David Robertson has remarked that '[c]ases … in one way or another, are nearly all about power imbalances'.[1] If that is the case, judges are the arbiters of where the balance of power should fall. If legal cases regularly feature such imbalances, whose side are the judges on?

JAG Griffith[2] and other sceptical voices on the left[3] have argued that judges reinforce and strengthen societal power structures. This may not be the result of individual choices but part and parcel of the judicial role itself; as Moran puts it, 'the whole process of … becoming a judge and more specifically becoming a good judge is education and training for hierarchy … those who take on the role make an important investment in that elite status.'[4] Certainly, judges are often *perceived* by many as overly traditional figures who are deferential to structures of authority and power.[5] More recently, similar views have been expressed by those of a very different political persuasion to Griffith. In 2019 Nigel Farage appeared on national television arguing that the 'the establishment', which he defined as including the senior judiciary, held vested interests (including remaining in the European Union) which they would seek to implement above all else, saying 'I don't accept that the establishment of this country is independent'.[6] Paradoxically, at other times, judges have been criticised not for *protecting* the establishment, but for *threatening* it too much, being portrayed as unjustifiably interventionist and too readily meddling in the affairs of government.[7] It has been suggested that

[1] D Robertson, *Judicial Discretion in the House of Lords* (OUP, 1998) 28–29.

[2] J Griffith, *Politics of the Judiciary*, 5th edn (Fontana Press, 1997).

[3] See eg M Macnair, 'Can Judges Be Trusted with the Common Law?' and G Rosenberg, 'Protecting Privilege: The Historic Role of the U.S. Supreme Court and the Great Progressive Misunderstanding' in R Ekins and G Gee, *Judicial Power and the Left* (Policy Exchange, 2018); K Ewing and C Gearty, *The Struggle for Civil Liberties, Political Freedom and the Rule of Law in Britain 1914–1945* (OUP, 2000); EP Thompson, *Whigs and Hunters: The Origin of the Black Act* (Allen Lane, 1975).

[4] L Moran, 'In Conversation with Lord Justice Etherton: judicial legitimacy, diversity and the representation of judicial authority' [2010] *PL* 662, 668.

[5] P Darbyshire, *Sitting in Judgment* (Hart Publishing, 2011) 19–23.

[6] The Andrew Neil Show (BBC One, 11 September 2019).

[7] Lord Dyson, for example, has remarked that, at least in some respects, it has become common for judges to be viewed as an 'anti-establishment' force: Lord Dyson, 'Criticising Judges: Fair Game or Off-Limits?' (Third Annual Bailii Lecture, 27 November 2014) 19.

the Conservative Party's recent enthusiasm for restricting judicial review may be underpinned by such concerns.[8]

Judges, then, occupy a curious position in the minds of the public: they are simultaneously seen as part of the powerful elite as well as a vital tool to be used against it. They are both *for* the little guy and dead-set *against* him. In 1995, during a televised interview with the BBC, Peter Taylor, the (then) Lord Chief Justice, pointed out this irony, noting that judges were being framed as 'these great establishment figures' on a programme 'largely about how we are attacking the establishment'.[9] So which is the more accurate view? Whose side are they on? And, importantly, are all judges on the same side?

This chapter tries to answer these questions investigating the success rates of different types of litigant in the UKSC. Uncovering the approach of the judges – collective or individual – towards certain parties may allow some inference of underlying sympathies. If judges were all establishment figures, only very rarely would an individual succeed in an action against big business or the government. If judges are all bleeding-heart liberals, weaker parties and ordinary litigants might be expected to have an advantage over stronger ones. This may play out at a general level, or may be more acute at the level of an individual judge – are some more *establishment-minded* than others?

The state is the obvious analogue to 'the establishment' when it comes to parties before the UKSC, and as such Section I below looks at whether judges tend to side for or against the state, individually or as a whole. Section II takes a slightly different approach, exploring whether judges tend to side with, or side against, socio-economic underdogs. Section III, drawing on feminist jurisprudence, seeks to determine whether women are treated differently from others when they find themselves parties to UKSC cases, and whether certain judges, including women judges, treat these parties differently.

Whilst it would certainly be interesting to consider how judges tended to treat other sorts of litigants – including racial, religious and other minorities[10] – these additional dimensions are not considered here. First, whilst it is relatively easy

[8] C Falconer, 'This government has plans that would destroy the protection of law' *The Guardian* (12 February 2020) www.theguardian.com/commentisfree/2020/feb/12/protection-law-politicians-judges-courts.

[9] His Lordship suggested that 'you can't have it both ways': On the Record (BBC One, 26 February 1995).

[10] These questions have been examined in the context of other jurisdictions: see eg J Coons and R Espinoza, 'An Examination of Aversive Heterosexism in the Courtroom: Effects of Defendants' Sexual Orientation and Attractiveness, and Juror Gender on Legal Decision making' (2017) 5 *Psychology of Sexual Orientation and Gender Diversity* 36; D Ritenhouse, 'What's Orientation Got to Do With It? The Best Interest of the Child Standard and Legal Bias against Gay and Lesbian Parents' (2011) 15 *Poverty* 309; J Rachlinski and S Johnson, 'Does Unconscious Racial Bias Affect Trial Judges?' (2009) 84 *Notre Dame Law Review* 1195; D Pinello, *Gay Rights and American Law* (CUP, 2003) ch 4. In the UK context, concerns have been raised about racism in the judiciary: see K Monteith et al, 'Racial Bias and the Bench' (Centre on the Dynamics of Ethnicity, University of Manchester, November 2022).

to identify (eg) the gender of the parties to a case, it is more difficult to classify a litigant's race, nationality, religious beliefs, or similar factors from the case law unless this specifically features as part of the case. Second, the number of cases where these characteristics play a key part in the case itself would be too small, in the current dataset, for any meaningful analysis to occur. That is not to say that judging is unaffected by these kinds of litigant characteristics; it is simply that the present dataset could not investigate this adequately.

Studies concerning other jurisdictions have shown that the type of party to a case may indeed affect judicial behaviour, including case outcomes.[11] Whilst a small number of empirical studies of this type have been carried out in the UK context, the results have proven inconclusive; whilst one empirical study has found that the identity of parties did not make a difference to the outcome of cases on the Court of Appeal,[12] another more recent study found some differences at the Supreme Court level.[13] This chapter hopes to contribute to this literature, and establish whether there is any evidence that the judges of the UKSC, individually or collectively, adopt a particular approach to cases involving public authorities, socio-economic underdogs or women litigants.

I. Preferences: The State

Cases pitting the citizen against the state are some of the most important – and controversial – in the UKSC's docket.[14] One of the fundamental roles of the judiciary is to ensure that the government is held to account. Lord Neuberger has said that the Supreme Court's ability to 'counterbalance' the power of state actors constitutes one of its most important functions.[15] The Court's relationship with the state, therefore, is of paramount importance and the proper role that each of the judges sees for themselves is likely to be bound up with their view of the role of the state and the place of the judiciary in relationship to it.[16]

[11] See, in addition to references at n 10, eg R Flemming and G Krutz, 'Selecting Appeals for Judicial Review in Canada: A Replication and Multivariate Test of American Hypotheses' (2002) 64(1) *Journal of Politics* 232; D Songer and R Sheehan 'Who Wins on Appeal? Upperdogs and Underdogs on the United States Courts of Appeals' (1992) 36 *American Journal of Political Science* 235; R Sheehan, W Mishler and D Songer, 'Ideology, Status, and the Differential Success of Different Parties before the Supreme Court' (1992) 86 *American Political Science Review* 464.

[12] J Vidal and C Leaver, 'Social Interactions and the Content of Legal Opinions' (2013) 29(1) *Journal of Law, Economics and Organization* 78.

[13] C Hanretty, *A Court of Specialists? Judicial Behavior on the UK Supreme Court* (OUP, 2020) ch 9.

[14] This is also true in the US context: see S Lindquist and F Cross, *Measuring Judicial Activism* (OUP, 2009) 95–102. Indeed, sometimes attitudes towards the state were treated as a straightforward proxy for judicial behaviour as a whole: J Sprague, *Voting Patterns of the United States Supreme Court: Cases in Federalism, 1889–1959* (Bobbs-Merrill, 1968) see especially 154.

[15] D Neuberger and P Riddell, *The Power of Judges* (Haus Curiosities, 2018) 36.

[16] For an example of how widely individual judicial views in this respect may differ compare J Sumption, 'Judicial and Political Decision-making: The Uncertain Boundary' 16(4) *Judicial Review* 301 and S Sedley, 'Judicial politics' (2012) 34(4) *London Review of Books* 15–16.

Research suggests that the prevailing attitude to state parties differs depending on the jurisdiction under examination. For example, Alarie and Green found that apex courts tend to side with the government in Canada, but not in Australia.[17] When it comes to senior UK courts, studies have reached differing conclusions on this question depending on the exact time period studied.[18] Empirical studies have also examined how *individual* judges approach cases involving the state. Bondy and Sunkin have conducted a masterful empirical examination of judicial review cases over time,[19] outlining a number of observations including, intriguingly, that certain judges were more likely – sometimes considerably – to allow cases to proceed against public bodies.[20] In one of the very few UK studies to measure individual judicial behaviour quantitatively using case outcomes, Arvind and Stirton[21] ranked judges according to how likely they were to find for the state (using 'red light' and 'green light' dimensions borrowed from Harlow and Rawlings).[22] The authors argue that this dimension serves as an institutionally appropriate analogue to the left/right dimension commonly found in US scholarship; they found, much like Bondy and Sunkin, that the judges do indeed differ from one another when it comes to their attitude towards the actions of public bodies.

A. Measuring State Preferences

In the dataset, 'state cases' were marked as those which include, as direct parties to proceedings, state actors or public bodies of any kind. This includes government ministers, local authorities and public agencies, regulators such as the Financial Services Authority and Legal Services Board as well as the BBC. Because this exercise seeks to uncover judicial preferences towards the state compared to non-state bodies, it excluded from consideration those fairly rare cases which involve two different state parties pitted against one another.

The salient dimension being measured here was the influence of the state as a party to proceedings rather than the exact nature of those proceedings. Therefore, it did not matter, for now, which kind of action was brought or how the case was categorised formally; although naturally many of the cases in this part of the dataset were judicial review cases, many others involved claims for (eg) breach of legislation, tort, or less commonly, contract law. As Arvind and Stirton put it,

[17] B Alarie and A Green, *Commitment and Cooperation on High Courts* (OUP, 2017) ch 7.

[18] Compare Alarie and Green (ibid ch 7) with Hanretty (n 13) ch 9 and see also C Hanretty, 'Haves and Have-Nots Before the Law Lords' (2014) 62 *Political Science* 686.

[19] See eg V Bondy and M Sunkin, 'Accessing Judicial Review' [2008] *Public Law* 647; V Bondy, L Platt and M Sunkin, *The Value and Effects of Judicial Review: The Nature of Claims, their Outcomes and Consequences* (Public Law Project, 2015).

[20] Bondy and Sunkin, ibid 664–65. See also L Bridges, G Meszaros and M Sunkin, *Judicial Review in Perspective*, 2nd edn (Cavendish, 1995) 164–90.

[21] TT Arvind and L Stirton, 'Legal ideology, legal doctrine and the UK's top judges' [2016] *PL* 418.

[22] C Harlow and R Rawlings, *Law and Administration*, 3rd edn (CUP, 2009).

'of central significance to all cases against the state, regardless of whether they are brought in public or private law, is the extent to which the law gives discretionary powers to executive bodies'.[23]

A state 'win' was straightforwardly coded according to whether (public authority) liability was found in those cases where this was a live issue. In the smaller number of cases where liability was not a relevant question, identifying a 'win' would otherwise depend on the question arising. For example, in some cases, the Court ruled on issues such as the extent of a public body's powers or obligations, the proper remedies or awards available in actions against a public body, or a party's competency or jurisdiction to bring actions against the state, without having to rule directly on whether any liability had, or would have, occurred. A win in each case was coded according to whether the state party was treated advantageously in each respect. For example, in *Pinnock*[24] the Court was asked to determine whether the ECHR required that proportionality-based defences be available in certain public eviction cases. In ruling that they were, the Court was clearly siding with the claimant (who had a new remedy available to them) and against the state (whose obligations were, in theory, enlarged). Where multiple non-state parties were involved in a case, and some, but not all, were found to be successful the 'success rate' was marked as a fraction of the whole.[25] Where cases raised multiple clearly demarcated issues, and some, but not all, were found to be successful, the same rule applied.

B. State Preferences: Results

A total of 422 cases were identified as involving the state or a public body according to the metric described above. As Figure 1 sets out, the Court was more likely to rule in the state's favour than it was to hold against it.

Figure 1 Court determinations: state parties

Applicable cases	Majority for state	Majority against state	Mixed finding
422	215	159	48

Importantly, it seems that some judges were more likely to side with the state than others. Figure 2 shows how likely each judge was to side with the state across all cases in which they sat (as with all figures in this chapter, judges who sat on too small a number of cases are excluded from analysis, and judges who sat on a comparatively small, but still meaningful, number of cases are appended with an asterisk and coloured in grey). Their positions range from finding for the

[23] Arvind and Stirton (n 21) 426.
[24] *Manchester City Council v Pinnock* [2011] UKSC 6; [2011] 2 AC 104.
[25] See similar discussions in ch 2.

state in just over 41 per cent of cases (Lady Black) to almost 67 per cent of cases (Lord Neuberger), averaging at a rate of 55.93 per cent (the judges sitting closest to this number were Lords Dyson and Reed).[26] The results show *some* divergence between individual judges, especially when comparing judges at both 'ends' of the spectrum (the 24-point difference between the highest-placed and lowest-placed judges remains notable) but overall there is a fairly low degree of variance, with judges clustered quite tightly around the mean. This may be expected given the high number of cases featuring the state, the wide range of public bodies defined as a state party, and the diversity of issues involving state parties.

Figure 2 Party preferences: state (all cases)

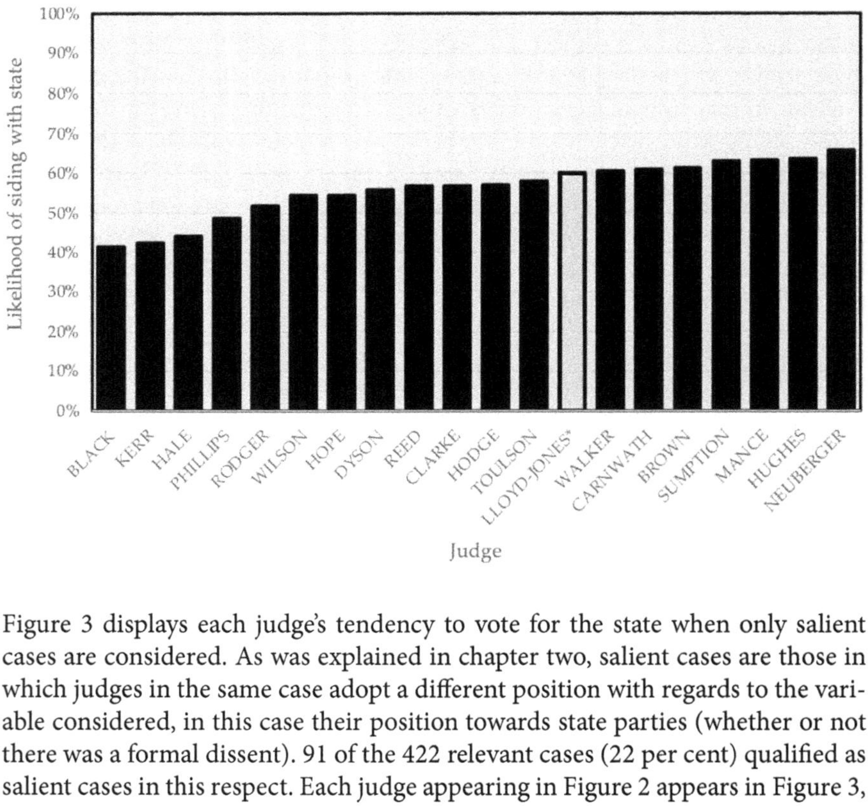

Figure 3 displays each judge's tendency to vote for the state when only salient cases are considered. As was explained in chapter two, salient cases are those in which judges in the same case adopt a different position with regards to the variable considered, in this case their position towards state parties (whether or not there was a formal dissent). 91 of the 422 relevant cases (22 per cent) qualified as salient cases in this respect. Each judge appearing in Figure 2 appears in Figure 3, but for three judges – Lady Black, Lord Collins and Lord Lloyd-Jones – who did not decide enough salient cases and were dropped due to insufficient data.

As would be expected, the spread of positions here is more notable than that of Figure 2. Individual positions showing state 'friendliness' range from around 20 per cent to over 80 per cent. The average 'score' of salient judges also differs

[26] By contrast, a sum count of each vote cast in cases in which the government was a party reveals that 53.46% of all judicial votes were in favour of the government.

from the general dataset, rising to 61.88 per cent (this time, Lord Clarke sits closest). Interestingly – and reassuringly – these results fall in line, more or less, with the results presented by Arvind and Stirton in their study of how likely each judge was to side with the state in split cases.[27]

Figure 3 Party preferences: state (salient cases)

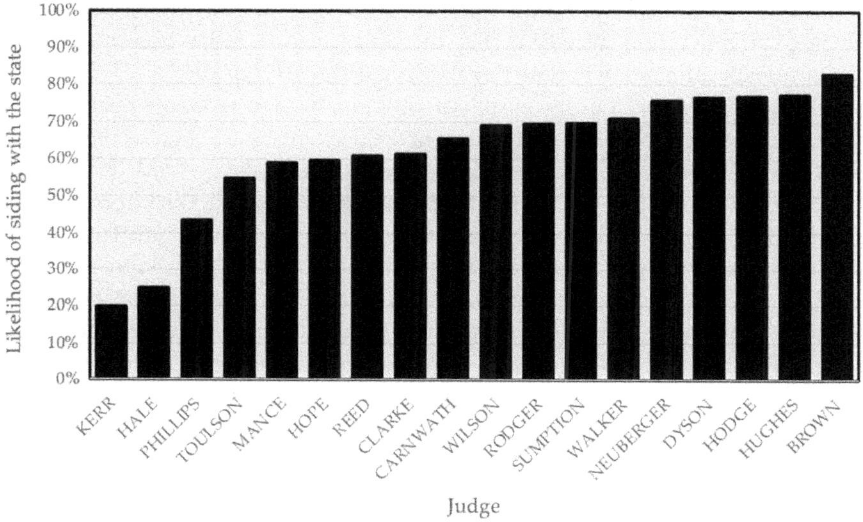

There are some particularly striking numbers in Figure 3. As can be seen, Lord Kerr was the judge who was most likely to side against the state in salient cases. His 'score' of 20 per cent means that, in cases involving the state where the judges on the panel differed in approach, he would advocate a position which was less favourable to the state than that of his colleagues four times out of five. This quite remarkable record caused Lord Reed to suggest (likely with tongue in cheek) that 'he sometimes appeared to apply a presumption that the government was in the wrong'.[28] Other judges who tended to side against the state in salient cases include Lady Hale, and to a lesser extent, Lord Phillips.[29] Lord Brown's records are

[27] Arvind and Stirton (n 21). Whilst there are clear differences between the studies in terms of methods used, cases included and judges examined it is encouraging to see that many of the judicial rankings are relatively similar to one another; the correlation between the two rankings is .752** (t-test, two-tailed, significant at the 0.01 level).

[28] Lord Reed, 'Foreword' in B Dickson and C McCormick (eds), *The Judicial Mind: A Festschrift for Lord Kerr of Tonaghmore* (Hart Publishing, 2021) viii.

[29] If cases involving Lady Hale and/or Lord Kerr are excluded from the dataset, and percentages are recalculated, Lord Phillips becomes the most anti-state judge (33%) showing that Lord Phillips would side against the state generally, and *not just* when he was influenced by Lady Hale and Lord Kerr. Interestingly, in this same modified dataset, Lord Dyson's pro-state tendencies shrink considerably compared to his position in Figure 3 (from 77% to 55%) which suggests that Lord Dyson might best be seen as holding a more pro-state position compared to Lady Hale and Lord Kerr, rather than a pro-state position more generally.

the inverse of Lord Kerr's: in salient cases, he would side *with* the state in four out of every five cases. Lord Brown's records are not quite so out of step with many of his colleagues as Lord Kerr's are, with a total of five judges siding with the state in salient cases more than 75 per cent of the time. Lord Rodger's records here are also of note: his first four votes in salient cases each fell *against* the state, but in every single vote thereafter he aligned himself with the state. Given that his voting record only spans two years, this may not quite show that he underwent some ideological conversion over time, but the prospect of a judge becoming more institutionally-minded over time remains interesting to consider.[30]

Given that Figure 3 focuses on split cases, it may be seen as a more reliable indicator of each judge's personal preferences in the trickiest cases. Many of the relative positions of judges are consistent between the two sets of data – Lords Brown and Hughes hold a pro-state position in both, and Lady Hale and Lord Kerr hold an anti-state position in both. But there are divergences elsewhere. Lords Hodge and Dyson hold a very moderate score in Figure 2 but appear to adopt a more pro-state position in Figure 3. The opposite is true for Lord Mance, who moves from one of the most pro-state judges in Figure 2 to a position nearer the other end of the scale in Figure 3. This might suggest, for example, that these judges do not hold a particularly strong preference with regards to state behaviour most of the time, but this preference can manifest in more important, complicated cases.

As a whole, the positions of each judge in Figures 2 and 3 will not be too surprising to those with a cursory familiarity with the Supreme Court's public law jurisprudence. A number of Lord Kerr's many dissenting judgments saw him holding the state to higher standards, and subjecting it to a greater degree of scrutiny, than his colleagues did, evidenced for example in his review of devolved legislative competences in *Martin*,[31] immigration rules in *Ali*,[32] and closed material procedures in *Tariq*.[33] It is no surprise to see Dickson and McCormick describing Lord Kerr as 'adjudicating in a predominantly pro-claimant fashion'.[34] Likewise, many of Lady Hale's judgments line up with her pro-claimant, anti-state tendencies; for example, she sometimes interpreted the classic judicial review ground of irrationality as imposing a comparatively high standard upon decision-makers, finding, on a number of occasions, public authority decisions to be unreasonable, against the contrary views of her colleagues.[35] She was particularly alert to the need to hold local authorities to account, delivering important dissents[36] in

[30] This may have happened in Lord Brown's case: see his profile in ch 9.

[31] *Martin v HM Advocate* [2010] UKSC 10; 2010 SC (UKSC) 40.

[32] *Ali v Secretary of State for the Home Department* [2016] UKSC 60; [2016] 1 WLR 4799.

[33] *Home Office v Tariq* [2011] UKSC 35; [2012] 1 AC 452.

[34] B Dickson and C McCormick, 'The Development of Lord Kerr's Judicial Mind' in Dickson and McCormick (n 28) 23.

[35] *Keyu v Secretary of State for Foreign and Commonwealth Affairs* [2015] UKSC 69; [2016] AC 1355, *R (McDonald) v Royal Borough of Kensington & Chelsea* [2011] UKSC 33; [2011] 4 All ER 881.

[36] Even in decisions where she did not dissent from her colleagues, she would often emphasise the importance of holding the state to account and ensuring that patients in hospitals are not let down: see *R (Modaresi) v Secretary of State for Health* [2013] UKSC 53; [2013] 4 All ER 318.

favour of strengthening duties in the field of social care,[37] children's services[38] and education.[39] She would also depart from her colleagues when they were reluctant to examine claims concerning sensitive fields such as foreign policy[40] and macro-economic decisions.[41] Whilst accepting that sensitivity may be required on the part of the judge when reviewing some public authority actions, she chastised those judges who seemed unprepared to scrutinise the executive at all in these areas, reminding them that for judges 'there are no "no go" areas'.[42] In state cases in which both Lady Hale or Lord Kerr sat, they would very often vote (and dissent) together. Noteworthy examples include their blistering dissents on matters such as the liability of police,[43] the fairness of discriminatory benefits schemes,[44] the government's approach to the consideration[45] and disclosure of evidence[46] in relation to the evacuation of the Chagos Islands, and the lawfulness of Northern Ireland's abortion laws.[47] In each of these cases, both judges clearly wished to hold public bodies to a higher standard than their colleagues would have done. It is no surprise that they each sit at the far end of Figure 3.

The same is true when it comes to the output of judges sitting at the other end of the table. In the case of *Quila* concerning the lawfulness of a set of immigration controls, Lord Brown revealingly dissented from the majority, on grounds that those decisions ought to be made by politicians rather than judges, and that judges should always be slow to interfere with government policies.[48] Elsewhere, he was more reluctant to find secondary legislation concerning asset freezing orders ultra vires, applying a more limited conception of the legality principle in the national security context,[49] and disagreeing with his colleagues on multiple occasions on the circumstances under which the state could be held liable for false imprisonment.[50] Lord Hughes was one of the dissenters in the famous *Miller* case, advocating a comparatively wide conception of the prerogative (with a smaller

[37] *McDonald* (n 35).
[38] *Re B* [2013] UKSC 33; [2013] 1 WLR 1911.
[39] *A v Essex County Council* [2010] UKSC 33; [2011] 1 AC 280.
[40] *Secretary of State for Foreign and Commonwealth Affairs v Rahmatullah* [2012] UKSC 48; [2013] AC 614.
[41] *R (SG) v Secretary of State for Work and Pensions* [2015] UKSC 16; [2015] WLR 1449; *R (Carmichael and Rourke) v Secretary of State for Work and Pensions* [2016] UKSC 58; [2016] WLR 4550.
[42] *R (DA and DS) v Secretary of State for Work and Pensions* [2019] UKSC 21; [2019] WLR 3289 at [113].
[43] *Michael v Chief Constable of South Wales Police* [2015] UKSC 2; [2015] 1 AC 1732.
[44] *SG* (n 41) and *DS* (n 42).
[45] *R (Bancoult) v Secretary of State for Foreign and Commonwealth Affairs (No 2)* [2016] UKSC 35; [2017] AC 300.
[46] *R (Bancoult) v Secretary of State for Foreign and Commonwealth Affairs (No 3)* [2018] UKSC 3; [2018] 1 WLR 973.
[47] *Re Northern Ireland Human Rights Commission* [2018] UKSC 27; [2019] 1 All ER 173.
[48] *R (Quila) v Secretary of State for the Home Department* [2011] UKSC 45; [2012] 1 AC 621, see especially [91] and [97].
[49] *HM Treasury v Ahmed* [2010] UKSC 2; [2010] 4 All ER 829.
[50] *R (Lumba) v Secretary of State for the Home Department* [2011] UKSC 12; [2012] 1 AC 245; *Kambadzi v Secretary of State for the Home Department* [2011] UKSC 23; [2011] 1 WLR 1299.

scope for judicial review into its exercise)[51] as well as the controversial *Evans* case, where he rejected his colleagues' suggestions that there could be constitutional limits on the government's ability to veto information requests.[52] He also voted to allow the state greater powers to deprive mental health detainees of their liberty,[53] and adopted a narrow construction of the police's investigative duties.[54] Whilst these individual decisions prove little in and of themselves, especially as they are drawn from a vast corpus of decisions, they do help to add credulity to the positions tentatively set out in Figures 2 and 3.

As such, whilst it seems that the Court, as a whole, was more likely to side with the state than it was to rule against it, the figures do not suggest that all judges subscribe to the kind of absolute institutional loyalty diagnosed by Griffith, although some perhaps come close. Different judges showed different tendencies in this regard. State 'sympathisers' appear to include Lords Brown, Hughes and Hodge Conversely, Lord Phillips and (especially) Lady Hale and Lord Kerr were the most likely to side against the state. Judges such as Lords Toulson and Wilson appeared as moderate 'middle of the pack' judges who were neither particularly likely, nor particularly hesitant, to side with the state.

II. Preferences: Socio-economic Underdogs

The citizen-state relationship is only one way to measure the power dynamic between parties and is in many ways a narrow one. Another option is to take account of the parties' respective socio-economic positions. For one thing, 'party capability theory'[55] suggests that the more 'capable' a party is, the more likely they will be to succeed in court ('capable' in this context is, in effect, an American euphemism for 'wealthy'). Studies have established considerable empirical evidence of differential treatment between the 'haves' and 'have nots' in the US context[56] as well as in other jurisdictions.[57] Socio-economically advantaged parties will be able to draw upon greater resources than socio-economic underdogs. Those with

[51] *R (Miller) v Secretary of State for Exiting the European Union* [2017] UKSC 5; [2018] AC 61.

[52] *R (Evans) v Attorney General* [2015] UKSC 21; [2015] AC 1787.

[53] *Secretary of State for Justice v MM* [2018] UKSC 60; [2019] AC 712.

[54] *Commissioner of Police of the Metropolis v DSD* [2018] UKSC 11; [2019] AC 196.

[55] M Galanter, 'Why the Haves Come Out Ahead: Speculations on the Limits of Social Change' (1974) 9 *Law and Society Review* 95.

[56] J Szmer, D Songer and J Bowie, 'Party Capability and the US Courts of Appeals: Understanding Why the "Haves" Win' (2016) 4(1) *Journal of Law and Courts* 65; H Kritzer and S Silbey (eds), *Litigation: Do the 'Haves' Still Come Out Ahead?* (Stanford, 2003); D Songer, A Kuersten and E Kaheny, 'Why the Haves Don't Always Come Out Ahead: Repeat Players Meet Amici Curiae for the Disadvantaged' (2000) 53(3) *Political Research Quarterly* 537.

[57] H Xin and Y Su, 'Do the Haves Come Out Ahead in Shanghai Courts?' (2013) 10(1) *Journal of Empirical Legal Studies* 120; P McCormick, 'Party Capability Theory and Appellate Success in the Supreme Court of Canada, 1949–1992' (1993) 26(3) *Canadian Journal of Political Science* 523; S Muro et al, 'Testing Representational Advantage in the Argentine Supreme Court' (2018) 6(1) *Journal of Law and Courts* 1.

greater financial means will be able to make more informed decisions in the litigation process, including whether to bring legal proceedings in first place, and are more likely to be able to afford to instruct more expensive lawyers to act on their behalf. This, studies suggest, leads to the 'haves' being treated more favourably in court compared to the 'have nots'.

There is also a more sociological consideration in play. Senior judiciaries tend not to be very diverse. This certainty applies to the UKSC; Lord Neuberger has admitted that 'the socio-economic background of the senior judiciary is almost monolithic'.[58] Before being appointed to the bench, most judges were senior barristers, often dealing with highly profitable (often, but not exclusively, commercial) cases. Most attended Oxbridge, and many attended elite schools such as Eton.[59] As one commentator put it, the career trajectories of senior judges tend to conform to a distinct pattern, with a typical judge moving from 'the cloistered environments of English public schools, Oxford colleges, [to] the Inns of Court and latterly in Parliament Square'.[60] It can be said, therefore, that most judges occupy an immensely privileged socio-economic position. It is easy to see why some have therefore suggested that judges tend to side with certain parties out of self-interest, behaving in a manner which protects their own social interests as well as those of a similar status.[61]

As a result, there is a strong case for measuring how likely judges are to side with socio-economic underdogs.[62] Importantly, some studies have already explored similar questions in the UK context, including Burton Atkins' examination of the Court of Appeal in the late 1980s[63] and Chris Hanretty's study of appeals to the Judicial House of Lords during its final years.[64] Both authors found some evidence that socio-economically powerful parties fared more favourably than weaker ones before appellate judges, but each argued that this effect was most pronounced in cases involving private parties against the government, with less obvious evidence

[58] Lord Neuberger, 'Judges and Policy: a delicate balance' (Institute for Government, 18 June 2013).

[59] According to the Sutton Trust, as of June 2019, 65% of senior judges were privately educated and 71% attended Oxford or Cambridge; just 13% attended a comprehensive school (although the figure in 2014 was even lower, at just 4%) – see The Sutton Trust, 'Elitist Britain 2019' (24 June 2019), available at www.suttontrust.com/wp-content/uploads/2019/12/Elitist-Britain-2019.pdf.

[60] M Loughlin, 'What would John Griffith have made of Jonathan Sumption's Reith Lectures?' (2019) 90(4) *Political Quarterly* 785, 793.

[61] See generally Griffith (n 2).

[62] It is arguable that this dimension maps well onto common understandings of ideological behaviour: J Laponce, *Left and right: the topography of political perceptions* (Toronto, 1981) 135. In one UK-based poll investigating popular conceptions of the term 'left-wing' and 'right-wing', of the five policies most associated with being 'left-wing', four directly related to ameliorating wealth disparities or strengthening the socio-economic underdog (support for minimum wage, trade unions, wealth redistribution and progressive taxation): YouGov, 'Left-wing vs right-wing: its complicated' (14 August 2019) yougov.co.uk/politics/articles/24767-left-wing-vs-right-wing-its-complicated. See further ch 9.

[63] B Atkins, 'Party Capability Theory as an Explanation for Intervention: Behavior in the English Court of Appeal' (1991) 35 *American Journal of Political Science* 881.

[64] Hanretty, 'Haves and Have-Nots' (n 18). In his later work, Hanretty found that a judge's political preferences played a significant role in their decision-making, at least in non-unanimous cases, and his definition of left-wing and right-wing politics somewhat aligns (however imperfectly) with the notion of siding with or against socio-economic underdogs: Hanretty (n 13) ch 7 and ch 8.

in other cases, for example, in cases involving workers against employers, or individuals against powerful private companies. The present dataset allows for a more thorough assessment into the treatment of the 'socio-economic underdog' in the as-yet unexamined context of the UK Supreme Court.

A. Measuring Underdog Preferences

How, then, should 'underdogs' be defined? However intuitive the concept, choosing a workable definition which can be applied across all cases for the purpose of coding is far from straightforward.[65] Ultimately, 'underdog' status was defined according to whether, in a given case, there existed a recognised social or financial disparity between the parties. In such a case, the weaker party would be coded as the underdog. There is an unavoidable level of ambiguity when it comes to applying such a criterion, and the question of whether a particular individual or group faces socio-economic disadvantage was sometimes tricky to determine, especially at the margins. Nonetheless, the following is an attempt to outline the contours of the definition adopted. First, the 'underdog' label was applied to those who tend to hold a particularly disadvantaged position in society more generally, such as homeless people, prisoners, immigrants or those facing deportation and those relying on social welfare. Otherwise, the existence of a hierarchal relationship between the parties was often illustrative; parties identified in the dataset as underdogs include tenants in cases against their landlords, users of land in cases against landowners and clients or workers in cases against their employers or corporations. Those accused by the state of having committed a crime usually fell into the underdog category, at least in cases where this was relevant to the subject-matter of the case at hand. The 'underdog' in a discrimination case was generally treated as the party claiming unfair treatment due to a protected characteristic. Generally, an 'ordinary' citizen was considered, at least for the purposes of this section, to be in a weaker position than public authorities or the government; whilst this may be obvious in a case involving agencies such as the police, the same applied whenever an ordinary individual was party to a case against a public body or agency, even if that body was not acting in an expressly coercive manner. In cases between two parties with significant and obvious wealth disparities between them (for example, a dispute between a private individual and a large multinational company in a patent dispute) the underdog was considered to be the financially weaker party.

On the other hand, it cannot be the case that every party facing some sort of disadvantage relative to their opponent should be labelled as a 'socio-economic

[65] Given the ambiguities in the margins of the definition of 'socio-economic underdog', coding in this context was undertaken cautiously. Cases where the relationship between parties was disputed or ambiguous, where there existed competing minority rights claims between parties, or where the identity of a socio-economic underdog was otherwise particularly contentious or troublesome, were excluded from the dataset.

underdog' and this was not done in this dataset. Cases between a powerful (private) body such as a large insurance company and the state, for example, were not treated as involving an obvious underdog dimension. For similar reasons, disputes between two large private companies were generally not deemed to include an underdog dimension, even if those companies were of different sizes. Equally, no underdog dimension was recognised in cases such as *Ashers Bakery*[66] where no large company was involved (the bakery in this case was small and family-ran) and both sides relied on competing discrimination claims.

Once an underdog was identified, a 'win' was marked in the same way it was in any other section, usually according to whether liability was found by the court on the facts, or in cases where this was not relevant, whether the live issues in the case were resolved in favour of the underdog (eg where greater damages were awarded). Partial wins, or wins for some parties but not others, were expressed as such in the usual way.

B. Underdog Preferences: Results

The data in Figure 4 does not suggest a robust application of 'party capability theory' in the UKSC context, when the Court's output is examined as a whole. Whilst the Court sided against the underdog more often than it sided with them, the numerical difference is only slight. Further, since cases with a 'mixed finding' involve the Court siding with at least one underdog party, this suggests that there are more cases where the Court sided *with an underdog in at least one respect* than cases in which it did not do so.

Figure 4 Court determination: underdog preferences

Applicable cases	Majority for underdog	Majority against underdog	Mixed finding
389	163	184	42

Regardless of the application of party capability theory to this context, as the above section on state preferences shows, it is unlikely that all judges behave the same way when it comes to underdog parties. American studies have shown differences between judges in this respect, with some judges aligning themselves with the 'haves' and others showing more sympathy to the 'have nots'.[67] As such, Figure 5 shows how likely each judge was to find for or against the socio-economic underdog across all relevant cases as defined above. 20 judges decided enough cases to produce data; their positions adopted ranged from siding with the underdog

[66] *Lee v Ashers Baking Company* [2018] UKSC 49; [2020] AC 413.

[67] See eg R Black and C Boyd, 'US Supreme Court Agenda Setting and the Role of Litigant Status' (2012) 28(2) *Journal of Law, Economics and Organization* 286.

in just under 35 per cent of cases (Lord Neuberger) to over 60 per cent of cases (Lord Kerr). The average 'score' of judges here was 47.77 per cent. The results, like those relating to state preferences above, show relatively minor variance. However, the results do suggest that at an individual level, judges are – if only just – more likely to side against the underdog than they are to side with them.

Figure 5 Party preferences: socio-economic underdog (all cases)

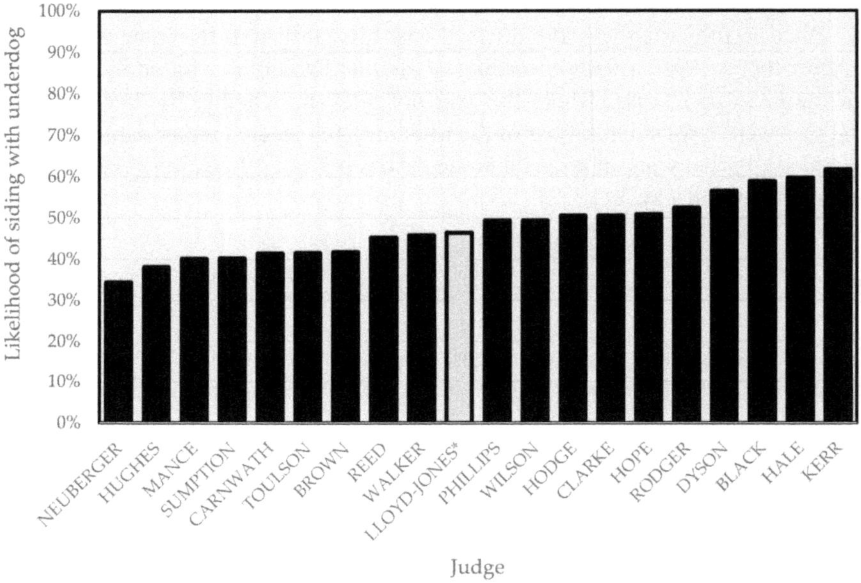

Much like the group of cases involving the state, the database of cases involving a socio-economic underdog features a significant number of salient cases (those cases where the judges differ as to their treatment of the underdog). Figure 6 therefore shows how likely each judge was to side with the underdog in relation to salient cases only. Here, 87 relevant cases were identified and 18 judges decided enough cases to produce data (Lady Black and Lord Lloyd-Jones were dropped, and Lords Hodge, Rodger and Toulson produced less significant data). As expected, the range of positions here is a lot wider than those found in Figure 5. Bookending the scale are Lords Hodge and Kerr: when it came to salient cases, the former sided with the underdog in just over 10 per cent of cases, whereas Lord Kerr did so over 80 per cent of the time.[68] Noteworthy rank differences include that of Lord Toulson, whose relative sympathy for the underdog in Figure 6 was not evident in Figure 5, and Lord Rodger, whose reluctance to side with the underdog as shown in Figure 6 was likewise seemingly hidden in

[68] Lord Kerr's score is significantly above average. Judges were likely to find for the underdog in these cases just 35.86% of the time (a difference of over 10 points from the average shown in Figure 5).

Figure 6. Lord Phillips also appears relatively likely to side with the underdog in salient cases when compared to the general dataset.

Figure 6 Party prefrences: socio-economic underdog (salient cases)

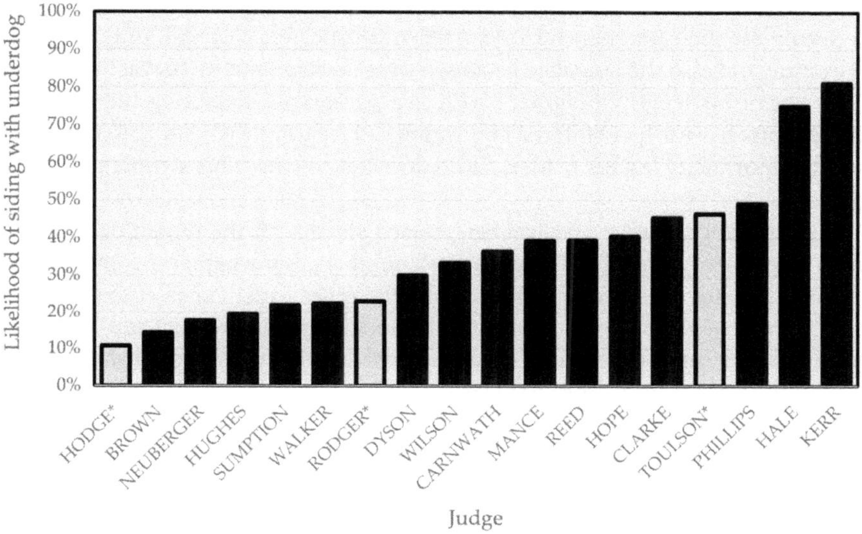

Lady Hale and Lord Kerr once again appear to show distinctive behavioural preferences here; they both sit over 25-points above the nearest judge. They are definitely the Court's two most 'pro-underdog' judges.[69] Given that many underdog cases involve the state in some way, this should not be too surprising, given their respective positions in the data set out in Section II above. Evidence of Lady Hale's particular sympathy for the underdog may be seen in cases such as *Edwards*, where she prefaced her contribution with a reminder that she was the 'only member of [the] court to have spent a substantial portion of her life' as an employee[70] and *McDonald*, where she carefully detailed the she circumstances affecting the claimant, including her limited mobility and bladder issues, in a challenge to the adequacy of her care plan. She emphasised that such a disability 'could affect any one of us'[71] and chastised her colleagues for failing to ensure

[69] Once again, their influence likely pushed their colleagues into a more 'anti-underdog' position; by removing any cases involving these judges from the dataset and recalculating each judge's tendency to side with the state, it can be discovered which judges were more inclined than their colleagues to side with the underdog, but whose preferences are 'lost' in a dataset featuring the much stronger preferences of Hale and Kerr. The rankings did not differ significantly from Figures 6, but both Lord Clarke and Lord Phillips sided with the state in 58% of cases. Lord Dyson appeared much more sympathetic to the underdog once Hale and Kerr were excluded, siding with the underdog in half of all salient cases (compared to around 25% in Figure 6).

[70] *Edwards v Chesterfield Royal Hospital NHS Foundation Trust* [2011] UKSC 58; [2012] 2 AC 22.

[71] *R (McDonald) v Royal Borough of Kensington & Chelsea* [2011] UKSC 33; [2011] 4 All ER 881 at [61].

that she received the dignified care required in a 'civilised society'.[72] Lord Kerr's clear sympathy for the underdog comes through in multiple judgments, perhaps most notably his powerful dissenting judgment in the *NIHRC* case, where he ruled that Northern Ireland's abortion restrictions breached not only Article 8 but also Article 3 ECHR.[73] His 'admiration and sympathy'[74] for women unable to terminate their pregnancies in Northern Ireland was clear not only from his reasoning but also the language he adopted; as Dickson put it: 'the fact that Lord Kerr began his lengthy judgment with five paragraphs depicting the plight of three women who had suffered the trauma of bearing foetuses suffering fatal foetal abnormality left his readers in no doubt as to where his sympathies lay in this case.'[75]

Lords Hodge, Brown and Neuberger each sided with the underdog in fewer than 20 per cent of cases.[76] These are stark numbers. But whether this means that these judges are particularly influenced by the more experienced counsel which can be employed by socio-economically advantaged parties, respect and deference to companies and state actors, or a personal buy-in to the established socio-economic order, is impossible to determine.

C. Relationship between the State and Underdog Dimensions

Clearly, there is significant overlap between the results in Section II and those in Section III.[77] Given that the definition of underdog used in Section III includes many claimants going against state parties, it might be hard to tell whether a judge who sides with one party over another in such cases is doing so because of their views on the state, their perception of the underdog, or both. This very issue muddied the conclusions drawn in earlier studies on this issue.[78]

Figure 7 therefore compares each judge's likelihood to side with the state overall with their tendency to side with the state in cases involving an underdog dimension, as well as those cases without an underdog dimension. Figure 8 does the same, centralising the underdog dimension and comparing those cases which

[72] ibid 79.

[73] *NIHRC* (n 47).

[74] See Lady Hale, 'Women and Children First' in Dickson and McCormick (n 28) 42.

[75] B Dickson, 'Lord Kerr and Articles 2 and 3 of the ECHR' in Dickson and McCormick (n 28) 109.

[76] If cases involving Lady Hale and Lord Kerr are excluded, both Lord Hodge and Lord Brown remain below 20%, suggesting that their reluctance to side with the underdog can be interpreted as a more general preference, rather than something exclusively understood in relation to the preferences of Lady Hale and Lord Kerr.

[77] There is a significant (negative) correlation between the judges in this respect, when it comes to their records in all cases (–.900** (t-test, two-tailed, significant at the 0.01 level)); salient cases (–.965** (t-test, two-tailed, significant at the 0.01 level)) and salient cases excluding Hale and Kerr (–.933** (t-test, two-tailed, significant at the 0.01 level)).

[78] See Atkins (n 63) and Hanretty (n 64).

feature the state with those which do not. This produces results for three case groupings: underdogs against the state, underdogs against non-state actors, and non-underdogs against the state.

It seems that judges are, on average, more likely to side with the state in those cases which do *not* involve an underdog dimension (for example, in disputes between a regulatory authority and a for-profit business organisation, or in a challenge to a tax decision by a large, private company) compared to those cases which do. In other words, the presence of an underdog has a moderating effect on a given judge's likelihood of siding with the state. However, there are exceptions: Lords Wilson, Toulson, Sumption and Hughes were each more likely to find for the state in cases against an underdog than those without one. The judges most likely to side with the state in cases without an underdog are Lords Walker and Hope; those least likely to do so in such cases are Lords Toulson and Wilson.

Regarding the underdog dimension, it can be seen that most judges were more likely to side with the underdog in cases in which the state was involved (eg individual challenging state detention) compared to those involving private actors only (eg employer challenging dismissal). There are exceptions, however, such as Lord Hope and Lord Reed. Overall, once the state dimension is removed, Lord Dyson becomes the judge most likely to side with the underdog, above even Lady Hale and Lord Kerr (although Lord Dyson decided fewer cases than the other judges, making his records somewhat less reliable). Those least likely to do so are Lords Neuberger and Reed. It appears, then, that the picture is complicated: *some* judges exhibit a sympathy for the underdog; for some of those judges, this mainly manifests in cases involving challenges against the state. But this is not true for all judges, who side with underdogs across the board; and indeed, it seems some judges were, in fact, *more* likely to side with the underdog in non-state cases. On the Supreme Court, attitudes towards socio-economic underdogs are far from uniform.

Figure 7 Party preferences: state (underdog versus non-underdog cases)

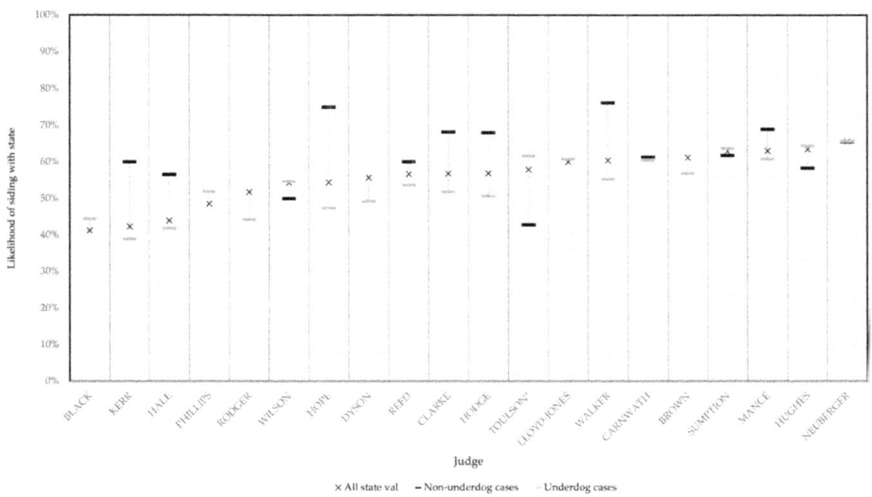

Figure 8 party preferences: socio-economic underdog (state versus non-state cases)

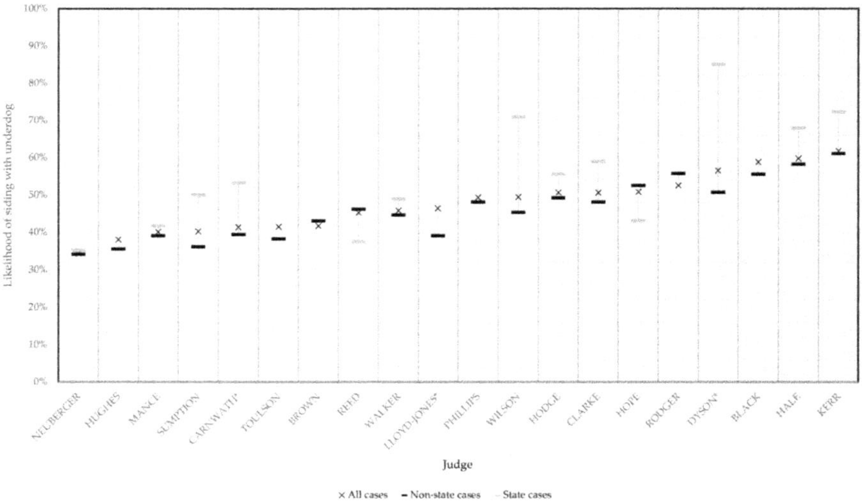

III. Preferences: Gender

At the end of the period surveyed, women made up less than a third of all full-time judges employed in England and Wales[79] and just three UKSC judges featured in the dataset were women.[80] The courts have a (now well-recognised) gender diversity problem. But does this mean that the judges themselves – so often derided as 'pale, male and stale' – have a gender problem of their own?[81] There is some evidence that judges, to at least some extent, are at least *perceived* to be sexist and unsympathetic towards women, and particularly towards female victims of crime.[82] But do those perceptions, however entrenched, match reality? And would this necessarily be the case for all judges, women included?

[79] Ministry of Justice, 'Judicial Diversity Statistics 2019', www.judiciary.uk/wp-content/uploads/2019/07/Judicial-Diversity-Statistics-2019.pdf.

[80] At time of writing, only five women have ever been appointed to the Court, and the Court has never included more than three women in its full-time roster at any given point. In addition to Lady Hale, Lady Black and Lady Arden, all of whom sat during the period studied, Lady Rose has since been appointed (in 2021), as has Lady Simler (in 2023). She sat on the court for the entire duration of the dataset used in this work and retired in 2020. The second woman to be appointed was Lady Black (appointed in 2017 and retired in 2021), followed by Lady Arden (appointed in 2018 and retired in 2022), Lady Rose (appointed in 2021) and Lady Simler (appointed in 2023).

[81] Feminist scholars have convincingly argued, for example, that there exists a gendered dimension to the judicial role itself: E Rackley, 'Representations of the (Woman) Judge: Hercules, the Little Mermaid and the Vain and Naked Emperor' 22(4) *Legal Studies* 602.

[82] Darbyshire (n 5) 24–25.

This section looks at whether judges tended to vote for or against women claimants. It therefore adds to the voluminous literature investigating whether the gender of litigants makes any meaningful difference to case outcomes in a variety of different circumstances. Some of these studies found that, within the specific contours of the study parameters, there *was* evidence that judges tend to treat women litigants differently to men (this effect seems to be particularly evident in the field of criminal sentencing). However, other studies concluded that gender had no particular influence in this respect.[83] Results, then, are mixed, and positive findings in earlier studies, looking at specific courts and narrow subject areas, cannot be presumed to carry over to the generalist work of the UKSC.

For the avoidance of doubt, this section does not seek to answer the bigger – and arguably much more difficult – question of whether women judges judge differently than their male counterparts,[84] although empirical studies can certainly make insightful contributions in this respect.[85] Tackling this question would be impossible using the current dataset, given the lamentable paucity of women who sat on the UKSC during the relevant period.[86]

A. Measuring Gender Preferences

At the outset, it should be remembered that this chapter is focusing on the influence of the characteristics of the *parties* involved in Supreme Court cases, rather than judges. Nonetheless, for the reasons described above, special attention will be paid to the women who sat on the Court: Lady Hale, Lady Black and Lady Arden.

[83] See eg P Coontz, 'Gender and judicial decisions: Do female judges decide cases differently than male judges?' (2000) 18 *Gender Issues* 59 (the study found that the gender of the judge made a difference, but the gender of the litigant did not).

[84] On which, see C Gilligan, *In a Different Voice* (Harvard, 1982); R Hunter, 'More than Just a Different Face? Judicial Diversity and Decision-making' (2015) 68 *Current Legal Problems* 119.

[85] For examples see eg C Boyd and A Rutkowski, 'Judicial Behaviour in Disability Cases: Do Judge Sex and Race Matter?' (2020) 8(4) *Politics Groups and Identities* 834; N Gill et al, 'The Limits of Procedural Discretion: Unequal Treatment and Vulnerability in Britain's Asylum Appeals' (2018) 27(1) *Social & Legal Studies* 49; L Graham, 'Lady Justices and Dissent on the Court of Appeal of England and Wales' (*UK Constitutional Law Association Blog*, 15 November 2018) ukconstitutionallaw.org/2018/11/15/lewis-graham-lady-justices-and-dissent-on-the-court-of-appeal-of-england-and-wales/; C Boyd, 'Representation on the Courts? The Effects of Trial Judges' Sex and Race' (2016) 69 *Political Research Quarterly* 788; Hunter, ibid; S Johnson, D Songer and N Jilani, 'Judge gender, critical mass, and decision making in the appellate courts of Canada' (2011) 32(3) *Journal of Women, Politics & Policy* 237; S Johnson and D Songer, 'Judge gender and the voting behavior of justices on two North American Supreme Courts' (2009) 30(3) *Justice System Journal* 265; M Belleau and R Johnson, 'Judging gender: difference and dissent at the Supreme Court of Canada' (2008) 15(1) *International Journal of the Legal Profession* 57.

[86] Remarkably, before 2017, the only woman to have sat as a full-time judge on the UKSC was Lady Hale, who was appointed to the Judicial House of Lords in 2004 and sat on the UKSC from its inception in 2009. The Court has never sat with more than three full-time women judges.

Regretfully, however, both Lady Black and Lady Arden joined the Court a short while before the cut-off period for this dataset, meaning insight into their behaviour towards women parties is necessarily much more limited than that which can be attributed to Lady Hale, who sat on the Court for the entire period surveyed.

To generate a dataset looking at approaches to women parties, the term needed to be defined. For present purposes, a qualifying case was one in which one party to the case was a woman and the other was not. The gender identification of parties was sourced from the judgment itself.[87] Where there were multiple parties to the case, all parties on one 'side' must have been women to be counted. Therefore, cases such as *Carmichael*[88] were not included, because the claimants were not all women, despite the fact that the case involved a claim relating to sex discrimination in the context of economic sanctions being applied to victims of domestic violence. Indeed, cases involving feminist issues, or claims which might focus on the particular position of women compared to men, were not automatically counted for the purposes of this section unless the parties themselves were women. Corporations and public bodies generally did not count as women parties, even if, for example, the CEO of a company was a woman at the time of the case. Equally, government ministers acting in their official capacity were not included, even if they happened to be a woman. As ever, wins and losses were coded as a binary mark, with partial wins (eg one woman winning, one losing) coded in the usual way.

Obviously, this is a very blunt way to evaluate cases. As the exclusion of *Carmichael* demonstrates, it filters only for 'cases involving women' rather than cases specifically raising feminist or gender issues.[89] As such, a vote for a woman is not necessarily a *feminist* or a *pro-woman* judgment. Lady Hale's dissenting judgment in the case of *Radmacher*[90] is illustrative: it was explicitly informed by her lived experience as a woman, and her scepticism about recognising and enforcing prenuptial agreements was based, in part, on worries that negatively and disproportionately affect women. Nonetheless, given that the party seeking to enforce the agreement on the facts of the case was herself a woman, Hale's vote in that case was marked as a vote *against* women parties. To be clear, then, this section examines the treatment of *women parties* rather than whether decisions are *good for women*.[91]

[87] In the present dataset, there were no issues relating to the definition of woman or gender, so no further definition was required.

[88] *R (Carmichael and Rourke) v Secretary of State for Work and Pensions* [2016] UKSC 58; [2016] WLR 4550.

[89] *cf* R Hunter and E Rackley, 'Judicial Leadership on the UK Supreme Court' (2018) 38 *Legal Studies* 191, 211.

[90] *Radmacher v Granatino* [2010] UKSC 42; [2011] 1 AC 534.

[91] On which see R Hunter and E Rackley, 'Feminist Judgments on the UK Supreme Court' (2020) 32(1) *Canadian Journal of Women and the Law* 85 and K McNeilly, 'Human Rights, Gender Equality and the Judge's Toolbox' in Dickson and McCormick (n 28).

B. Gender Preferences: Results

127 cases were marked as involving a woman party, according to the criteria outlined above. Figure 9 shows that in a majority of cases the Court sided with the woman party (72 cases).

Figure 9 Court determinations: women parties

Applicable cases	Majority for women parties	Majority against women parties	Mixed finding
127	72	50	5

As to individual judges, just 12 decided enough cases to produce data (nine of them significant). Their records are set out in Figure 10. The judges range from finding for the woman party in just 42.5 per cent of cases (Lord Carnwath) to over 72 per cent of cases (Lord Kerr), with an average likelihood of 56.77 per cent. Lady Hale, the sole female judge deciding enough cases involving women to produce meaningful data, scored relatively highly – 67.48 per cent – but was not the *most* likely judge to side with women. Lady Arden's records were too small to draw any conclusions from, and Lady Black decided just 13 cases involving women. However, it may be worth noting that the latter sided with the woman in 11 of those cases. Whilst this is clearly too small a dataset for any meaningful conclusions to be drawn, it could be the case that Lady Black, too, held something of a sympathy towards women parties.

Figure 10 Party preferences: gender (all cases)

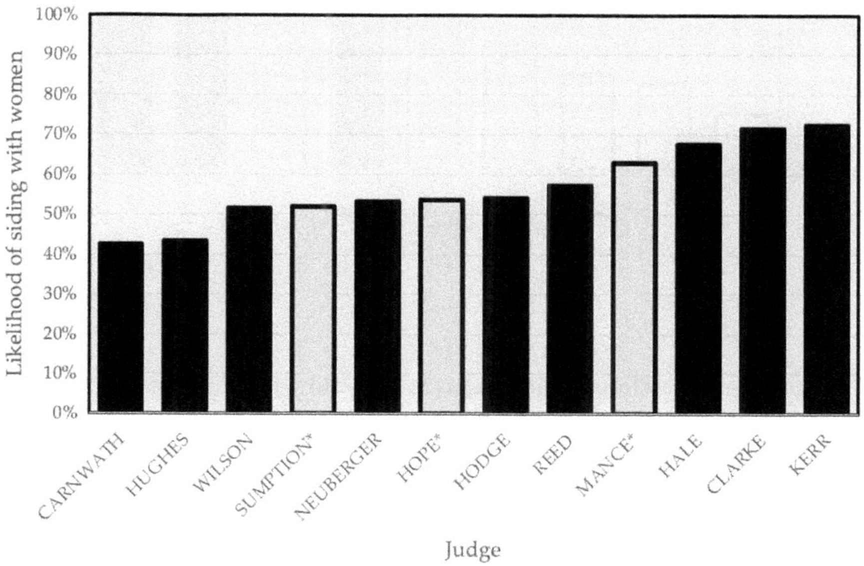

Figure 11 shows each judge's record when considering salient cases only. As can be seen, the relatively low number of cases here (just 26 salient cases in total) means that most judges were characterised as having less reliable data (marked with an asterisk and coloured in grey). This may cast some doubt on the overall reliability of results.

Despite this, it is notable that Lady Hale's likelihood of siding with women increased to 82 per cent, placing her amongst the judges most sympathetic to women parties, alongside Lord Kerr (82 per cent) and Lord Clarke (83 per cent), although the data for Lady Hale and Lord Kerr was based on a higher number of cases than that of Lord Clarke. In addition, something not captured by Figure 11 is that Lady Hale seems to have become more likely to side with women parties in salient cases over time. She sided with the woman party in all of the 17 most recent salient cases and did not cast a single vote *against* a woman party in a salient case since Hilary Term 2013. Additionally, she sided with the woman in every one of her dissenting opinions in this dataset bar one, and that case was the *Radmacher* case detailed above, where her reasoning was based in part on her concern that the majority's position would disadvantage other women parties.

Figure 11 Party preferences: gender (salient cases)

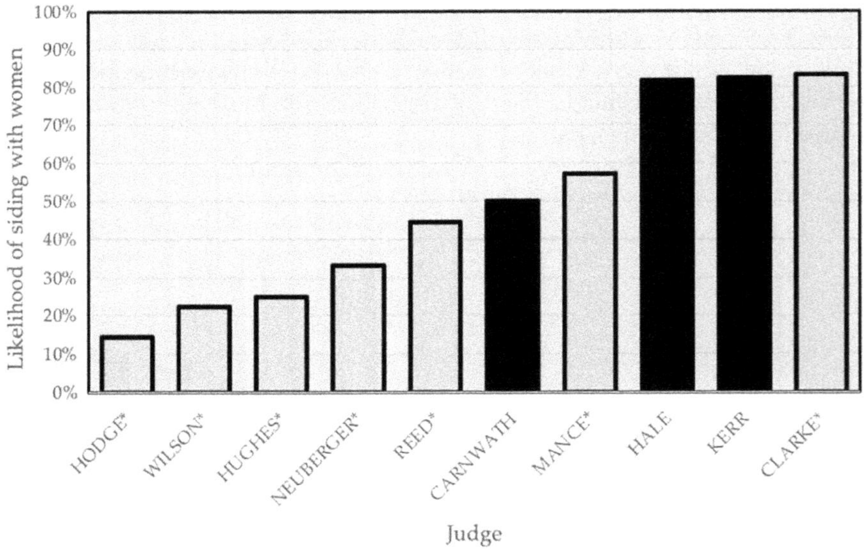

The data might therefore be interpreted as suggesting that Lady Hale is particularly likely to side with women. But if that is the case, she is not alone, as both Lord Kerr and Lord Clarke have comparable records (as the only woman in Figures 10 and 11, conclusions about gendered judging are even harder to draw, although it may be noteworthy that Lady Black sided with the woman in both salient cases in which she sat). There is also a significant overlap between the question of whether a given judge sides with a woman in a given case and whether they side with the state, or the underdog, in that case. In the vast majority of cases involving a woman and an underdog dimension, for example, the woman *was* the party identified as the underdog;[92] in only one of the salient cases involved in Figure 11 was a woman classed as the stronger socio-economic party. Given that Lady Hale and Lord Kerr (and to some extent, Lord Clarke) appear to side with the underdog and against the state in Sections II and III above, and the close relationship between the gender variable and both state and underdog variables, it becomes difficult to establish whether the judges in Figures 10 and 11 are siding with women *because they are women* or siding with women because of their anti-state or pro-underdog preferences.

With the important caveat that splitting the dataset into state and non-state cases and filtering for women parties results in some low numbers from which it would be difficult to draw any strong conclusions, it is nevertheless notable that when looking at cases involving women in private law cases (that is, cases involving a woman party but no state party), Lady Hale sided with the woman around 68 per cent of the time which is, significantly, only slightly above the average figure of 67 per cent. Lord Reed, by contrast, did so 83 per cent of the time. When looking at non-underdog cases (that is, cases involving a woman party but no underdog dimension), Lady Hale sided with women 70 per cent of the time (the average here was 63 per cent), although again, other judges, such as Lords Collins (83 per cent), Clarke (80 per cent) and Kerr (74 per cent) were more sympathetic. In those cases which involved a woman party but neither the state nor an obvious underdog, Lady Hale's likelihood to side with women (66 per cent) again sits just above the average (65 per cent) and falls below that of colleagues such as Lord Clarke (75 per cent) and Lord Reed (82 per cent). It is clear, then, that the relationship between gender and other attributes is a complicated one, and that, taken by itself, it is not necessarily evident that Lady Hale found for women parties simply because of their gender.

What did emerge from that dataset, however, was that Lady Hale sat a lot of cases featuring women.[93] She sat on 103 of 123 cases featuring a woman party (84 per cent) and 22 of 26 split cases (85 per cent). She sat on 42 of the 49 cases (86 per cent) which involved a woman but not the state, 30 of the 34 cases (88 per cent) which involved a woman but not an underdog, and 28 of the 31 cases (90 per cent) which involved women but neither the state nor an underdog. No other judges had a remotely comparable record. This is remarkable even

[92] In cases which feature both a woman and an underdog dimension, the relationship between the two was strongly positively correlated: .938** (t-test, two-tailed, significant at the 0.01 level).

[93] This may be due to a conscious policy of the court registrar. Writing in 2020 (when three women judges sat on the Court), Lord Reed said that 'it is … considered appropriate to have to have both female Justices sit on appeals where female participation is especially important (eg equal pay cases)': Lord Reed, 'Collective Judging in the UK Supreme Court' in B Häcker and W Ernst, *Collective Judging in Comparative Perspective* (Intersentia, 2020) 27 fn 16.

considering Lady Hale's tendency to sit on a greater number of cases across the board.[94] Whilst it is true that a number of the cases involving women fall within the topic of family law, an area in which Lady Hale holds a special interest, these figures remain distinct from those of Lord Wilson, the other family law specialist on the Court. The family law connection does not, in and of itself, explain Hale's sitting figures here. It does not seem too much of a stretch, therefore, to draw a connection between the fact that Lady Hale was, for a very long time the only woman on the Supreme Court, and the fact that she participated in the vast majority of cases involving women.

As such, whilst Lady Hale *sat* on a greater number of cases involving women, it is harder to show that she systemically *sided* with women, at least to a greater extent than her colleagues did. It is also hard to determine whether this possible pro-woman position is better explained by a preference for siding with women rather than siding against the state or siding with socio-economic underdogs. Nor is she the only judge to exhibit what looks, on its face, to be a pro-woman tendency. Whilst this does not mean that that women do not judge differently,[95] nor forecloses the possibility that Lady Hale judges differently because of her gender,[96] it is not true to say that, according to her voting records, Lady Hale is more likely to side with women *simply because* they are women. Her judicial philosophy is much more sophisticated than this.[97]

IV. Conclusions

This chapter looked through the voting records of UKSC judges and has suggested that there is evidence – at least to some extent – of certain judges having a tendency to vote for or against certain types of party to a case. Some judges show a sympathy for the underdog (others go the opposite way); others are typically likely to side with the state (and again, others do the opposite). Not all judges who side with the underdog also tend to side with the state, but there is a clear correlation between the judges' records in this respect. And whilst there is some evidence that different judges are more or less likely to side with women parties, the data in this case is much weaker and definitive conclusions cannot be made. An overview of findings in relation to each of the factors examined, including the

[94] See ch 3.

[95] For a convincing argument that there are many reasons as to why women's voices may not 'show up' in statistical analyses, see Hunter (n 84).

[96] Or indeed her feminist philosophy: see R Hunter and E Rackley, 'Lady Hale: A Feminist Towering Judge' in R Abeyratne and I Porat, *Towering Judges: A Comparative Study of Constitutional Judges* (CUP, 2021).

[97] When discussing the predictability of judicial determinations Lady Hale remarked that 'You can't look at Hale and say she always sides with the women. Because she doesn't!': Lady Hale, 'Safeguarding London's Standing in International Dispute Resolution' (Prospect Webinars, 6 October 2020).

most prominent judges in each case, is set out below in Figures 12–14. What is clear is that the identity of the parties in a case *may well matter* when it comes to judicial decision-making.

Does this mean that judges are foregoing their role and siding with whichever party attracts their sympathy? Not at all – stony-faced stalwarts and bleeding hearts are each bound by all kinds of restrictions and are committed to applying the law as they see it. In addition, a voting record which reveals a sympathy – or otherwise – for certain kinds of parties does not indicate that a judge is working outside the law. Rather, party sympathy affects how core aspects of the judicial role operate in practice: the exercise of discretion, the application of law to the facts, and the degree to which judicial law-making powers are exercised. Holding attitudes towards particular parties is not necessarily antithetical to the judicial role; it is, in fact, in many ways, central to it.

Figure 12 State approach overview

Results	
UKSC tendency as a whole	More likely to side with state
Likely to side with state	*Lord Brown, Lord Hughes*
Unlikely to side with state	*Lord Kerr, Lady Hale*

Figure 13 Underdog approach overview

Results	
UKSC tendency as a whole	Slightly more likely to side against underdog
Likely to side with underdog	*Lord Kerr, Lady Hale, Lord Dyson*
Unlikely to side with underdog	*Lord Hodge, Lord Brown, Lord Hughes*

Figure 14 Women parties overview

Results	
UKSC tendency as a whole	Slightly more likely to side with women
Likely to uphold challenge	*Lord Clarke, Lady Hale, Lord Kerr*
Unlikely to uphold challenge	*Lord Hodge, Lord Hughes*

6

Legal Subject-Areas

In the previous chapters, a case was made that some individual judges are more likely than others to allow appeals from certain courts, and that some tend to favour certain kinds of parties to others. In this chapter, the focus turns to how the Court approached different substantive areas of law, and whether any significant patterns can be identified in relation to each individual judge's approach: a focus upon *what* is being argued before them, rather than *who* is arguing it.

It may be the case that some areas of law provide more fertile settings for the manifestation of preferential behaviour. Some areas of law, by their nature, invite a lot of judicial discretion, whereas others may focus on the application of more rigid and settled rules.[1] Some areas may involve a notable degree of ambiguity, or raise problems which give rise to particular controversy. Some judges may therefore feel that it is more appropriate to exercise discretion or develop the law in certain fields rather than others. Lord Reed, for example, has suggested that he is more comfortable with taking a more activist approach in areas guided primarily by the common law than those chiefly guided by statute.[2] He is unlikely to be the only one to distinguish the cases before him in such a way. This chapter investigates how the judges have approached different subject areas, and whether the judges differ from one another in this respect.

The existing literature, the majority of which does not, of course, look at UK courts, has produced mixed answers to the question of whether judicial behaviour is subject-dependent and, if so, to what extent. Some studies have found that judges apply different approaches and show different preferences across different subject areas, whereas others have diagnosed consistent judicial attitudes across the board.[3] A number of studies have found that the degree of consistency across subject areas differs between the judges themselves.[4] This latter possibility may be especially likely in the present context given that each of the UKSC judges have

[1] Lord Sales, for example, has contrasted, the 'black letter law' of the work of the Chancery Division with the 'touchy-feely principles' of public law: P Sales, 'Reflections on legal life' (*Counsel*, April 2020).

[2] Law in Action, 'The Supreme Court' (*BBC Radio 4*, 26 February 2019).

[3] Compare eg R Posner, *How Judges Think* (Harvard, 2008) 93–94 with G Nelson, *Pathways to the US Supreme Court* (Macmillan, 2013) 197.

[4] L Epstein, W Landes and R Posner, *The Behavior of Federal Judges: A Theoretical and Empirical Study of Rational Choice* (Harvard, 2013) 112; G Schubert, *The Judicial Mind: Attitudes and Ideologies of Supreme Court Justices* (Northwestern, 1965) 99; W Farnsworth, 'Signatures and Ideology: The Case of the Supreme Court's Criminal Docket' (2005) 104 *Michigan Law Review* 67, 96–99.

their own areas of speciality and expertise. This chapter will investigate whether this is, in fact, the case. As with surrounding chapters, the core question remains: do the judges, as individuals, have a voting record which suggests their preferences influence their work?

The analysis below examines seven discrete subject areas in the UKSC's jurisprudence. The Court's case load is not naturally separated into subject categories or groups, so a note on how the 'subject' of each case was identified in the dataset may be useful. Perhaps the most intuitive route, adopted in some other studies,[5] involves labelling each case at the outset according to its content: this way, a list of 'tort cases', 'contract cases', etc can be compiled. But not only is it difficult to characterise cases objectively into discrete categories, but many cases before the UKSC feature multiple issues and overlapping controversies. Therefore, rather than labelling each categorically as a 'tort case' or a 'contract case', the present study marked each of the discrete subject-issues set out below separately whenever they arose. Rather than asking, 'is this more of a tort case or more of a contract case?', the question becomes 'does a tort liability issue feature? Does it involve a contract?' and so on. This meant that cases featuring more than one distinct issue could be considered appropriately; multiple issues could be recorded within the same case, and mixed results would still be marked accurately.

The analysis below examines, in turn, the UKSC's approach to tort liability, contractual liability, criminal liability, EU law, devolution claims, immigration and asylum challenges and tax liability. Human rights liability is assessed in its own dedicated chapter, which follows this one. Of course, the output of the UKSC extends far beyond the cases captured by these seven categories. The categories of case examined here were selected partly for pragmatic purposes, and were not necessarily the seven most important areas of law tackled by the UKSC (although it is submitted each is interesting in its own right). No doubt approaches to other subjects could be examined, such as property law, equity and discrimination law, but these categories proved either too difficult to operationalise (what unites land law cases and what common metric could be used to measure success in this area?) or did not attract enough cases to contribute to meaningful analysis in the current context.

Of particular note when interpreting the results presented in this chapter is that examining judicial records by subject area necessarily creates some fairly small datasets, particularly when filtering for salient cases. In some cases, each judge's record boiled down to just a handful of cases. Naturally, this reduces the reliability of what might otherwise seem to be some fairly striking results. Nevertheless, so long as the limitations of the dataset are borne in mind (each dataset size is provided in the discussion below), it is suggested that the results presented below can still reveal some interesting *indications* of judicial behaviour, which are well worth taking seriously.

[5] See eg C Hanretty, *A Court of Specialists* (OUP, 2020) ch.2; R Hunter and E Rackley, 'Judicial Leadership on the UK Supreme Court' (2018) 38 *Legal Studies* 191; A Paterson, *Final Judgment: The Law Lords and the Supreme Court* (Hart Publishing, 2013).

I. Tort

Tort law is laden with concepts which invite value-judgments and discretion on the part of judges.[6] It is common, for example, for a judge deciding a tort law case to determine such questions as whether an action is intentional, a consequence foreseeable, or conduct can be deemed 'rational' or, 'fair, just and reasonable' (the latter of which has been described light-heartedly by Lady Hale as an invitation to judges to 'do what [they] like').[7] Such standards are, by their very nature, indeterminate, and even the question of *which* standard to apply in a given context may be an open one.[8] There is therefore ample room for judicial manoeuvring within the field of tort, and scope for the influence of extra-legal factors, including judges' own 'conscious or unconscious biases'.[9]

The dataset includes cases involving torts of all types, including those originating in both statutory and common law. Examples include negligence, defamation, deceit, false imprisonment, harassment, breach of confidence and the rule in *Wilkinson v Downton*.[10] A tort 'win' was most straightforwardly awarded when a claimant successfully convinced the Court that the opposing party committed a tort, or that tortious liability otherwise lay against them. If a breach was not found, where a breach was indemnified or where a defence was successful, the tort claim was marked as a loss for the claimant. As with other areas, tortious liability was only marked where this was a live issue between parties and the coding focused exclusively on the existence of, or extent of, liability in each case, thus excluding judgments in which the sole question for the judges related to the quantification of remedies. In vicarious liability cases, a finding that an employer was liable for the tort on the facts was deemed a tort 'win'.

In the dataset, 60 cases were coded as involving a relevant tort issue. Overall, 21 judges were deemed to have contributed to a relevant number of tort law pronouncements; 13 of those were deemed to have contributed a *significant* number. Figure 1 shows that, on average, judges made a finding of tortious liability 51 per cent of the time.[11] When adjusted to exclude less significant records, this figure increases to around 55 per cent. Thus, the Court's judges were about as likely to rule in favour of finding tortious liability as they were to find against it.

[6] Brice Dickson put it neatly by saying that it involves mechanics which 'leave the practical outworking of the principles to the discretion of individual judges': B Dickson, 'Apex Courts and the Development of the Common Law' in P Daly (ed), *Apex Courts and the Common Law* (Toronto, 2019) 37.

[7] Lady Hale, 'Principle and pragmatism in developing private law' (Cambridge Freshfields Lecture, 7 March 2019).

[8] It has been implied that the divergent approaches regarding how duties of care should be conceptualised in the area of negligence may owe something to the appearance of different 'judicial personnel' on panels in landmark cases: J Morgan, 'Nonfeasance and the end of policy? Reflections on the revolution in public authority liability' (2019) 35(1) *Public Negligence* 32, 45.

[9] Lady Hale (n 7).

[10] *Wilkinson v Downton* [1897] EWHC 1 (QB); [1897] 2 QB 57.

[11] This contrasts with the findings of P Laleng, 'Winners and Losers in the Court of Appeal: An Empirical Study of Personal Injury Cases, 2002–16' (2018) *JPIL* 36, who found a pro-defendant bias in personal injury cases before the Court of Appeal.

There is a moderately high level of variance between the judges. Lord Kerr voted in favour of finding tortious liability 79 per cent of the time. Lord Rodger was the least likely judge to do so (finding liability in just 14 per cent of cases), although many of the judges sitting at the lower end of Figure 1 had less significant records. The judge with the lowest likelihood of finding tort liability amongst judges with *a more significant record* was Lord Neuberger, with a much higher likelihood of 45 per cent. The majority of judges, and the vast majority of those with more significant records, tend to fall around the average.

Figure 1 Tort liability (all cases)

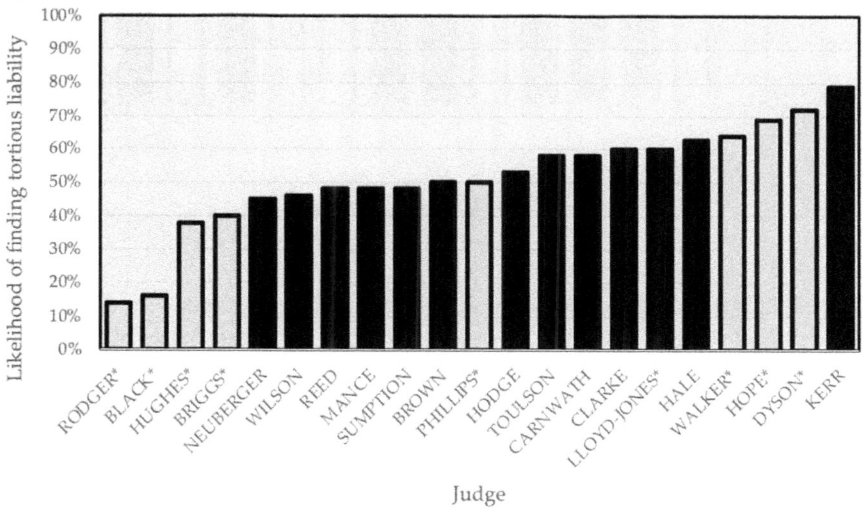

A number of cases (15) featured some sort of division between the judges on an issue relating to tort liability and were marked as *salient cases*.[12] Excluding those who sat on too few cases to produce meaningful data, each judge's record with regards to salient tort cases is set out in Figure 2.

As expected, the judges' positions here are more spread out than with the general data; this results in a higher degree of variance, but a fairly even spread. Lord Rodger's tendency to find against tortious liability in the general dataset is reflected in the salient dataset, too; whilst he only decided three salient tort cases, he found against liability in all of them. Lords Brown and Neuberger both appeared to be more reluctant to recognise a tort breach in salient cases, too. Whilst the general data showed Lord Kerr to be notably more likely to find liability than Lady Hale (79 per cent to 63 per cent), in terms of salient cases they seem to stand equally with each finding tortious liability in nine of the ten cases in which they sat.

[12] No salient tort case was handed down between October 2017 and the dataset cut-off point, October 2019.

Figure 2 Tortious liability (salient cases)

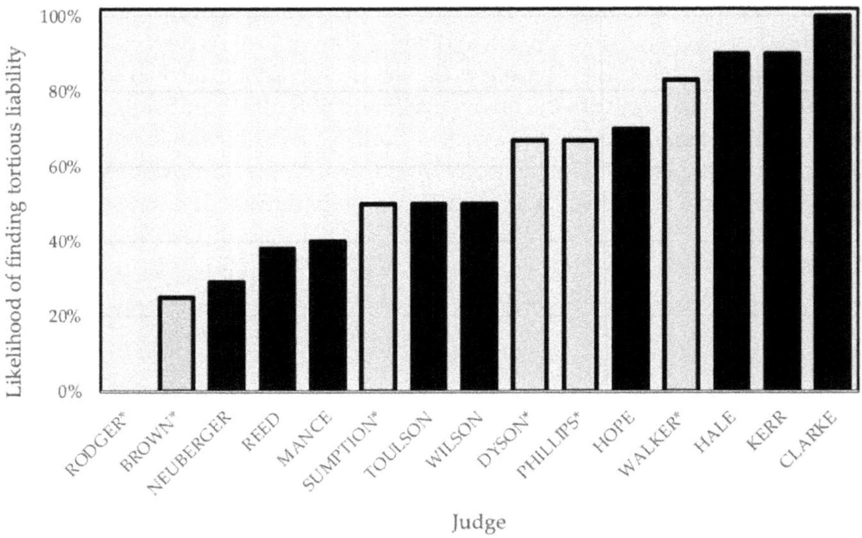

Interestingly, Lord Clarke, who found liability in around 60 per cent of cases in Figure 1, did so in *all* of the salient cases in which he sat. Otherwise, Lords Phillips and Walker both appear to be more likely to find tortious liability in salient cases than the numbers in Figure 1 might otherwise suggest. It should, of course, be borne in mind that this salient dataset includes just 15 cases, and each judge's score was computed on as few as six individual cases. Nevertheless, the judicial records shown here, especially at the upper end, remain striking.

Figure 3 Tort liability overview

Results	
UKSC tendency as a whole	Neither likely nor unlikely
Likely to find tort liability	*Lord Kerr, Lady Hale, Lord Clarke*
Unlikely to find tort liability	*Lords Rodger, Brown, Neuberger*

II. Contract

It is difficult to define what a 'typical' UKSC contract law case might look like. For example, the dataset included cases where the Court was asked to determine: the validity of a contract, whether its terms had been breached, whether (and at which point) it had been terminated, whether its conditions had been satisfied, and the validity and operation of implied terms and exclusion clauses. Fundamentally, however, in each case the Court was being asked to determine whether the terms of a voluntary agreement entered into between two parties was legally valid and enforceable. That seemingly simple enterprise hides, just beneath the surface, a myriad of complicated and sometimes ill-defined rules and principles, some of which invite a surprising degree of judicial discretion (when is a mistake *unconscionable*? When is a contract term *unfair?*) and creates ample space for judges to adopt their own individual approaches. Despite what some might suggest,[13] there is no reason why a judge's personal preferences and ideological priors should not have a space to influence contract law just as much as any other area.[14]

For present purposes, the term 'contract' has been construed widely to include those arrangements which, although similar in nature to contract (in that they basically give effect to an explicit agreement between parties) may technically operate under different legal rules: in addition to 'traditional' contractual arrangements, the dataset included more general undertakings, certain express trusts, lien and construction consent documents.

Unlike some of the other areas in this chapter, the 'contract win' variable was marked according to whether the disputed contract in question was deemed to be valid and operational, rather than whether liability occurred in the abstract. This is because a number of key contractual disputes did not give rise to questions of liability in a straightforward manner, in a comparable sense to cases involving tort and criminal law. If a certain contractual clause is declared invalid, for example, this may alter the parties' obligations, but may not result in a contractual breach. Contracts are often reciprocal, with their provisions affecting both parties rather than causing one of them to 'lose'. Sometimes, a party will seek to invalidate a contract in order to avoid undertaking an obligation, which does not fit easily with the idea of liability or blameworthiness. It is also common, especially in commercial cases, for a patchwork of contractual obligations to be involved; to try and ascribe 'liability' to a single party in this context feels particularly artificial. As noted above, the determination of whether an agreement is effective unites most contrast and quasi-contract cases. For that reason, a contract 'win' in this section was based on whether a given contract was found by the Court to be *lawful, valid, enforceable or effective*.

Broadly, then, a contract 'win' was coded as such whenever a contract was upheld as valid, or its terms were found to have been breached on the facts. Conversely, a successful challenge to the validity of a contract (including a modification of

[13] It has been suggested by Geoffery Lane LJ that there is no place for 'sympathy and politics' in contractual disputes: *Gibson v Manchester City Council* [1978] 2 All ER 583, 591 (as noted in J Adams and R Brownsword, 'The Ideologies of Contract' (1987) 7(2) *Legal Studies* 205, 214–15, this may be true of 'formalist' judges, but this leaves the question as to which judges, if any, really qualify as such).

[14] Indeed, there may be good reason to think that in certain respects decision-making in cases concerning contract law may be *more* ideological than other areas, especially when contract questions are framed as exercises in determining the balance between 'market-individualism' and 'consumer-welfarism': Adams and Brownsword, ibid 213–17. Note also Lord Reed's comments in this respect: see text to fn 2.

a key clause), an inability to enforce it, or a failure to show that any terms were breached was marked in each instance as a contract 'loss'. If the dispute involved a contract but the legal issue exclusively concerned ancillary issues, such as the consequences of breaching it, or whether the breach itself gave rise to other liability, for example statutory liability, it was not coded here. Where the issue concerned the subject matter or effect of the contract rather than its validity, and each party was arguing for a different construction, this was not ordinarily marked, unless the construction adopted affected whether the contract was effective at all. As with other areas, if a challenge was considered partly successful (for example, if certain aspects of a contract were declared invalid but not others) a partial mark was given.

117 cases in the dataset raised a relevant contract issue as defined above. 17 judges decided enough contract cases for meaningful analysis, 14 of them a significant number. Figure 4 shows how likely each judge was to vote for a contract 'win'.

Figure 4 Contract win (all cases)

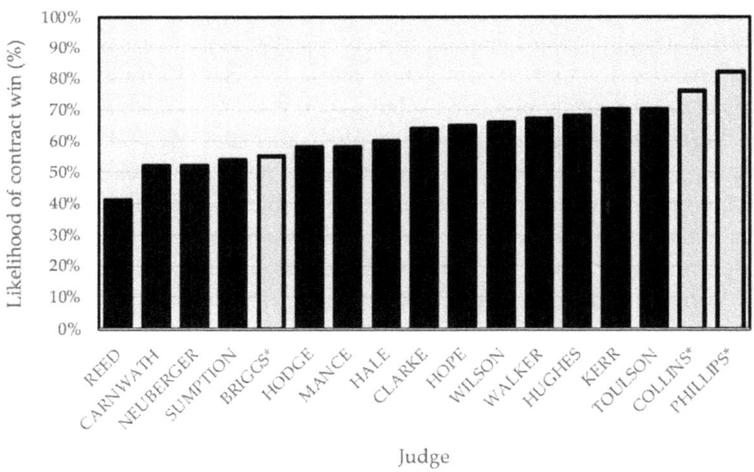

On average, judges seemed to generally prefer to uphold and enforce contracts, voting for a contract 'win' 62.29 per cent of the time (60.43 per cent of the time when only more significant records are included). Lord Reed was the only judge who voted for a contract win in fewer than half of the relevant cases in which he sat. Lord Phillips seems to be the most pro-contract judge based on this data (although his data is limited, ruling in just 12 cases involving contract issues). He voted to support a contract 'loss' only one single time although he adopted a 'mixed' approach (ie some, but not all parties succeed) in some cases. The most contract-friendly judge with a significant record is Lord Toulson, upholding a contract around 70 per cent of the time.

As with tort liability, above, the picture changes somewhat when only salient cases are analysed. Figure 5 sets out each judge's position in this respect, although note that 7 of the 15 judges here sat on five or fewer cases, and were treated as producing less significant records as a result (as usual, their records are coloured in grey and their names feature an asterisk). Unsurprisingly, when comparing Figure 4 and Figure 5, the latter features a higher spread of scores. Lord Hughes achieved a 'pro-contract' score of 100 per cent in this dataset, although this was the result of sitting in only three relevant cases (he was treated as having less significant data, but fell on the very outer cusp of relevance). Lady Hale adopted a 'pro-contract' position with respect to at least one of the relevant parties in all salient cases in which she sat (she does not sit at 100 per cent because in some cases she adopted a pro-contract position with respect to certain parties but not others). Lord Reed once again appears at the opposite end of the scale, although like Lord Hughes he sat on too few cases to draw robust conclusions from. Otherwise, Lords Neuberger, Carnwath and Mance were also unlikely to vote for a contract 'win'.

Figure 5 Contract win (salient cases)

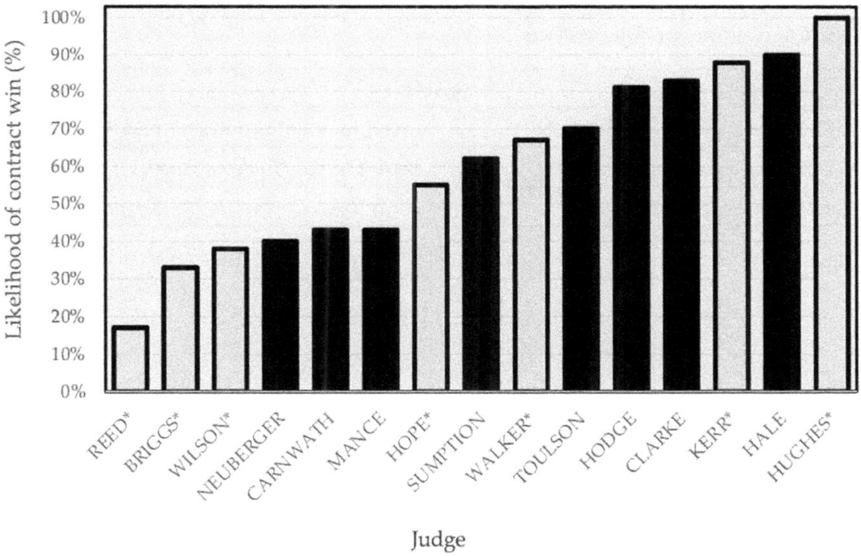

In terms of position, no obvious pattern emerges. There is no correlation between time of appointment and rankings in Figures 4 and 5. Whilst each judge's professional history will doubtless have some influence on their approach to contract law, and whilst judges such as Lords Carnwath and Neuberger spent time in the Chancery Division of the High Court dealing with lots of contract cases, virtually all judges of the judges in the dataset had significant commercial experience.

One interesting question is whether there is any relationship between the likelihood of a judge finding a contract 'win' and their preferred approach to contractual interpretation more generally. Whilst further research is required, at first blush this does not seem to be the case. Lord Carnwath, who was not likely to uphold and enforce a contract according to Figure 5, has expressed a preference for interpreting contracts in an expansive and contextual way, paying heed to the wider context in which they operate, rather than upon the specific wording of specific section.[15] Lord Sumption, on the other hand, has emphasised the importance of a textual, almost literalist approach to contractual interpretation,[16] but despite this, he was more likely than Lord Carnwath to uphold a contract, and sits in the middle of the pack when it comes to contracts overall. Further exploration of each individual judge's preferred approach to contractual interpretation falls beyond the scope of this chapter,[17] but it would certainly be an interesting avenue to explore, especially given that it has already been ascertained that there is some divergence between the judges in this respect.[18] Indeed, looking at how judges *interpret* contracts may tell us something more interesting about judicial behaviour than the slightly clunky measure of whether they upheld the contracts before them adopted here. Nonetheless, based only on case outcomes, Figure 6 summarises which judges appear to be 'pro' contract, and which do not.

Figure 6 Contract rulings overview

Results	
UKSC tendency as a whole	Likely to uphold contract / find liability
Likely to be 'pro' contract	*Lords Phillips, Toulson, Hughes, Lady Hale*
Unlikely to be 'pro' contract	*Lords Reed, Carnwath, Neuberger*

III. Criminal

The level of discretion available to judges in the field of criminal law is in one sense obvious. Whilst trial judges ordinarily bear the ultimate responsibility for determining the factual truth of what has occurred, as well as whether criminal

[15] See eg *Airtours Holidays Transport v HMRC* [2016] UKSC 21; [2016] 4 WLR 87 at [81] and his dissenting judgment in *Arnold v Britton* [2015] UKSC 36; [2015] AC 161. Lord Clarke delivered the lead judgment in *Rainy Sky v Kookmin Bank* [2011] UKSC 50; [2015] AC 1619, in which the Court adopted a contextual approach to contractual interpretation; this *does* appear to correlate with his pro-contract tendency.

[16] Lord Sumption, 'A Question of Taste: The Supreme Court and the Interpretation of Contracts' (Harris Society Annual Lecture, 8 May 2017).

[17] Whatever the position with regards to individual judges, it seems to be the case that the UKSC's earlier judgments on contractual interpretation (eg *Rainy Sky* (n 15)) disclose a more contextual approach, whereas more recent judgments (eg *Arnold* (n 15)) reflect a more literal approach. See D McLauchlan, 'The lingering confusion and uncertainty in the law of contract interpretation' (2015) *LMCLQ* 406; D McLauchlan, 'Continuity, not change, in contract interpretation?' (2017) 133 *LQR* 546.

[18] See Lord Sumption (n 16); L Hoffmann, 'Language and Lawyers' (2018) 134 *Law Quarterly Review* 553.

responsibility has arisen on those facts, appellate judges are by no means bound by formalism in this area. They are tasked with outlining both the necessary elements of a crime (which may be based on ambiguous statutory wording or more amorphous common law cases) as well as reviewing whether the lower courts were correct in understanding the law and applying it to the facts. Further, in criminal cases, judges necessarily deal with matters beyond those directly affecting the parties to a case; criminal law adjudication involves determining how the state relates to citizens in its most coercive context.[19] Over time, many jurisprudential controversies relating to criminal matters have been resolved in the UK's highest court, on matters such as criminal intent, the nature of dishonesty, and the inner workings of joint enterprise liability.

In the present dataset, the only cases marked as raising criminal issues were those which involved the determination of criminal *liability*, rather than appeals from the Court of Appeal (Criminal Division) per se. Criminal cases which dealt only with ancillary issues such as the jurisdiction of courts or the procedural requirements of jury directions were not included where they did not involve determinations of criminal liability directly. Cases where the extent of any criminal liability was considered alongside other forms of liability such as tort were normally included, so long as criminal liability remained a live and distinct controversy in each instance.

Criminal liability was marked whenever a case involved a finding that a defendant committed criminal conduct on the facts, but also, for example, where an interpretation of the criminal law was adopted that placed the defendant in a position where they attracted – or were made more likely to attract – criminal liability. A finding which upheld a criminal defence fell the other way. The coding for each case was in each instance adopted with the range of options legitimately open to the Court borne in mind – if, for example, the Court was asked to consider whether to order a retrial or to let an existing conviction stand, the pro-criminal liability position would be the latter one. However, where different options were canvassed to the Court, the same action may have been coded differently.

Criminal matters which directly engaged questions of liability were a rarity before the UKSC during its first decade. In the entire dataset, just 20 cases were considered to involve a concrete issue relating to criminal liability.[20] As a result, only a handful of judges decided enough cases for meaningful analysis, and just five decided more than ten applicable cases. Nevertheless, Figure 7 shows how each judge voted in criminal cases.

[19] J Griffith, *Politics of the Judiciary*, 5th edn (Fontana Press, 1997) 291.

[20] This low number is perhaps surprising given the high likelihood of success that criminal cases achieve at the permission to appeal stage: Hanretty (n 5) ch 3. The Court decides far fewer criminal cases than it used to; according to Paterson, criminal cases made up around a quarter of its docket from the 1970s until the early 21st century: Paterson (n 5) 17.

Figure 7 Criminal liability (all cases)

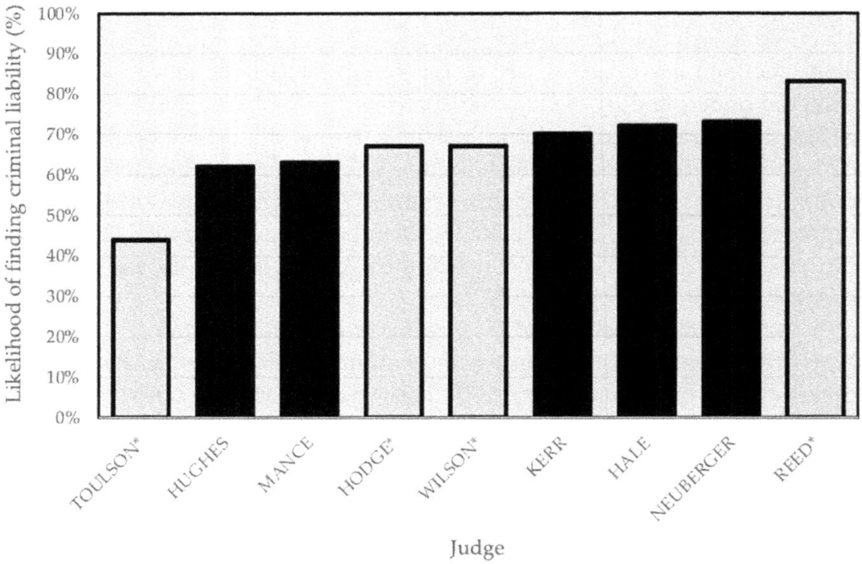

Despite the small numbers, some trends can be noted amongst the judges surveyed: the Court tended to favour finding criminal liability, with only Lord Toulson being more likely to find *against* criminal liability than for it. The average judge voted in favour of finding criminal liability 67 per cent of the time across all cases, rising slightly to 68 per cent when considering only the significant data. Whilst the highest-scoring judge (Lord Reed) was almost twice as likely to find criminal liability than the lowest-scoring judge (Lord Toulson) both decided only a handful of relevant cases. There is a relatively small spread between the judges when looking exclusively at the records of judges that produced more significant data; the results show a very low degree of deviation and variance. Thus, criminal liability seems to be one area where judges do not differ from one another too significantly.

Analysis of salient cases in this area is limited by the fact that the UKSC only decided down *three* criminal liability cases which were salient (ie the Court was split on the criminal liability issue). This further adds to the idea that the Court's judges held a fairly homogenous attitude towards criminal matters. These cases, outlined in Figure 8, were all decided in the Court's earlier period; it has not issued a salient criminal liability case since early 2013.

It can be seen that the majority in all three salient cases ruled in favour of finding criminal liability, matching with the general pro-liability trend identified in Figure 7. No single judge sat in all three cases. Lords Dyson, Mance and Wilson each sat in two and found liability in both. Lord Brown found liability in one case but not the other. This is not particularly illuminating. We are left, therefore, with the very rough positions set out in Figure 7, where Lords Reed

Figure 8 Criminal liability (salient cases)

Name of case	Result	Judges
Maxwell [2010] UKSC 48	Liability	Dyson, Mance and Rodger (majority) for liability; Brown and Collins (minority) against liability.
Gnango [2011] UKSC 59	Liability	Brown, Clarke, Dyson, Judge, Phillips and Wilson (majority) for liability; Kerr (minority) against liability.
Hayes [2013] UKSC 17	Liability	Mance, Neuberger, Sumption and Wilson (majority) for liability; Reed (minority) against liability.

and Toulson bookend the rankings. However, due to their placements being based on a low number of cases, and the dataset including all cases rather than salient ones, it is difficult to argue that their placements reveal anything particularly reliable about their attitude towards criminal law. For that reason, when it comes to criminal liability, the judges can be said to hold fairly consistent attitudes with no obvious outliers.

Whether it is because the judges do not hold particularly strong attitudes towards criminal law, the circumstances under which criminal liability issues arise are just too varied to generate a consistent approach based on judicial preferences, or simply that criminal law cases before the UKSC are just too few and far between for any meaningful analysis to occur, we cannot say that there is evidence that the individual judges on the UKSC showed a preference or tendency for finding for or against criminal liability.

Figure 9 Criminal liability overview

Results	
UKSC tendency as a whole	Likely to find criminal liability
Likely to find criminal liability	*n/a*
Unlikely to find criminal liability	*n/a*

IV. EU Law

During the examined period,[21] the UKSC held significant responsibility regarding EU law in the domestic setting. Although in one sense the ultimate arbiter of many EU law issues was the Court of Justice of the European Union, the UKSC had the important responsibility to not only decide if and when to refer questions to that court, but also how to interpret its rulings and the corpus of EU law more generally in the national context. EU law, like any other law, is full of ambiguities, and gives ample opportunities for judges to exercise discretion.

[21] The role of the UKSC 'post-Brexit' is not tackled here; EU law was fully applicable during the period surveyed.

The role of EU law in the UK legal system was significant and complex. For present purposes, however, each judge's approach to EU law was measured according to the simple metric of whether or not they found that a breach of EU law had occurred in a given case. This included situations in which the Court examined whether domestic provisions – primary or secondary – were compatible with EU law, as well as situations where it was asked to determine whether an individual or state actor breached some specific EU law provision. Where there was a live question as to whether the state is acting within the scope of EU law (and liability was dependent on the answer), this was coded as an 'EU law win' where the answer was affirmative. Cases in which judges cite EU guidance as an aid for interpreting domestic provisions were, however, *not* treated as relevant EU law cases, absent some further qualifying feature. Cases involving some consideration of general principles of EU law were generally included here, including those dealing with issues of proportionality or due process, but those dealing explicitly with human rights issues, arising either from the Charter of Fundamental Rights of the European Union or general principles of law, were excluded and are considered separately in chapter seven.

Overall, 83 cases involving EU law liability were identified across the dataset. Figure 10 shows how likely each judge was to find a breach of EU law. 15 judges cast enough votes to generate meaningful data, and all but one provided *more significant* data.

Figure 10 Breach of EU law (all cases)

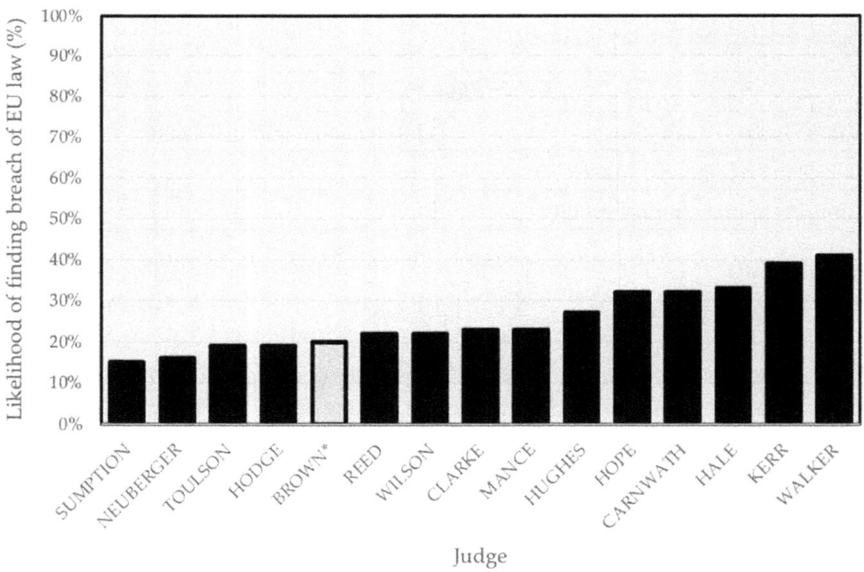

It is clear that, as a whole, UKSC judges were reluctant to find that a breach of EU law had occurred. The average likelihood of finding a breach was just

25.53 per cent (or 25.93 per cent if Lord Brown is excluded due to his less significant data). No single judge ruled to find a breach more frequently than they ruled against finding one: the judge most likely to do so, Lord Walker, did so 41 per cent of the time. The most reluctant judge to find EU law liability was Lord Sumption, doing so in just 15 per cent of cases. Overall, judges did not differ too much between one another when it came to EU liability questions, with the vast majority staying relatively close to the average position; it seems that only Lords Kerr and Walker deviated somewhat in this respect.

There were only a relatively small number of salient cases – eight in total – concerning EU law in the dataset. Whilst it is unwise to place too much weight on trends in such a small dataset, some observations have nevertheless been set out in Figure 11. Lords Hughes, Kerr and Toulson each sat in two of the salient cases and voted in favour of finding a breach of EU law in each. This may be unsurprising for Lord Kerr, who ranks as the second-most likely judge to find a breach of EU law in Figure 10, but is perhaps unusual for Lord Toulson, who found such a breach less than 20 per cent of the time across the board. Lords Carnwath and Walker each found a breach in two of the three cases in which they sat, which aligns with their comparatively high ranking in Figure 10. Of all judges deciding multiple salient cases, Lord Sumption seems the most reluctant to find a breach of EU law, doing so on only one occasion in the four cases in which he sat. This matches with his general reluctance to do the same across all cases, as evidenced in Figure 10.

Figure 11 Breach of EU law (salient cases)

No. of cases sat	Judge	EU law breach findings
5 cases	Hale	3 *(60%)*
	Wilson	2 *(40%)*
4 cases	Clarke, Reed	2 *(50%)*
	Sumption	1 *(25%)*
3 cases	Carnwath, Walker	2 *(67%)*
	Hope	1 *(33%)*
2 cases	Hughes, Kerr, Toulson	2 *(100%)*
	Brown, Mance, Neuberger	1 *(50%)*

If anything can be taken from Figures 10 and 11, it is simply that most judges are relatively reluctant to find a breach of EU law. In salient cases, the judges appear fairly balanced: of the eight judges that sat on at least three salient cases, no judge found a breach of EU law in every case, nor did any judge find against a breach of EU law in every case. This, alongside the small number of salient which produced splits in the first place, and the relatively tight spread of each judge's position in EU cases in general (see again Figure 10) may indicate that preferences regarding EU law do not play a particularly significant part in judicial decision-making.

Much like with criminal law, cases concerning EU law liability appeared to unite rather than divide the judges: there was little appetite for finding a breach in this context from any of the judges on the Court.

Figure 12 EU law overview

Results	
UKSC tendency as a whole	Unlikely to find breach of EU law
Likely to find breach of EU law	*Lord Kerr, Lord Walker*
Unlikely to find breach of EU law	*Lord Sumption*

V. Devolution

One important aspect of the Supreme Court's work is to act as a final arbiter on devolution disputes (a function that was previously given to the Privy Council). Devolution cases are a somewhat idiosyncratic aspect of the Court's case load. First, they provide one of very few avenues for the UKSC to sit as a first-instance court (when considering devolution references). Second, they provide a rare opportunity for the Court to scrutinise the actions of democratic legislatures, an issue which is fraught with political sensitivities. Some devolution cases even require the Court to take sides on issues which divide *different* legislative bodies. Devolution cases require judges to not only determine whether a given institution acts lawfully, but often to choose between competing arguments about constitutional competencies (which are themselves often based on competing *conceptions* of the constitutional settlement in question). A judge's preferences when it comes to devolution matters may reflect views about the Court's institutional position within the devolution settlement (if not their views on devolution itself): the Court is frequently being asked to both define and, in some cases, police, a settlement which is politically, and constitutionally, of the highest importance. The 'specialness' of devolution cases merits their separate examination here.

In terms of defining a devolution case, it is important to note that not all cases originally arising from one of the devolved institutions necessarily involve devolution issues; for present purposes, a devolution challenge was defined as a challenge to the legitimacy of an act of one of the devolved *institutions*, rather than against actions originating within that jurisdiction (appeals from courts in Scotland and Northern Ireland in 'ordinary' civil matters, and some criminal matters, can be made to the UKSC; these matters were *not* considered to involve devolution matters for the purposes of this section). Devolution cases before the UKSC typically involved claims that the devolved institutions legislated outside of their proscribed areas of competency as set out in the devolution statutes, acted incompatibly with EU law or failed to comply with human rights obligations under the ECHR or EU Charter of Fundamental Rights. A 'devolution issue' as defined here encompassed both challenges to specific provisions passed by the devolved institutions, as well as more direct challenges against the actions adopted by the devolved governments via their executive function.

25 cases were identified as raising a relevant devolution issue. Figure 13 shows the voting records of the judges deciding those cases. The average judicial 'score' here (ie likelihood of finding a devolution challenge successful) was low, at 31.23 per cent, rising to 33.75 per cent if only more significant data is considered. The relatively uncommon success rate in this area may be unsurprising in light of the Court's judgments in cases like *AXA*[22] which endorse a relatively deferential approach to devolution cases, with great importance placed on respecting the democratic legitimacy of the devolved institutions.

Figure 13 Devolution challenge outcome (all cases)

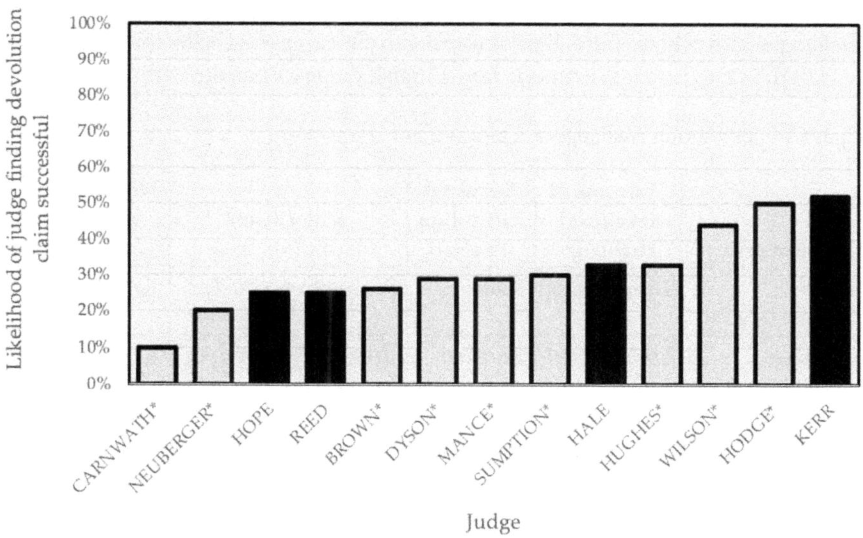

Only four judges cast 10 or more relevant votes during this period, so most fall into the less reliable data category. Nonetheless, the data shows something of a variation between judges. As can be seen, Lord Kerr was the most likely judge of all to find that a devolution challenge successful (he was the only judge to vote *in favour of* a devolution challenge than against it) whereas Lord Carnwath was the least likely to do so (just 10 per cent of the time, although this figure is based on just a few cases). There is no obvious evidence here that judges hailing from devolved jurisdictions exhibited particular attitudes towards devolution challenges; whilst Lord Kerr and Lord Hodge were (comparatively) comfortable with upholding them, Lords Hope and Reed were unlikely to do so.[23]

[22] *AXA General Insurance v Lord Advocate* [2011] UKSC 46; [2012] 1 AC 868.

[23] On the relationship between the nationality of judges deciding a case and the jurisdiction of the court being reviewed, more generally see ch 4.

Lord Kerr's tendency to uphold devolution challenges very likely comes not from being Northern Irish, but by virtue of being Lord Kerr.

There were just seven cases featuring some salient division between the judges in this area, listed in Figure 14. Lords Dyson, Hope and Brown each appeared multiple times, and each voted to reject the devolution challenge in each instance. Indeed, most judges clearly favoured rejecting devolution challenges; in six of seven salient cases, this was how the majority voted. One judge once again clearly stands out from the rest. Lord Kerr sided with the challengers on each of the six cases in which he sat.[24] In each of those six cases, the majority voted to reject the devolution claim, and he dissented, either alone or with the support of another judge, voting to uphold it. His record here is therefore significant, despite the small number of cases considered. As with the general dataset, there is no evidence that the non-English judges considered are particularly sympathetic to devolution challenges as a whole; Lord Kerr's record can be contrasted with the fact that in each of the cases listed, at least one non-English judge cast a vote with the majority.

Figure 14 Devolution challenge outcome (salient cases only)

Name of case	Outcome of devolution challenge	Devolved institution involved	Majority on devolution issue	Minority on devolution issue
Martin [2010] UKSC 10	Unsuccessful	Scotland	Brown; Hope; Walker	Kerr; Rodger
Ambrose [2011] UKSC 43	Unsuccessful	Scotland	Brown; Dyson; Hope; Matthew Clarke (ad hoc)	Kerr
McGowan [2011] UKSC 54	Unsuccessful	Scotland	Brown; Dyson; Hope; Hamilton (ad hoc)	Kerr
Birnie [2011] UKSC 55	Unsuccessful	Scotland	Brown; Dyson; Hope; Hamilton (ad hoc)	Kerr
Moohan [2014] UKSC 67	Unsuccessful	Scotland	Hale; Hodge; Neuberger	Kerr; Wilson
Welsh Asbestos [2015] UKSC 3	Successful	Wales	Hodge; Mance; Neuberger	Hale; Thomas
A and B [2017] UKSC 41	Unsuccessful	Northern Ireland	Hughes; Reed; Wilson	Hale; Kerr

Importantly, however, it should be noted that most devolution cases in the dataset involved human rights issues. Devolved institutions are not authorised to act in a way which is incompatible with the European Convention and doing so will bring them outside their legislative competence. Challenges on this basis made up the majority of devolution cases in the dataset. In fact, of the 25 devolution cases

[24] Once with Lady Hale, once with Lord Wilson, once with Lord Rodger, and three times on his own.

identified in the dataset, only seven did not feature some kind of live human rights issue. Lord Kerr's propensity to uphold devolution challenges therefore becomes difficult to disentangle from his approach to human rights issues more generally (chapter seven deals with human rights voting records for Lord Kerr and all other judges in more detail but suffice it to say for present purposes that Lord Kerr very much falls on the *pro-human rights claim* side of the spectrum). Further, of the seven devolution cases heard by the Court which did *not* concern human rights, just one involved a *successful* claim (and even in that instance, the case was only *partially* successful and was coded as a mixed result in the dataset). Further, just one of these seven cases split the Court, with Lord Rodger and, naturally, Lord Kerr dissenting. Lord Kerr's act of breaking with his colleagues to find in favour of a devolution challenge, of course, fits well with Figures 13 and 14, but it is difficult to draw too much from this single case. From what little information we have, it does seem to be the case that Lord Kerr's records with respect to devolution cannot be *entirely* attributed towards his pro-human rights attitude.

Figure 15 Devolution challenge overview

Results	
UKSC tendency as a whole	Unlikely to uphold
Likely to uphold challenge	*Lord Kerr*
Unlikely to uphold challenge	*n/a*

VI. Immigration and Expulsion

Immigration and expulsion cases provide for a particularly interesting case study of judicial behaviour; not only are these matters typically considered to be politically controversial, but a significant degree of judicial discretion operates in this area.[25] Both the nature of such cases (where the factual circumstances affecting claimants in each case differ – often significantly – from each other) and the legal frameworks operating here invite individualised, context-specific decision-making. Judges must decide cases against the background of rapidly changing (national and international) policy and constantly evolving global affairs. Each case also potentially raises considerations relating to the appropriate level of discretion to be afforded to national authorities, initial decision-makers and the diplomatic institutions of other countries. Even relatively straightforward immigration cases raise significant opportunities for judicial preferences – and judicial *individuality* – to take effect.

[25] V Federico, 'Going Against the Grain? The Growing but Uneven Role of Courts in Framing Principled Migration Law' (ECPR General Conference, 25 August 2020). Griffith (n 19) dedicates a significant amount of time to assessing the judicial approach to immigration matters; unsurprisingly, he finds that judges have largely taken a conservative approach to these issues: 182–204.

For present purposes, 'immigration cases' will be used as shorthand for immigration, expulsion and deportation cases, regardless of whether the case at hand involves an individual entering or leaving the country. They were coded according to whether an immigration or removal decision actually arose for determination before the UKSC, rather than whether they were dealt with at some stage by the Immigration and Asylum Tribunal or engaged a particular Act. Cases which were not directly concerned with the lawfulness of the immigration or expulsion of persons, but were instead exclusively related to matters arising prior to removal (eg immigration detention) or following arrival (eg accommodation duties), were treated as ancillary matters and were not coded here. Disputes relating to child custody in international cases were also excluded for the most part. As ever, where the determination of multiple cases was involved, each judge's position in respect of each was recorded; coding in this case was expressed as a figure reflecting the success rate as part of the outcome as a whole.

The UKSC decided 59 cases coded as involving an immigration/expulsion issue. Figure 16 shows how likely each judge was to adopt a pro-immigration position. On this occasion, 19 judges decided enough cases to provide meaningful analysis, and 14 decided enough to produce *more significant* data. On average, a 'pro-immigration' vote was cast around 45 per cent of the time, or around 41 per cent of the time when only the more significant cases are included.[26]

Figure 16 Immigration and expulsion win (all cases)

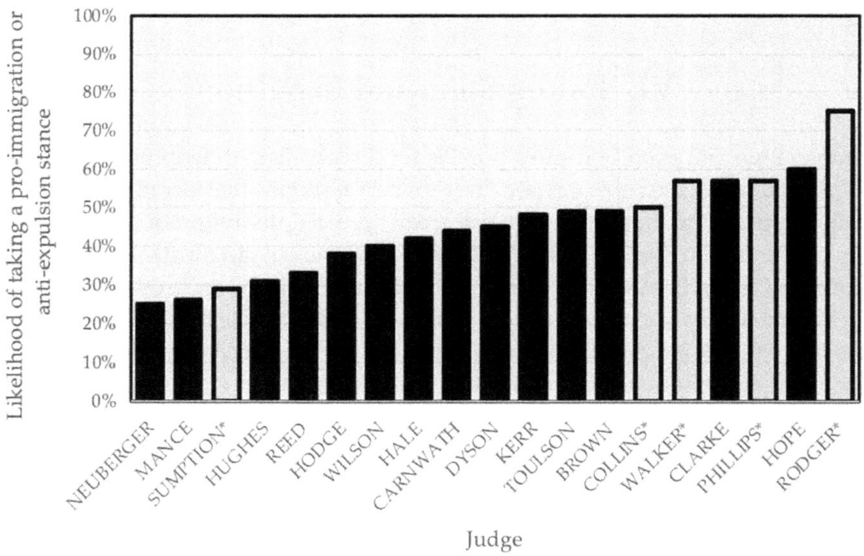

[26] According to Paterson, the government's success rate in the Supreme Court's initial years was significantly lower than its success rate during the late House of Lords era. However, looking at the date as a whole, the government appears to fare much better; a pro-immigration 'score' of 45% gives the government a rough 'win rate' of 55%, similar to that during the Bingham era: Paterson (n 5) 290.

The data suggests that the judge with the most immigration-friendly record is Lord Rodger. However, as can be seen, the significance of this observation is limited by the fact that he decided relatively few immigration cases in this period, sitting on just eight in total and taking a pro-immigration position in six of them. Lord Hope's position – taking a pro-immigration stance 60 per cent of the time – is based on more significant data and is more reliable. The least likely judge to adopt a pro-immigration position is Lord Neuberger.

It is worth repeating that the aim of this section, and indeed of this book, is to determine whether judicial records differ significantly from one another, and whether any inferences about judicial preferences more generally can be made out from that, rather than a wholesale account of judicial influence. However, in the current case, the individual judicial positions in Figure 16 seem to conform to a pattern. This is set out in Figure 17, which shows a correlation between each judge's record in this area and the median point of their tenure.

Figure 17 Relationship between likelihood of pro-immigration vote and median point of Supreme Court tenure

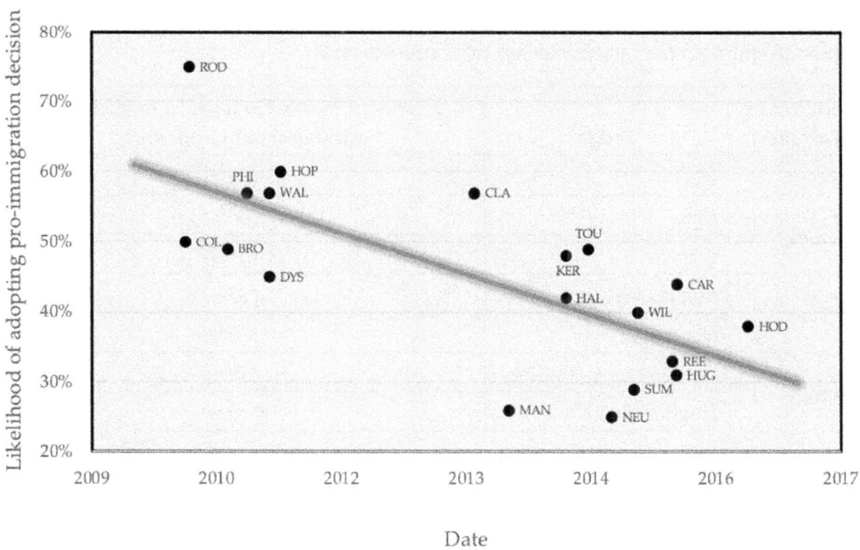

The values set on the vertical axis are simply the likelihood of each judge to adopt a pro-immigration position, taken from Figure 16; the values set on the horizontal axis are the median points of each judge's time on the Court, rounded to the nearest month.[27] A clear negative correlation can be identified.[28] This trend can be explained in a number of ways, for example:

[27] For example, Lady Hale's median date is set to October 2014 as she sat from the beginning of the examined period – October 2009 to the end of it in September 2019. Lord Neuberger, sitting from October 2012 to September 2017, has a median mark of March 2015.

[28] p=-.696**. t-test, one-tailed, significant at the 0.01 level.

- Judges in the earlier period of the Supreme Court, on the whole, simply held stronger pro-immigration preferences than later judges.
- Governmental policy and practice changed over time, so that successful challenges to policy decided by judges in the later period were less likely to succeed.[29]
- The law changed over time, so that government actions relating to immigration and deportation, which may have been suspect at an earlier stage, would later become lawful under more recently-enacted statutes or immigration rules.[30]
- Other judicial trends, such as a more cautious approach to human rights claims, and more deference to governmental authorities, both of which play a frequent role in immigration cases, may have taken hold.

As was set out in chapter one, it would be impossible to compile a list of influences affecting judicial behaviour. But in this case, whilst the judges' voting records may reveal some indication of personal preferences, the temporal aspect of these decisions cannot be ignored.

Figure 18 Immigration and expulsion cases (salient cases)

Number of cases sat	**Judge**	**Number of votes for a proimmigration / antideportation position**
6 cases	Hale	3 *(50%)*
4 cases	Kerr	2 *(50%)*
	Brown	1 *(25%)*
3 cases	Mance, Wilson	1 *(33%)*
	Neuberger	0 *(0%)*
2 cases	Clarke, Hope, Phillips	1 *(50%)*
	Hughes, Reed	0 *(0%)*

Can a look at the salient immigration cases help matters? As with EU law above, the number of salient cases in this category is low: just seven cases. The voting records of the judges that sat in at least two of those cases are set out in Figure 18. In these salient cases, no judge adopted a pro-immigration position more than half the time. Lord Hope, the judge with the most immigration-friendly record out of all the judges providing more significant data in Figure 16, cast one

[29] A related possibility may be that more significant, and obviously problematic, issues in this area were litigated and resolved during the Court's earlier period, with less obviously unlawful policies and actions dealt with in later proceedings.

[30] Over the course of the Supreme Court's life, the government party switched from Labour to Conservative, a party typically associated with a stricter approach to immigration and deportation matters. The party came to power first as part of a coalition and then as the largest majority party in this period.

pro-immigration vote and one against this position in each of the two salient cases in which he sat. The same occurred with Lord Clarke, the next most immigration-friendly judge in that set. In purely numerical terms, Figure 18 does not paint any judges as having a particular tendency to support immigration cases. However, Lord Kerr's voting record can be unpacked somewhat; his two pro-immigration votes were cast in cases where he dissented against a strong majority, and he was the only judge to do so in each instance[31] which may suggest that his votes in these two cases were particularly important to him. At the other end of the scale, and correlating somewhat with the general data in Figure 16 above, Lords Neuberger, Hughes and Reed did not cast a pro-immigration vote in any of the admittedly small number of salient immigration cases in which they sat.

Figure 19 Immigration and expulsion overview

Results	
UKSC tendency as a whole	Neither likely nor unlikely
Likely to adopt pro-immigration position	*Lord Hope, Rodger, Clarke*
Unlikely to adopt pro-immigration position	*Lords Neuberger, Hughes, Reed*

VII. Tax

Tax liability may seem to some as something of an esoteric area to examine, but there were a surprisingly high number of tax cases before the UKSC during its first decade. In fact, both Robinson and Paterson singled out tax cases as one area in which differences between judges sitting on the House of Lords, the predecessor to the UKSC, were more readily apparent.[32] Whilst the House of Lords determined a greater number of tax cases compared to the UKSC,[33] it is still worth considering whether, as a field, it continues to present a battleground for judicial attitudes to butt against one another.

Tax cases were defined simply as those where a requirement to pay tax, or the amount of tax to be paid, was questioned in proceedings. Usually, HMRC was one party to the claim, although other parties do occasionally bring claims. A 'pro-tax' position was coded where a judge voted to order the payment of tax, or for the higher sum of tax where the amount to be paid was disputed. Although less common in tax cases than in other areas, where multiple issues were involved, and the outcome was not uniform, the resulting coding was once again reflected in a partial score. Coding was, in the vast majority of cases, uncomplicated. Each judge's record is set out in Figure 20.

[31] In the only two salient cases in which Lord Kerr did not cast a pro-immigration vote, he was part of a majority group, with the dissenting judge being Lady Hale.

[32] See D Robertson, *Judicial Discretion in the House of Lords* (Clarendon, 1998); A Paterson, *The Law Lords* (Macmillan, 1982).

[33] Paterson (n 5) 17.

Figure 20 Tax liability (all cases)

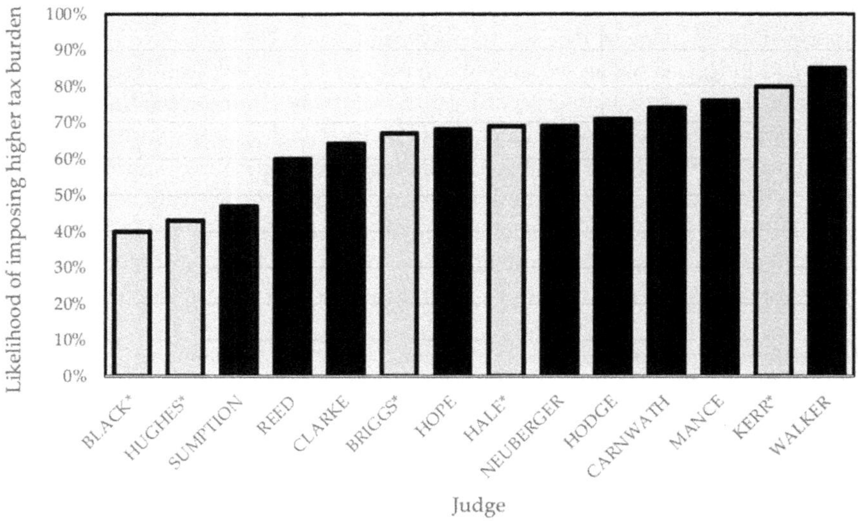

The dataset contains 46 cases and shows that the UKSC judges tended to favour a pro-tax position overall. Only three judges voted against imposing tax liability more frequently than for it, and only one of those judges' records was based on more significant data. Of the 14 judges with qualifying records, the average 'score' sits as a relatively high figure of 65.21 per cent, and rises to 68.22 per cent if less significant data is excluded. Lord Walker is the most pro-tax judge, adopting such a position 85 per cent of the time – in only one tax case did he adopt an unambiguously anti-tax position. Even at this stage, before filtering for salient cases, some degree of divergence between the judges can be seen.

Judicial positions on the basis of only salient cases are set out in Figure 21. There are just eight overall. Lord Wilson voted in favour of tax liability in both of the salient cases in which he participated but he sat on too few tax cases overall for any meaningful conclusions to be drawn.[34] Lords Carnwath and Walker appear, from the limited data available, to lean towards a pro-tax position, even in cases where their colleagues disagreed with them. This aligns with their respective positions in Figure 20; Lord Carnwath's pro-tax position (voting in favour of tax liability 74 per cent of the time) is no fluke – he sat in 28 of the 46 tax cases decided over the ten-year period, and nearly every single tax case during his tenure on the Court. There therefore seems to be more variance between the judges when it comes to their positions on tax issues compared to criminal and EU law cases.

[34] Although taking a pro-tax position in both salient tax cases in which he sat, Lord Wilson actually did not sit on enough tax cases more generally to create even less meaningful data.

Figure 21 Tax liability (salient cases)

Number of cases sat	Judge	Number of pro-tax votes
4 cases	Carnwath, Walker	3 (*75%*)
	Clarke, Hope, Reed	2 (*50%*)
3 cases	Hodge, Mance, Neuberger	2 (*67%*)
2 cases	Wilson	2 (*100%*)
	Briggs, Lloyd-Jones	1 (*50%*)
	Sumption	0 (*0%*)

Figure 22 Tax liability overview

Results	
UKSC tendency as a whole	More likely than not
Likely to adopt pro-tax position	*Lords Walker, Carnwath*
Unlikely to adopt pro-tax position	*Lord Sumption*

VIII. Correlations and Conclusions

This chapter has sought to uncover trends and tendencies when it comes to judicial approaches to cases of different subject-matter. For each different area of law, the tendency of the Court as a whole has been described where possible; further, judges who are particularly likely, or unlikely, to find liability in a given area have been listed. The results show that judicial individuality is not limited to certain areas of law (although the influence of individual judicial preferences seems to be stronger in some areas compared to others). Certain judges have appeared repeatedly as particularly likely – or in some cases unlikely – candidates for finding liability, or a case 'win', across different sections. A more wholesale look at how these preferences might come together to form composite judicial profiles is offered in chapter ten, but this section briefly looks at the correlation between judicial approaches in relation to subject-area.

On the one hand, each of the sections above involve distinct areas of law. On the other it has been argued that legal categories are to some extent artificial and that the values and ideals which underpin preferences in one area will likely translate to others.[35] Is there some evidence of this? Only in some cases. There is a strong positive correlation, for example, between a judge's likelihood to vote in favour of finding tortious liability and their likelihood to find a breach of both EU law[36]

[35] In the words of Duncan Kennedy, 'It isn't random. You can predict from a person's position on one issue what his position is likely (not certain) to be on the next': D Kennedy, 'The Political Significance of the Structure of the Law School Curriculum' (1983) 14 *Seton Hall Law Review* 1, 15.

[36] Comparing the data from the general dataset, rather than that filtered for salient cases: p =.708** (t-test, two-tailed, significant at the 0.01 level). When less significant results are excluded, the positive correlation becomes stronger: p =.822** (t-tailed, two-tailed, significant at the 0.01 level).

and tax liability.[37] Approaches to immigration law are positively correlated with a judge's position in relation to both contract law[38] and EU law.[39] Some of these correlations are unsurprising. For example, a judge who tends to find immigration appeals successful may also be predisposed to finding EU law claims successful because both, to some extent, involve disputes upon the proper 'boundaries' of UK law. The positive relationship between judicial approaches to immigration law with those relating to contract law is, admittedly, perhaps less obvious.[40]

Further, there is a significant *negative* correlation between each judge's likelihood to award a contract win and their likelihood to recognise criminal liability.[41] Again, some potential reasons may be floated as to why this might be the case (contract law usually involves relationships between private parties whereas criminal law largely involves the state intervention; contract law is often conceptualised on the notion of individual freedom whereas criminal law prohibits certain actions), but this is ultimately speculative. For the vast majority of examined factors, there is no statistically significant correlation between the attitudes, and relative positions, of individual judges. This does suggest that insofar as the results set out above can be construed as reliable indicators of individual judicial behaviour, judges do have different approaches to subject areas and are more likely to find in favour of some species of liability than others.

Of course, there are limitations to the utility of the above conclusions. They cannot take a whole host of unobserved influences into account. The granulation of cases can be awkward and blunt.[42] Many subject areas involved a small number of cases, limiting the strength of the conclusions drawn. But it is hoped that some of the results show that there are at least some notable and interesting trends and tendencies when it comes to the behaviour of the judges of the Supreme Court, whether examined as a collective (the Court's general reluctance to find breaches of EU law is noteworthy, for example) or individually (Lord Kerr's records in particular).

The following chapter continues to explore individual approaches to particular kinds of cases, undertaking an in-depth examination into each judge's attitude towards human rights claims. This field, perhaps more than any other, gives rise to significant legal and political controversy, and the discretion available to judges when it comes to questions of balance and proportionality makes it a prime site for examining judicial decision-making. It is perhaps the field in which the tensions between the Court's individual and collective roles are most acute.

[37] p =.735** (t-test, two-tailed, significant at the 0.01 level). When less significant results are excluded, the correlation seems to fall away: p =.202 (t-test, two-tailed, with no statistical significance: 0.635).

[38] p =.621* (t-test, two-tailed, significant at the 0.05 level).

[39] p =.544* (t-test, two-tailed, significant at the 0.05 level).

[40] The correlation between these results loses statistical significance once less significant results are excluded. Contract and immigration: p =.475 (t-test, two-tailed, with no statistical significance: 0.119); Immigration and EU law: p =.437 (t-test, two-tailed, with no statistical significance: 0.155).

[41] p = -.722* (t-test, two-tailed, significant at the 0.05 level). Again, once less significant results are excluded, the relationship loses statistical significance: p = -.381 (t-test, two-tailed, with no statistical significance: 0.527).

[42] On the other hand, it may be useful to granulate subjects even further. Laleng (n 11), for example, found differences in success rates of different *types* of tort claim in cases before the Court of Appeal.

7

Human Rights

It is undeniable that one of the most significant avenues by which UK judges can exercise power and discretion in the UK is within the field of human rights law.[1] Not only do human rights carry considerable rhetorical power, but they grant courts, including the UKSC, a degree of unique legal power, too. For example, judges can use powers under the Human Rights Act 1998 (HRA) to declare legislation – including primary legislation – incompatible with human rights.[2] Although this does not alter the validity of the impugned measure, the declaration does act as a powerful 'feedback mechanism from the courts to the sovereign legislature',[3] and one which is not available to judges outside the human rights context. Human rights standards emanating from EU law can be used by judges to disapply and invalidate primary legislation in the event of a conflict.[4] Human rights, including judge-made common law rights, can also be used to impose limitations (and obligations) upon public bodies, and in some cases alter the plain meanings of statutes.[5] Human rights are powerful tools.

Further, human rights laws have arguably brought within the judicial scope certain issues of political controversy which may have otherwise been considered off-limits for the courts and cases often require judges to consider issues which go far beyond the case at hand.[6] They often arise against the backdrop of, and sometimes require directly engaging with, the Court's role in relation to other institutions such as Parliament,[7] the executive,[8] lower

[1] See eg R Stevens, *The English Judges: Their Role in the Changing Constitution* (Hart Publishing, 2002) 138, 180–81; J Sumption, 'Judicial and Political Decision-Making: The Uncertain Boundary' (2011) 16(4) *Judicial Review* 301, 307–308.

[2] Human Rights Act 1998, s 4. On the discretion available to judges under this section see C Mallory and H Tyrrell, 'Discretionary space and Declarations of Incompatibility' (2021) 32(3) *Kings Law Journal* 466.

[3] Lady Hale, 'Principle and Pragmatism in Public Law (Sir David Williams Lecture 2019) 7.

[4] *Benkharbouche v Secretary of State for Foreign and Commonwealth Affairs* [2017] UKSC 62; [2019] AC 777.

[5] J Varuhas, 'The Principle of Legality' (2020) 79(3) *CLJ* 578.

[6] This is why Lady Hale's answer to the question: 'are human rights political' was 'they are and they aren't': Lady Hale, The Emma Barnett Show (*BBC Radio 5*, 11 June 2019).

[7] Lord Toulson has said that there are cases where 'law and politics butt up against each other and that may give rise to a question [of] how far ought the court to intervene in this area or how far ought the court to say, actually, we are not the most appropriate forum for dealing with this, it is a matter which should be left to the politicians.' UK Supreme Court Blog, Interview with Lord Toulson (28 July 2016) ukscblog.com/interview-with-lord-toulson/.

[8] See *R (Lord Carlile) v Secretary of State for the Home Department* [2014] UKSC 60; [2015] 1 AC 945 at [57].

courts,[9] expert bodies,[10] and other human rights courts.[11] As Lord Sumption put it, 'when it comes to reviewing the compatibility of executive decisions with the [ECHR], there can be no absolute constitutional bar to any inquiry which is both relevant and necessary to enable the Court to adjudicate.'[12] These comments, spoken in relation to cases brought under the HRA, may well be said to be applicable to cases involving human rights issues more generally. As a result, human rights feature heavily in some of the most high-profile and controversial cases in the Supreme Court's history.[13] Challenges have been made – not always successful ones – before the UKSC on human rights grounds in matters relating to issues as controversial as abortion,[14] euthanasia[15] and prisoner voting.[16]

Further, human rights are ambiguous and amorphous concepts. When deciding human rights cases, judges have to answer a number of related, open-ended questions. What form does a given right take? How far does a given right stretch? Under which circumstances can a right be relied upon? Others arise in the circumstances of a given case: which rights, if any, are engaged? Has that right been interfered with? Can that interference be justified? What role does 'public interest' play?[17] Answering these questions – or as is often the case, *deciding who should answer them* – is far from straightforward, and the answer is likely to differ between judges. Indeed, Lord Dyson has suggested that because of the prominence of such questions, human rights cases are unique in allowing judges to make the sort of value-judgments which would be considered improper elsewhere.[18]

The UKSC considered human rights claims very frequently. There was a human rights component present in about 30 per cent of the judgments it handed down during the examined period.[19] Human rights cases were particularly likely

[9] See *AR* [2018] UKSC 48 [53]–[64].

[10] See *Lord Carlile* (n 8) at [105] (Lady Hale): 'the Government has much greater expertise [than the court] in assessing risks to national security or the safety of people for whom we are responsible'.

[11] See L Graham, 'The Modern Mirror Principle' [2021] *Public Law* 523.

[12] *Lord Carlile* (n 8) [30].

[13] Of the 15 UKSC cases to feature in Judicial Power Project's list of 50 'problematic' judicial decisions, 11 of them involve human rights issues: Judicial Power Project, *50 Problematic Cases* judicialpowerproject.org.uk/50-problematic-cases/.

[14] *Greater Glasgow Health Board v Doogan* [2014] UKSC 68; [2015] 1 AC 640.

[15] *R (Nicklinson) v Ministry of Justice* [2014] UKSC 38; [2015] 1 AC 657.

[16] *R (Chester) v Secretary of State for Justice* [2013] UKSC 63; [2014] 1 AC 271.

[17] Griffith noted that 'judges differ in their view as to where the public interest lies' when adjudicating human rights cases: J Griffith, 'The Brave New World of Sir John Laws' (2000) 63(2) *MLR* 159, 159.

[18] Lord Dyson, 'Are the judges too powerful?' (Bentham Association Presidential Address, 12 March 2014) 11: the HRA 'requires [judges] to make value judgments which are different from those which, as custodians of the common law, they have been accustomed to making'.

[19] This is a significant increase from the previous decades. For example, between 1970 and 1972, just 2% of cases raised human rights issues; between 1980 and 1982, just 5% did: A Paterson, *Final Judgment: the Last law Lords and the Supreme Court* (Hart Publishing, 2013) 17.

to attract larger judicial panels,[20] and human rights judgments were both longer than average[21] and more likely to divide the Court.[22] This suggests that human rights claims were not just common, but contentious.

In light of this, it is perhaps unsurprising that much of the scholarship focusing on the UK Supreme Court as an institution has examined its approach to human rights issues.[23] Some of the empirical literature has even tried to identify the preferences of particular judges when it comes to human rights issues. For example, Dickson analysed non-unanimous human rights cases decided across a single legal year of the UK Supreme Court's tenure,[24] whereas Poole and Shah did the same with judgments of the House of Lords across a number of years.[25] Both studies found some evidence of differences in approaches between individual judges regarding human rights issues[26] and were even able to separate judges into broad groupings according to their propensity to invoke and find breaches of human rights. This chapter pursues similar aims but, of course, looks at the approach adopted across the whole of the Court's first decade.

Human rights arguments made before the Court invoke rights found in a number of different sources. Each of these sources operate in different ways, and different considerations may well apply to the application of each. For the purposes of the present study, 'human rights laws' will be separated into three categories: (1) those arising under the Human Rights Act or the European Convention on Human Rights (ECHR); (2) those arising by way of EU law; and (3) those emanating from other sources, such as the common law. Cases involving ECHR claims are by far the largest group; the number of cases handed down concerning each category is set out in Figure 1. Each type of human rights claim will be dealt with in its own section below, beginning with rights under the HRA//ECHR. At the end of the chapter, each judge's approach to human rights claims as a whole, irrespective of their nature and source, is set out. At the outset, however, some methodological choices are set out.

[20] See M Blackwell, 'Indeterminacy, Disagreement and the Human Rights Act: An Empirical Study of Litigation in the UK House of Lords and Supreme Court 1997–2017' (2020) 83(2) *MLR* 285. In the examined period, over half of the cases dealt with in panels of seven featured a human rights component and 65% of nine-panel cases did so.

[21] 105 paragraphs (the average length is 80.96 paragraphs for all Supreme Court cases).

[22] C Hanretty, *A Court of Specialists* (OUP, 2020) ch 7; R Cahill-O'Callaghan, *Values in the Supreme Court* (Hart Publishing, 2020) 62–63. 31.43% of cases featuring a human rights issue featured at least one dissenting opinion, higher than the average (around 20% of all cases are split).

[23] See eg B Dickson, *Human Rights and the United Kingdom Supreme Court* (OUP, 2013); Blackwell (n 20). For the approach of the House of Lords, see eg D Feldman, 'Human Rights' in L Blom-Cooper, B Dickson and G Drewry (eds), *The Judicial House of Lords 1876–2009* (OUP, 2009) and T Poole and S Shah, 'The Law Lords and human rights' (2011) 74(1) *MLR* 79.

[24] Dickson, ibid.

[25] Poole and Shah (n 23).

[26] Although Poole and Shah posit that whilst cases decided under the Human Rights Act are more likely to feature multiple concurring judgments than those that came before, they are *less* likely to feature dissenting views: ibid 89–94.

Figure 1 Number of human rights cases per year

Year	All HR	ECHR	EU	Other
2009–10	19	18	0	2
2010–11	20	15	2	6
2011–12	21	17	0	4
2012–13	23	17	2	11
2013–14	24	17	3	11
2014–15	25	18	5	8
2015–16	15	11	3	5
2016–17	25	23	1	4
2017–18	21	16	3	4
2018–19	16	14	0	6
Average	**21 (*20.9*)**	**17 (*16.6*)**	**2 (*1.9*)**	**6 (*6.1*)**

I. Methodology: Coding 'Rights'

Identifying cases involving rights can be tricky, especially outside the realm of those prescribed in the European Convention or EU Charter. 'Rights' can mean different things for different people and elude objective definition. The overlap between rights, interests, values and principles is considerable and the contours of each concept is not obvious; the choice of which particular label to adopt in a judgment may itself be amenable to ideological preferences.[27] As such, whilst the language found in the Court's judgment can certainly be helpful when it comes to identifying whether a case involves a human rights claim, for the purposes of identifying 'rights cases' in the dataset, the language adopted was not presumed to be determinative in and of itself.[28] Each classification depended on the full context of the case and the legal purpose to which each term was used.

In line with the practice adopted throughout, a binary coding scheme was adopted, with successful human rights claims coded to the value 1, and unsuccessful claims to 0. Mixed results were coded accordingly. Identifying a human rights 'success' depended to a significant degree on the details of each case and what each

[27] There may be a political aspect as to which sorts of rights are recognised and which ones are not: see Griffith (n 11) 172–74.

[28] Cases involving established human rights were coded as such even in the absence of a specific language to this effect; conversely, some cases invoked human rights language but were not treated as human rights cases. For example, in *Jones v Kaney* [2011] UKSC 13; [2011] 2 AC 398 the court described the rule that a witness should not be intimidated as a 'fundamental principle' ([130]–[131]), which despite the nomenclature, was not used in the context of some fundamental justiciable right.

party claimed, but it generally aligned with a positive finding of a breach,[29] or the adoption of a human-rights compliant interpretation of a provision. There were a small number of cases concerning *potential* or prospective breaches of human rights. Although somewhat artificial, these cases were marked according to what the position would be if the actions had been carried out. Any action which the Court indicated could not take place because it would breach rights was treated as indicating a human rights success. More specific guidelines as to how successes were evaluated in relation to specific kinds of human rights claims are set out in each of the sections below.

It is common for rights to clash and for opposing parties to rely on different, directly competing human rights claims. In such cases, no human rights 'win' was coded (as one right would *necessarily* have to succeed and one would fail). However, it is standard in cases involving the ECHR for the Court to ask whether a given interference with rights can be justified through *protecting the rights of others*. Such cases were deemed to involve only one direct human rights claim (the 'rights of others' being a consideration which could be used to justify interference with the claimed human right, but not as a standalone rights claim in and of itself). There is obvious overlap between situations the two situations. Nevertheless, they are treated as distinct in the eyes of the ECHR and EU case law, and so a similar approach has been adopted here.

As ever, it is important to remember that correlation is not causation. The following exercise can show patterns of voting behaviour, but not why those judges vote the way they do. As with other parts of this work, however, inferences can be drawn from particularly notable records; for example, a particularly low 'win rate' may demonstrate 'a significant statement of hostility to the very idea of human rights',[30] whereas a higher 'success rate' may indicate some allegiance to the wider human rights project.

II. European Convention on Human Rights

The first type of human rights claim involves those rights stemming from the ECHR, usually via the application of the Human Rights Act. That Act effectively incorporates the core rights found in the European Convention on Human Rights (ECHR) into domestic law;[31] each of the applicable rights is set out in Schedule 1 of the domestic Act.

[29] In one case (*Chester* (n 16)) the Court accepted that the ECHR was breached but refused to grant relief on the specific facts of the case; a mixed score (usually 0.5) was recorded.

[30] Poole and Shah (n 23) 100.

[31] The exact relationship between HRA rights and ECHR rights remains somewhat ambiguous: see L Graham, 'Taking Strasbourg jurisprudence into account' (2022) 2 *EHRLR* 163, 171–72 and compare *R (Elan Cane) v Secretary of State for the Home Department* [2021] UKSC 56; [2022] 2 WLR 133 at [87] and [101] with *Re McQuillan* [2021] UKSC 55; [2022] 2 WLR 49 at [156], *Re McKerr* [2004] UKHL 12; [2004] 1 WLR 807 at [64]–[65].

The HRA undoubtedly gives judges a lot of power. Lord Neuberger has stated that 'the biggest factor in increasing judicial power … has been the Human Rights Act'[32] and Lord Sumption went so far as to say that it modifies 'traditional notions of the constitutional distribution of powers'.[33] Whilst the UKSC cannot use the Act to invalidate primary legislation, it can issue a 'declaration of incompatibility' which signals to Parliament that certain provisions run afoul of human rights standards, something which has been compared to a de facto strike down power.[34] It can invoke a special power in order to interpret legislation in far-reaching ways, departing from what would otherwise be a passage's natural meaning, in order to secure Convention-compliance.[35] In addition, subject to some limited exceptions flowing from section 6(2), the Act allows the Court to invalidate any *secondary* legislation which it deems incompatible with the rights in Schedule 1. Public bodies also have a statutory duty to comply with the Act and not to breach the rights therein, which the courts can enforce.[36]

The Act also provides judges with considerable discretion. The HRA gives rise to debates such as whether judges always hold the institutional competence to decide the cases brought before it,[37] how far interpretive obligations ought to stretch, and how much weight should be placed on the jurisprudence of the European Court of Human Rights (ECtHR).[38] Indeed, during the passage of the original Human Rights Bill which would eventually become the HRA, Lord Mackay argued against the incorporation of the ECHR because he feared that this would vest the judges with too great a discretionary power to act within politically-sensitive areas.[39] Whether his fears have proven to be well-founded is not a question tackled here. However, the fact that such questions arose at that time shows that the HRA was considered to be a very important, impactful piece of legislation from its inception. It provides a perfect setting for determining the divergence of individual judicial approaches on the Court.

In order to measure how judges have exercised their powers under the Act, for present purposes, a case involving a relevant 'ECHR claim' was defined as one in which a judge includes within their judgment some substantive consideration of an issue arising under the HRA or ECHR. The Convention issue had to be a 'live' issue before the Court; some cases feature judges discussing ECHR case law in

[32] D Neuberger and P Riddell, *The Power of Judges* (Haus Curiosities, 2018) 32. *cf* T Etherton, 'Liberty, the archetype and diversity: a philosophy of judging' [2010] *PL* 727, 742: even before the advent of the HRA, the judges had a significant discretionary power, and the impact of the HRA should not be overstated in this respect.

[33] *Lord Carlile* (n 8) at [29].

[34] Human Rights Act 1998, s 4; A Kavanagh, *Constitutional Review Under the UK Human Rights Act* (CUP, 2009) 281–92; see also N Petrie, 'Indications of Inconsistency' (2019) 78 *CLJ* 612.

[35] Human Rights Act 1998, s 3.

[36] Human Rights Act 1998, s 6.

[37] See the approaches of different judges in *Nicklinson* (n 15).

[38] Under section 2 of the Act, national courts must 'take into account' relevant Strasbourg jurisprudence, but it has no strict obligation to emulate it. The UKSC's practical approach to this provision has varied: see Graham (n 11).

[39] as referenced by Stevens (n 1) 104.

some detail for some purpose other than determining liability (eg when tracing the development of the law)[40] and these cases were not treated as ECHR claims. Similarly, in cases in which ECHR case law was used to interpret another source of human rights (such as a common law right or right derived from EU law) this was not marked as an ECHR claim in and of itself.[41]

Two specific cases require further clarification. First, since the tort of misuse of private information was designed to 'import' Convention standards into the common law, the one case which considered this tort in detail was accordingly treated as involving an ECHR matter.[42] Second, in one case concerning the extent of police powers, the Court found that the domestic authorities had misconstrued the extent of their ECHR obligations in relation to police powers.[43] Whilst the proper approach to the ECHR was clarified in that case, the Court did not consider whether any rights breaches had occurred on the facts, and the resulting declaration only clarified the extent of the statutory powers available. No ECHR issue was marked in that case.

As ever, each judge's overall likelihood to find in favour of an ECHR claim was quantified as a percentage, based on their votes across all qualifying cases in which they sat. There were 164 cases in the dataset which involved an ECHR claim; each judge's own position is set out in Figure 2.

Figure 2 ECHR success (all cases)

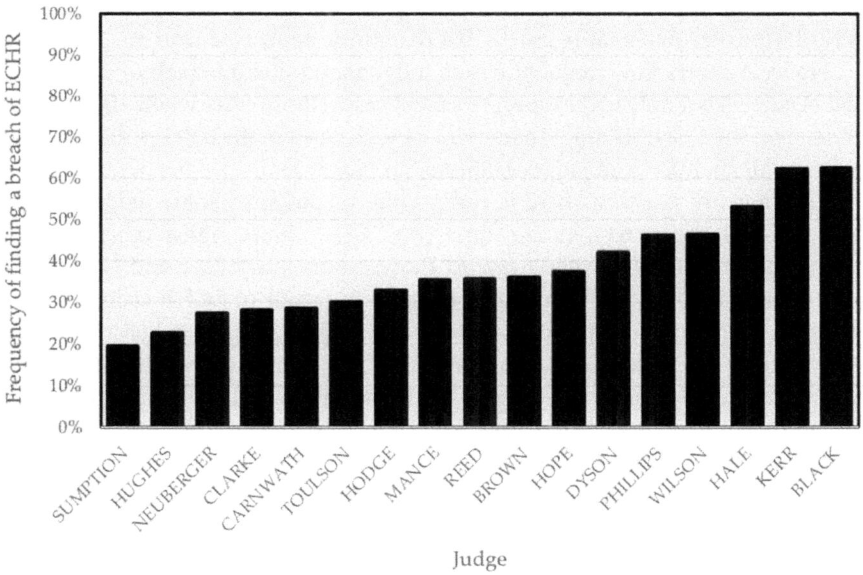

[40] *Flood v Times Newspapers* [2012] UKSC 11; [2012] 2 AC 273.
[41] *R (Nouzali) v Secretary of State for the Home Department* [2016] UKSC 16; [2016] 1 WLR 1565.
[42] *PJS v News Group Newspapers* [2016] UKSC 26; [2016] 1 AC 1081.
[43] *DB v Chief Constable of Police Service of Northern Ireland* [2017] UKSC 7; [2017] NI 301.

The results show that judges would side with an ECHR claim, on average, around 40 per cent of the time. Lord Kerr and Lady Black were the most ECHR-friendly judges, each of them finding a breach in over 60 per cent of the relevant cases in which they sat. Whilst Lord Kerr sat on many more cases than Lady Black, the latter nonetheless sat on enough cases during the relevant period to produce reliable data. The judge who was least likely to find a breach of the ECHR was Lord Sumption, who did so in less than 20 per cent of cases. Lord Hope sits closest to the mean score. Notably, there is a relatively high range of positions here, especially given that the results in Figure 2 were not filtered to include only salient cases. There is some notable skewing towards judges that sat closer to the beginning of the Supreme Court's tenure; Lords Walker, Dyson and Brown all sat in the initial few years of this period and achieve high scores, whereas low-scorers Lords Sumption, Hughes and Carnwath joined later in this period. Judges who sat for a long time covering both the early and later periods (eg Lady Hale, Lord Kerr, Lord Mance, Lord Clarke) are placed in a range of positions. The increased likelihood to find in favour of an ECHR claim during the Court's early years may be explainable by any number of reasons, including the advent of a new Court creating a mood which was particularly receptive to human rights claims, a greater level of compliance with human rights standards over time on the part of public authorities, a rolling back over time, at the Strasbourg level, as to the level of protection states must secure in order to comply with the Convention. There may also be something in the straightforward answer that judges appointed nearer the beginning of this period were personally more pro-ECHR than those appointed later on.

Figure 3 shows how frequently each judge found that a breach of the ECHR had occurred, but only with respect to salient cases (those cases where the Court is divided on the ECHR claim). There were 44 such cases in the dataset, allowing for meaningful analysis of all judges examined in Figure 2.

The range of positions here is really quite remarkable. Some judges almost always found themselves in the more pro-ECHR camp, whilst others almost always found themselves siding against those claims. Lady Hale and Lady Black both appear to take a fairly consistent position in favour of ECHR claims, solidifying the inferences which can be drawn from Figure 2. But it is Lord Kerr who stands out as the most ECHR-friendly judge, by a significant margin. If a single statistic in the book had to be singled out for attention it is likely this: Lord Kerr cast a pro-ECHR vote in salient cases 96 per cent of the time. In fact, in only two cases did he find himself against the comparatively pro-ECHR 'side' of a split case; in both of these cases, he formed part of the majority who did not see fit to join Lady Hale's sole dissenting voice.[44]

It is perhaps unsurprising that Lord Kerr appears to be the most likely judge to find a breach of the ECHR; he often makes statements that are markedly

[44] *HH v Italy* [2012] UKSC 25; [2013] 1 AC 338; *Re B* [2013] UKSC 33; [2013] 1 WLR 1911.

Figure 3 ECHR success (salient cases)

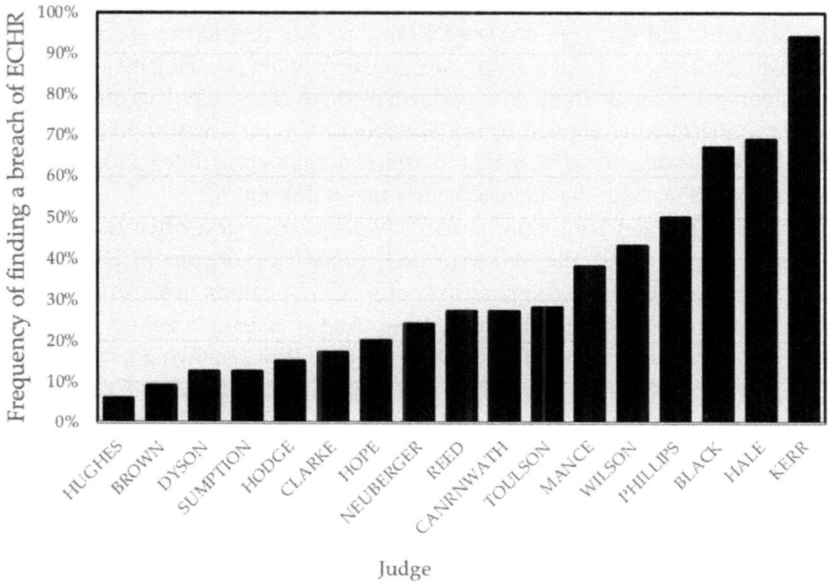

'Strasbourg-friendly' (even in those cases where he agrees with his colleagues as to the result of the case). *Gallagher*[45] is a good example. Whilst all members of the Court found that some narrow aspects of the national scheme regulating the retention of criminal records breached Article 8, the majority of the Court did so hesitantly, Lord Kerr's judgment exhibited no such uncertainty; he openly acknowledged that he shared few of the apprehensions held by his colleagues and came to his conclusion – that the scheme was disproportionate *and* that it was not properly prescribed by law – with little hesitation. In *G*, he adopted a wider, more general understanding of when Article 6 would apply to decisions of domestic public bodies than that of his colleagues.[46] In *Birnie*, he was willing to grasp the nettle and declare that the purported waiver of legal assistance examined in that case had not been properly established. His colleagues would have preferred to remit that question to a lower court judge to decide.[47] In *Ambrose*, he emphatically argued, again without the support of his colleagues at that time, that the UKSC should not be afraid to go beyond the confines of the Strasbourg should justice require it.[48] His blistering dissent in the *Northern Ireland Human Rights*

[45] *Re Gallagher* [2019] UKSC 3; [2020] AC 185.

[46] *R (G) v Governors of X School* [2011] UKSC 30; [2012] 1 AC 167.

[47] *Birnie v HM Advocate* [2011] UKSC 55; 2012 SC (UKSC) 222.

[48] *Ambrose v Harris* [2011] UKSC 43; [2011] WLR 2435. Other judges followed Lord Kerr in this respect: see *Moohan v Lord Advocate* [2014] UKSC 67; [2015] AC 901 (Lord Wilson); *Re McLaughlin* [2018] UKSC 48; [2018] 1 WLR 4250 (Lord Mance). Lord Kerr was able to re-state his view in his majority judgment in *Commissioner of Police of the Metropolis v DSD* [2018] UKSC 11; [2019] AC 196.

Centre case was long and intense, and his finding that Northern Ireland's abortion laws breached both Articles 8 and 3 of the ECHR put him in a minority of two.[49] The list could, and does, go on. Lord Kerr was also unafraid to stake his claim alone when it came to human rights cases – many of his *solo* dissents were issued in this context.[50] Incidentally, in a number of these cases, the disgruntled losing claimant subsequently applied to the Strasbourg Court, where the judges sided with Lord Kerr's dissenting view that the state's actions constituted a breach of the Convention rather than the majority's view that it did not.[51]

Lords Hughes and Sumption remain low-ranking judges; when ECHR issues cause a split in the Court, they reliably voted *against* the more pro-ECHR position. In fact, Lord Hughes took a comparatively pro-ECHR position in just one split case. Lord Sumption's position may be predictable, to some extent, in light of the critical comments made before and after his time on the UKSC, showing a clear scepticism about the apparent over-reach of Convention rights.[52] He has also criticised certain aspects of the Strasbourg machinery in the judgments he handed down,[53] as has Lord Hughes on number of occasions.[54] The positions of Lords Dyson and Brown are more interesting. Despite scoring relatively averagely when it comes to finding a breach of the ECHR overall (with a score of 42 per cent and 36 per cent respectively), they too seem to favour a more conservative approach in split cases, moving to a very low position in Figure 3. Interestingly enough, as has been shown in chapter three, Lord Dyson has a very low dissent rate, whereas Lord Brown has a very high one. It seems, therefore, that very few of Lord Dyson's votes against finding a breach of the ECHR went against the majority view. However, Lord Brown's high dissent rate suggests that he often found himself opposing his more ECHR-friendly colleagues as part of a minority bloc.[55] Indeed, in his memoir, Lord Brown admitted that during his time on the UKSC, he became 'troubled' by the 'excessive

[49] *Re Northern Ireland Human Rights Commission* [2018] UKSC 27; [2019] 1 All ER 173. Lord Wilson concurred with his judgment.

[50] See eg *Lord Carlile* (n 8); *Gaughran v Chief Constable of the Police Service of Northern Ireland* [2015] UKSC 29; [2016] AC 345, *Beghal v DPP* [2015] UKSC 49; [2016] AC 88; *Gallagher* (n 45). He also dissented frequently with Lady Hale: see eg *R (Smith) v Secretary of State for Defence* [2010] UKSC 29; [2011] 1 AC 1; *Nicklinson* (n 15); *R (DA and DS) v Secretary of State for Work and Pensions* [2019] UKSC 21; [2019] WLR 3289.

[51] See eg *Gaughran v United Kingdom* Application 45245/15 (13 February 2020), *Gaughran v United Kingdom* Application 4755/16 (28 February 2019) and see also *JD and A v United Kingdom* Applications 32949/17 and 34614/17 (24 October 2019) in effect endorsing the dissenting judgment of Lord Kerr and Lady Hale in *DA and DS*, ibid.

[52] See J Sumption, 'Law's Expanding Empire' (Reith Lectures, 21 May 2019) and J Sumption, *Trials of the State* (Profile Books, 2019). In 2023, Lord Sumption publicly, albeit 'reluctantly', advocated withdrawing from the ECHR: 'Tonight With Andrew Marr' (*LBC Radio*, 6 September 2023) 6 pm.

[53] *Chester* (n 16) at [112]. His statements in this case were strongly rebutted by Lord Clarke, who nonetheless appears in this dataset as a judge relatively unsympathetic to ECHR claims.

[54] See eg *DSD* (n 48) and *R (Hallam and Nealon) v Secretary of State for Justice* [2019] UKSC 2; [2020] AC 279.

[55] See eg *R (Quila) v Secretary of State for the Home Department* [2011] UKSC 45; [2012] 1 AC 621, where Lord Brown adopted a much more deferential approach when it came to assessing the lawfulness of immigration rules compared to the one preferred by his colleagues.

soft-heartedness ... of a number of ... colleagues', particularly in cases 'supposedly raising human rights concerns'.[56] Lord Brown's records indicate that he himself was in little danger of acceding to such soft-heartedness in salient cases.

Some judgments provided very neat illustrations as to the different judges' individual positions on matters relating to the ECHR. The 'camps' that tended to form in such judgments broadly aligned with the results set out above. In *Lord Carlile*,[57] for example, the judges considered the circumstances under which it would be appropriate for the UKSC to intervene when the executive has already made a determination of the relevant human rights issues themselves. Lord Kerr adopted the most activist stance, supporting the position that the Court has a duty to intervene wherever the executive has not come to the right conclusion.[58] Lord Sumption was the most restrained, finding that courts should only disagree with the executive's decision on rights where that decision is not at all tenable.[59] The other judges fell in-between, stressing both the need to protect rights and the need to respect expert policy decisions.[60]

The case of *DA and DS*[61] also concerned the proper approach to be given to policymakers' decision-making powers. Lord Kerr adopted the most overtly interventionist stance as well as finding a breach of the ECHR on the facts.[62] Lady Hale (second place only to Kerr in terms of her tendency find a breach of the ECHR) adopted a more deferential test, but still found a breach on the facts.[63] The other members of the Court adopted the more deferential standard and found no breach on the facts[64] although Lord Wilson did appear to express far greater doubt about this than his colleagues.[65] In *DSD*,[66] although all judges came to the same overall conclusion in finding that the state breached Article 3 ECHR in relation to its (lack of) investigation into the actions of John Worboys, their judgments were markedly different. Lord Kerr (with whom Lady Hale agreed) applied the strongest approach, endorsing the fullest account of the relevant ECHR obligations in play. Lord Neuberger agreed with Lord Kerr, albeit with considerably less enthusiasm. Lord Hughes, on the other hand, was very critical of the ECHR case law, and severely limited the scope of the positive obligations in play in this case, and police investigation cases, considerably. Lord Mance expressed sympathy with Lord Hughes's argument, but accepted that the state of the Strasbourg case law compelled him to adopt a more robust approach, a position part-way between

[56] S Brown, *Playing off the Roof* (Marble Hall, 2020) 192.
[57] *Lord Carlile* (n 8).
[58] ibid [159].
[59] ibid [49].
[60] ibid [80] and [105].
[61] *DA and DS* (n 50).
[62] ibid [169]–[177].
[63] ibid [132], [147], [152].
[64] ibid [65], [110], [115].
[65] ibid [39].
[66] *DSD* (n 48).

that of Lord Kerr and Lord Hughes. It is suggested that there is a clear alignment between the judicial camps evident in these judgments and the position of the judges involved in Figures 2 and 3 above.

A. Sections 3 and 4 of the HRA

One juncture worth exploring is whether, in those cases where legislation is considered incompatible with rights under the HRA, some judges prefer to use certain remedial tools over others. As noted above, judges have two unique powers in this respect: section 3 HRA, which allows the extensive (re)interpretation of offending provisions, and section 4 HRA, which allows the issuance of a declaration of incompatibility.[67] Opinion is divided on the issue of which of these tools is the stronger or more 'activist',[68] but in theory, certain judges may prefer to use one remedy over another.

However, this proved difficult to measure for a number of reasons. First, whilst there are already a limited number of cases in which a prima facie incompatibility is found, there are even fewer where judges expressly consider which of section 3 or section 4 is to be preferred. In addition, presenting a selection between the two as an open choice is somewhat false. Whilst difficult to pin down precisely, in theory the circumstances under which it is more appropriate to use each provision are different.[69] Further, in some cases, only one remedy will be sought by parties.[70] Perhaps as a result, it is very uncommon for judges on the same panel to differ between one another as to the appropriate remedy to be given in a relevant case. Nevertheless, Figure 4 shows how often each judge was to accede to an invitation to apply sections 3 and 4 of the HRA, in cases where such an option was presented to them explicitly.[71]

[67] See text to n 33 to n 36.

[68] Whilst some judicial statements suggest that section 4 should be used only as a 'last resort': (eg *R v A* [2001] 3 All ER 1 at [44] (Lord Steyn) and *R v W & B (Children)* [2001] HRLR 50 at [50] (Hale LJ)), academics have questioned how strong each respective section is in practice: T Hickman, 'Bill of Rights Reform and the Case for Going Beyond the Declaration of Incompatibility Model' [2015] 35; S Stark, 'Facing Facts: Judicial Approaches to Section 4 of the Human Rights Act 1998' (2017) *LQR* 631; F Powell and S Needleman, 'How Radical an Instrument is Section 3 of the Human Rights Act 1998?' (*UK Constitutional Law Association Blog*, 24 March 2021).

[69] See A Young, *Parliamentary Sovereignty and the Human Rights Act* (Hart Publishing, 2009) 129–30: section 3 and section 4 put in place 'a model that focuses on the different institutional features of the legislature and the judiciary. Section 3 is more suited to situations where the judiciary is more likely to reach a correct conclusion as to the scope and application of Convention rights. Section 4 is more suited to cases where the legislature is more likely to reach a correct conclusion concerning the scope and application of Convention rights.' See also E Adams, 'Judicial discretion and the declaration of incompatibility: constitutional considerations in controversial cases' [2021] *PL* 311; C Chandrachud, 'Reconfiguring the discourse on political responses to declarations of incompatibility' [2014] *PL* 624 and see more generally, Stark, ibid.

[70] For example both parties agreed that the Court should invoke section 3 rather than section 4 in the cases of *Principal Reporter v K* [2010] UKSC 56; [2011] 1 WLR 18 and *Pomiechowski v Poland* [2012] UKSC 20; [2012] 4 All ER 667.

[71] Only those judges deciding five or more relevant cases were included.

Figure 4 s3 and s4 success rates

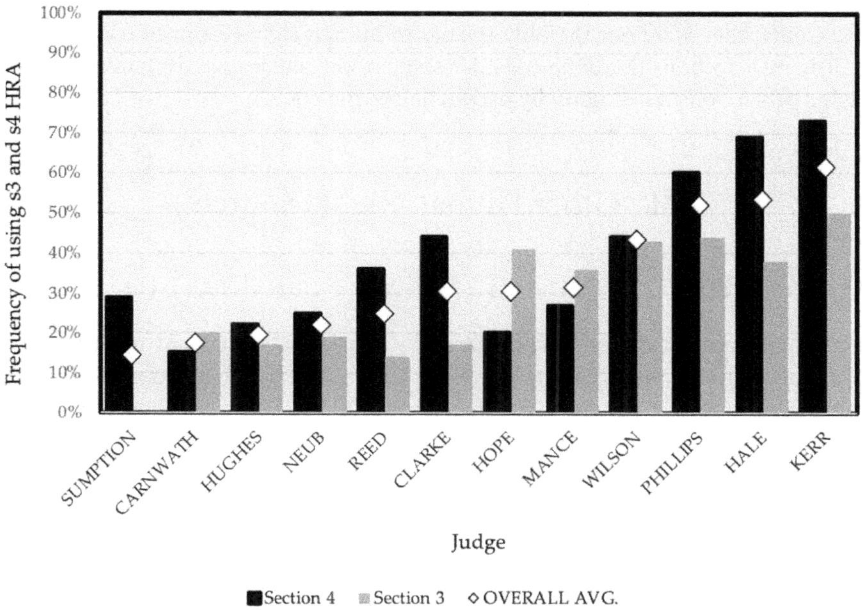

So what does Figure 4 tell us, given the limited number of cases which fed into the data? First, perhaps unsurprisingly, the positions in Figure 4 correlate strongly with those in Figure 3; those judges likely to find a breach of the ECHR generally were likely to vote in favour of a human rights remedy when it came to primary legislation. Second, and again unsurprisingly, the judges who were generally more likely to accede to an invitation to invoke section 3 were also similarly likely to issue declarations under section 4. Third, despite not filtering for salient cases (the low number of relevant cases made this impossible) there is considerable variation between the judges, with, for example, the likelihood of a given judge to accept an invitation to issue a declaration of incompatibility in a given case ranging from 15 per cent to nearly 75 per cent. Fourth, with the exception of Lords Hope and Carnwath, all judges tended to be more likely to use section 4 than section 3, which throws into doubt certain judicial suggestions that section 4 should be resorted to exceptionally. Fifth, and finally, not all judges appear due to sitting on too low a number of cases involving section 3 or section 4 arguments. However, it is worth noting that neither Lord Brown nor Lord Hodge voted to issue a declaration of incompatibility under section 4 during the entire surveyed period (Lord Brown expressly declined to do so on three occasions, Lord Hodge on six) and that Lord Toulson never elected to use the interpretive powers under section 3 (he refused to do so in four cases), putting him in a similar position to Lord Sumption (who *is* represented in Figure 4).

Whilst the rights under the HRA/ECHR are of utmost importance, and formed the basis of the clear majority of human rights claims (see Figure 1) considered by the Court, they were not the only species of human rights claim to come before it. The next sections therefore consider some of the alternative sources of human rights protections relied upon by parties before the UKSC.

III. Other Human Rights Sources

A. EU Rights

One important set of rights considered by the UKSC emanated not from the Council of Europe, but from the European Union. The two main sources of rights protection in the EU framework – henceforth 'EU rights' – are those which are found in the EU's Charter of Fundamental Rights and those which are separately identified by EU courts as emerging, either explicitly or implicitly, from the various laws, treaties and case law of the European Union as 'general principles of EU law'.[72]

Although the position of EU rights has since changed following the UK's departure from the EU, the UK remained a full member for the whole period surveyed. During this time, and in contrast to the situation with those rights under the HRA and ECHR, national courts, including the UKSC, could invalidate even primary legislation which was deemed to be incompatible with EU rights. National courts could also use strong interpretive powers similar to those under section 3 HRA, to construe legislation in line with EU rights standards.[73] EU rights gave national courts significant (and in some ways unique) power.

Whilst the supremacy of EU law means that the question of *whether* to follow EU law was, at the time, not one which was open to national judges to decide, this did not remove their discretion in relation to how to interpret EU rights, the compatibility of national rules with those rights, and how certain qualified rights should be balanced. National judges were also required to deal with issues unique to the framework in which EU rights appear; for example, there are tricky questions relating to the circumstances in which the Charter applies as well as how EU rights should be interpreted and applied in light of EU law as a whole. As a result, cases involving EU rights before the UKSC were rarely straightforward and presented judges with multiple occasions in which their preferences can take hold.

However, once the dataset was properly filtered, there remained very few cases in which a human rights claim based on EU law was actually invoked by parties or

[72] These rights both pre-date and survive the application of the Charter in EU law.

[73] *Marleasing SA v La commercial Internacional de Alimentacion* [1990] WCR I-4135. As with section 3 HRA, these powers are not unlimited: *R (Z) v Hackney LBC* [2020] UKSC 40; [2020] 1 WLR 4327 at [112]–[115].

considered by the judges.[74] There were just 19 such cases overall, and most judges considered between 5 and 10 EU rights claims during their entire tenure. Most judges were therefore considered to have decided too few cases to generate meaningful data. Figure 5 sets out the likelihood of the (only) four judges who decided 10 or more relevant cases to adopt a position in favour of EU rights.

Figure 5 EU rights success (all cases)

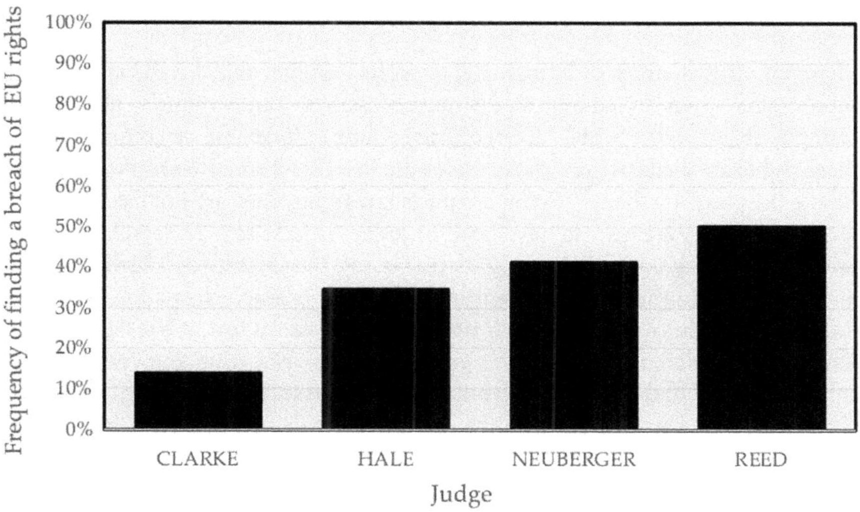

The average of these results is just under 35 per cent. Lady Hale sits closest to the median. These bare results show little correlation to those in the ECHR category above, except perhaps that Lord Clarke generally takes a position which is unenthusiastic about rights under either the ECHR or EU law. Lord Reed would appear to be more comfortable when it comes to finding a breach of EU rights compared to those found in the ECHR. Interestingly, the limited data shows that the lowest ranking judge in the ECHR table, Lord Sumption, found for a breach of EU rights in 40 per cent of the five cases in which he sat, and Lord Hughes, who ranked similarly, found for a breach in 60 per cent of the five in which he sat; by contrast, Lord Kerr, the judge most likely to find a breach of the ECHR, was less likely to find a breach of EU rights than Lords Neuberger, Reed and Hughes (although his results were based on nine cases). As interesting as it may be to consider whether the EU context makes a difference to the attitudes of domestic judges when it comes to

[74] Not all issues involving the EU or its Charter constituted a relevant EU rights claim under this section. For example, some UKSC cases mentioned and discussed EU case law, but as an aid to interpreting a domestic statute or a right under the ECHR. These were not counted for present purposes. For example, the principle of certainty, derived from EU law, was considered in one UKSC case, but its purpose was to aid the interpretation of a statute rather than to act as a standalone rights claim (*BCL Old Co v BASF Plc* [2012] UKSC 45; [2012] 1 WLR 2922).

human rights protection (judges may, for example, feel like they have less discretion when it comes to following judgments of the Court of Justice of the European Union compared to the Strasbourg Court) the very limited number of cases available (and even fewer salient cases – there were just two such cases in the entire dataset) unfortunately reveal very little.

B. Other Rights

There are other sources of human rights protection, beyond the EU and ECHR. These rights – here styled admittedly quite messily as 'other rights' – include, for example, those rights which are recognised and enforceable at common law.[75] These rights are distinct from those under the ECHR, although in some cases they may be 'inspired' by them.[76] Being common law rights, they are not listed in some document;[77] they are instead developed by judges in case law. The resulting ambiguity surrounding common law rights (including the identity of which common law rights exist in the first place) ensures that there is ample scope for individual judicial choices in cases where such rights are invoked. In fact, it has been argued that judicial preferences may play a greater role in cases featuring common law rights compared to those involving other rights, as in such cases, judges are generally subject to fewer textual restraints and there are fewer precedents binding on them.[78] This will be tested below.

A related concept, relevant for present purposes, is the so-called principle of legality. When invoked by judges, this compels the adoption of a rights-consistent interpretation of a statute or policy, at least insofar as that provision was otherwise vague or ambiguous. In most cases, the legality principle attaches to a specific identified 'right', such as access to justice or freedom of expression. Where this is so, the case was deemed to raise a human rights issue in the current dataset. This category also includes rights claims which are based in international law. The UK is a signatory to a number of international instruments including treaties, some of which create obligations which can be litigated before the UKSC. For example, the Court has examined whether the executive acted in accordance with the UN Convention against Torture (UNCRC)[79] and whether family law judges acted

[75] M Elliott, 'Beyond the European Convention: Human Rights and the Common Law' (2015) 68 *Current Legal Problems* 85; M Elliott and K Hughes, 'The Nature and Role of Common Law Constitutional Rights' in M Elliott and K Hughes (eds), *Common Law Constitutional Rights* (OUP, 2020).

[76] *Kennedy v The Charity Commission* [2014] UKSC 20; [2015] AC 435 at [46] (Lord Mance).

[77] A list of currently recognised common law rights can be found in *De Smith's Judicial Review*, 8th edn (With 4th supplement, 2021) 11-054.

[78] Elliott and Hughes (n 75) 9–10.

[79] United Nations Convention against Torture and Other Cruel, Inhuman or Degrading Treatment or Punishment. See *Youssef v Secretary of State for Foreign and Commonwealth Affairs* [2016] UKSC 3; [2016] AC 1457, especially the judgment of Lord Carnwath.

consistently with international law rights under the Abduction Convention.[80] In some cases, parties voluntarily entered into agreements or arrangements which required compliance with other national or international human rights standards. In this way, there are also a small number of cases in which the Court was asked to assess compliance with human rights frameworks of other jurisdictions. Those cases also fall into the nebulous category of cases concerning 'other rights'.

Although these sources of human rights are very different, and it is artificial to treat them in the same way, the limited number of cases raising, for example, a common law rights issue, or the interpretation of an international human rights treaty, was in each case too small to allow for meaningful analysis. As such, the 'other rights' category here is simply meant to capture human rights thinking on the UKSC outside the realm of the EU and ECHR frameworks. To do this, as with other areas, cases involving such rights were only considered relevant under this section if they formed a substantive part of the case rather than being an incidental consideration. Further, there is some limit as to what 'other rights' can constitute. Whilst other studies have considered cases involving, for example, actions against the police as constituting 'rights' claims,[81] this has not been done here (there are many possible actions which can be – and have been – brought against the police, many of which do not have the appearance of a 'rights' claim). Direct reliance on the conception of natural justice was a relatively common occurrence in the case law, which would only count as an example of the courts engaging with 'human rights' where a specific right, such as access to justice, was invoked, rather than in cases where natural justice was used as a synonym for procedural fairness in judicial review cases.

Sometimes, particular effort was required in order to determine exactly which tools the Court was using in a given case, and whether any of them could reasonably be said to involve 'rights'. The distinction between the use of general principles, guiding values, good practice and specific rights was not always obvious. Here, certain language choices were often indicative of whether a case was relevant, with references to 'fundamental rights', 'basic domestic law rights' or, in the right context, 'constitutional principles' obviously indicating relevance.[82] However, language alone never acted as the sole determiner in this respect, as the language of 'rights' is both slippery and subject to be applied in a range of different contexts.[83] If rights simply formed part of the *background* to statutory interpretation without

[80] The Hague Convention on the Civil Aspects of International Child Abduction. See *Re C* [2018] UKSC 8; [2019] AC 1.

[81] T Poole and S Shah, 'The impact of the Human Rights Act on the House of Lords' [2009] *PL* 347.

[82] See eg *HM Treasury v Ahmed* [2010] UKSC 2; [2010] 4 All ER 829 at [60], [61], [75], [145], [146], [174], [196] and [240]; *R (Lumba) v Secretary of State for the Home Department* [2011] UKSC 12; [2012] 1 AC 245 at [35], [101] and [219].

[83] In *Jones v Kaney* [2011] UKSC 13; [2011] 2 AC 398 the Court opined that the rule that a witness should not be intimidated is some sort of 'fundamental principle' ([130]–[131]) but this is not used in context of some fundamental justiciable right. In *Montgomery v Lanarkshire Health Board* [2015] UKSC 11; [2015] AC 1430, the judges mention the 'common law right' to self-determination – it is

more, or vague references to (eg) the rule of law underpinned the Court's reasoning, this was not normally treated as an explicit consideration of human rights. However, whenever rights were expressed and invoked directly, including a small number of instances in which otherwise vague 'rule of law' principles were translated into enforceable rights standards,[84] the case was considered to involve rights.

The usual coding principles and binary marking scheme applicable to Section II above, and indeed the rest of the book, applied in much the same way here. A total of 61 cases were considered to involve qualifying 'other rights'. Figure 6 sets out how frequently each judge found a breach of these rights standards, looking first at all cases in which they sat.

Figure 6 Other rights claim success (all cases)

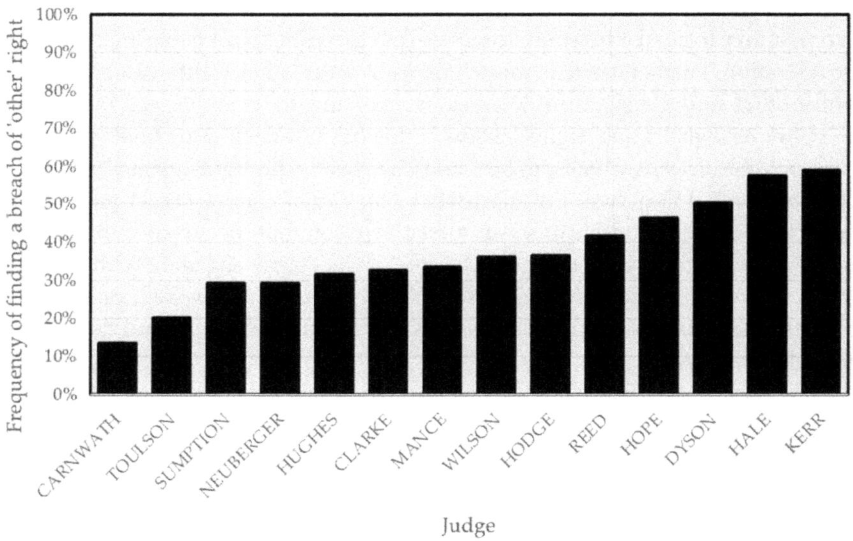

The results show that, as with the ECHR data, Lord Kerr was the most rights-friendly judge, finding a breach in just under 60 per cent of the relevant cases. Lady Hale ranks just beneath him; both she and Lord Dyson voted in favour of upholding qualifying rights in at least half of the cases in which they sat. Lord Carnwath ranks the lowest here, finding a breach of rights in just over 13 per cent of cases.

reflected in the approved quotes authored by Lord Scarman ([43]) and mentioned in the judgment of Lords Reed and Kerr ([80]). But both are confirmed to be manifestations of the tort, not a standalone right (at [56], Kerr and Reed suggest Scarman 'drew on the language' of human rights but really the reasoning focused on the existence of a duty of care; at [82] they confirm that they are working 'within the traditional framework of negligence'). Equally, in *Re B* [2009] UKSC 5; [2009] WLR 2496 there is some discussion over a child's 'right' to be raised by a biological parent (at [19]). But it is clear that this is not a justiciable legal right in any real sense, but just nomenclature to deal with the balancing of interests in family law cases.

[84] eg *R (UNISON) v Lord Chancellor* [2017] UKSC 51; [2020] AC 869.

Lord Hodge sits closest to the mean result. The variance between judges when considering claims under this heading is slightly higher than the variance between them when considering ECHR claims, although there is perhaps a slightly stronger cluster around the centre mark (35 per cent or so).

There is a fairly high correlation between these results and the ECHR data for all cases. Lady Hale, Lord Kerr and Lord Dyson remain at the top of the table; Lords Sumption, Hughes and Neuberger all continue to fall on the lower end. There are, however, some differences. Lords Hodge and Reed appear to be more comfortable with finding a violation of rights arising under this heading than they are rights under the ECHR. Lord Carnwath dropped from a position indicating a *relative* reluctance to find in favour of rights to the very bottom position in Figure 6. Lord Wilson similarly appears less enthusiastic about non-ECHR rights.

Figure 7 filters the above results to include only salient cases (that is, cases in which judges sitting on the same case disagreed as to the approach to be adopted to 'other rights'). There were 19 such cases overall, which led to the exclusion of a number of judges appearing above due to insufficient data. Lord Kerr and Lady Hale remain the friendliest judges with respect to these non-ECHR, non-EU rights claims, but Lord Dyson moves down the rankings significantly, just like he did with respect to salient ECHR claims. Conversely, Lord Clarke seems to be much more positive towards 'other' rights claims where the issue effects a split in the Court. Lord Carnwath remains at the bottom of the table.

Figure 7 Other rights success (salient cases)

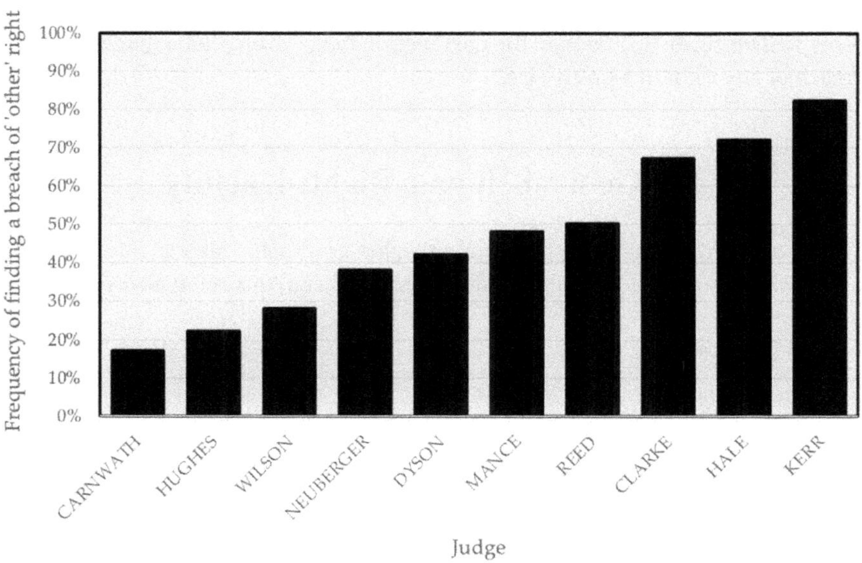

The placement of a number of judges here aligns with some important comments made in their judgments. For example, in some cases Lord Kerr took quite a radical view of domestic obligations towards international law. In one instance, he found, despite the fact that the parties had not put it to the Court, that the UNCRC was directly enforceable at national law.[85] In the same case, Lord Hughes took the opposite view, and was the only judge in that case to find that international standards had not been breached at all.[86] Lords Kerr and Hughes also sparred in the context of common law rights; in the case of *Beghal*,[87] whilst both judges found that the common law included a right against self-incrimination, the former found that it was breached (alongside provisions of the ECHR), dissenting from Hughes' contrary view.[88] Lord Kerr adopted a similarly expansive approach to the scope and application of common law rights in cases such as *Moohan*, concerning voting rights,[89] and the more recent case of *Elgizouli* (a case which was argued during the period covered by the database, but handed down outside of it) where he was the only judge to recognise a common law right to life in the context of information sharing to a foreign country.[90]

Because of the varied nature of the rights included in this category, it is hard to draw too many discrete conclusions about judicial behaviour here – a judge may adopt a very different attitude towards rights under international law compared to those they find in the common law. Nonetheless, the majority of the results in Figures 6 and 7 are fairly unsurprising in light of the judges' tendencies towards the ECHR. Judges who tend to uphold rights arguments based on the ECHR tend to uphold rights arguments based on the common law, international law and other sources. Given that correlation, it seems likely that the results of this category can be explained largely by reference to the judicial attitudes towards rights generally, rather than reflecting a specific attitude towards the origin of those rights.[91] In order to investigate this further, the next section looks at whether a judge finds any breach of any right in a given case.

IV. General Human Rights Liability

Whilst in many instances, when human rights arguments appear in a case, the Court will only consider a claim made under one 'head', this is not always the case.

[85] *R (SG) v Secretary of State for Work and Pensions* [2015] UKSC 16; [2015] WLR 1449 at [255]–[256]. In *DA and DS* (n 50), he left the point open, but implied that he had not changed his mind about it: [178] and [181].

[86] *SG*, ibid [148]–[155].

[87] *Beghal* (n 50).

[88] ibid [60] and [112]–[113].

[89] *Moohan* (n 48). See also *R (Evans) v Attorney General* [2015] UKSC 21; [2015] AC 1787, where Lord Kerr agreed with Lord Neuberger's lead judgment, which advocated the strongest position on common law rights in that case.

[90] *Elgizouli v Secretary of State for the Home Department* [2020] UKSC 10; [2021] AC 937.

[91] Although some judges have expressed a greater willingness to develop common law rights compared to rights in the ECHR, including Lord Toulson: see UK Supreme Court Blog (n 7).

In *HM Treasury v Ahmed*, the legality of certain asset freezing orders was challenged by way of both ECHR and common law rights;[92] a majority of judges found a breach of natural justice and common law rights but did not find a breach of the ECHR.[93] Counting such cases as human rights 'losses' may give an impression that a judge is something of a rights-sceptic when, in fact, they might be much more willing to find that a breach has occurred using a different human rights 'tool'. Therefore, Figure 8 shows how frequently judges found *at least one violation of at least one right* across all cases which raises qualifying human rights issues of any kind.

Figure 8 Percent of cases in which any rights violation is found

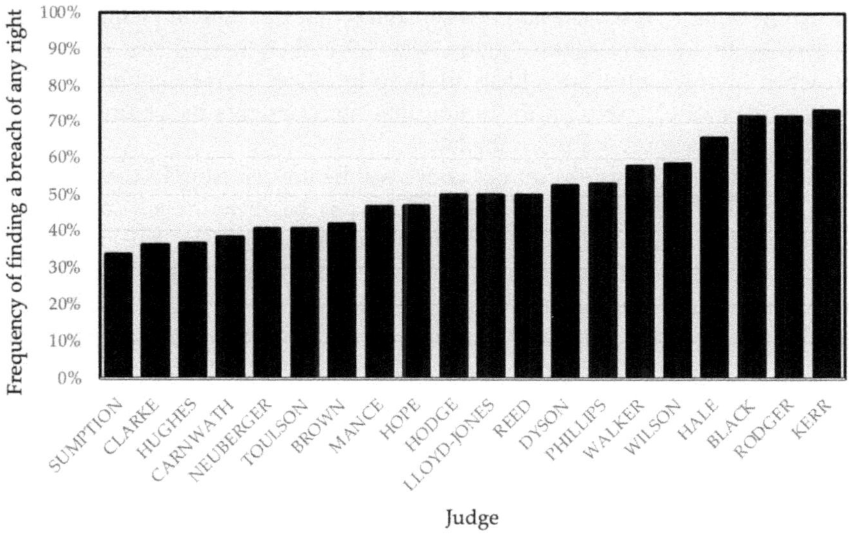

Due to the increased size of relevant data inputs, some judges appear for the first time here: Lord Lloyd-Jones appears in the middle, finding a breach of human rights in exactly half of the relevant cases in which he sat; Lord Walker did so in around 58 per cent of cases and Lord Rodger in about 71 per cent of cases. There is a slight skew towards the judges who sat on the Court during its earlier period, who were more likely to find a breach of some human right overall than those appointed later. Apart from that, these results are broadly similar to those set out above; Lords Sumption, Hughes and Carnwath sit at the lower end of the table, and Lady Hale and Lord Kerr sit at the top. Lord Wilson places a little higher than might have otherwise been expected, and Lord Clarke a little lower. Figure 8 therefore confirms that variance between the judges' voting records in this area can be

[92] *Amhed* (n 82), see [65]–[74] (Convention rights) and [75]–[82]; [145]–[157] ('other' rights).
[93] The precise identity of the tools used to declare the Order in this case unlawful is a little vague, but the judgment features frequent reference to terms like 'fundamental rights', 'common law rights' and 'natural justice': ibid [60], [61], [75], [145], [146], [174], [196], [240].

best explained by their attitude towards human rights claims as a class of claim, rather than because of a specific view towards their source. It seems that some judges are simply more sympathetic towards human rights claims than others.

V. Conclusions

This chapter compliments the previous one, showing that some judges are particularly likely to recognise certain kinds of claims and arguments put before them, whilst some are comparatively more reluctant to do so. Each judge's likelihood to find a breach of the HRA/ECHR, (where applicable) breach of EU law, and a breach of other rights was examined separately, but the general picture was one of continuity across categories: judges who were likely to find that rights were breached in one context were likely to do so in others. Conversely, some judges were comparatively resistant to finding that human rights had been breached, regardless of the source of rights in play.

Some of the conclusions set out above will be unsurprising to those familiar with the UKSC's human rights jurisprudence; as has been noted, some of the judges' positions align with what they have said during, or after, their time on the bench. After all, as Moses LJ has admitted, '[some] judges mask their views … more successfully than others'.[94] Lord Sumption, for example, has openly criticised Strasbourg for its supposed tendency to be too prescriptive and overbearing on states.[95] Whilst delivering an extrajudicial speech in 2012, Lord Kerr took the opportunity to implore domestic courts not only to follow the ECHR jurisprudence, but to go further than the Strasbourg Court had done where justice required it.[96] It might therefore be unsurprising to discover that number-crunching shows Lord Sumption to be quite unlikely to find human rights breaches compared to his colleagues, whilst the very opposite is true for Lord Kerr.

In a sense, for the reasons outlined at the beginning of this chapter, finding such variance when it comes to human rights is unsurprising: there is so much room for judges to make their own evaluations and apply their own discretion, and, perhaps more than any other area of law, questions like justification and proportionality invite value-judgments which are likely to engage personal preferences. Many human rights cases require judges to engage with issues central to our constitutional set-up: should all legal standards be set domestically, or is an international dimension relevant? Should legislative and executive discretion go untrammelled? Who ultimately should have the final say when it comes to justifying rights

[94] Moses LJ, 'Hitting the Balls out of Court: Are Judges Stepping Over the Line?' (Creaney Memorial Lecture, 24 February 2014) 15.

[95] J Sumption, 'Judicial and Political Decision-making: The Uncertain Boundary' 16(4) *Judicial Review* 301, 309.

[96] Lord Kerr, 'The UK Supreme Court – the modest underworker of Strasbourg?' (Clifford Chance Lecture, 25 January 2012).

infringements? In approaching human rights cases in different (sometimes *radically different*) ways, it need not be assumed that judges are disregarding the law by siding with their favoured parties or otherwise acting inappropriately; they are, rather, giving different answers to these fundamental questions. That the judges do not speak with one voice on these matters does not make their actions illegitimate, however varied those voices may turn out to be in practice.

Having found that some judges tend to be more or less likely to come to certain conclusions in cases (this chapter and the previous one), and side with certain parties (chapter five), the next chapter will turn to whether the same can be said with regards to the application of legal reasoning. In particular, each judge's approach to statutory interpretation and *stare decisis* will be examined, as well as their approach to questions of jurisdiction and remedies, in order to determine whether any preferences can be inferred in this respect, too.

8

Legal Tools and Cross-Cutting Questions: Statutes, Precedent, Jurisdiction and Remedies

This chapter will evaluate the Court's use of different legal 'tools' and the judges' approach to some specific kinds of legal questions. It will examine, in turn, their approach to statutory interpretation, precedent, jurisdiction and remedies. Readers may think that there is little to unite these themes, and that this chapter disguises something of a clean-up exercise, looking at aspects of judicial behaviour which do not fit elsewhere in this work. There is some truth to this. Yet I suggest that not only are the insights from the data set out below interesting in their own right, but that this is not quite the 'miscellany' chapter some may expect. Each subject examined involves a distinct *cross-cutting* legal issue which arises in a variety of different cases, and a judge's attitude towards each one may shed light on general preferences not tied to the holder's attitudes towards particular subject matter or the presence of certain parties.

Notably, the questions examined in this chapter have often been framed as being, somehow, more purely legal in nature compared to others. Human rights questions might be seen as involving wishy-washy political values, but questions about statutory interpretation and precedent are a *proper lawyer's* bread and butter. Historic clashes between Lord Denning and Lord Simonds feature on the typical undergraduate Law syllabus, with their respective views on both stare decisis[1] and statutory interpretation[2] being well-known and well-respected. Divergence between judges on these matters tends to be acknowledged as legitimate, rather than denied or derided. Nevertheless, in their own way, the issues examined in this chapter clearly relate to ever-present constitutional questions including what the most appropriate relationship between the court, the executive, the legislature and the parties to a case is and ought to be. The issues identified in earlier chapters, such as whether the identity of the judge sitting on a case makes a difference to its outcome, and how far this challenges the idea of a mythical judiciary, therefore continue to be apposite. Legal reasoning is not – or at least need not always be – some detached technical exercise.

[1] *Magor and St Mellons v Newport Corporation* [1952] AC 189 and see H Carty, 'Precedent and the Court of Appeal: Lord Denning's views explored' (1981) 1(1) *Legal Studies* 68.

[2] R Dworkin, 'Stare decisis in the House of Lords' (1962) 25(2) *MLR* 163, 166–74.

The following sections explore, in turn, individual judicial records in relation to: first, questions of statutory interpretation; second, invitations to depart from earlier precedents; third, issues relating to the extent of the Court's own jurisdiction; and fourth, generosity of discretionary remedies provided. This chapter therefore explores the same questions as were posed in the preceding chapters, albeit in the slightly different context of legal reasoning, namely: do UKSC judges show consistent preferences on the relevant issues, and how significant, if at all, is the difference between individual judges in this respect?

I. Statutory Interpretation

Statutory interpretation is a staple of the judicial diet. During the UKSC's first ten years, a total of 276 cases (around 40 per cent of all cases) involved at least one judge performing an act of 'statutory interpretation' (as defined below). Few judges, despite telling us that they are searching for a statute's 'correct' or 'true' meaning, could seriously entertain the idea that statutory interpretation is some wholly objective exercise. It is trite to say that much of language is inherently ambiguous and amorphous. And in the specialised and esoteric realm of legal interpretation, even the most seemingly straightforward of terms may give rise to different – sometimes unintuitive – interpretations and meanings, depending on their statutory provenance.[3] Any judge taking up the task of statutory construction is likely to consider questions such as the following: should interpretation focus on the specific words used in the statute or on the general thrust of the terms? Should language be interpreted as it would have been understood at time of enactment, or as it is understood at the time of interpretation? Should specialist terms be given a particular technical or legal meaning?[4] Should recourse be made to dictionaries or historical documents, or should judges simply rely on 'common sense'? How far should the context of the terms be taken into consideration (whether in terms of other parts in the same statute, or the wider legal framework)? Should the intention of Parliament or the purpose of legislation be taken into account? What weight should be given to the way the terms are understood by other actors: Parliament, expert bodies, other courts, or the 'general public'? Should there be any presumptions involved in interpretation and when should they be rebutted? Should statutory terms be open to what Andrew Burrows has termed 'conforming interpretation':[5] modifying the meaning of otherwise straightforward provisions

[3] A Gearey, W Morrison and R Jago, *The Politics of the Common Law*, 2nd edn (Routledge, 2013) 164–87; J Bell, *Policy Arguments in Judicial Decisions* (OUP, 1983) 84–93; *Re Nortel Companies* [2013] UKSC 52; [2014] AC 209 at [70] (Lord Neuberger).

[4] Legal formulae can be just as slippery as any other statutory words: 'A phrase begins life as a literary expression, its felicity leads to its lazy repetition, and repetition soon establishes it as a legal formula, undiscriminatingly used to express different and sometimes contradictory ideas' – *Tiller v Atlantic Coast Line Railroad Co* (1943) 318 US 54 at 68 (Frankfurter J).

[5] A Burrows, *Thinking About Statutes* (CUP, 2018) 11–13.

in light of concepts such as human rights, legality, international obligations and the rule of law? And how should the exercise of statutory interpretation relate to the interpretation of other legal instruments, such as contracts?[6]

As such, what at first may seem like a simple question – what does *term x* mean? – can in fact mask quite a complex exercise, involving, in the words of Lord Mance, 'the identification, evaluation and weighing of principles which quite often pull in different directions'.[7] In answering such questions, judges rely on different 'tools' – canons of interpretation – but they must always choose which tool to use in each situation. And, as Lord Reid once pointed out, sometimes the outcome of a case will entirely depend on which method of interpretation is adopted and applied.[8] A judge's preferred approach to interpretation can, therefore, be of crucial importance. That choice will also inform their view on certain fundamental constitutional questions – how tightly-bound should the judiciary be to legislative pronouncements? How much creative power should a judge hold? How great is the scope for ensuring justice and fairness in the context of statutory law?[9] A judge who believes, for example, that judges should be careful to avoid becoming 'lawmakers' and should generally defer to Parliament's view may well find themselves adopting a certain method of statutory construction – in this case, a narrow approach to avoid developing the law beyond that which Parliament had intended – as a result. Therefore, even seemingly innocuous questions of statutory construction may be related to principles such as legislative supremacy, the separation of powers and the rule of law. It makes it interesting to examine whether judges place particular weight on certain canons and approaches when they interpret statutes: this may reveal something deeper about how they conceive of the judicial role in the wider constitutional context.

It may be thought unlikely that a given judge would exhibit some consistent and universal approach when it comes to statutory interpretation; arguably, the question of which interpretative approach to adopt should always depend, at least to some extent, on the statute being examined, the context of the legal dispute in question and the wider area involved.[10] John Burrows has suggested that statutory interpretation is primarily a pragmatic exercise, and that it is unlikely that interpretation is informed by any 'coherent philosophy' on the part of the judges.[11] However, given the potential relationship between statutory interpretation and constitutional fundamentals described above, it would be surprising if judges did not hold *some* more general preferences, even if they are not applied

[6] See eg L Hoffmann, 'Language and Lawyers' (2018) 134 *LQR* 553; Lord Sumption, 'A Question of Taste: The Supreme Court and the Interpretation of Contracts' (Harris Society Annual Lecture, 8 May 2017); Burrows, ibid 34–40.

[7] Lord Mance, 'Should law be certain?' The Oxford Shrieval Lecture, 11 October 2011).

[8] *Maunsell v Olins* [1975] AC 373, 382 (Lord Reid).

[9] On which see P Sales, 'Modern Statutory Interpretation' (2017) 38(2) *SLR* 125.

[10] P Sales, 'Legalism in constitutional law: judging in democracy' [2018] *PL* 687, 695–96.

[11] J Burrows, 'The Changing Approach to the Interpretation of Statutes' (2002) 33(3) *Victoria University of Wellington Law Review* 981, 981.

as consistently as others. Certainly, Lord Neuberger has claimed that during his time as the Court's President, he had some idea of the way his colleagues would *generally* approach questions of statutory interpretation, saying that they fell on a 'spectrum' although he admitted that this intuition as to where they fell on this spectrum was not always reliable.[12] The next section tries to identify what that spectrum might look like.

A. Measuring Statutory Interpretation

For the purposes of this section, all cases involving the interpretation of a statute, regardless of its kind or type, were coded according to the kind of interpretation adopted. This included primary legislation, but also secondary legislation including formal regulations but not (eg) guidance, administrative codes of practice or contracts. Cases involving interpretations under section 3 of the HRA were excluded as they were dealt with separately in chapter seven. Any discrete instance of statutory interpretation in a case was recorded, so long as it was a live issue in the case, even if it was dealt with in part of a judgment which technically constituted obiter dicta, or if the statute was otherwise not relied upon to reach the outcome in the case.

Whilst in many cases, the interpretation and application of a particular statutory term was dealt with as one exercise, this dataset excluded those cases where the correct interpretation of a statute was not in question, and the court's task was exclusively related to a provision's application to the facts. As is the case with other coding schemes in this thesis, where a judge adopted a mixed approach (in that some aspects of the reasoning points towards one method of interpretation and other aspects point towards another, *or* there are multiple statutory provisions to be interpreted, and the judge applies a different method to each), each judge's approach was marked as a partial score. However, where a certain method of interpretation was adopted in the main, but the judge subsequently employed an alternative method as a means of 'checking' the correctness of that initial interpretation, only the former reasoning was treated as the judge's preferred approach.[13]

The big question, of course, was how the many examples of statutory interpretation across the Court's case law should be categorised and recorded for the purpose of the coding exercise. It is common (if somewhat antiquated) for statutory interpretation to be understood as involving a choice between a number

[12] Lord Neuberger, 'Judicial Impartiality: Essential or Impossible?' (Clare College Cambridge, 12 March 2018).

[13] See eg in *Re I (A Child)* [2009] UKSC 9; [2010] AC 319 Lady Hale adopted a narrow approach focusing on the specific and sometimes technical language used ([17]–[18], [27]), although afterwards she suggested that the conclusion was bolstered by principle ([28]). In *R v Rollins* [2010] UKSC 39; [2010] 1 WLR 1922, a purpose-driven approach was used ([15], [17]–[19]; [21]–[24]) but a textual reasoning was then used at the end of the passage as a 'check' on correctness: [25].

of different tools, usually including the 'literal rule',[14] the 'golden rule'[15] the 'purposive approach[16] and so on. Whilst these approaches are useful enough in demonstrating some of the different approaches to statutory interpretation and how they might differ from one another, they do not necessarily provide an accurate, and certainly not an exclusive, account of the choices available to judges when they interpret statutes in practice.[17] For that reason, rather than relying on named canons, for the present exercise, each instance of statutory interpretation was categorised as falling into one of three broad categories: 'narrow', 'wide', or a 'mixed' approach involving both.[18] Whilst judges sometimes spelled out and labelled the specific approach they then applied in their judgments, in most cases an informed (although ultimately subjective) evaluation was required. It is accepted that, perhaps more than in any other instance, labelling judicial behaviour in this context involves an inevitable degree of subjectivity. I do not doubt that some may well think it simply too subjective an exercise to be of use. I hope not, not least because of the implementation of the checks set out in chapter two, including blind cross-checking and the involvement of second reviewers. To minimise the risk of arbitrariness, and in the interests of transparency, the following guidance was adopted.

An exercise in interpretation was coded as involving a 'wide approach' when it involved placing limited weight on the precise words or terms used in the statute being interpreted.[19] This sometimes saw the judge question the idea that words can be given some objective definition.[20] In addition, rather than focusing exclusively on the language adopted and interpreting the statute in isolation, this approach focused instead on what the statute was intended to mean ('what goes in …') and

[14] *Abley v Dale* (1850) 20 LJCP 33 at 35 (Jervis CJ); *Magor and St Mellons* (n 1) 190–91 (Lord Simonds). Note, however, that it is very hard to find many examples of an *exclusively* literal approach to statutory interpretation in practice; for example, it is commonly said that the case of *Fisher v Bell* [1961] 1 QB 394 exemplifies this approach, because of Parker CJ's focus on the language of the statute (and the application of the principle of *inclusion unius exclusio alterius*) as well as the fact that the result seems to run directly contrary to both common sense and the clear intention of Parliament. However, in that case Parker CJ also drew on wider sources, including other statutes and the underlying aims behind the law of contract, and ultimately chose to interpret the statutory term according to how a similar term would be understood as a contractual term under the common law. As such, even this case does not provide an example where the terms of a statute are applied literally.

[15] *Attorney General v Lockwood* (1842) 9 M & W 378, 398 (Alderson B); *R v Warner* [1969] 2 AC 256, 286 (Lord Morris).

[16] *R (Quintavalle) v Secretary of State for Health* [2003] UKHL 13; [2003] 2 AC 687 at [9] (Lord Bingham). The 'purposive approach' is similar to the so-called 'mischief rule' as set out in *Heydon's Case* (1584) 3 Co Rep 7a.

[17] Burrows (n 6) 4–5.

[18] Thus adopting a much blunter approach than that adopted in some of the US literature, which codes decisions according to the specific interpretive 'tools' used: see J Brudney and C Distlear, 'Canons of Construction and the Elusive Quest for Neutral Reasoning' (2005) 58(1) *Vanderbilt Law Review* 1.

[19] Sometimes the Court's policy-based approach is so strong that it dismisses certain provisions which seem out of step as drafting errors: *All Stars Nursery v Scottish Commission for Regulation of Care* [2013] UKSC 12; SC (UKSC) 186 at [37] (Lord Hope); *Goluchowski and Sas v Poland* [2016] UKSC 36; [2016] 1 WLR 2665 at [28] (Lord Mance).

[20] See the remarks of Wright MR comparing the meaning of 'free speech, free love, free dinner and free trade': *James v Commonwealth of Australia* [1936] AC 578, 627.

what effect the statute would have ('what comes out …') in different contexts. With regard to the former, a wide approach tended to examine the policy underpinning the statutory term, its legislative history, or the specific reasons for its enactment. The wider purpose behind the provision typically featured in the reasoning (but, as noted above, a 'wide' approach to statutory interpretation was not necessarily treated as synonymous with the so-called purposive approach). In terms of its effects, a wide approach would try to interpret the law in a way which will bolster predictability and certainty, and avoid results which were surprising, capricious or unworkable. Sometimes an approach would be adopted which sought to promote justice and fairness, howsoever construed, or at least to mitigate undue harshness, which might follow from a more direct or literal interpretation. A wide approach often sought to interpret provisions harmoniously with other laws, including international laws and obligations,[21] and might have modified or 'imported' approaches or tests from other areas of law. Finally, a wide approach was sometimes recognised by reliance on external influences, such as Law Commission reports and academic opinion.[22]

In addition to these general pointers, a number of specific terms used would typically signal that a judge was adopting a 'wide' approach to statutory interpretation. Most obviously, sometimes a narrow or literal approach is expressly discarded in favour of one which is described as 'wider' or 'purposive'. Beyond this, a wide approach was sometimes signposted by, for example: reference to an 'expanded'[23] or 'extended'[24] definition of a statutory term; a provision being described as 'loose',[25] 'practical'[26] or 'functional';[27] reference to a statutory 'gloss';[28] words being 'read in'[29] to a passage; the adoption of meanings which are 'incidental'[30] to or 'implicit'[31] within an initial interpretation; reference to the meaning of a term having been 'imported' from elsewhere;[32] and/or references to the 'spirit'[33]

[21] See K Stanton, 'Comparative Law in the House of Lords and Supreme Court' (2013) 42 *Common Law World Review* 269.

[22] See K Stanton, 'Use of Scholarship by the House of Lords in Tort Cases' in J Lee (ed), *From House of Lords to Supreme Court* (Hart Publishing, 2011); Paterson, *Final Judgment* (Hart Publishing, 2013) 213–21.

[23] See eg *Yemshaw v London Borough of Hounslow* [2011] UKSC 3; [2011] 1 All ER 912 at [34] (Lady Hale).

[24] See eg *Akers v Samba Financial Group* [2017] UKSC 6; [2017] AC 424 at [56] (Lord Mance).

[25] See eg *Eclipse Film Partners No 35 v HMRC* [2016] UKSC 24; [2016] 1 WLR 1939 at [23] (Lord Neuberger).

[26] See eg *Secretary of State for Work and Pensions v MM* [2019] UKSC 34; [2020] 1 All ER 829 at [41] (Lady Black).

[27] See eg *Campbell v Gordon* [2016] UKSC 38; [2016] AC 1513 at [30] (Lord Toulson).

[28] See eg *Clyde & Co v van Winklehof* [2014] UKSC 32; [2014] 1 WLR 2047 at [39] (Lady Hale).

[29] See eg *All Stars Nursery* (n 19) at [37] (Lord Hope).

[30] See eg *R (New London College) v Secretary of State for the Home Department* [2013] UKSC 51; [2013] 1 WLR 2358 at [33], [35]–[37] (Lord Carnwath).

[31] See eg *Hotak v London Borough of Southwark* [2015] UKSC 30; [2016] AC 811 at [51] (Lord Neuberger).

[32] See eg *Office of Fair Trading v Abbey National* [2009] UKSC 6; [2010] 1 AC 696 at [112] (Lord Mance).

[33] See eg *R (ZO) v Secretary of State for the Home Department* [2010] UKSC 36; [2010] 1 WLR 1948 at [31] (Lord Kerr).

of legislation, its 'general message',[34] or 'what really matters'.[35] Wide interpretations sometimes saw statutory provisions undergo a 'remoulding',[36] or an interpretation would be adopted 'despite the words'[37] of the statute, or read 'as if' they meant something else.[38] Finally, a wide approach was sometimes described in more accusatory terms, often by judges adopting a more narrow approach; an impermissibly wide approach was described as 'highly artificial',[39] 'strained'[40] or even 'through the looking glass'.[41]

By contrast, judges adopting a narrow approach tend to emphasise the primacy of the language and words used in the statute, over and above other more purposive considerations. Often, the focus would be upon the meaning of a specific term or phrase, sometimes subjecting even the most seemingly inconspicuous of terms to forensic examination. The syntax and grammar, or even the chosen tense of the statute was examined under this approach. Sometimes judges have even had recourse to dictionaries when defining statutory terms.[42] Under a narrow approach, the meaning and effect of statutory terms were often found wholly within the statute itself. In this respect, it was common to see judges reasoning that a statute could not authorise a certain power or action because it did not explicitly contain authority for that power or action within its text, and it was common to find the adage that, were Parliament to have intended the statute to be interpreted in a certain way, it would have spelled it out specifically. Not only were public policy concerns downplayed under the narrow approach, but extrinsic aids such as academic opinion, the approach of other areas of law and the workings of other statutes also tended to be given limited weight. Sometimes, judges applying a narrow interpretation noted that a different (wider) interpretation may have produced desirable results, but that this was irrelevant for the purposes of statutory interpretation. In such situations, changes were ringfenced for Parliament rather than the courts, and those who stepped over that line were chastised for indulging in judicial policy-making.

As with a wider approach, there are a number of linguistic terms which would often indicate that a judge was adopting a narrow approach to statutory interpretation. These included when an interpretative choice is described as ordinary',[43]

[34] See eg *AXA General Insurance v Lord Advocate* [2011] UKSC 46; [2012] 1 AC 868 at [46] (Lord Hope).

[35] See eg *Lukaszewski v Poland* [2012] UKSC 20; [2012] 1 WLR 1604 at [18] (Lord Mance).

[36] See eg *HMRC v Marks and Spencer (No 2)* [2014] UKSC 11; [2014] 1 WLR 711 at [28] (Lord Neuberger).

[37] See eg *Goluchowski* (n 19) at [39] (Lord Mance).

[38] See eg *Marley v Rawlings* [2014] UKSC 2; [2015] AC 129 at [66] (Lord Neuberger).

[39] See eg *Loveridge v London Borough of Lambeth* [2014] UKSC 65; [2014] 1 WLR 4516 at [26] (Lord Wilson).

[40] See eg *R v McCool* [2018] UKSC 23; [2018] NI 181 at [144] (Lord Reed).

[41] See eg *Assange v Swedish Prosecution Authority* [2012] UKSC 22; [2012] 2 AC 471 at [238] (Lord Mance).

[42] See eg *R v Golds* [2016] UKSC 61; [2016] WLR 5231 at [27] (Lord Hughes) and see also *R v Copeland* [2020] UKSC 8; [2021] AC 815 at [52].

[43] See eg *SL v Westminster City Council* [2013] UKSC 27; [2013] 1 WLR 1445 at [40]–[41] (Lord Carnwath).

'plain',[44] or 'pure';[45] when appeals were made to the virtues of 'ordinary English';[46] when interpretation was described as a 'linguistic'[47] or 'textual'[48] exercise; when judges alleged that 'nothing in the language' supported a rival interpretation;[49] or when a statute was interpreted 'according to its own terms',[50] 'as it stands',[51] 'on its face'[52] or 'as [the judges] find it'.[53] Often, a narrow approach was identified where a judge refused to adopt a wider approach: when there was 'no room' for a wider approach to be adopted,[54] or when doing so would go 'against the grain'[55] of the legislation or 're-write' the law.[56] All of the above was taken into consideration during the coding exercise.

B. Statutory Interpretation: Results

Each judge's record regarding statutory interpretation, across all cases, is set out in Figure 1. The judges are organised according to their respective propensity to adopt a wide approach to interpretation – in other words, those with a high percentage score, placed towards the right-hand side of the graph, were more likely to adopt a wide(r) interpretation across the board. Those with a low 'score', placed on the left-hand side of the graph, were, by contrast, more likely to adopt a narrow(er) interpretation. As always, regarding those judges associated with comparatively less robust, data are marked with an asterisk (*).

At first blush, Figure 1 suggests a fair degree of homogeneity between the judges, with most being *only very slightly more likely* to adopt a wider approach compared to a narrower one.

[44] See eg *McDonald v National Grid Energy Transmission Plc* [2014] UKSC 53; [2015] AC 1128 at [64] (Lord Kerr).

[45] See eg *Re Peacock* [2012] UKSC 5; [2012] WLR 550 at [23] (Lord Brown).

[46] See eg *Torfaen County BC v Douglas Willis Ltd* [2013] UKSC 59; [2013] 4 All ER 1 at [24] (Lord Toulson).

[47] See eg *Rhuppiah v Secretary of State for the Home Department* [2018] UKSC 58; [2018] 1 WLR 5536 at [43] (Lord Wilson).

[48] See eg *R (Ismail) v Secretary of State for the Home Department* [2016] UKSC 37; [2016] 1 WLR 2814 at [25] (Lord Kerr).

[49] See eg *Haralambous v Crown Court at St Albans* [2018] UKSC 1; [2018] AC 236 at [15] (Lord Mance).

[50] See eg *Grays Timber Products v HMRC* [2010] UKSC 4; [2010] WLR 497 at [56] (Lord Hope).

[51] See eg *R v Guraj* [2016] UKSC 65; [2017] 1 WLR 22 at [37] (Lord Hughes).

[52] See eg *R (Trail Riders Fellowship) v Dorset CC* [2015] UKSC 18; [2015] 1 WLR 1406 at [19] (Lord Clarke).

[53] See eg *R (A) v London Borough of Croydon* [2009] UKSC 8; [2010] 1 All ER 469 at [54] (Lord Hope).

[54] See eg *KO (Nigeria) v Secretary of State for the Home Department* [2018] UKSC 53; [2018] 1 WLR 5273 at [21] (Lord Carnwath).

[55] See eg *Phoenix Engineering v UK Insurance Ltd* [2019] UKSC 16; [2020] AC 1025 at [40] (Lord Hodge).

[56] See eg *Project Blue v HMRC* [2018] UKSC 30; [2018] WLR 3169 at [115] (Lord Briggs).

Figure 1 Likelihood of adopting a wide approach to statutory interpretation (all votes)

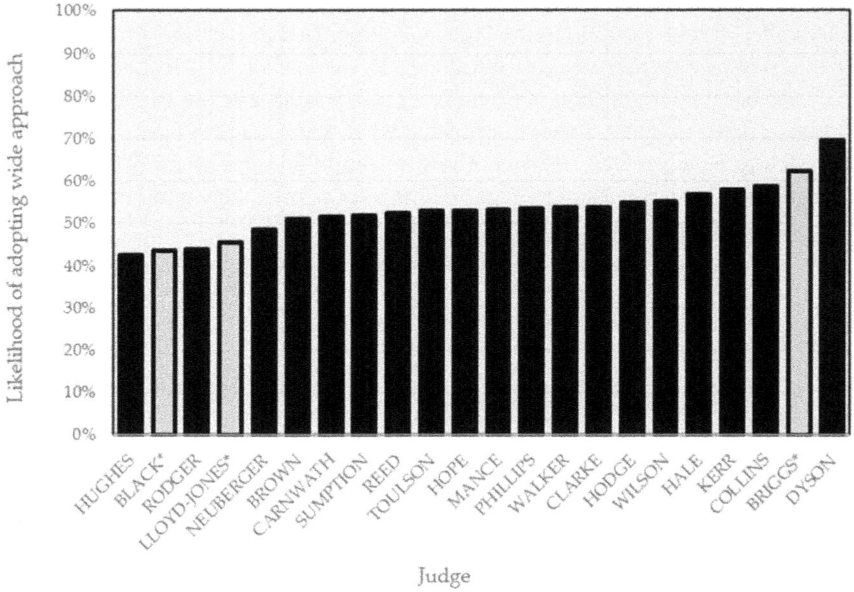

However, variance can be detected at the margins, with Lords Hughes and Rodger seeming particularly likely to have adopted a narrow approach, and Lord Dyson in particular having being more likely to adopt a wider one. However, an important point should be noted: in the unique context of statutory interpretation, presenting each judge's position in terms of a binary choice (1 or 0; wide or narrow) can be distorting. Usually, the coding scheme would allocate a mixed position (0.5) to a judge only where they take different (binary) positions towards different parties within the same case. As noted above, however, this section involves a 'mixed' approach label, which was applied when a judge invoked a number of distinct considerations during the interpretive exercise, some emblematic of a wider approach, some a narrower one. As might be expected, such a mixed approach prevailed in many cases. In fact, preferring to adopt a mixed approach to statutory interpretation may be just as much a distinct judicial preference as adopting a wide or a narrow one. For this reason, Figure 2 sets out, for each judge, how often they applied a wide, narrow *and* a distinctly mixed approach to statutory interpretation.

The data here reveals something slightly more nuanced than Figure 1 might suggest. For example, Lady Black initially seemed to be an advocate for interpreting statutes narrowly according to Figure 1, and indeed Figure 2 shows that she was the judge who was least likely to adopt an exclusively 'wide' approach (around 13 per cent of the time). But Figure 2 shows that she was *not* very likely to adopt a narrow approach, either – she was, by far, most likely to adopt a 'middle ground'

Figure 2 Statutory interpretation (order: likelihood of adopting wide approach)

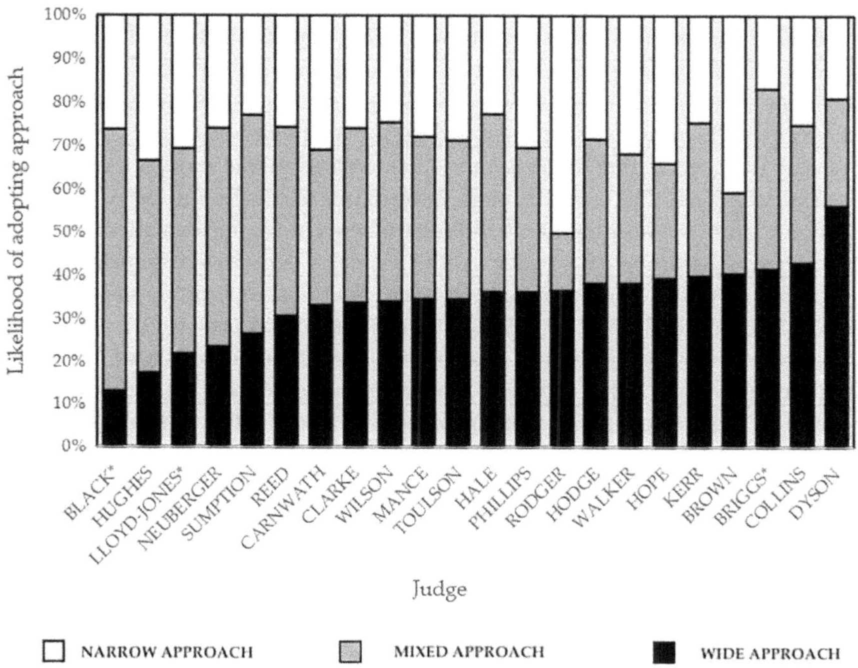

approach, borrowing from both wide and narrow canons of interpretation. The same applies to Lord Neuberger, who emerges as a much more balanced figure than Figure 1 might initially suggest, who adopted a distinctly mixed approach more than 50 per cent of the time.

Also interesting in this respect are the records of Lords Brown and Rodger. They both sit at the lower 'end' of Figure 1, and might be considered to prefer narrow interpretations on the whole, but whilst they are the two judges most likely to adopt an exclusively narrow position in Figure 2, they were each also more likely than the average judge to adopt an exclusively wide position, too – in fact, Lord Brown is the fourth-most likely judge to do so. It seems that both judges tended to adopt quite firm, committed positions, *either* sticking to a wide approach or a narrow one, and rarely a more holistic approach borrowing methods from both canons. Lord Brown was, in fact, equally as likely to adopt a wide position as he was a narrow one, but he was twice as likely to adopt *either* a narrow or a wide position than he was a mixed one involving both strands of reasoning.

One useful aspect of the current enquiry is that so many cases involved statutory interpretation to some extent, producing a lot of datapoints and, in theory, more reliable data. This means that not only can the data be filtered to include only salient cases, as was the case in previous chapters, but that there is also enough data to assess which approaches judges adopted in their lead opinions.

As with salient cases, assessing lead opinions may allow, to some extent, a greater degree of insight into a judge's more sincerely held preferences. As was set out in chapter three, judges signing up to the majority opinion in a case may concur with the lead opinion-writer for many reasons. This means, for example, that a judge who is comfortable with a wide approach to statutory interpretation may very well choose to simply agree with the lead opinion author in a certain case (at least when they believe they have arrived at the correct conclusion) even if they reach that result through interpreting the statute using particularly narrow methods. Things are very different when a judge authors a lead opinion themselves. Not only does a judge exhibit a greater degree of responsibility and 'ownership' over an opinion they themselves author compared to one authored by a colleague which they merely sign their name to, but they would have more scope to employ their preferred method of statutory interpretation in practice. In short, the relationship between a judge and the content of their own lead opinion is more direct than one they agree with, and it can be inferred that they feel more strongly about the content (including methods of statutory interpretation) contained within it.

In any case, Figure 3 sets out each judge's overall likelihood of adopting a wide approach to statutory interpretation but only when considering the lead opinions they authored. As with the above data, each judge's voting records has also been set out (in terms of whether their approach was wide, narrow or mixed), set out in Figure 4. Again, those judges with reliable but less robust data are marked with an asterisk (*).

Figure 3 Likelihood of adopting a wide approach to statutory interpretation (leads only)

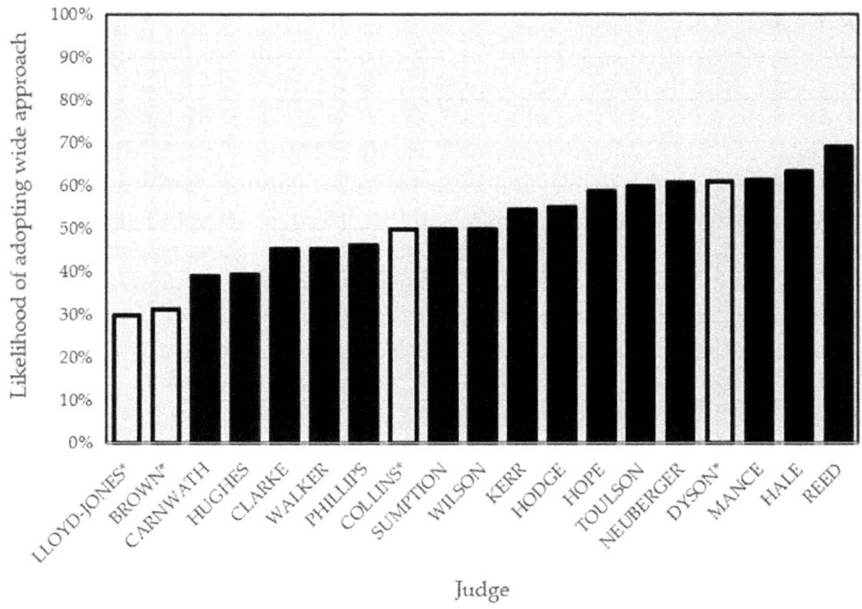

There are some noteworthy changes compared to the general data presented above. In addition to exhibiting a more varied spread of positions, the judges' respective placements also differ. Whilst Lord Dyson remains to appear a clear advocate for a wider approach, Lord Collins slips down the rankings (although neither judges decided enough cases to produce particularly robust data). By contrast, Lady Hale and (especially) Lord Reed appear much more likely to have adopted a wider approach in their lead opinions.

Additional nuance is again revealed through marking 'mixed' approaches separately. For example, whilst Lord Brown is indeed the judge who was most likely to construe a statute narrowly in a lead judgment (and by a significant margin at that), this did not mean that he was also the judge who was least likely to adopt a wide approach – that judge is Lord Lloyd-Jones (or Lord Hughes if only more robust data is included). Other judges of note here include Lord Dyson, who, like Lord Brown, tended to adopt either a wide or a narrow approach, rather than a mixed one, and as such was more likely to employ a wide construction than, say, Lord Clarke, despite their relative positions in Figure 3.

One potentially interesting observation is that there appears to be something of a trend for Court Presidents and Deputy Presidents to adopt a wider approach to statutory interpretation when they author lead judgments. Indeed, when comparing their data, five of the six judges who have held a senior position were notably

Figure 4 Statutory interpretation (order: likelihood of adopting wide approach), leads only

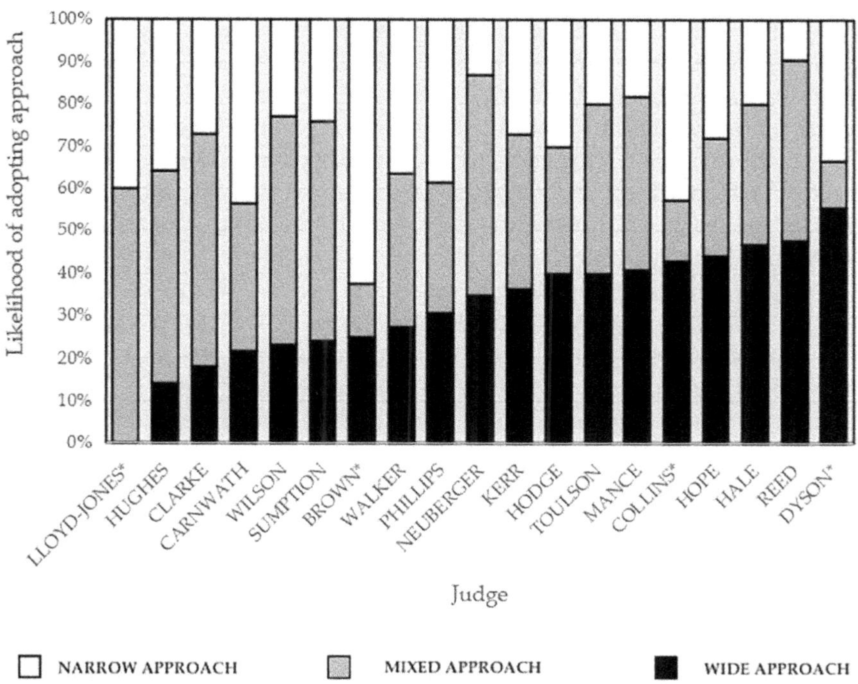

more likely to adopt a wide approach when writing a lead judgment than they would in general (whereas Lord Phillips, the Court's first President, seemed to take a balanced approach in both contexts). This could simply be evidence that lead judgments provide a better landscape for the identification of a judge's true preferences, and that each of these judges naturally leaned towards a wider approach to statutory interpretation. However, this could also be evidence that the adoption of a formal leadership position might have *some* impact upon judicial behaviour – in that court leaders, for one reason or another, tend to employ a wider (perhaps more contextual, purposive) approach to statutory interpretation in this context compared to non-title holders.

In addition to looking at each judge's lead judgments, we can also look to their votes in salient cases – those cases in which members of the panel deciding a case differed in their approach to statutory interpretation (in the context of statutory interpretation, the difference between split cases and salient cases becomes very important, not least because in many cases the judges were unanimous as to the case outcome, but divided according to their approach to statutory interpretation).[57] When looking at salient cases, the three-pronged approach adopted above (marking wide, narrow and mixed approaches separately) was abandoned in favour of a *relative* measure – put simply, in relevant cases, how often did a judge adopt a *wider* or *narrower* approach than their colleagues did? The answer is set out in Figure 5.

After considering the previous data, some of the judges' positions in Figure 5 are unsurprising. Judges like Lord Rodger, Hughes and Brown continue to sit at one end of the table and others such as Lord Kerr, Lord Toulson and Lord Dyson sit at the other. Other positions are somewhat more surprising. The seemingly quite moderate Lord Hodge edges up to become one of the Court's more consistent employers of a wider interpretation in divided cases, whereas Lord Hope appears to be notably more inclined to adopt a narrow position compared to his colleagues. Perhaps most significant is Lord Reed – whilst he was the judge who was most likely of all to adopt a wide approach to statutory construction in a lead judgment, he was much less likely to do so in split cases, adopting a comparatively wide approach around 31 per cent of the time. What exactly this means is unclear, but it is possible to stipulate that Lord Reed considers different types of judgments to have different utility. For example, might it be the case that he considers that utilising narrow construction techniques may be more likely to convince (some) wavering colleagues in divided cases, whereas the adoption of a wide interpretation is more likely to result in a more authoritative judgment overall?

It is also noteworthy that whilst in some of the above figures, the differences between judges when it comes to statutory interpretation have been fairly slight,

[57] And vice versa – whilst Lord Kerr came to a different conclusion from his colleagues in *Morge v Hampshire CC* [2011] UKSC 2; [2011] 1 WLR 268 he seemed to adopt their approach to statutory interpretation.

Figure 5 Likelihood of adopting wide approach to statutory interpretation (salient cases only)

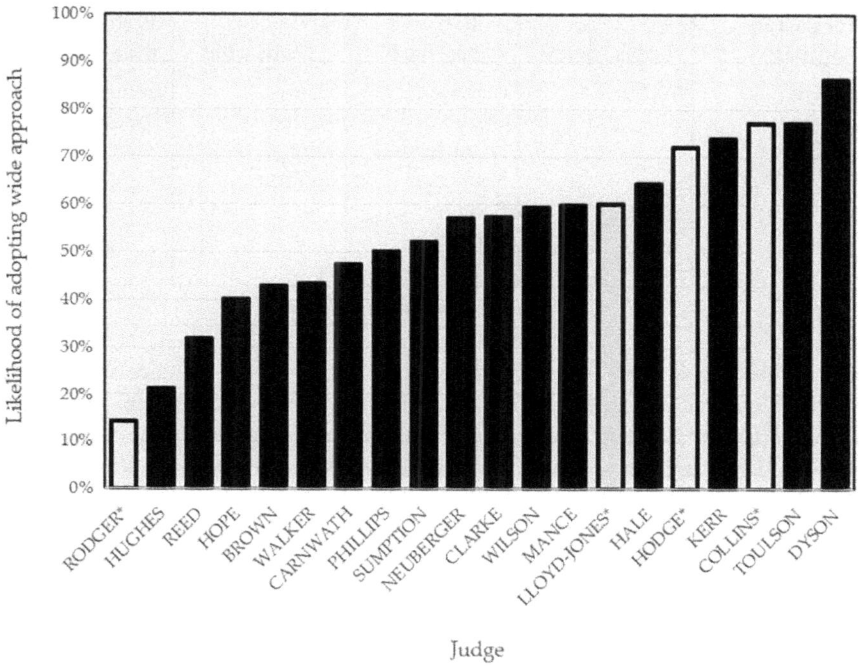

the same cannot be said here. Even if Lord Rodger's data is put to one side due to its low level of reliability, we find Lord Hughes adopting a *comparatively* wide approach to interpretation just over 20 per cent of the time, whereas, by contrast, three judges did so *over 75 per cent of the time*. Lord Dyson, remarkably, adopted a wide approach in over 86 per cent of the salient cases he was involved in. Not only do the judges differ from one another quite substantially in Figure 5, but in some cases, their records disclose a preference regarding statutory interpretation which was applied consistently across salient cases.

Each of the figures above demonstrate how far individual judges vary when it comes to statutory interpretation, and what each judge's preference in this respect may be. However, judicial preferences are inevitably subject to different influences and constraints depending on which of their votes are being examined, and as such each figure above 'places' judges slightly differently. It may therefore be helpful to draw an overall picture as to where each judge sits when it comes to statutory interpretation. This is set out in Figure 6. These categorisations are very blunt but operate (roughly) on a scale from those judges most likely to exhibit a 'narrow' approach to those most likely to adopt a 'wide' one.

Figure 6 Statutory interpretation: summary

Preference for narrow approach	Leans narrow	Balanced approach	Leans wide	Preference for wide approach
Brown Hughes Rodger	Walker	Camwath Clarke Lloyd-Jones Neuberger Phillips Sumption Wilson	Hale Hodge Kerr Toulson	Collins Dyson
Difficult to categorise: Hope, Reed				

The difference between placement categories is merely one of consistency and degree. However, as can be seen, most judges sit in the middle area, indicating a preference for a balanced approach. This means that those judges either: (a) tend to adopt a 'mixed' approach to statutory interpretation, using both wide and narrow strands of reasoning when interpreting a given provision; (b) tend to adopt a narrow approach in some cases and a wide approach in others, so that neither dominates overall; (c) lean towards one approach (wide or narrow) in some contexts (eg in divided cases) but towards the other in another context (eg in their lead judgments), but only to a limited degree. In any case, they cannot be said to advocate a *particularly wide or narrow approach* to statutory interpretation overall.

The positions of some of the judges here are unsurprising given some of their judicial statements on the topic of statutory interpretation. For example, Lord Brown has stated that when interpreting statutes, 'the court must, of course, be guided principally by the language of the section itself',[58] a notion which aligns neatly with his position in the tables above. Similarly, in the famous case of *Evans v Attorney-General*, Lord Hughes stressed that:

> The rule of law is of the first importance. But it is an integral part of the rule of law that courts give effect to Parliamentary intention. The rule of law is not the same as a rule that courts must always prevail, no matter what the statute says.[59]

In light of such remarks, it is unsurprising that Lord Hughes tended to take a narrow approach to statutory construction as a whole. Those remarks can be

[58] *Peacock* (n 45) at [19].

[59] *R (Evans) v Attorney General* [2015] UKSC 21; [2015] AC 1787 at [154]. Another example of Lord Hughes applying a very strong narrow approach is *R v Mackinlay* [2018] UKSC 42; [2019] AC 387. There, he read the statute in a 'plain' and 'natural' manner ([27]; [28]; [21]) and let only those words dictate his approach ([17]). He confirmed that there was 'no room' for alterative interpretations ([19]) nor for 'importing' more content ([26]); if this had been Parliament's wish, express words could have been used ([20]). 'Consequentialist' arguments were also rejected ([27]). His duty was to apply the plain meaning of the statute regardless of what he or anyone else thought would be a normatively preferable ([28]).

contrasted to those of Lord Kerr, a judge who, the data suggests, tended to apply a wide approach, who has said that when it comes to statutory interpretation, statutes 'can, and should, be given a purposive construction'[60] and that it is 'well-established' that applying a literal, narrow approach is not appropriate for modern judges.[61]

In addition, some placements align, to some extent, with the data in previous chapters. Lady Hale and Lord Kerr showed similar preferences to one another in other contexts, so it is perhaps unsurprising that they are grouped together here, too. The same can be said for the now-familiar pairing of Lords Brown and Rodger. There also seems to be some sort of conceptual relationship between the measures examined in previous chapters – how likely a judge is to side with certain parties, or how likely they are to find liability in a certain area or to recognise a wider jurisdiction for the Court – and the measures set out above. Perhaps a judge who is more likely to adhere to the specific, straightforward language of the statute is also more likely to side with powerful parties (especially if one subscribes to the idea that the law, generally, does not sufficiently protect weaker parties). But such a relationship is neither straightforward nor applicable to all judges. Whilst Lord Brown, for example, generally adopted a narrow approach to statutory construction *and* tended to side with stronger parties, Lord Dyson, the strongest adherent of a wide interpretive approach, was not particularly likely to side with weaker parties. These connections are necessarily speculative. A more in-depth examination of each judge's individual profile is conducted in chapter ten.

II. Precedent

Another frequent – perhaps *surprisingly* frequent – issue for the judges of the UKSC relates to whether it ought to follow its own previous case law or whether to depart from it in full or in part. Broadly, the notion of stare decisis dictates that judges sitting in a court should ordinarily follow the case law of more senior courts, and, sometimes, courts of equal rank. The Supreme Court has its own rules of precedent, and is considered to be generally (but not absolutely) bound by the decisions of its predecessor, the House of Lords, in addition to its own decisions.[62]

There are many reasons for a court to adhere to precedent; the main ones are that doing so ensures 'coherence, clarity and predictability' in the law,[63] and ensures

[60] *Robertson v Swift* [2014] UKSC 50; [2014] 1 WLR 3438 at [30] (Lord Kerr), citing *Quintavalle* (n 16) at [8] (Lord Bingham).

[61] *Re Northern Ireland Human Rights Commission* [2018] UKSC 27; [2019] 1 All ER 173 at [202]–[207] (Lord Kerr).

[62] See *Austin v London Borough of Southwark* [2010] UKSC 28; [2011] 1 AC 355 at [24]–[25]. Slightly less straightforward is status of decisions handed down by the Privy Council: see *Willers v Joyce (No 2)* [2016] UKSC 44; [2015] 3 WLR 534.

[63] *Willers*, ibid [4].

that its development is controlled and incremental.[64] It also operates as something of a brake on judicial activism and creativity. Ultimately, if judges truly do have the ability to rule according to their own 'doctrinal dispositions', the requirement to adhere to precedent may act as a potentially significant restraint upon this.[65] As Lord Toulson put it in one case:

> Particularly in a difficult case in which the panel is narrowly divided, it is always possible that a small change of constitution would have produced a different outcome. That is itself a powerful reason to be very slow to depart from a fully considered previous decision. To do otherwise would not only lead to uncertainty but would also risk the rule of law being seen as the rule of individual judges.[66]

Precedent plays an integral part of common law reasoning. Indeed, it is not altogether uncommon for a judge to signal a preference for a certain outcome, and to dictate that they would have otherwise ruled in a way which would have led to that outcome, *but for* their duty to follow an applicable precedent.[67]

However, as with virtually every other aspect of legal reasoning, the operation of stare decisis in practice is far from straightforward. Ironically, despite its supposed utility in promoting restraint and ensuring legal certainty, the application (and, more controversially, the *non-application*) of precedent often proceeds in quite an unpredictable manner. When considering questions relating to precedent, judges must ask themselves a number of questions, each of which inherently invites a degree of discretion. These include:[68]

(i) Which constitutes a legitimate precedent?
(ii) Is the precedent applicable?
(iii) Would it be possible to depart from it?
(iv) Would it be appropriate or desirable to depart from it?

The first two questions are related and essentially concern the relevant conditions required to identify an authoritative precedent applicable to the case at hand. The practical difficulties encountered when trying to resolve these questions are substantial. For example: was a contested point approved by a majority

[64] For much more developed insight, see N Duxbury, *The Nature and Authority of Precedent* (CUP, 2011).

[65] *Lewis v AG of Jamaica* [2001] 2 AC 50 at [90] (Lord Hoffmann). There is, however, something of an irony in Lord Hoffmann's caution against letting personal preferences dictate the outcome of cases, especially in a case such as *Lewis* involving the death penalty. Lord Hoffmann consistently adopted a pro-death penalty position in many (usually divided) cases before the Privy Council, *notwithstanding* the existence of precedent to the contrary: see eg *John v Trinidad and Tobago* [2009] UKPC 12; 75 WIR 429, *Smith v The Queen* [2005] UKPC 43; [2006] 1 WLR 243; *Matthew v Trinidad and Tobago* [2004] UKPC 33; [2005] AC 433; *R v Watson* [2004] UKPC 34; [2005] 1 AC 472, and in *Lewis* itself. See L Graham, 'Lessons from Lord Hope's Diaries' (UK Constitutional Law Association Blog, 18 June 2020).

[66] *Khan v The State* [2015] UKPC 33; 40 BHRC 633 at [65].

[67] See eg *British Car Auctions Ltd v Wright* [1972] 1 WLR 1519 at 1525–26 (Stephenson J). For a contemporary example in the US context, see the concurring opinion of Roberts CJ in *June Medical Services LLC v Russo*, 591 US___ (2020).

[68] Adapted from R Cross and J Harris, *Precedent in English Law*, 4th edn (Clarendon, 1991) 49–52.

of judges in the earlier case?[69] Was that observation part of the ratio decidendi of the case?[70] Do those observations remain authoritative in light of more recent case law and legislation? How should conflicting authorities be treated?[71] Is the earlier case applicable to the factual and/or legal situation arising in the later case? Does the previous decision foreclose further development or does there remain room for expansion without necessitating departure from the previous law?[72] Has an otherwise non-binding statement, such as that set out in obiter dicta, become so authoritative as to render it 'almost virtually binding' in practice?[73]

The second two questions invite an even greater level of discretion. Even after a precedent is identified, can it be departed from, and if so, should the Court do so under the circumstances arising in the later case? The Supreme Court can overrule itself in certain defined circumstances set out in the Practice Statement.[74] But this power has, at least expressly, been invoked only a handful of times in the Supreme Court. However, as noted above, a departure from precedent can take many forms[75] and, indeed, in a majority of cases where the Supreme Court has declined to follow its earlier case law, the Practice Statement was not mentioned

[69] See *Sevilleja v Marex* [2020] UKSC 31; [2020] 3 WLR 255 at [174] (Lord Sales).

[70] A Goodhart, 'Determining the Ratio Decidendi of a Case' (1930) *Yale Law Journal* 161; Lord Wright, 'Precedents' (1943) 8(2) *CLJ* 118, 126–29; *Jacobs v London County Council* [1950] AC 361, 369 (Lord Simonds); J Montrose, 'The Ratio Decidendi of a Case' (1957) 20(6) *MLR* 587; AWB Simpson, 'The Ratio Decidendi of a Case' (1958) 21(2) *MLR* 155; A Goodhart, 'The Ratio Decidendi of a Case' (1959) 22(2) *MLR* 117; J Stone, 'The Ratio of the Ratio Decidendi' (1959) 22(6) *MLR* 597; Cross and Harris (n 68) 52–84. For good examples in practice compare the majority and minority in *Khuja v Times Newspapers* [2017] UKSC 49; [2019] AC 161 and the contrasting views of the High Court and Court of Appeal in *R (Youngsam) v Parole Board* [2019] EWCA Civ 229; [2019] 3 WLR 33 (on appeal from [2017] EWHC 729 Admin); [2017] WLR 2848 and Edis LJ in *London Borough of Barking and Dagenham v Argos Ltd* [2022] EWHC 1398 (Admin); [2022] AC 659 at [40]. See also, more generally, the discussion between John Morris and Robert Megarry on the authority of the famous *High Trees* case ('The Authority of the Central London and High Trees Case' (1948) *LQR* 28 at 28 and 29 respectively). Megarry acerbically put it that if one believes that 'if a judge lays down wide propositions of law and then makes findings of fact which prevent those propositions of law from arising, the propositions of law nevertheless constitute the radio decidendi' then he 'may well look forward with pleasure to cases still undecided in which the legal effect of a contract for the sale of a car by an English lunatic to a French infant will logically fall to be decided before it is held that, in fact, both parties were of full capacity and that the contract (if any) did not relate to the car in question' (at 31).

[71] This is not a new problem. 'If one pleader bring the case under any former law or precedent … the opposite pleader is not at a loss to find an opposite analogy or comparison: and the preference given by the judge is often founded more on taste and imagination than on any solid argument … where several rules, nearly equal and indifferent, present themselves, it is a very slight turn of thought which fixes the decision in favour of either party': D Hume, *Enquiries Concerning the Human Understanding and Concerning the Principles of Morals*, 2nd edn (reprod. Selby-Begge, 1892) 307–308.

[72] For example, in some cases an 'exception' to the previous case law is made out: *VB v Westminster Magistrates' Court* [2014] UKSC 59; [2015] 1 AC 1195 at [94] (Lord Toulson).

[73] See, in the context of vertical application of precedent, *Moss v Information Commissioner* [2020] UKUT 242 (AAC) at [63] and *APPGER v ICO and FCO* [2015] UKUT 377 (AAC); [2016] AACR 5 at [49].

[74] See L Blom-Cooper, '1966 and All That: the Story of the Practice Statement' in L Blom-Cooper, B Dickson and G Drewry, *The Judicial House of Lords* (OUP, 2009).

[75] F Emmert, 'Stare Decisis: A Universally Misunderstood Idea' (2002) 6(2) *Legisprudence* 207, 221–24; Cross and Harris (n 68) 129–35.

at all.[76] In these cases, the Court often simply announced that it was choosing to 'depart from' its previous pronouncements, or that the previous authority should be considered 'incorrect' or 'unsatisfactory'. Other linguistic markers which might indicate that the Court was departing from its earlier case law are set out in the following section.

Whether or not the Practice Statement is expressly invoked, it remains ambiguous as to exactly what the appropriate threshold for departing from an earlier case ought to be, and judges may – *and do* – disagree with one another as to exactly where the line falls (either in general or on the facts of a specific case). One fairly common view amongst the judges on the UKSC is that an earlier decision should not be departed from just because it is considered to be incorrect, or that a modern court may not reach the same conclusion in the abstract;[77] some further reason for departure must also be present. However, what that further reason must be, and how it is to be weighted and evaluated, remains an open question, and in any case it is not obvious that all judges even adhere to this view,[78] nor that they always apply this threshold in practice.[79]

Further issues in this field include whether certain types of precedent should be afforded greater weight than others; whether questions about the status of authorities can be considered by a judge of their own motion or whether this must be raised by parties; and whether certain precedents ought only to be over-ruled by an enlarged panel of judges.[80] A judge's view on any of these issues may well affect the extent to which they feel able to depart from precedent in practice.

As such, decisions relating to precedent are not straightforward; the application of stare decisis is much more of a discretionary exercise than some may think. Even the most celebrated and entrenched of precedents can be distinguished, undermined, and eventually overturned; in Llewellyn's words, 'absolutely binding no decision ever was'.[81] The rules of precedent allow, and indeed require, *choices* to be made by judges. This raises the obvious possibility that different judges will tend to make different choices in this regard, informed by their individual propensities and philosophies – *should the law prioritise certainty or justice?* This certainly seems to be the case with judges on certain US courts.[82] Of course, there is a collegiate

[76] See Paterson (n 22) 267–68.

[77] *Haile v London Borough of Waltham Forest* [2015] UKSC 34; [2015] 1 AC 1471 at [72] (Lord Neuberger); *Knauer v Ministry of Justice* [2016] UKSC 9; [2016] AC 908 at [22] (Lord Neuberger and Lady Hale).

[78] Lord Rodger has suggested that precedent is not always adhered to for the simple reason that 'judges change their minds from time to time': A Rodger, 'A time for everything under law: some reflections on retrospectivity' (2005) 121 *LQR* 57, 79.

[79] Lee suggests that 'a change is deemed judicially appropriate when the judge agrees with the substantive result': J Lee, 'Fides et ratio: Precedent in the early jurisprudence of the UK Supreme Court' (2015) 21(1) *European Journal of Current Legal Issues*.

[80] See eg *Welsh Ministers v PJ* [2018] UKSC 66; [2020] AC 757 at [21] (Lady Hale).

[81] See Karl Llewellyn's scathing review of AL Goodhart's work: (1935) 83(3) *Pennsylvania Law Review* 396, 398.

[82] see L Baum, *The Puzzle of Judicial Behavior* (Michigan, 1997) 72–74; W Eskridge and L Baer, 'The continuum of deference: Supreme Court treatment of agency statutory interpretations from Chevron

dimension to judicial decision-making in this context, as there is with so many others[83] and the facts, law and wider context of each individual case will heavily influence each judge's decision as to whether to follow the existing law. However, individual preferences may still play a part. Some judges will naturally think that incorrect cases should be corrected readily, so that 'ghosts of the past' should not 'stand in the path of justice',[84] whereas for others a departure from existing precedent should only occur in a truly 'exceptional' case'.[85] Indeed, Lord Dyson has suggested that certain judges are 'acutely conscious of precedent and the need for certainty' when it comes to stare decisis, whilst others show 'an altogether more adventurous spirit' in this respect;[86] other judges, past and present, have expressed similar sentiments.[87] The remainder of this section investigates whether there is any evidence of such differences when it comes to the judges of the UKSC, and if so, which kind of approach is favoured by which judges.

A. Measuring Approaches to Precedent

For present purposes, cases considered to raise a relevant 'precedent issue' were those in which the correctness of a previous decision of the Supreme Court and/or the House of Lords was actively considered. Usually, those cases considering previous decisions of the Court of Appeal did not count as a relevant decision as such authorities do not constitute a binding precedent upon the Supreme Court in and of themselves, although they may on occasion constitute a useful tool for identifying whether a strong line of authority exists. Exceptionally, however, cases which evaluated the status of very longstanding precedents originating in lower courts (particularly if that precedent was decided at a time before the current hierarchy of the courts was established) were marked as relevant for this section. Cases

to Hamdan' (2008) 96(4) *Georgetown Law Journal* 1083, 1120. However, at least one study found no particularly strong attitudes towards precedent: E Segal and H Spaeth, 'The Influence of Stare Decisis on the Votes of United States Supreme Court Justices' (1996) 40(4) *American Journal of Political Science* 971.

[83] For example, in *Lukaszewski* (n 35) Lady Hale suggested that she would be prepared to depart from precedent but that, owing to her colleagues' lack of enthusiasm, she ultimately chose not to ([54]).

[84] The quote is Lord Atkin's. In full, it reads: 'When … ghosts of the past stand in the path of justice clanking their medieval chains, the proper course for the judge is to pass through them undeterred': *United Australia v Barclays Bank* [1941] AC 1, 29. Indeed, in one case, Lord Bridge felt able to depart from precedent which he himself authored simply by saying that 'the opinion I expressed was simply mistaken': *R v IAT ex p Patel* [1988] AC 910, 922.

[85] See Lords Hoffmann, Carswell and Mance in *Gibson v USA* [2007] UKPC 52; [2007] 1 WLR 2367 at [38].

[86] Lord Dyson, 'The Shifting Sands of Statutory Interpretation', (Statute Law Society, 9 October 2010) 3. See also Lord Dyson, 'Are the Judges Too Powerful?' in *Justice: Continuity and Change* (Hart Publishing, 2018) 56: 'It is an inescapable fact that some judges are more conservative than others. Some are cautious and prefer to paddle in the warm and safe shadows of clear precedent. Others are more adventurous and are prepared to give it a go in the far more treacherous waters of the open sea'.

[87] See eg Lord Wright (n 70) at 138–39. Academics have also said as much: 'there seem to be differences as to precedential reasoning from Justice to Justice and from case to case': Lee (n 79).

which examined the propriety of earlier – otherwise binding – case law in light of subsequent decisions of the European Court of Human Rights were also treated as relevant. Whilst most cases naturally dealt with questions of precedent as part of the ratio decidendi of the case, in the very few cases where a definitive view as to the appropriateness of following precedent was expressed as part of obiter dicta, this was also marked as relevant.

As with other areas, approaches were coded according to a binary scale (1 for following precedent, 0 for departing from it, 0.5 for any mixed or conflicting approach). On a practical level, coding often followed the arguments of the parties; sometimes, the Court was specifically asked to depart from precedent, and sometimes the prospect of departure was foreclosed by the nature of submissions. Otherwise, the main issue related to what exactly constituted a *departure* from precedent in practice. A case which is strongly and firmly distinguished (or indeed, distinguished on a 'fine basis')[88] can seem no different, in practice, from a case which is considered to have been overruled in practice, despite there being no explicit judicial statement to this effect. Similarly, a disputed precedent may be formally upheld by a court, but it may have been reinterpreted to such a degree that the actual substance of the earlier decision seems to have been abandoned. In cases like these, the question of whether there has been a departure from an earlier case becomes difficult to determine.[89] For the purposes of this section, to be considered relevant, the judge in a given case must *actually* choose whether or not to follow an earlier authority; criticism of that earlier case, no matter how trenchant, was treated as immaterial. Equally, cases where a judge simply raised the possibility that an earlier case may have been wrongly decided, or suggested that a case may be overruled at some future point, were not counted. However, departure was sometimes recognised, exceptionally, where an authority had for all practical purposes, been totally abandoned in reality. Again, a pragmatic approach was adopted where a departure was marked in cases where a line of precedent was technically upheld but made subject to such a significant degree of qualification or modification that it no longer really resembled the original authority.[90]

Something of an identification bias may have been in play when identifying and coding these issues. When an otherwise binding authority was departed from, this was usually fairly easy to spot as it was typically mentioned explicitly in the judgment, even if the Court considered it a relatively obvious and uncontroversial move. However, when an authority was followed, the Court did not always necessarily draw attention to this because following existing authority was considered the expected course in a precedent-based system. The Court does not necessarily

[88] *Haile* (n 77) at [69] (Lord Neuberger).

[89] See Cross and Harris (n 68) 129–35.

[90] An example of a case where this kind of practical departure occurred was the case in *ParkingEye v Beavis* [2015] UKSC 67; [2016] AC 1172, where the classic approach in *Dunlop Pneumatic Tyre Co Ltd v New Garage and Motor Co Ltd* [1915] AC 79 was technically upheld but modified to such an extent that the law had, in effect, changed significantly.

make it explicit which authorities are questioned or challenged in argument; where the notion of departing from existing precedent is considered particularly remote or fanciful, the fact that said authority was questioned in the first place may not even appear in the written judgment. As such, there is a possibility that certain decisions in which judges choose to uphold precedent slip 'under the radar' to some extent. Whilst unavoidable to a degree, awareness of this possibility meant that the coding exercise was done more carefully, with particular attention given to any statements suggesting that departure was put forward by parties, or was otherwise seriously argued or contemplated by the Court.

As was the case with the coding of approaches to statutory interpretation in Section I above, sometimes certain uses of language could provide 'clues' as to whether a judge was choosing to depart from the law. Sometimes the Court explicitly confirmed that precedent 'should not be followed'[91] or that it would 'depart'[92] or 'decline to follow'[93] it. In others, the Court declared that the previous authority was 'mistaken'[94] 'incorrect'[95] or 'wrongly decided';[96] that subsequent developments had 'fatally undermined'[97] its authority; that it had 'no basis'[98] or represented a 'wrong turn';[99] that it should be 'consigned to history',[100] that a 'contrary' approach should be adopted,[101] or that the case had been 'replaced'[102] or 'superseded'.[103] On the other hand, when adhering to precedent, in addition to using language indicating the converse of the above, for example, that the Court should 'not depart' from precedent or that it would be 'wrong' to do so, occasionally the Court used positive language to connote adherence to law, such as where authorities were described as being 'clearly right'.[104] The use of such language by judges was rarely completely prescriptive, but nevertheless often provided a useful indicator of the approach adopted.

[91] See eg *NML Capital v Argentina* [2011] UKSC 31; [2011] 2 AC 495 at [78] (Lord Phillips).

[92] See eg *Michael v Chief Constable of South Wales Police* [2015] UKSC 2; [2015] 1 AC 1732 at [128] (Lord Toulson).

[93] See eg *Lukaszewski* (n 35) at [17] (Lord Mance).

[94] See eg *Takhar v Gracefield Developments* [2019] UKSC 13; [2020] AC 450 at [65] (Lord Sumption).

[95] See eg *Williams v Central Bank of Nigeria* [2014] UKSC 10; [2014] AC 1189 at [89] (Lord Neuberger).

[96] See eg *R (Lord Carlile) v Secretary of State for the Home Department* [2014] UKSC 60; [2015] 1 AC 945 at [81] (Lord Neuberger).

[97] See eg *Zurich Insurance v International Energy Group* [2015] UKSC 33; [2016] AC 509 at [27] (Lord Mance).

[98] See eg *Khuja* (n 70) at [56] (Lords Kerr and Wilson).

[99] See eg *R v Jogee* [2016] UKSC 8; [2017] AC 387 at [67] (Lords Hughes and Toulson).

[100] See eg *Robinson v Chief Constable of West Yorkshire Police* [2018] UKSC 4; [2018] AC 736 at [113] (Lord Hughes).

[101] See eg *Prudential Assurance Company v HMRC* [2018] UKSC 39; [2019] AC 929 at [71] (Lords Mance, Reed and Hodge).

[102] See eg *Mohamud v WM Morrison Supermarkets* [2016] UKSC 11; [2016] AC 677 at [51] (Lord Dyson).

[103] See eg *Al-Waheed v Ministry of Defence* [2017] UKSC 2; [2017] AC 821 at [307] (Lord Reed).

[104] See eg *Re B* [2016] UKSC 4; [2016] AC 606 at [80] (Lord Sumption).

B. Precedent: Results

To begin, Figure 7 sets out the base statistics for each judge according to how likely they were to uphold and follow existing precedent. Those judges more likely to uphold precedent score highly and are placed to the right of the scale; those more likely to depart from it have a lower 'score' and are placed towards the left.

Figure 7 Likelihood of upholding precedent (all votes)

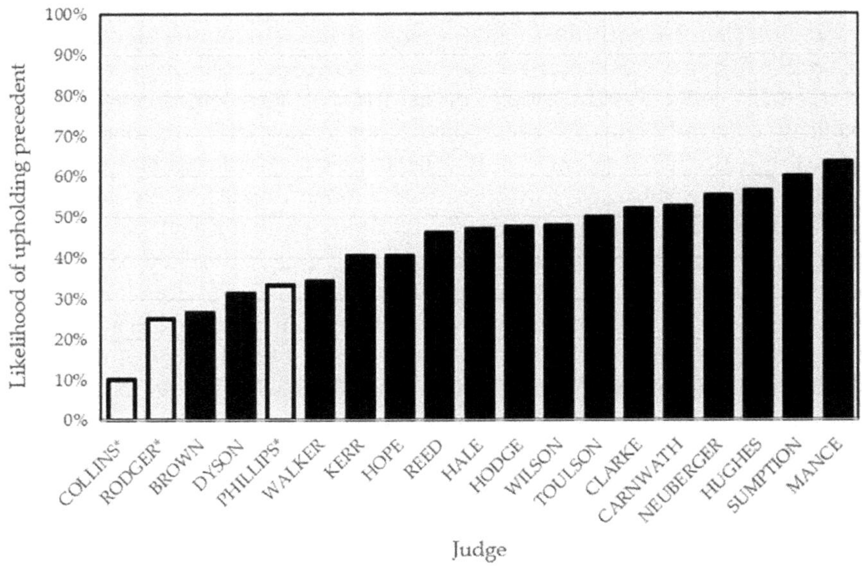

Lee has suggested that the Supreme Court has shown something of a reluctance to overturn existing precedent[105] but the data presented here suggests that this is not necessarily the case overall.[106] According to Figure 7 the average judge was more likely to depart from an earlier authority than to follow it when the status of the earlier authority was expressly considered[107] (however, this may, at least in part, result from the inherent identification bias mentioned above).

With regard to the positions of individual judges, Figure 7 shows something of a variance between them (the variance is greater than that which can be seen in in Figure 1 with respect to statutory interpretation, for example). The judge who

[105] Lee (n 79).

[106] Lee adopted a stricter definition of what constitutes a 'departure from precedent' than the more holistic one used in the current study, and looks at overall case outcomes rather than the sum of individual votes. In another article, Lee suggests that the UKSC cases involving precedent issues illustrate the differing attitudes held by individual judges: J Lee, 'Judging Reformers and Reforming Judges' (2019) 21 *European Journal of Law Reform* 15.

[107] Average = 43.09%; when less robust data is excluded, average = 46.9%.

was least likely to follow existing precedent, and thus most likely to depart from contested authorities, was Lord Collins. Although his data is somewhat less robust than that of others, he followed the previous case law in just one of the ten relevant cases he decided (which means that he voted to *depart from* an earlier decision in nine of the ten cases in which he sat, where this was an express consideration). He and Lord Rodger upheld existing precedent less than one-quarter of the time, whereas Lords Sumption and Mance chose to adhere to contested authorities more than 60 per cent of the time. As with other areas, further granulation was achieved by looking first at each judge's approach to precedent in salient cases (those where the judges involved were divided as to the treatment of existing authorities). As with other assessments of salient cases in this work, each judge's score was based on how their position in a case compared to that of their fellow judges.[108] The results are set out in Figure 8.

Figure 8 Likelihood of upholding precedent (salient cases only)

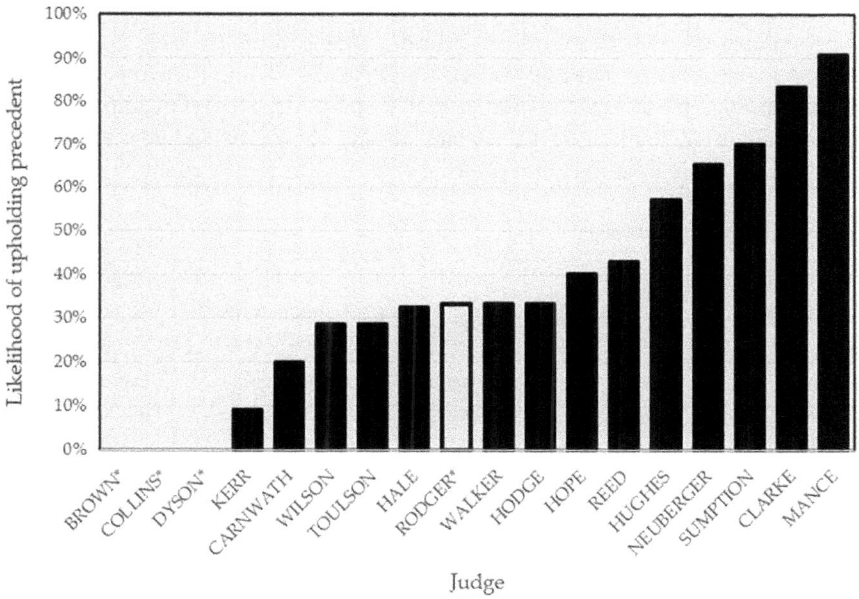

We once again see familiar judges at both ends of the table; Lords Mance and Sumption, relatively likely to adhere to precedent according to Figure 7, once again appear as 'pro-precedent' judges in Figure 8, whilst judges such as Lords Collins, Brown and Dyson appear again at the other side of the table, indicating a 'pro-departure' position.

[108] Because the question of whether precedent is followed is usually expressed as a binary output, this usually only necessitated modifying the coding where multiple precedents were evaluated within the same case, or the occasional case in which the judges differed as to whether to depart from an authority in part or in full.

Indeed, some of the judges' positions here are fairly remarkable; in salient cases, Lord Clarke voted to follow established authorities more rigorously than his colleagues just over 83 per cent of the time, whilst Lord Sumption did so in just under 91 per cent of cases. When it came to hard cases which pulled the judges in different directions, these judges clearly placed a premium on certainty and consistency. On the other end of the scale, Lords Brown, Collins and Dyson each voted to depart from precedent in every single salient case in which they sat (although given that each decided only three relevant cases, perhaps too much should not be gleamed from this). Lords Kerr and Carnwath, however, *did* decide enough cases to generate reliable data, and they only voted to follow contested precedents less than 10 per cent and 20 per cent of the time, respectively. These low numbers stand in contrast to their much more moderate positions in the general precedent dataset (Figure 7) above – Lord Carnwath was in fact one of the few judges more likely to follow precedent than to depart from it overall. It seems that whilst Lords Kerr and Carnwath were happy enough with following their colleagues in voting to uphold precedent much of the time, they were nonetheless prepared to adopt a more adventurous stance in the trickiest cases, where it became particularly necessary to stake a particular claim. Their records aside, the data in Figure 8 strengthens rather than disputes the general positions set out above in Figure 7. Looking at the available results, the following table categorises, very broadly, each judge's general position with regards to precedent.

Figure 9 Precedent: summary

Most likely to depart from precedent	Leans towards departure	Middle ground position	Leans towards adherence	Most likely to adhere to precedent
Brown Collins Dyson	Kerr Rodger Walker Wilson	Carnwath Hale Hodge Hope Reed Toulson	Neuberger	Clarke Hughes Mance Sumption

As with other areas, some of the judges' positions in Figure 9 match with the tenor of their judicial and extrajudicial statements on precedent. Lord Neuberger, who, it is suggested, shows a preference for adhering to precedent, chose to emphasise, in his opening address as President, the importance of certainty in the law, for the benefit of the public as well as judges, which required caution when developing the law.[109] Elsewhere he has argued that that judges should be 'very slow' to depart from existing case law when invited to do so by parties.[110] Similarly, Lee has argued

[109] As cited by Lee (n 79) 4.
[110] *Haile* (n 77) at [73].

that Lord Sumption's extrajudicial speeches reveal an approach to the treatment of authority which is 'essentially a conservative one'.[111] That seems an accurate label for Lord Sumption's approach to precedent in practice, too. By contrast, it is hard to detect the same reverence for continuity in Lord Kerr's extrajudicial speeches. In one, he provocatively declared that 'certainty or finality in the law is an over-rated concept'.[112] This certainly fits with the results in this section, which show that Lord Kerr's more limited appreciation for finality was frequently outweighed by his desire to do justice in a particular case or to change the law to keep up with the times. Finally, writing extrajudicially, Lord Dyson once remarked:

> It is an inescapable fact that some judges are more conservative than others. Some are cautious and prefer to paddle in the warm and safe shadows of clear precedent. Others are more adventurous and are prepared to give it a go in the far more treacherous waters of the open sea.[113]

Not only would this chapter suggest that Lord Dyson is correct, but that he himself is a prime example of such an 'adventurous' judge, prepared to depart from precedent even in those circumstances where his colleagues may prefer to hold onto it.

Finally, it is worth noting something about the temporal aspect of the data above. It appears that those judges appointed at the beginning of the period surveyed were more likely to depart from precedent than those appointed more recently. Five of the seven judges occupying the 'likely to depart' or 'leans towards departure' columns in Figure 9 formed part of the Court's inaugural roster, whereas only two of the five judges in the 'likely to adhere' or 'leans towards adherence' columns formed a part of this initial line-up. Whilst the numbers suggest that there may be *some* positive correlation between a judge's date of appointment (and/or date of tenure) and their likelihood to depart from precedent (in short, older judges tend to be more likely to depart, newer appointments tend to be more likely to adhere), the correlation is not strong.[114] One temporal trend which did emerge was that the judges were given many more *opportunities* to consider its earlier case law during its earlier period, leading to a greater number of votes cast both for and against departing from precedent. This should not, in theory, affect the results in Figures 7 and 8 which show how *likely* each judge was to adhere to precedent, rather than how many opportunities they had to vote on this issue. Insofar as there is a *modest* correlation between early appointees and a tendency to depart from case law, one explanation could be that the creation of a new Supreme Court, which (correctly or otherwise) was portrayed as being newly independent

[111] J Lee, 'The Judicial Individuality of Lord Sumption' 31 *UNSW Law Journal* 862, 862.

[112] Lord Kerr, 'Dissenting judgments – self-indulgence or self-sacrifice?' (The Birkinhead Lecture, 8 October 2012) 12.

[113] Lord Dyson, 'Are the judges too powerful' (n 86) 56.

[114] Using a very crude measure (where each judge was given a numerical score between 0 and 1 depending on their column placement in Figure 9), there is a broadly positive correlation between adherence to precedent and recentness of appointment (.801** (0)). There was, however, no significant correlation between the results presented in this section and the binary question of whether a judge sat on the Court's starting roster or not.

of the executive, may have implicitly encouraged a more 'activist' approach to precedent in the minds of its inaugural judges. This may also have influenced litigants, resulting in more adventurous arguments being made before the Court. Alternatively, the reason may simply be that the judges appointed during the Court's earlier period simply held different attitudes towards precedent, certainty and continuity than those appointed during its later years.

As such, the answer to the question of what explains the variance in judicial attitudes towards precedent demonstrated in this chapter is a complicated one. The judges' individual preferences towards precedent are unlikely to provide a sufficient explanation for their voting behaviour in and of themselves, given that something as simple as the time of appointment may also play a considerable role. Indeed, the temporal aspect described here is likely to constitute one of many, largely unobservable, competing influences on judicial behaviour in this context. To claim that individual judicial preferences provide the *only* explanation for judicial behaviour would be extremely naïve (and, indeed, this has never been the claim of this chapter, or any chapter in this work). However, whilst individual preferences cannot tell the whole story, the data presented in this section strongly suggests that individual preferences do have *some* role, and perhaps a more significant role than was previously thought, when it comes to determining questions relating to precedent. Preferences may not play out in a vacuum, but neither are they completely drowned out by the noise of other influences. Certain judges clearly show greater reluctance, *across the board*, to depart from authorities compared to their colleagues. This finding is significant in and of itself.

III. Jurisdiction

Before a judge can examine issues such as the status of precedent and the meaning of a statute, they must first determine that they have the jurisdiction to consider the dispute before them. The exercise of determining whether the court is empowered to answer certain kinds of questions is intensely important from a constitutional perspective, not least because the question often requires the court to determine whether they are *better placed* to answer certain questions than other bodies, such as the legislature, public bodies, or other courts. The issue is, naturally, also important for the parties in a case: without demonstrating that the court has jurisdiction to consider their legal claim, they can have no chance of getting the outcome they want (or indeed, any outcome at all). This next section examines how likely each judge is to recognise or expand the Court's jurisdiction across various contexts, and whether this indicates anything about their view as to the Court's institutional (or even *constitutional*) competency to address certain issues.[115]

[115] The terms *institutional* and *constitutional* competency are borrowed from the speeches in the case of *R (Nicklinson) v Ministry of Justice* [2014] UKSC 38; [2015] 1 AC 657 (see especially Lord Neuberger's judgment).

Because the Court ordinarily proceeds to assess the substance of a claim before it without expressly considering the existence of, or the extent of, its jurisdiction beforehand, it is clearly the case that the Court has jurisdiction in the vast majority of cases it considers (indeed, if the Court self-evidently lacked jurisdiction to consider a particular issue, it would be unlikely to grant permission to bring the corresponding claim in the first place). Therefore, in line with the approach taken elsewhere, only those cases in which the extent of the Court's jurisdiction arose as a distinct, live issue in proceedings were marked under this section. This section also includes cases where the jurisdiction of the courts in general, rather than the Supreme Court specifically, was challenged, but *only* where the dispute required determining whether a *judicial body* had jurisdiction to decide the case rather than *a non-judicial body* (for example, a dispute as to whether a national security decision could be reviewed by courts *at all* would be treated as a relevant case for the purposes of this section, whereas a dispute as to whether a certain claim should be heard by the Civil or Criminal Division of the Court of Appeal would not; this latter issue would not involve determining whether a judicial body as opposed to a non-judicial body had jurisdiction to hear the case). The source of the jurisdiction (in some areas the Court derives its authority from statute, but it holds inherent jurisdiction in others) was generally considered irrelevant for present purposes. A 'jurisdiction question' would sometimes arise in the abstract, or on the facts of a given case, or both. All instances where a court considered its jurisdiction in some detail were marked (even if the answer to the question did not, strictly speaking, affect the outcome in the case).

On a number of occasions, the Court has described the question of whether an individual is able to bring a case to the Court on the facts (for example, whether the case was brought within a certain period of time) as raising a 'jurisdictional' issue. Therefore, the present dataset also included those cases which concern matters such as time bars and immunities, as well as cases where it is claimed that issues were conclusively determined at an earlier stage or are unsuitable for legal determination. Where appropriate, cases which dealt with questions of standing or an individual's right of action to bring a case were also included, so long as the determination of these issues was required as a preliminary issue to govern whether the court could consider the claim at all.

A jurisdiction 'win' was recognised wherever the Court's jurisdiction was recognised or expanded. Coding cases involving jurisdictional clashes was difficult and resolved as follows: if the question considered by the Court was whether the national or foreign *court* should deal with issues, this was coded as a jurisdiction 'win' if it was found that the issue should be dealt with by the Court itself or another domestic court. Where cases involved a question of which laws apply (eg national or foreign law) to the case, this was not usually treated as raising a jurisdictional issue for present purposes unless there was an active dispute as to whether the Court had the competence to apply one or more of these laws. The same applied to cases in which the Court's task was to determine *which* rules or legal frameworks applied to the case; this was not treated as a relevant jurisdiction case, because in such cases the Court's jurisdiction to determine matters under *some* framework was not questioned.

The dataset contained enough cases to generate workable records for 22 judges, 15 resting on more significant data. Overall, judges seemed quite comfortable with the concept of an enlarged jurisdiction, with 17 judges being more likely to recognise rather than reject jurisdiction in a given case on average. The lowest-ranked judge whose position was based on comparatively reliable data – Lord Walker – still voted in favour of recognising jurisdiction nearly half the time. The judicial spread here is not huge, although Lord Kerr notably stands out from the pack, voting in favour of recognising jurisdiction in 82 per cent of cases, a very high number even in the context of a relatively generous attitude towards jurisdiction held by judges in general in this set.

Figure 10 Finding jurisdiction (all cases)

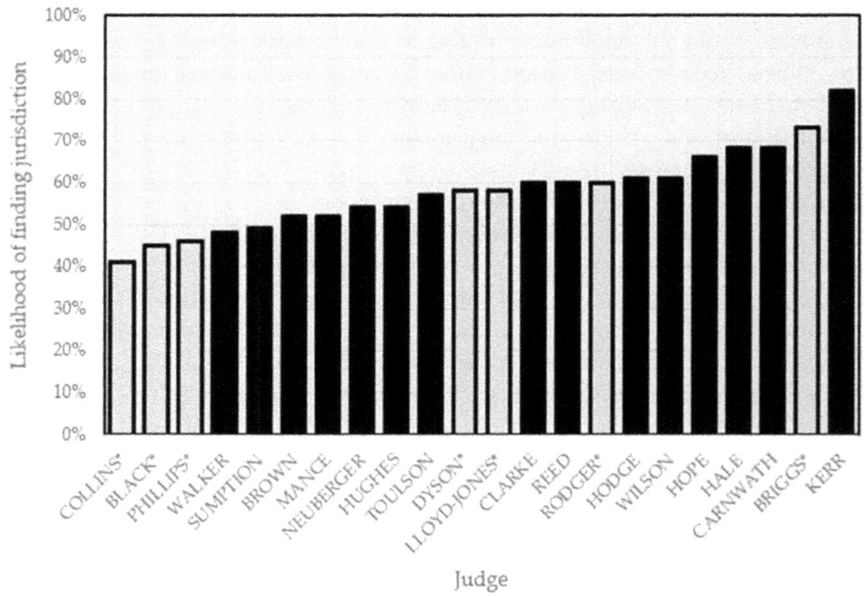

Of these cases, 31 were identified as salient, in that they featured an internal division on the panel as to the jurisdiction issue. Sixteen judges decided enough of these cases to be worth counting, and ten judges decided enough cases to generate *more reliable data*. Each judge's approach to salient cases is set out in Figure 11.

In this table, the judges' positions are now spread much more widely; although the higher-placing judges have comparable 'scores' in both Figure 10 and Figure 11, the lowest-scoring judge in the latter, Lord Sumption, who voted in favour of jurisdiction across all cases (Figure 10), falls 40 points to a 'score' of just 8 per cent in salient cases. This is a particularly striking record (based on more significant data no less) – only in one salient case did he vote for recognising a comparably wider

Figure 11 Finding jurisdiction (salient cases)

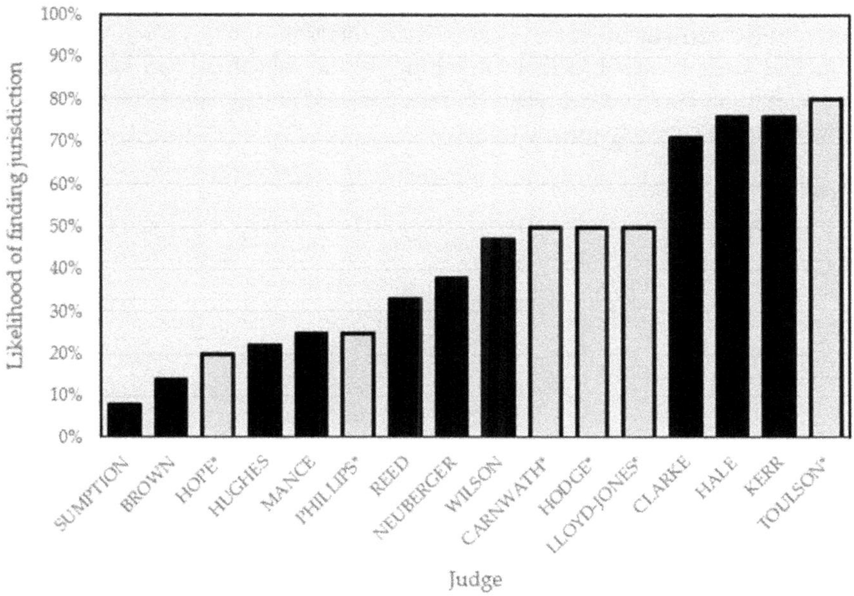

conception of the Court's jurisdiction compared to his colleagues.[116] On the other end of the scale, Lord Toulson's score of 80 per cent is also impressive, although his inclusion in the dataset here is based on votes in a fairly small handful of salient cases (the records of other high-scorers in Figure 11 did not suffer from this problem, however; both Lady Hale and Lord Kerr sat on more than half of the salient jurisdiction cases in the dataset). Although it is wholly expected that filtering for salient cases would produce a more significant spread of data-points, the difference in Figure 11, with records spanning from 8 per cent to 80 per cent, is particularly noteworthy.

As ever, many of the results outlined in this section seem to match with judicial statements by certain judges. Lady Hale, for example, has suggested that, in human rights cases, 'there are no "no go" areas' for the Court, even when issues such as economic policy are concerned,[117] and seemed to accept, with relative ease, something of a 'universal jurisdiction' for the Court in *B*, a family law case.[118] In that same case, Lord Sumption expressed a distinct lack of ease with Lady Hale's position.[119] This lines up neatly with the views he has expressed extrajudicially,

[116] Although in two further cases he was technically marked as advocating a mixed approach, owing to multiple distinct issues arising in those cases.

[117] *R (DA and DS) v Secretary of State for Work and Pensions* [2019] UKSC 21; [2019] WLR 3289 at [133].

[118] *B* (n 104).

[119] *B* (n 104) at [81]–[87].

favouring a recalibration of political power away from the judiciary and towards the province of the executive and legislature.[120] Adopting a narrower conception of the Court's jurisdiction in cases where this is disputed is surely consistent with that vision. Indeed, it is unsurprising to find that these two judges, Hale and Sumption, bookend the relatively wide range of positions held by individual judges when it comes to jurisdiction.

Figure 12 Jurisdiction overview

Results	
UKSC tendency as a whole	Likely to recognise
Likely to recognise jurisdiction	*Lady Hale; Lord Kerr, Clarke*
Unlikely to recognise jurisdiction	*Lords Sumption, Brown, Hughes, Mance*

IV. Remedies

Finally, this section examines judicial approaches to remedies and damages: supposing the Court recognises a legal wrong, how far should it go, if at all, to remedy that wrong? How far should it ensure that its findings are adhered to and followed properly? Should a judge limit themselves to merely identifying unlawful action and declaring that a wrong has occurred, or should the court also play a further role in punishing, compensating or rewarding parties?

The question of whether an action is lawful, or otherwise gives rise to liability of some kind, is distinct from the question of which remedy, if any, should be given in relation to this. As such, preferences relating to remedies may be distinct from the kind of subject outcome preferences examined in elsewhere in this chapter, and the chapters before it. Preferences relating to remedies may also reflect a distinct set of considerations relating to the judicial role and the position of judges compared to other constitutional actors: who should be responsible for determining the consequences of adverse legal findings? How prescriptive should the court be, when determining the kind of response which should follow? Is the court's role to simply restore any losses, or to compensate for something further? Judges may differ between themselves as to what the answers to such questions ought to be. Further, judges generally have quite a significant discretion as to which remedies to award and how significant they ought to be (indeed, it has been found that judges exhibit a greater variance when it comes to awarding punitive damages in tort compared to juries).[121] As such, there is ample room in this context for the 'seepage' of personal preferences and victim sympathies on the part of the judges.

[120] See Sumption J, *Trials of the State* (Profile Books, 2019).

[121] J Goudkamp and E Katsampouka, 'An Empirical Study of Punitive Damages' (2018) 38 *Oxford Journal of Legal Studies* 90.

Remedies, whether potential or actual, are part and parcel of almost all cases decided by the UKSC. Therefore, qualifying cases in this section are limited to those where the question of which remedy to impose or reward arises as a distinct live issue, separate from any consideration of liability (as such, cases where the Court's determination of the applicable remedy was *entirely dependent* on whether there had in fact been a breach of law did not qualify for the purposes of this section, because in such cases there was no consideration of damages as a *distinct issue separate from liability*).

Each judge's approach was recorded according to the generosity of their approach. A 'generous' approach was recorded: first, in cases where the judges were asked to determine whether a remedy should be given or not, when a judge did in fact award a remedy; second, in cases where the judges were asked whether the court has the power or the jurisdiction to award a certain remedy, when a judge recognised that they were able to award that remedy; third, in cases where there was no dispute that a remedy should be awarded, when a judge awarded a comparatively more substantial award, generosity was also determined by reference to what the parties sought and what the Court considered. Therefore, for example, an award of fairly moderate damages may be considered 'generous' in the context of a case where the only possible alternative would be for the Court to grant no damages at all, but might not be considered so 'generous' in the context of a case where some measure of compensation was reasonably anticipated, and the moderate amount was selected by the Court in preference to some higher sum claimed by parties. Cases where the Court considered issues surrounding remedies which did not relate to their existence or their generosity (eg where the Court determined which agency would pay damages) were not considered relevant to this section. Cases where different kinds of non-monetary remedies were considered by the Court, and one was chosen over another, were also generally discarded, unless one of the remedies was self-evidently more substantial than the other (for example, a mandatory order was considered to be more generous than declaratory relief). Defining the generosity of remedies with respect to party arguments and contemplated alternatives is, of course, somewhat artificial, but it is suggested that it is much less problematic an approach than one which attempts to proscribe some artificial dividing line between an objectively generous amount and an objectively ungenerous amount in the abstract.

Figure 13 shows each how likely each judge was to vote in favour of awarding a generous remedy, defined in these terms. The judges falling to the right-hand side of the graph, with a higher 'score', tended to award more generous remedies overall; those to the left, with a lower score, were less generous overall.

The average score is just over 48 per cent, meaning that on average judges tended to be just as likely to award a generous remedy as they were to award a less generous one. Lords Hodge and Wilson appear to be the judges most inclined to grant generous remedies, whilst Lords Hope and Phillips were the least likely to do so. Having said that, the range of positions amongst the judges is not significant. There is, however, a broadly positive correlation between the time period of

Figure 13 Likelihood of adopting a wide approach to statutory interpretation (all votes)

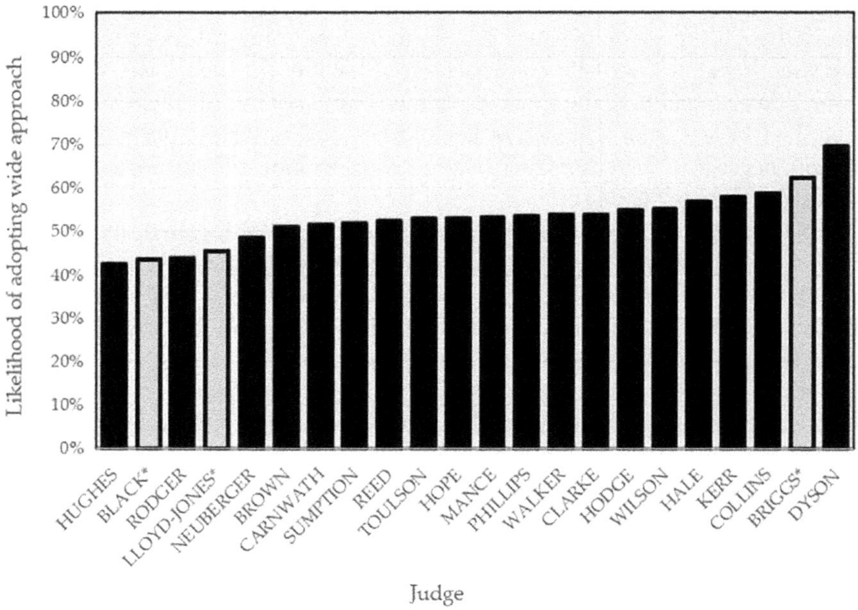

a judge's tenure and their propensity to award more generous remedies, with the four most generous judges sitting on the Court during the end-point of the dataset (October 2019) and judges such as Lords Hope and Phillips, less generous judges, sitting during its earlier period. This correlation is notable but imperfect.[122]

Turning to salient cases, 21 cases can be identified across the ten-year period surveyed; 14 judges decided enough cases to provide usable data, and nine enough to provide more significant data. Their records are shown in Figure 14.

In this case, as with many others, the salient dataset reveals judicial records featuring a much more significant spread. Lady Hale stands out here, who opted for a comparatively generous remedy in over 70 per cent of salient cases in which she sat, leapfrogging the colleagues who 'outranked' her in Figure 13. Lords Hodge and Carnwath continue to remain relatively likely to adopt a generous position according to Figure 14. The same cannot be said for Lord Wilson; despite his placement in Figure 13, when it comes to salient cases he exhibited a tendency to show far greater conservatism, as he was coded as preferring to award a more generous remedy than his colleagues only 21 per cent of the time, making him the second-lowest ranking judge. In contract to the results in Figure 13, there appears to be little correlation between the judges' period of tenure and their likelihood to grant higher damages in salient cases.[123]

[122] p=.48* with a significance of .035 (one-tailed t-test, significant at the 0.05 level).
[123] p=.024 with no statistical significance (.467).

Figure 14 Generosity of remedies (salient cases)

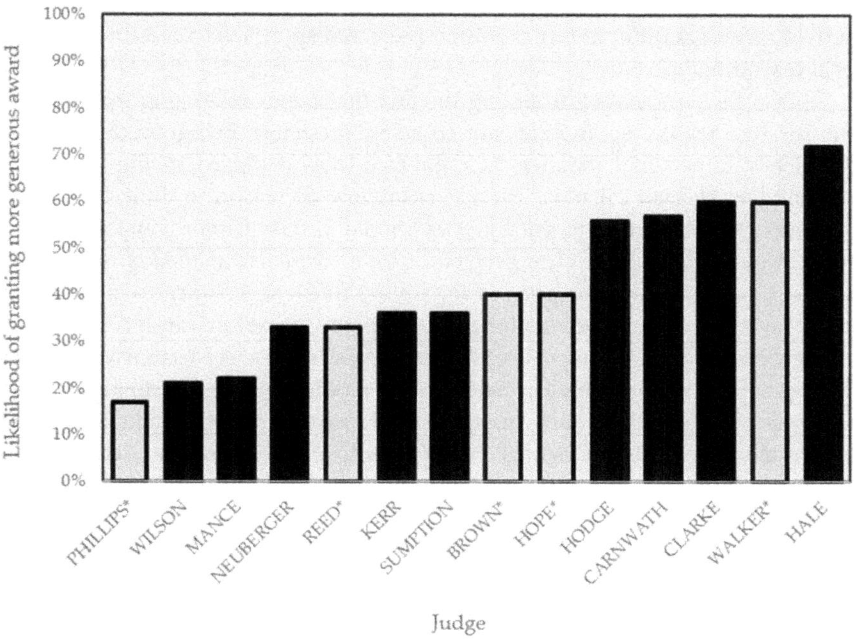

Figure 15 presents a final overview of the judges' positions in relation to remedies.

Figure 15 Remedies overview

Results	
UKSC tendency as a whole	Neither generous nor ungenerous
Likely to grant more generous remedy	*Lady Hale; Lords Carnwath, Hodge*
Unlikely to grant more generous remedy	*Lords Wilson, Mance, Phillips*

V. Conclusions

This chapter has explored the records of individual judges when it comes to questions surrounding statutory interpretation, precedent, jurisdiction and remedies. These issues are absolutely central to the determination of legal questions across case law boundaries and the judges' approach to them may matter just as much as, if nor more than, specific doctrinal positions or party sympathies. It has been shown that even the most fundamental judicial tasks – the interpretation of statute, the application of own case law – cannot in practice be completely separated from the identity of the individual judges performing such tasks and the values and preferences they hold. It is not only in terms of case outcomes that the preferences of individual judges can be measured. Rather, there is evidence that individual judges differ in terms of their preferred approach to certain aspects of legal reasoning, too.

This is the case, notwithstanding the fact that issues relating to *legal reasoning*, for one reason or another, are so often presented being conducted in a completely impersonal manner, as value-free tools deployed in the pursuance of some Dworkinian calculus. There is absolutely no reason to think that this is any more true in relation to the issues examined in this chapter compared to any other. A judge may have a clear preference for a *particular method of interpreting statutes* or a *particular conception of the Court's inherent jurisdiction* in much the same way as they might have an inherent sympathy for certain kinds of party, or a strong view as to the proper role of the executive. Indeed, as I have tried to claim throughout this chapter, these preferences are very likely to be interlinked; a judge may resist widening the Court's jurisdiction *precisely because* they take a sceptical, conservative view as to the rightful extent of judicial power. They may cling tightly to precedents because they prize certainty and consistency over the desirability of following changing norms. We may think it more *legitimate*, or certainly less inappropriate, for all kinds of reasons, for judges' views on the kinds of legal questions assessed in this chapter to affect their judging role, as opposed to factors such as party sympathy. But the influence remains all the same.

Further, the variety between the judges when it comes to their approach to interpretation, precedent, jurisdiction and remedies may cause us to find more attractive the realists' claim that legal reasoning is simply deployed as 'an illusion … to convey the delusive impression that … law can be settled by virtue of a set of objective rules'[124] (for how objective can a rule like stare decisis be, if the judges apply it in totally different ways in practice?); constructs such as precedent and Parliamentary intention surely have the *potential* to provide judges with useful artefacts under which to employ a more creative mode of reasoning, or perhaps, in the eyes of some, a lack of reasoning altogether.[125] But we should also consider that the above results make a strong claim in their favour: they show that (some) judges take these legal tools *seriously*, even if they do not all apply them in the same way.[126] A judge may take a particular approach to precedent which is different from that of their colleagues, but in applying that approach consistently, across

[124] A Ross, *On Law and Justice* (California Press, 1959) 88.

[125] Commitment to legal realism is not needed to imagine this prospect. In *Haile* (n 77) Lord Carnwath criticised Lord Reed for adopting a new position under the guise of 'clarifying' the existing law and having 'undertaken his own re-analysis of [the case law] in a way which had not suggested by the parties before us, nor (to my knowledge) by anyone else in the three decades since it was decided' ([89]).

[126] JAG Griffith theorised that individual judges do not apply legal reasoning in a consistent manner: J Griffith, *Politics of the Judiciary*, 5th edn (Fontana Press, 1997) 283–85. On this, at least when it comes to *some* of the UKSC judges, Griffith appears to be mistaken.

different areas of law, that judge is applying *their understanding of how precedent should work* above other considerations, such as party sympathy.

If, as I have argued in this work, it is practically inescapable that a judge's personal preferences will affect what they do in the courtroom, it becomes more important to consider which *kinds* of preferences – political or legal, doctrinal or ideological – we might be more comfortable expecting to see in practice, and what consequences this may, or may not, have when it comes to the authority and legitimacy of the judiciary.

9

Politics and Personalities

I. Introduction

In one interview, Lord Sumption professed: 'I don't have a judicial ideology'.[1] Not only is this denial unsurprising, but it is also representative of the position adopted by most judges, at least on the record.

There may, of course, be good reasons to doubt whether what Lord Sumption, and other judges, say is true. Griffith (in)famously painted the judiciary as conservative and out of touch with its members, even the so-called reformers and progressives amongst them, principally concerned with protecting their own status and social class more than anything else.[2] Griffith's judges certainly had a judicial ideology. The conventional perception in the UK seems to be that our senior judges are: (a) traditional figures, (b) part of the establishment (however this is conceived), and (c) on the right of the political spectrum.[3] As Stevens put it, '[o]ne suspects most normally voted Tory'.[4] If this is true, why would these conservative ideologues tip their hand? It would make great sense for them to try and portray themselves as apolitical and neutral. They could, *of course*, deny any judicial ideology.

However, more recently there has been something of a shift to a popular vision of the UK judiciary as a more liberal institution overall.[5] The senior judges are viewed in some quarters as 'soft' in some areas, such as where human rights are concerned,[6] in immigration cases,[7] or when it comes to sentencing

[1] W Steavenson, 'Jonathan Sumption: the brain of Britain' *The Guardian* (6 August 2015) www.theguardian.com/law/2015/aug/06/jonathan-sumption-brain-of-britain.

[2] J Griffith, *Politics of the Judiciary*, 5th edn (Fontana Press, 1997).

[3] R Stevens, *The English Judges: Their Role in the Changing Constitution* (Hart Publishing, 2002) 462; 116; L Moran, 'In Conversation with Lord Justice Etherton: judicial legitimacy, diversity and the representation of judicial authority' [2010] *PL* 662, 668; P Darbyshire, *Sitting in Judgment* (Hart Publishing, 2011) 19–23.

[4] Stevens, ibid 58. Backed up by J Waltman, 'The Courts in England' in J Waltman and K Holland, *The Political Role of Law Courts in Modern Democracies* (Macmillan, 1988) 117.

[5] A Gearey, W Morrison and R Jago, *The Politics of the Common Law*, 2nd edn (Routledge, 2013) 190, 193.

[6] Lord Dyson has remarked that in human rights cases, the senior judiciary has been seen as a threat to the establishment: Lord Dyson, 'Criticising Judges: Fair Game or Off-Limits?' (Third Annual Bailii Lecture, 27 November 2014).

[7] Campbell has claimed that 'tribunals and courts hearing asylum and immigration cases have repeatedly refused to give effect to government policies the substance of which they do not favour, and

matters.[8] In light of successful challenges to the government's Brexit strategy, some media outlets characterised the senior judiciary as a whole as holding a liberal, pro-EU position.[9] Certainly, Boris Johnson's judicial reform plans seemed to be inspired, at least in part, by his feeling that the judges were straying too far into the political arena, producing decisions which were at odds with Conservative Party policy.[10] More generally, framing the judiciary as an institution espousing political values (usually liberal views or some pro-EU sentiment) which contrast to those of the government (and therefore their voter base) has seemingly proved to be a useful tool for senior Conservative party politicians facing pushback from the judiciary over their policies as well as for more outspoken Members of Parliament.[11] If this is true, and the judges hold a *liberal* judicial ideology, it makes sense that they would try very hard to portray themselves as politically neutral, too.

Paradoxically, it seems that judges are simultaneously portrayed as old guard conservatives as well as soft-hearted members of the chattering classes.[12] No doubt the political persuasion of the government of the day plays a significant part on which of these dual identities comes to the fore during any given period. But even if we thought that any of these characterisations holds true of the judiciary as a whole, this does not tell us about the views and positions of the individual judges sitting on the Supreme Court. Even if it is accepted that the Court is some hyper-conservative institution, or full of bleeding-hearts, some of its judges would surely embody that spirit more than others. This work has sought to explore the attitudes of the individual judges on the Court. This remains true in this chapter, when trying to thread together some of the political and ideological positions on

have frustrated the legislative intent of Parliament in order to do so': D Campbell, 'Decency, disobedience and democracy in immigration law' [2018] *PL* 413, 413.

[8] Darbyshire (n 3) 27–31; I Burnett, 'Lord Chief Justice: why accusations that judges have gone soft are unfounded' (Prospect, 22 January 2021). Philip Davies MP openly criticised the 'lily-livered, wet, soft, liberal judges who hand out … unduly lenient sentences' in the House of Commons (HC Deb, 10 July 2012, col. 161).

[9] See eg 'judges who will rule on Brexit impact' *Daily Mail* (7 November 2016). There is some limited support for this view from certain academics; Nicol has criticised the 'well to-do' judges with a 'class interest in Britain's continued EU membership' for supporting the neoliberal project of 'intensified capitalist globalisation': D Nicol, 'Supreme Court Against the People' (UK Constitutional Law Blog, 25 September 2019).

[10] For an example, see S Braverman, 'People we elect must take back control from people we don't. Who include the judges' (ConservativeHome, 30 January 2020) conservativehome.com/2020/01/27/suella-braverman-people-we-elect-must-take-back-control-from-people-we-dont-who-include-the-judges/. Soon after the High Court of Justiciary ruled on matters relating to Boris Johnson's decision to prorogue Parliament, Kwasi Kwarteng MP suggested that their ruling may have been influenced by their own anti-English or pro-EU sympathies: BBC News, 'Kwasi Kwarteng criticised for biased judges comment' (12 September 2019) www.bbc.co.uk/news/uk-politics-49670901.

[11] For example, Aidan Burley MP responded to a judgment of the House of Lords ruling that the structure of a scheme for registering sex offenders was unlawful by decrying the judges as being 'out-of-touch' and siding with dangerous paedophiles (HC Deb. 16 February 2011, vol. 523, col. 965).

[12] M Potter, 'Do the Media Influence the Judiciary?' (Foundation for Law, Media and Society) ora.ox.ac.uk/objects/uuid:e38939d4-17ba-415b-bbdb-f9721390fef4, 2.

the Court (even if, for some, this will always be viewed in a relative sense: the most progressive member of a conservative institution may well still be considered pretty conservative overall).

This chapter attempts to draw together composite 'profiles' of judges. These profiles may well be best understood using some kind of political or ideological lens. A judge who routinely sides against the state, readily finds that human rights have been breached, and usually sides with socio-economic underdogs, looks like a very different *type* of judge to one who frequently defers to the state, rarely finds human rights breaches, sides with powerful parties and is reluctant to impose obligations on them. From this we might even infer, contra Sumption, that at least some judges do indeed have a judicial ideology of some sort.

These profiles rely primarily on the data set out in earlier chapters of this book, alongside any noteworthy extrajudicial comments or actions taken by the judges which might affect our understanding of this data. It does not, in the main, rely on or compare the judges' actual party-political affiliations or their positions on major political controversies for the main reason that these are, understandably, almost always kept private.[13] The judges' political affiliations are not *entirely* unknown, however: some of them freely identified with political associations or political parties before (and only very occasionally after)[14] becoming a judge. Where this is on the public record, it has been considered below.[15]

First, a note on politics. Whilst it might be expected that the findings in the previous chapter should be straightforwardly translated into some basic ideological scale, perhaps of the kind found in some of the comparative literature, which sees the judges placed on a line from 'most liberal' to 'most conservative',[16] this would not be fruitful. As exciting as the idea might be, it would be very difficult to do in this context: there is an inherent ambiguity in the core terms, especially

[13] This did not prevent Peter Lilley from claiming to know that most UKSC judges hold anti-Brexit views: 'Supreme Court justices expressed strident disbelief over Brexit vote, Tory peer claims' *The Express* (27 September 2019). In late 2019, an account began to circulate on *Twitter* which, it was claimed, was based on insider information, alleging that all but one of the UKSC judges sitting on the *Miller* case had voted to Remain in the EU Referendum, but, bizarrely, that Lord Wilson had in fact voted Leave. The post gained significant attention on Twitter and other social media sites, but the origin of the source could be traced back to the Facebook page 'We Support Jacob Rees-Mogg'.

[14] Following his retirement, Michael Tugendhat wrote a number of publications for the influential 'liberal conservative' think tank *Bright Blue*. The group is not formally affiliated with the Conservative Party but it does seek – often successfully – to influence that party's policy: brightblue.org.uk/.

[15] As to whether the judges themselves know the political persuasions of their colleagues, the answer appears to be, on the whole, no: see Lord Neuberger, 'Tweaking the Curial Veil' (Blackstone Lecture 2014, 15 November 2014) para 52. Lord Sumption once suggested that he could accurately guess the 'views' of his colleagues, but not the way they would vote in elections: 'British Institutions: The Supreme Court' *Financial Times* (19 April 2013). By contrast, whilst Lady Hale admitted in a 2019 speech that she did not know which way her colleagues voted, she did admit that she could make a 'very good guess in some cases': Lady Hale, 'Principle and pragmatism in developing private law' (Cambridge Freshfields Lecture, 7 March 2019).

[16] The most well-known of these measures – even getting its own *Wikipedia* page – has its origins in S Segal, A Cover and D Albert, 'Ideological Values and the Votes of U.S. Supreme Court Justices' (1989) 83(2) *American Political Science Review* 557. The measure is updated frequently to reflect more recent SCOTUS decisions.

when they are applied to the realm of judicial behaviour[17] – what constitutes 'liberal' judging or a 'conservative' judgment? How might these labels be applied consistently to a judge's favoured legal reasoning methods alongside their outcome preferences? How might two reasonable manifestations of one kind of ideology be set against one another (if one judge upholds the freedom of a newspaper to publish details about a criminal defendant, but the other considers this a disproportionate invasion of privacy, which is the more 'liberal' approach)? What is the relationship between a so-called liberal approach and an activist one? Ultimately these labels are simply too vague and too slippery to be used as the *sole* way of displaying and understanding different judicial preferences. This is not necessarily to say, as Burrows does, that 'the judges do not split on political lines'[18] at least in some cases. It is, rather, that this phenomenon would be too difficult to translate into some unidimensional ideological scale, and would not capture the fuller range of relevant and interesting judicial behaviour which is of interest to me (and, it is hoped, the reader) in this book.

At the same time, political language should not be discarded entirely. The use of some political or ideological terms might seem particularly appropriate when describing the voting records and behavioural tendencies of at least some judges. After all, legal reasoning and political ideology share a 'basic similarity'[19] and 'shed significant light on each other'.[20] As has been argued in previous chapters, even seemingly mundane legal decisions reflect deeper views about the proper role of the individual and the state, the use and abuse of power, and the respective merits of continuity and change. It would be naïve to suggest that there would never be identifiable political and ideological dimensions to each judge's behavioural profile. A judge who consistently holds the state in breach of human rights obligations, interprets statutes in line with changing social conditions and awards generous damages would seem to hold very different ideological preferences to a judge who, for example, always rules in favour of the state, frequently defers to the executive, and interprets rights and obligations very narrowly. A bespoke definition of ideology is not needed to justify calling the former judge a liberal one and the latter judge a conservative.[21]

[17] G Gaus, 'Ideological dominance through confusion: liberalism in the twentieth century' in M Freeden (ed), *Reassessing Political Ideologies: The Durability of Dissent* (Routledge, 2001) 15–26; R Posner, *How Judges Think* (Harvard, 2008) 9; L Epstein W Landes and R Posner, *The Behavior of Federal Judges: A Theoretical and Empirical Study of Rational Choice* (Harvard, 2013) 46; J Fischman and D Law, 'What is judicial ideology and how should we measure it?' (2009) 29 *Washington University Journal of Law and Policy* 133, 135–36; 143–50.

[18] A Burrows, 'Numbers Sitting in the Supreme Court' (2013) 129 *LQR* 305, 308. See also D Robertson, *Judicial Discretion in the House of Lords* (Clarendon, 1998) 35: '[i]t would be impossible to infer a judge's ideology from his voting pattern'.

[19] L Baum, *The Puzzle of Judicial Behaviour* (Michigan, 1997) 61.

[20] TT Arvind and L Stirton, 'Legal ideology, legal doctrine and the UK's top judges' [2016] *PL* 418, 419.

[21] In my defence of this approach, I place shameless reliance on the words of Blackburn J, who justified his application of a very vague term (in that case, remoteness) because although to define that term precisely would be 'like having to draw a line between night and day' he was nonetheless

As such, where there is a compelling case to do so, some of the judicial profiles below do include descriptions couched in the following ideological or political language. The reader is, of course, free to disagree with, or entirely disregard, these labels.

- Liberal-conservative scale: a liberal judge is likely to side against the state; side with the underdog;[22] adopt pro-immigration outcomes[23] and adopt pro-human rights outcomes.[24] A conservative judge is likely to do the opposite.
- Activism-restraint scale:[25] an activist judge is likely to interpret statutes broadly; overturn or decline to follow precedent; widen or expand the court's jurisdiction; expand or otherwise develop the common law. A restrained judge is likely to do the opposite.
- Institutional-independent scale: an institutional judge is likely to side with state parties; uphold existing decisions including the decisions of lower courts; dismiss devolution-based challenges and narrow the court's jurisdiction. An independent judge is likely to do the opposite.

These definitions are not meant to be particularly robust, and too much reliance should not be placed on them. They are to be understood only as secondary descriptors (ie the dataset was *not* generated with them in mind) and as a useful way describe how the conclusions in previous chapters might fit together. They are neither exhaustive, nor necessarily the most important, ways of understanding and measuring behaviour.[26] Further, these terms should be understood *in the*

able to apply it to the clear facts before him, because 'athough you cannot draw the precise line, you can say which side of the line the case is': *Hobbs v London and Southwestern Railway Co* (1874–75) LR 10 QB 111 at 121.

[22] Left-wing policies have long been associated with reducing inequality and remedying socio-economic disadvantage. Siding with the weaker socio-economic party is often correlated with a 'liberal' ideology in quantitative studies: N Tate and P Sittiwong, 'Decision Making in the Canadian Supreme Court: Extending the Personal Attributes Model Across Nations' (1989) 51(4) *The Journal of Politics* 900, 902–903; R Dudley and C Ducat, 'The Burger Court and Economic Liberalism' (1986) 38(2) *Western Political Quarterly* 236, 238; D Robertson, 'Judicial Ideology in the House of Lords: A Jurimetric Analysis' (1982) 12(1) *British Journal of Political Science* 1, 12–13.

[23] Wishing for tighter controls on immigration is, in the eyes of the British public, a markedly 'right-wing' view: YouGov, 'Left-wing vs right-wing: it's complicated' (14 August 2019) available at yougov.co.uk/topics/politics/articles-reports/2019/08/14/left-wing-vs-right-wing-its-complicated.

[24] But see D Kennedy, 'The Political Significance of the Structure of the Law School Curriculum' (1983) 14 *Seton Hall Law Review* 1, 3–9, who argues that public law success should be seen as left-leaning, because it is 'inseparably connected' with ideas like state responsibility and the promotion of the welfare state, whereas successful arguments based on 'doctrine' – ie contract, tort, property – can be seen as right-wing, crudely, because it serves to upholds private property norms.

[25] The use of this scale is preferred by Arvind and Stirton (n 20) 420–24 and B Dickson, 'Activism and Restraint in within the UK Supreme Court' 21(1) *EJCLI*. This is notwithstanding the adoption of 'activist' as a term of derision in UK politics as of late. Also note that some disagree that 'activism' is any more commensurable than 'politics': see A Paterson, *Final Judgment: The Last Law Lords and the Supreme Court* (Hart Publishing, 2013) 261: 'activism is too much in the eye of the beholder to serve as a useful mechanism for discrimination'.

[26] For example, studies have shown that different judges play different 'roles' on the bench – this cannot be easily captured by the kind of data presented in this chapter: J Gibson, 'The Role Concept in Judicial Research' (1981) *Law and Policy Quarterly* 291.

particular context of the judicial landscape in which they operate. As Arvind and Stirton put it, judicial ideologies:

> do not merely represent *personal* philosophies as to desirable outcomes or objectives. They are 'institutionalized', in that they are part of an identifiable legal and judicial culture, which in turn is a component of the overall approach of governance taken within a state.[27]

A judge who is considered 'conservative' in the context of their judicial behaviour on the UKSC would likely not be considered 'conservative' in the very different context of party-politics. A judge who shows 'activist' tendencies may not be considered an 'activist' in the way some politicians allege. And even the most 'independent' judge is not independent in any true sense; they are still restrained by the conditions of their office, bound by judicial oath, and so on.

The judicial positions explored here are, importantly, relative in nature. The labels applied to a given judge are accurate only insofar as they describe that judge's approach *in relation to the other judges examined here.* A moderate judge surrounded by more activist colleagues might appear to be particularly conservative by comparison. A judge who is considered a liberal amongst colleagues may appear much more moderate if they had instead sat years later.

With those caveats in mind, I submit that there remains something intuitive about their use, and that their deployment might be useful going forwards, even if I earn the chagrin of political scientists by doing so. As such, what follows is an attempted 'profile' of each of the UKSC judges, primarily based on their records and attitudes towards the various issues explored in previous chapters.

II. The Judges

A. Lord Phillips

As the Supreme Court's first President, Lord Phillips took charge as a leader; not only did he deliver the lead judgment in almost 40 per cent of the cases in which he sat, but he was also particularly likely to deliver the lead in cases which were 'difficult' and drew splits in the Court (around 40 per cent of cases in which he delivered the lead judgment were non-unanimous).[28] He was quite comfortable with both leading *and* dissenting, and his dissents were quite long. Cahill-O'Callaghan's description of him as a confident reformer whose leadership rejected notions of traditionalism certainly seems accurate.[29] He was in this way

[27] Arvind and Stirton (n 20) 423.

[28] This is in spite his apparent tendency to change his mind and reach a conclusion at a late stage: see Paterson (n 25) 162; 194; 197; 200 fn 152.

[29] R Cahill-O'Callaghan, *Values in the Supreme Court* (Hart Publishing, 2020) 142–45 and 171.

the perfect candidate to hold the position of Presidency during the Court's early transitional years.[30]

It is fairly difficult to predict how Lord Phillips would cast his vote, as he adopted a range of different positions across his judgments. He was, however, the most likely judge of all to uphold disputed contracts[31] but tended to be quite conservative when it came to remedies. He had a tendency to both vote against the state and for the socio-economic underdog, but this inclination in this respect was fairly moderate. In line with some of his extrajudicial statements,[32] he adopted a comparatively liberal position when it came to human rights issues, especially in cases relating to the ECHR.[33] On a number of issues, such as his approach to statutory interpretation and view of precedent, he adopted a moderate, middle-ground position, disclosing no favoured approach across the board and preferring to adopt different tools depending on the cases at hand. Overall, he could be described as a moderate regarding judicial activism, but probably falls towards the liberal end[34] of the political scale, and is one of the Court's less institutionally-minded judges.[35]

B. Lord Hope

Lord Hope was an extremely busy judge during his time on the Court. Not only did he sit on a high number of cases (as might be expected of a Scottish judge, he sat on many Scottish appeals) but he penned his own substantive contribution in almost three-quarters of them (and almost always said something of his own in Scottish cases, contributing to them some 93 per cent of the time). He authored the lead judgment in over 40 per cent of the cases in which he sat (and in almost 70 per cent of Scottish appeals), added his own written concurrence 50 per cent of the time, and contributed a substantive judgment each time he

[30] Lord Phillips certainly had significant leadership experience: prior to the opening of the Supreme Court, he had sat Master of the Rolls (from 2000 to 2005) and Lord Chief Justice (from 2005 to 2008) and Senior Law Lord (2008 to 2009).

[31] This may be related to the fact that Lord Phillips specialised in commercial law before becoming a judge, and regularly worked on civil and commercial cases during his time on lower courts.

[32] Lord Phillips, 'Strasbourg Has Spoken' in A Burrows, D Johnston and R Zimmerman (eds), *Judge and Jurist: Essays in Memory of Lord Rodger of Earlsferry* (OUP, 2013) 119.

[33] Again, he was the judge most likely to find a breach of the ECHR, behind Lady Hale and Lord Kerr.

[34] Editors of *The Times* seemed to agree, having once labelled Phillips a 'liberal' judge: 'Seven may be the general's lucky number' *The Times* (18 January 1999) 18. In fact, he was 'perhaps the most liberal' judge on the Court at the time. This would not be the last time the same publication used this label to describe Phillips: D Woodhouse, 'The constitutional and political implications of a United Kingdom Supreme Court' (2004) 24 *Legal Studies* 134, 144. A small insight into Lord Phillips' political preferences might be seen when considering the relatively small number of votes he has case in the House of Lords, where he voted against the Conservative government's proposals in areas such as immigration, court reform and smoking laws.

[35] This aligns with Arvind and Stirton's characterisation of him as a more 'red-light' judge: n 20, 428–30.

issued a dissenting vote. Although this level of activity might be *partially* explained by the fact that Hope sat as a member of the Judicial House of Lords, where multiple judgments and written concurrences were much more the norm, for some 13 years before its transformation into the Supreme Court, his record still stands out from his contemporaries in this respect (Hope *was* the longest-serving member of the Lords when it came to an end in October 2009, but not by much: Lord Saville joined one year later than him, Lord Phillips two years later).

He is quite a difficult judge to place in terms of his general preferences and behaviour; like Lord Phillips, he tended to adopt different positions on different jurisprudential issues. He was somewhat more likely to vote in a way which was sympathetic to the plight of the socio-economic underdog than some of his colleagues[36] – he certainly tended to side with the state in cases *without* an obvious underdog, but far less so in cases with an underdog dimension present. In terms of subject areas, in most respects he held quite a moderate voting record, but often leaned slightly towards the more conservative side of things. In particular, he seemed relatively reluctant to recognise a wide jurisdiction for the Court, often leaving matters to state bodies, independent agencies or the parties themselves.

Can Lord Hope's voting record be evaluated in political terms? In his published diaries, he offered a rare glimpse into his views on some party-political matters, but characteristically revealed no consistent ideological allegiance. He expressed disquiet over the conservative criminal policies pursued by the Major government (particularly those championed by Michael Howard)[37] and was concerned about the later Conservative government's hostility to human rights and legal aid.[38] However, he held a positive view of Ruth Davidson, leader of the Scottish Conservatives from 2011–19,[39] and criticised policies adopted by the Labour Party[40] and (especially) the SNP.[41]

His judicial voting record discloses a similar approach. He was just as likely to opt for a more liberal position than his colleagues as he was to vie for a comparably conservative one. This places him squarely in the 'moderate' category (although the language of moderation should not be taken to mean that he showed *no* strong viewpoints; rather, when he did so these positions were

[36] Despite being notably sympathetic to the plight of the 'private landlord' in his diaries: D Hope, *House of Lords 1996–2009: Lord Hope's Diaries* (Avizandum, 2018) 63.

[37] D Hope, *UK Supreme Court 2009–2015: Lord Hope's Diaries* (Avizandum, 2019) 26, 29. Hope was also 'pleased' to be described as a liberal judge by *the Independent*: 34. See further 'Rights: how the law lords line up' *The Times* (25 July 1997) 18, labelling him a 'liberal' judge. Further, sitting as a member of the House of Lords post-retirement, he issued a number of notable speeches against the length of criminal sentences and poor prison conditions: HL, 7 September 2017, vol.783, col.2080–2081; 26 March 2015, vol.760, col.1580–1581.

[38] Hope, ibid 310.

[39] Hope, ibid 309.

[40] His main gripe against the Labour party seemed to be its 'disgraceful bias against landlords' (ibid 180) and see n 36.

[41] Hope (n 37) 309–310.

neither consistently liberal nor conservative).[42] Appropriately enough, Arvind and Stirton designate him the 'median judge' in their study of judicial attitudes towards public bodies.[43] He did, however, seem to favour a more restrained approach to judicial activism in particular, preferring to keep the law as it stood at the time rather than expanding it unnecessarily.[44] He also seemed to be a relatively institutional figure, showing greater respect for state institutions and other decision-making bodies compared to his colleagues.[45] He might, therefore, be described as a moderate, but institutional-leaning, judge. On the other hand, as all law students know, Lord Hope was one of very few judges who have suggested that there may be limits to the sovereignty of Parliament.[46] The fact that these provocative remarks should be made by a judge who I suggest should be considered a fairly institutional figure suggests that both the idea of an 'institutional judge' and the task of trying to pigeonhole someone like Lord Hope into a fixed category are fraught with difficulty.

C. Lord Rodger

Lord Rodger was another judge who was very likely to contribute something of his own to a case, speaking in around 60 per cent of the cases in which he sat. He was also the judge who was most likely to dissent overall (and those dissents were powerful and particularly likely to cause at least some of his colleagues to reconsider their own views).[47] As a Scottish judge, he very commonly sat on appeals from the decisions of Scottish courts. However, unlike the other Scottish judges on the UKSC, he was no more likely to author the lead judgment in *those* cases, nor was he any more likely than others to contribute his own judgment there.

Lord Rodger was one of very few modern judges to have held some kind of political office prior to becoming a judge – he was Scotland's primary legal officer under the Conservative Party during the late 1980s and early 1990s.[48] Of course, holding a government position does not *necessarily* require an endorsement, much less some strong and immutable allegiance to, the politics of that government. Yet Lord Hope has suggested that when sitting on the Supreme Court, he

[42] In 1999, *The Times* seemed to resile from its earlier opinion that Hope was a liberal (see n 37) and labelled him a 'middle of the road' judge instead: 'Seven may be the general's lucky number' *The Times* (18 January 1999) 11.

[43] Arvind and Stirton (n 20) 420–24.

[44] In *House of Lords* (n 36) he criticised some of his colleagues for dissenting too readily: 307–308, 345. See also Hope (n 37) 174.

[45] See further Cahill-O'Callaghan (n 29) 129–34, 165, 170.

[46] *Jackson v Attorney General* [2005] UKHL 56; [2006] AC 262.

[47] Lord Brown, 'Dissenting Judgments' in Burrows, Johnston and Zimmerman (n 32) 30, 37.

[48] Lord Rodger's apparent longstanding hostility to the Labour Party is noted in H MacQueen, 'Alan Ferguson Rodger' *Biographical Memoirs of Fellows of the British Academy XII* (2013) 372–73.

would display 'ideas rooted in the past Conservative government of which he was a member'[49] and Lady Hale suggested that she could 'make a guess' as to what Rodger's 'politics' were, not only from his history but because of his 'reverence for tradition in thinking and his views'.[50]

One strong view held by Lord Rodger was that he was, according to Lord Hope, 'deeply hostile to devolution'[51] and, per MacQueen, strongly averse to Scottish nationalism more generally.[52] He decided just three cases raising devolution issues during his time on the Court, giving him few opportunities to confront this issue jurisprudentially. It is nonetheless noteworthy that he voted to find that the Scottish Parliament had exceeded its competency, and had therefore acted unlawfully, in all three of those cases.

Devolution aside, did Lord Rodger's possible political sympathies carry over to his judgments more generally? Some scholars have suggested so, with both Hanretty and Arvind and Stirton placing him squarely in the conservative camp.[53] He certainly seemed to have a clear preference for siding with the government in public law cases, although he certainly was not the *most* hostile judge in this respect, and his tendencies in this respect are a lot more moderate than those of some of his colleagues. Further, in some ways, Lord Rodger's voting record goes *against* traditional conservative stereotypes. He seems, albeit based on a fairly small sample of cases, to have adopted the most *pro-immigration* position of all judges, and despite being considered a critic of the ECHR and the jurisprudence of the Strasbourg Court,[54] he would vote to find breaches of the ECHR fairly consistently (although it is notable that his votes in a number of important cases in which he found against the ECHR *also* involved finding against the Scottish government).

Lord Rodger's judicial behaviour may be better characterised by invoking notions of traditionalism[55] and restraint rather than conservatism per se. Lord Dyson has noted that Lord Rodger showed a 'reticence in developing the common law',[56] and that he thought that judges 'should leave exciting developments … to Parliament'.[57] His voting record confirms Dyson's assessment. He typically preferred to adopt a narrow approach to statutory interpretation and only very rarely chose to develop the scope of common law rights (but he did seem to be

[49] Hope (n 37) 28.
[50] Lady Hale, 'Lord Rodger's Mental Health Law' in Burrows, Johnston and Zimmerman (n 32) 51. See also Lord Dyson, 'Some Reflections on Lord Rodger's Contribution to the Development of the Common Law' in Burrows, Johnston and Zimmerman (ibid), noting Rodger's 'strong views' about 'political issues': 40.
[51] Hope (n 37) 28.
[52] MacQueen, (n 48) 387–88.
[53] C Hanretty, *A Court of Specialists* (OUP, 2020) 213; Arvind and Stirton (n 20) 420–24.
[54] Lord Phillips, 'Strasbourg Has Spoken' in Burrows, Johnston and Zimmerman (n 32) 119.
[55] See Cahill-O'Callaghan (n 29) at 165 and 170.
[56] Lord Dyson (n 50) 50.
[57] ibid 40.

more comfortable with overturning precedent than some of his colleagues).[58] Overall, he emerges as a strong advocate of *judicial restraint* and of upholding the *traditional roles of the courts, the executive and Parliament* rather than a conservative ideologue. Lord Rodger was certainly no 'revolutionary'[59] but neither was he dogged by some kind of ideological fealty.

D. Lord Walker

After sitting for six years as a Lord of Appeal in the Judicial House of Lords, it seems Lord Walker took something of a step back during his time on the Supreme Court. Whilst he did issue a modest number of concurrences and dissents, his output slowed compared to contemporaries like Lords Hope and Rodger. Identifying his judicial ideology is therefore difficult, but his voting record nevertheless discloses a *fairly* conservative approach. He was quite likely to side with the state, and was also quite likely to side with the stronger party against the underdog. Further, he seemed to generally apply existing precedents rather than depart from them and, albeit to a lesser extent, preferred to employ a narrower approach to statutory interpretation than his colleagues. At the same time, he tended to adopt a pro-immigration position, and whilst he did not sit in many human rights cases, he was fairly comfortable with finding a breach when he did so. Elsewhere, he was notably quite likely to find liability on the facts, across EU law, tax law and tort law.

Whilst other academics have described Lord Walker as a firmly conservative figure,[60] (a position which might well be picked up by law students encountering his sole dissent in *Belmarsh*,[61] a case which has become synonymous with the merits of a distinctly liberal vision of constitutional review), the voting records examined in this work do not reveal preferences of that kind of strength. He often adopted more moderate positions than his colleagues and his inclinations might be described as *pragmatic* rather than *dogmatic*. Indeed, in his extrajudicial writing he endorsed a careful approach to development of the common law, encouraging

[58] Even if this was not always done with enthusiasm: see *Secretary of State for the Home Department v AF (No 3)* [2009] UKHL 28; [2009] 3 WLR 74 at [94].

[59] Lord Dyson (n 50) 40.

[60] See Arvind and Stirton (n 20) 420–24 (describing him as particularly likely to side with public authorities); Hanretty (n 53) 213 (describing him as the Court's second-most conservative judge); Cahill-O'Callaghan (n 29) 170 (describing him as a traditionalist alongside Lords Rodger and Brown).

[61] *A v Secretary of State for the Home Department* [2004] UKHL 56; [2005] 2 AC 68. However, if the relative positions of the judges in that case were to set in stone our understanding of their ideologies, it would paint Lord Hoffmann as the Court's most progressive figure, an impression which has went to great lengths to undo in other cases: see *Secretary of State for the Home Department v Rehman* [2001] UKHL 47; [2003] 1 AC 153; *R v Watson* [2004] UKPC 34; [2005] 1 AC 472; [2004] 3 WLR 841; *R (Bancoult) v Secretary of State For Foreign and Commonwealth Affairs* [2008] UKHL 61; [2008] 4 All ER 1055 and see C Monaghan, 'Returning to Bancoult: New Perspectives' [2022] Judicial Review 337 see especially [22]–[23]; [27]–[28] and [62].

expansion in some areas and restraint in others,[62] and elsewhere offered an audience at Lincoln's Inn a balanced and even-handed overview of the impact of the ECHR.[63] Neither publication discloses views which are particularly rigid or extreme. The data here suggests that Lord Walker's conservatism should be acknowledged, but not overstated: he held a moderate-to-conservative position in terms of politics, a moderate-to-restrained position in terms of activism and development of the law; and a moderate-to-institutional position in terms of independence.

E. Lady Hale

Lady Hale is likely the most well-known judge to have sat on the UKSC.[64] Not only did she publicly represent the court as its Deputy President from 2013 and as its third President from 2017, but she was, for over 13 years, the *only* woman to sit on the UK's highest court,[65] signalling her 'difference' with pride.[66] She attracted more media attention than other judges, sometimes because of her judgments,[67] sometimes because of her feminist statements,[68] and sometimes because of her identity and background.[69] Seemingly, she was prolific enough that upon her upon her retirement in 2020, former Prime Minister Boris Johnson sought to frame her departure as somehow being something of his government's own doing, proudly telling the House of Commons that 'with iron determination we saw off Brenda Hale'.[70] That was, of course, nonsense: she had simply reached the mandatory retirement age.

[62] R Walker, 'Developing the Common Law: How far is too far?' (2013) 37(1) *Melbourne Law Review* 232, 250–53.

[63] Lord Walker, 'The Indefinite Article 8' (Thomas More Lecture, Lincoln's Inn, 9 November 2011).

[64] See C Hanretty, 'The celebrity judges of the UKSC?' (*Medium*, 19 February 2016) available at medium.com/@chrishanretty/the-celebrity-judges-of-the-uksc-7ab33eacb7bf. That piece was written before her elevation to President, her appearances on various TV and radio shows, and the unveiling of her 'black spider' brooch: 'How Lady Hale's spider brooch sent the web into a spin' *The Guardian* (28 September 2019).

[65] Lady Black joined the Supreme Court in October 2017. Lady Hale joined the House of Lords in January 2004. Lady Hale used her unique position and influence to support women judges: see L Cox 'Supporting and Inspiring Women Judges' in R Hunter and E Rackley (eds), *Justice for Everyone: the Jurisprudence and Legal Lives of Brenda Hale* (CUP, 2022).

[66] See R Hunter and E Rackley, 'Lady Hale: A Feminist Towering Judge' in R Abeyratne and I Porat, *Towering Judges: A Comparative Study of Constitutional Judges* (CUP, 2021) and more generally R Hunter, 'More than Just a Different Face? Judicial Diversity and Decision-Making' (2015) 68(1) *Current Legal Problems* 119. Lady Hale's choice to wear a broach during her judicial work was inspired, at least in part, by a desire 'to be a little bit different from the men and to show that there was a woman there': Cumberland Lodge, 'A Conversation with Baroness Hale' (16 March 2020), available at www.cumberlandlodge.ac.uk/whats-on/conversation-baroness-hale.

[67] 'Shout at your spouse and risk losing your home: it's just the same as domestic violence, warns woman judge' *Daily Mail* (27 January 2011).

[68] 'Lady Hale: at least half of judiciary should be female' *The Guardian* (24 March 2019).

[69] 'Ex-barmaid with a spider brooch who spun legal web that snared PM' *Daily Mail* (24 September 2019).

[70] HC Debate, 18 July 2022 vol. 718 col. 726.

Lady Hale is notable for her extensive judicial output. She sat on the Court for the entire ten-year duration of the dataset and sat on more cases than anyone else. She delivered more lead judgments, as well as dissenting judgments, than any other judge in terms of raw numbers. This work rate did not abate to any significant extent when she was promoted to court leadership positions (although there is some evidence that she was less likely to dissent when she presided over a case as Deputy President or President).[71]

Hale has something of a reputation as being a liberal, progressive judge. Sometimes this view was put forward by her former colleagues: she was described as 'forward and free-thinking' with 'a strong agenda of her own' by Lord Hope[72] and a judge 'on the more socially progressive end of the judicial spectrum' by Lord Neuberger,[73] whilst Lord Kerr has praised her 'determination to scrutinise the impact which the law has on the most vulnerable'.[74] Similar sentiments appear in academic works: Hunter and Rackley note her 'commitment to (social) justice';[75] Paterson has mentioned her 'liberal tendencies';[76] Hanretty described her as one of the most left-wing judges on the Court;[77] and Dickson places her in his liberal, 'activist' category.[78] Certain media commentators seem to agree, although often their preferred expressions are much less charitable: Quentin Letts called her a 'quintessential liberal bluestocking' in *The Sun*,[79] and the same publication elsewhere chided her for her 'radical liberal ideas'.[80]

To a considerable extent, Lady Hale's association with liberalism is borne out in her data. She was likely to award quite generous remedies where this was a disputed issue before the Court. She was fairly likely to find liability across the board, particularly tortious liability. Alongside her colleague Lord Kerr, she had a strong tendency to vote in ways which aligned her with the socio-economic underdog, and against the state, especially in contested cases which split the Court. She also seemed to sympathise with women parties, although was *not* the most 'pro-woman' judge on the Court. She was also significantly more likely than most of her colleagues to find that a breach of human rights had occurred, and especially likely to find a breach of the ECHR.

[71] A Paterson, 'Assessing Lady Hale's impact on the UK's final appeal courts' in Hunter and Rackley (n 65) 124–25.

[72] Hope (n 36) 232; 310.

[73] D Neuberger, 'On the Bench with Brenda' in Hunter and Rackley (n 65) 17–18.

[74] B Kerr in Hunter and Rackley (n 65) 134.

[75] R Hunter and E Rackley, 'Introduction' in Hunter and Rackley (n 65) 5.

[76] Paterson (n 71) 128.

[77] Hanretty (n 53) 213.

[78] Dickson (n 25).

[79] 'Judges blew their hallowed status with the Supreme Court ruling and will now be fair game for public scrutiny' *The Sun* (24 September 2019).

[80] 'The day free speech drowned in a paddling pool of olive oil … outrage at gagging verdict' *The Sun* (20 May 2016). In the same editorial it was suggested that she is 'thought not to read The Sun', an observation which is probably correct. See further J Rozenberg, *Enemies of the People? How Judges Shape Society* (Bristol, 2020) 183.

Further, there is considerable evidence that Lady Hale espoused what could be called an 'activist' approach, as well as a clear preference for independent rather than institutional decision-making. She tended to take a wide view of the Court's jurisdiction, and was unafraid to overturn decisions of the courts below. Paterson has noted her 'willingness to go further than some of her more cautious colleagues' in her judgments[81] and indeed she did appear more comfortable than most of her colleagues when it came to developing the law and applying common law protections. She tended to opt for a wide, more purposive approach to statutory interpretation. However, her approach to precedent was not *especially* activist: whilst she certainly did not see herself as rigidly constrained by earlier decisions, she was less likely to depart from authority than a number of her colleagues, and would often highlight the importance of maintaining certainty and consistency in this regard.

Paterson notes that 'Lady Hale set out to make her mark on the UK's highest court and to show that having a woman on the court makes a difference, and we have seen that she certainly did that'.[82] It would be impossible not to concur. There is plenty of evidence that in addition to her strong judicial leadership[83] and extensive output, Lady Hale's 'independent-mindedness'[84] and concern for the 'practical and human consequences' of her decisions[85] led to a rich jurisprudence of a strongly liberal, activist and independent character.

F. Lord Brown

Lord Brown's style of judicial communication was much more in line with the working practices of the House of Lords than that which would emerge in the later years of the Supreme Court. He frequently added his own concurrences, even if they were only a handful of paragraphs long, and his high dissent rate reveals a clear confidence in departing from the views of his colleagues when necessary. Interestingly, his judgments were typically very concise and to the point, regardless of whether he delivered a lead, concurrence or a dissenting judgment: during his time on the UKSC, not once did he author a contribution exceeding 50 paragraphs in length.

In many ways, Lord Brown epitomised a conservative approach to judging.[86] He tended to side with powerful parties over socio-economic underdogs, and

[81] Paterson (n 71) 126.

[82] Paterson (n 71) 132.

[83] See further R Hunter and E Rackley, 'Judicial Leadership on the UK Supreme Court' (2018) 38 *Legal Studies* 191, for dimensions of judicial leadership which cannot easily be captured through looking at votes.

[84] Kerr (n 74) 138.

[85] Neuberger (n 73) 17. See also D Feldman, 'Orthodox Principles and Unconventional Outcomes in Public Law' in Hunter and Rackley (n 65), who accurately characterises Lady Hale's jurisprudence as driven by a desire to protect the vulnerable and to hold decision-makers to account, using pragmatic methods to achieve this.

[86] Hanretty labelled him the most conservative judge on the Court in his book: n 53, 213.

was the most likely of all judges to side with the state against citizens in salient cases. He was, it seems, particularly unsympathetic to arguments relying on human rights and developed something of a scepticism towards the role of human rights in civil and legal discourse more generally.[87] In his memoir, Brown admitted that upon moving from the House of Lords to the Supreme Court, he had started to become 'sufficiently troubled by … the excessive soft-heartedness … of a number of [his] colleagues, particularly in any case supposedly raising human rights concerns'.[88] Lord Brown's record when it came to claims made under the ECHR[89] shows that he was certainly not prone to the same 'soft-heartedness' of his colleagues. He also adopted a strongly institutional approach. He was more likely than his colleagues to refrain from interfering with the decision of the court below, and adopted a restrictive view of the Court's jurisdiction. He also preferred to follow settled precedent rather than disrupt the certainty of the law. Notably, however, whilst he was certainly no judicial activist, he was often willing to change the law where necessary, and was an advocate of a wider, contextual approach to statutory interpretation.

Overall, Lord Brown emerges as a consistently conservative and strongly institutionally-minded judge. Little wonder, then, that upon his death in July 2023, Richard Ekins, head of Policy Exchange's Judicial Power Project,[90] praised his jurisprudence and sought to cast it as 'centrist' and 'orthodox' in nature.[91] Lord Brown's approach may reflect the Judicial Power Project's preferred orthodoxy, but it does not line up with the Court's. And, I suggest, Lord Brown would have been quite proud of that fact.[92]

G. Lord Mance

Lord Mance served on the UKSC for nine years, sitting as its Deputy President during the year immediately preceding his retirement in 2018. Despite his commercial background, he would sit in cases involving many different areas of

[87] See his speeches as a member of the (legislative) House of Lords eg his contributions to the discussion of the Investigatory Powers Bill, 11 October 2016, vol.774, as well as HL, 16 July 2018, vol.792, col.1092–1094 (mental health laws); HL, 10 May 2016, vol.771, col.1160–1161 (detention in immigration context). cf. his passionate defence of Strasbourg: HL, 2 July 2015, vol.762, col.2197.

[88] S Brown, *Playing off the Roof* (Marble Hall, 2020) 192.

[89] He did not sit on enough cases to produce meaningful data regarding other human rights sources.

[90] See judicialpowerproject.org.uk. The group operates as part of the conservative think tank *Policy Exchange* and seeks to promote 'political authority' against what it considers to be 'judicial overreach'. For criticism, see P Craig, 'Judicial Power, the Judicial Power Project and the UK' (2017) 36 *University of Queensland Law Journal* 355 and D Dyzenhaus, 'The Snake Charmers' (*Verfassungsblog*, 7 March 2022).

[91] R Ekins, 'In memory of Lord Brown' *The Spectator* (10 July 2023).

[92] There are many passages in *Playing Off the Roof* where Lord Brown shows that he was well aware of some of the jurisprudential differences between himself and his colleagues during his later years on the Supreme Court – it certainly did not seem to bother him (see eg n 88, 192–93) and see also Lord Brown, 'In Praise of Dissenting Judgments' (*Prospect Magazine*, 28 May 2020).

law. He would often contribute something of his own to a judgment, and would frequently issue a concurrence of his own, especially during the Court's earlier years. He was also fairly comfortable with issuing a dissenting judgment, including an occasional lone dissent.

During his time on the Court, he had a very balanced voting record and can be described as a model moderate judge. He was neither particularly likely to take a liberal nor a conservative approach to areas of law and did he did not disclose any strong tendency to side for or against particular parties. In split cases, he would often adopt a middle-way view between the more extreme positions of his colleagues.[93]

One notable outlier is that Lord Mance was particularly likely to vote to uphold and follow existing precedent rather than depart from it even when, on balance, he might disagree with it. Perhaps the most striking example of this position in practice is the *Bancoult* litigation.[94] In 2007, Lord Mance dissented from the majority, and would have held that there was an enforceable expectation which could be invoked by the indigenous groups expelled from the Chagos Islands. However, notwithstanding this, when the case came before the Court again in 2016, he declined the opportunity to re-open proceedings on the basis of subsequent findings despite the fact that two of his fellow justices would have allowed the case to proceed – Mance was in effect the deciding vote. It must surely have been tempting to reconsider the case and give effect to his (then rejected) view on the legal merits a decade later. Yet in that case as much as any other, certainty and consistency were of premium concern for him and he voted to uphold the settled position.

Overall, Lord Mance's judicial records are characterised by moderation and balance.[95] However, his attitude towards precedent might suggest that in some specific respects he can be more institutionally-minded.

H. Lord Collins

Although Lord Collins – notable for being the first solicitor to be appointed to the UK's highest court – spent just under two years on the Court, he was quite an active member during his time there. He authored the lead judgment in over 30 per cent of the cases in which he sat, and his lead judgments were, on average, the longest of all judges.

[93] It is therefore unsurprising that according to Cahill-O'Callaghan (n 29 at 141 and 171) he embraces both the (contrasting) values of 'self-direction' and 'security'.

[94] See *R (Bancoult) v Secretary of State For Foreign and Commonwealth Affairs* [2008] UKHL 61; [2008] 4 All ER 1055 and *R (Bancoult) v Secretary of State for Foreign and Commonwealth Affairs (No 2)* [2016] UKSC 35; [2017] AC 300.

[95] Cahill-O'Callaghan suggests that his judicial values prioritise freedom and self-direction above others, values which might not necessarily translate into a consistent voting pattern or a simple ideological axis: Cahill-O'Callaghan (n 29) at 165 and 171.

It is difficult to draw too many conclusions from the content of Lord Collins' judgments due to the relatively short duration of his stay on the Court. However, his limited records suggest that he was somewhat likely to recognise disputed contracts and adopt a pro-immigration position. In terms of judicial reasoning, he seemed to embrace wider, purposive construction techniques when it came to statutory interpretation and was comfortable with departing from precedent. Therefore, the very limited records for Lord Collins would tentatively suggest that he leaned towards an activist and liberal stance overall.[96]

I. Lord Kerr

Lord Kerr's time on the Supreme Court's first decade was in many ways remarkable. He was one of two judges – the other being Lady Hale – to sit as an active judge for the entire duration of the period.[97] He was the only permanent judge of that period to hail from Northern Ireland. Unsurprisingly, he was both disproportionately likely to sit on appeals from Northern Irish courts (which became more frequent as time went by) and to deliver the lead judgment in those cases. He was, notably, an 'unshrinking dissenter'[98] who was unafraid to break from the pack, and on many occasions did so on his own. His dissents, especially those involving human rights, were rarely technical disagreements: rather, they were stringent and powerful, often reflecting a position diametrically opposed to that which was supported by the majority. They were often lengthy – in fact, Lord Kerr's longest single contribution was a characteristically impassioned dissent in the *NIHRC* abortion case,[99] which dwarfed Lord Mance's lead judgment in length by a considerable extent. By contrast, he did not tend to produce as many lead judgments or overall contributions compared to his colleagues and was particularly unlikely to issue a written contribution in cases falling outside of his preferred subject areas of public and criminal law.

In addition to having a reputation as something of a *great dissenter*, Lord Kerr was also considered a strongly liberal and progressive judge. Lady Hale has described him as the 'most considerably liberal and forward-looking of the Supreme Court Justices'[100] whilst Lord Reed has suggested that he was guided by a 'strong and instinctive sense of justice'[101] and that his jurisprudence was characterised by

[96] In the House of Lords, the few votes he has cast seem to align him with the Labour and Liberal Democrat peers rather than the Conservative Lords eg supporting the Dubs amendment in immigration matters, voting for stricter climate change targets and supporting greater data protection safeguards. All data sourced from hansard.parliament.uk and publicwhip.org.uk.

[97] He would then go on to outlast her; Lady Hale retired in January 2020 and Lord Kerr followed in the summer.

[98] Paterson (n 25) 117.

[99] *Re Northern Ireland Human Rights Commission* [2018] UKSC 27; [2019] 1 All ER 173.

[100] Lady Hale, 'Women and Children First' in B Dickson and C McCormick (eds), *The Judicial Mind: A Festschrift for Lord Kerr of Tonaghmore* (Hart Publishing, 2021) 46.

[101] Lord Reed, 'Tribute for Lord Kerr' (UK Supreme Court, 30 September 2020).

a 'liberal approach to the law, [a] readiness to take the side of the underdog and … adventurousness in developing the law'.[102] This reputation extends beyond the judges themselves; academics have routinely cast him as a liberal,[103] and even *The Guardian* has quoted, albeit without attribution, a view that Lord Kerr was one of the Court's 'more liberal members'.[104] The voting records examined in earlier chapters would suggest that this reputation is well-earned. Lord Kerr was more likely than any other judge to side against public authority litigants,[105] as well as the most likely of all judges to side with the socio-economic underdog.[106] He was, further, very likely to hold that the Court had jurisdiction over disputed matters, and was indisputably the human rights 'friendly' judge on the Court, especially when it came to cases involving the ECHR.

In terms of his preferred legal reasoning, it seems that Kerr's preferences were less entrenched. However, he still showed a preference, overall, for adopting wider, more purposive modes of statutory interpretation and was more comfortable than some of his colleagues with departing from existing precedent. Overall, however, it seems like Kerr was guided more strongly by the desire to do justice in the case before him than with adherence to some strict legal doctrine; he would, for example, go so far as to employ dictionary definitions, and focus on the precise tense of applicable statutory terms, when performing statutory interpretation, if doing so would lead to achieving a fair result in his eyes.

Overall, Lord Kerr stands out as the Court's most liberal judge, as well as its most independent-minded one.[107] He is also clearly at the activist end of the judicial spectrum. His jurisprudential attitude is neatly encapsulated in a quote from a lecture he gave in 2019, reflecting on the first decade of the Supreme Court's operation. There, he suggested that judges must 'remain alive to [the] social values, standards and experiences of the society we serve' and that this, more than anything else, should direct the judge towards the judicial positions they endorse.[108] Lord Kerr certainly lived by his own words.

J. Lord Clarke

Lord Clarke's behaviour and preferences were, overall, quite measured, showing no strong preferences either way in terms of most of the categories examined.[109]

[102] Lord Reed, 'Foreword' in Dickson and McCormick (n 100) viii.

[103] See eg Hanretty (n 53) 213; Dickson (n 25), Arvind and Stirton (n 20) 420–24.

[104] 'Supreme court prorogation hearing: who are the judges?' *The Guardian* (17 September 2019).

[105] This is despite working as a lawyer acting on behalf of the government for 15 years.

[106] Lord Reed said that one of his great strengths was his 'humane response to the plight of the vulnerable': Lord Reed (n 101).

[107] This is particularly interesting in light of the fact that 'Lord Kerr is the only member of the Supreme Court to have practised law daily in a legal system that was operating … during an emergency threatening the life of the nation' (S Lee and J Lee, 'Humility in the Supreme Court' (2015) 16(2) *King's LJ* 165, 172).

[108] Lord Kerr, 'The Impact of the Supreme Court on the law of Northern Ireland' (UK Supreme Court Ten-Year Anniversary Lecture Series, 4 December 2019).

[109] This may be why Hunter and Rackley described him as lacking a distinctive voice: n 83, 213.

He was, however, notably more likely than a number of his colleagues to side with citizens against the state and, interestingly enough, more likely than any other judge to side with women parties (more so than Lady Hale, the only women to serve on the Court for a substantial time during the examined period). In addition, he generally adopted a pro-immigration position in applicable cases, was comfortable with affording a wide jurisdiction to the Court, and was very likely to find tortious liability (particularly in cases where the Court was split). Notably, Cahill-O'Callaghan identified him, alongside Lord Kerr, as one of the judges whose judicial values involve rejecting tradition in embracing universalism.[110] Whilst this appears much more explicit in Lord Kerr's voting record than Lord Clarke's, the latter's progressive values more than occasionally shine through.

Alongside Lord Mance (who, incidentally, shared a number of Lord Clarke's judicial preferences more generally) he showed a strong preference for upholding and applying existing precedent. As such, it seems Lord Clarke preferred a reformist, liberal approach to the exercise of discretion and development of the law, *where that possibility has not already been foreclosed by existing case law.* Taken altogether, the holistic evaluation above paints a picture of Lord Clarke as leaning towards a liberal political position, as having a slightly anti-institutional preference, but as neither particularly activist nor restrained in the round.

K. Lord Dyson

Lord Dyson was a very influential judge in many respects.[111] Despite his short tenure on the Court (he was appointed in 2010 but was soon promoted to Master of the Rolls in 2012) he quickly emerged as a significant influence on the Court during its early years, and would very often take on the lead judgment in challenging and complex cases, especially if they divided the Court. His lead judgments were significant and lengthy, and, despite being involved in many split cases, he had a remarkably low dissent rate overall. Paterson describes him as a particularly formidable figure, noting, for example, that he was 'not known for ducking challenges'[112] and that 'counter-punching came naturally to him'.[113] As such, he was able to both influence his colleagues to move closer to his views, and compromise effectively where he could not do so.

In terms of what his voting record reveals about his judicial preferences, Lord Dyson presents a relatively unique profile. On the one hand, he had something of a tendency to side with the state against the citizen, yet he also tended to side with socio-economic underdogs. In fact, in those cases involving an underdog

[110] Cahill-O'Callaghan (n 29) 165, 171.
[111] See eg Paterson (n 25) 146, 165, 202.
[112] Paterson (n 25) 22.
[113] ibid 201.

dimension, but absent any direct state involvement, Dyson emerged as the *most likely judge of all* to take the side of the disadvantaged party. His approach to human rights cases is also very interesting – his record is relatively moderate with respect to ECHR claims (and he seems particularly conservative in salient cases)[114] but he took a much stronger line in cases concerned with other kinds of rights, such common law rights, where he was much more likely to side with the claimant.

In addition, Lord Dyson was one of the most confident judges when it came to departing from existing precedent, and was more likely than any other judge to adopt a wide approach to statutory interpretation. He was certainly not restrained when it came to the use of legal tools: he adopted purposive, evolutive reasoning and did not wish to see legal progress hampered by formal constraints and technicalities.

In summary, Lord Dyson did not necessarily conform to the patterns of other judges, nor could his judicial behaviour be accurately summarised with simple labels. He has claimed that 'the middle ground is [his] natural habitat' and that he had been considered both 'progressive' as well as 'cautious' by others.[115] Politically, he exhibited some liberal characteristics as well as some conservative ones. He also exhibited a fair amount of institutional loyalty. However, perhaps most notable of all is that he was one of the least 'restrained' judges on the Court, being happy to decide things for himself and develop the law where necessary, even if this was not always done in one consistent and predictable ideological direction. He might therefore be described as an activist judge, but not a political one.

L. Lord Wilson

Lord Wilson was, in contrast to many of the Court's initial roster, a relatively quiet judge, who was unlikely to add a concurrence or his own separate remarks without good reason, contributing only when he had something of real substance to add. Although not a frequent dissenter – he admitted that his self-imposed threshold for dissenting rather than 'swallow[ing] hard and accept[ing] a majority decision' with which he disagreed was a high one[116] – he was, in fact, more likely to dissent than many of his colleagues, and those dissenting opinions were described as 'trenchant' by Lord Reed.[117]

Although he was not as consistent as some other judges in this respect, he generally showed sympathy for disadvantaged parties. Extrajudicially, he has described the Human Rights Act as 'brilliant' and has lauded the European

[114] Despite this, he has authored a robust defence of human rights, after a number of his colleagues were much more critical: see Lord Dyson, 'Human Rights?' in *Justice: Continuity and Change* (Hart Publishing, 2018).

[115] Dyson, *A Judge's Journey* (Hart Publishing, 2019) 238.

[116] Paterson (n 25) 117 (interview with author).

[117] Lord Reed, 'Tribute for Lord Wilson' (UK Supreme Court, 30 September 2020).

Convention as having 'enormous value', yet has also criticised Strasbourg for some of its more far-reaching decisions, complaining that they 'occasionally … stick in the throat'.[118] His judicial behaviour matches this rhetoric; whilst on the whole, he leaned towards a 'pro-ECHR' position in his judgments, he could occasionally strongly push back when he thought there was a danger of human rights arguments being stretched too far,[119] or where Strasbourg had, in his view, clearly overreached.[120] He was also less enthusiastic when it came to finding breaches of other kinds of rights, such as common law rights.

He seemed relatively comfortable with the notion of departing from existing authority, and generally preferred to adopt a wide, purposive approach to statutory interpretation. At the same time, there were, for him, clear limits to judicial creativity and he considered it very important to enunciate these in cases such as *Evans*[121] and *Privacy International*.[122] He clearly thought that statutes should not be read literally, and should be interpreted purposively and in light of modern conditions where possible, but emphasised that the court's role was fundamentally interpretive rather than legislative, and that tools such as the principle of legality should not be used to undermine the will of Parliament. He also cared about ensuring comity with judges in the courts below – according to Lord Reed, he would often remind his colleagues of the need for 'humility' towards the decisions of lower courts[123] – but despite this he was no more or less likely than his colleagues to allow appeals from those lower courts in practice.

Overall, despite the fact that he was considered by at least one of his colleagues as a traditional and conservative figure 'by virtue of his background and demeanour',[124] Lord Wilson's record did not straightforwardly accord with this impression. Overall, he was politically unpredictable, sometimes voting in a very liberal way, and sometimes adopting a markedly conservative stance. He was not a particularly institutional figure. He did, however, generally lean towards the more expansionist side of the activism scale. He was very comfortable with exercising his discretion in inventive and often liberal ways, and developed the law, where permissible, in a manner which would achieve justice, but was careful not to cross constitutional red-lines, and was more willing than most to question and push back against the authority of the Strasbourg Court when he disagreed with its decisions.

[118] Lord Wilson, 'Our Human Rights: A Joint Effort?' (Howard J Trienens Lecture, 25 September 2018) 11.

[119] See eg *R (DA and DS) v Secretary of State for Work and Pensions* [2019] UKSC 21; [2019] WLR 3289.

[120] See eg *Smith v Ministry of Defence* [2013] UKSC 41; [2014] 1 AC 52; *R (Hallam and Nealon) v Secretary of State for Justice* [2019] UKSC 2; [2020] AC 279.

[121] *R (Evans) v Attorney General* [2015] UKSC 21; [2015] AC 1787.

[122] *R (Privacy International) v Investigatory Powers* Tribunal [2019] UKSC 22; [2019] 4 All ER 1.

[123] Lord Reed (n 117).

[124] Lord Hope (n 37) 86.

M. Lord Sumption

Lord Sumption's appointment to the Court was a controversial one, being the first UKSC Justice to be appointed directly from the legal profession. Once he took up his position, he could hardly be charged with fading into the background.[125] He sat on a lot of cases, frequently delivering the lead judgment in them. His contributions were often succinct and to the point, and colleagues frequently signed up to them. Despite having something of a reputation as being a dissident figure,[126] his actual dissent rate was not particularly high compared to his colleagues. However, when he did vote with a dissenting bloc, he contributed something of his own on every occasion, and his colleagues have described his dissents as 'vigorous'[127] and thought-provoking.[128]

Sumption also held a reputation as something of a conservative figure[129] and not always of a 'small-c' kind: he wrote a book with a Conservative politician in the 1970s[130] and considered running as Conservative MP himself his youth.[131] Despite this, he admitted (prior to his appointment to the UKSC) that he had in fact voted for the Labour Party in the 1970s.[132] By the turn of the twenty-first century, he was 'basically … a Tory who votes Labour much of the time'[133] and once he retired from the Supreme Court he revealed that he no longer held any allegiance to a particular political party.[134] More broadly, he has come to be associated with the philosophy of libertarianism. In addition to openly identifying himself as such[135] (the book on equality which he wrote suggested that class distinctions could be overcome in a society committed to individualism as its core value),[136] his Reith lectures contain lamentations on state interference into the zone of 'autonomous decision making by individuals' and 'the area within which citizens take responsibility for their own destinies',[137] and it is not difficult to detect a libertarian undercurrent to his post-judicial writings on the government's

[125] See Hunter and Rackley (n 83) 212–13.

[126] Lady Hale, 'Valedictory for Lord Sumption' (UK Supreme Court, 12 December 2018).

[127] Lord Hope (n 37) 168.

[128] Lady Hale (n 126).

[129] 'Only the judiciary can save the Tories from themselves' *The Spectator* (18 September 2019): Sumption was called 'the most conservative of small 'c' conservative judges'.

[130] K Joseph and J Sumption, *Equality* (John Murray, 1979).

[131] Political Thinking with Nick Robinson, 'The Jonathan Sumption One' (*BBC Radio 4*, 29 May 2020) available at www.bbc.co.uk/sounds/play/p08fjy9j.

[132] 'Jonathan Sumption: Donnish but deadly' *The Independent* (15 October 2011); 'Lord Sumption: I have observed that lockdown scepticism goes with high levels of education' *The Daily Telegraph* (4 June 2021).

[133] 'Jonathan Sumption: Donnish but deadly' *The Independent* (15 October 2011). What this might tell us about Tony Blair's Labour party is left to the reader to determine.

[134] During a radio interview he suggested that he has no 'natural political home': Political Thinking with Nick Robinson, 'The Jonathan Sumption One' (*BBC Radio 4*, 29 May 2020), available at www.bbc.co.uk/sounds/play/p08fjy9j.

[135] ibid.

[136] Joseph and Sumption (n 130).

[137] J Sumption, 'Law's Expanding Empire' (Reith Lectures, 21 May 2019).

coronavirus response.[138] On the subject of the UK's constitutional arrangements, Sumption has advocated for a more limited judicial role in some areas and greater respect for the separation of powers.[139] In his view, judges should be particularly careful when reviewing political decisions and policy choices, including in the context of human rights litigation.[140]

But do those political preferences appear when looking at Sumption's judgments?[141] He was, perhaps in line with his views about the court's limited role, the least likely of all judges in the dataset to find that the Court had jurisdiction to determine a contentious issue, and generally proposed a more modest role for courts where this was questioned.[142] He was also more reluctant than many other judges to depart from settled law. He was significantly less likely than others to vote in favour of finding a breach of the ECHR, and was fairly reluctant to uphold human rights claims more generally.[143]

However, his record on matters concerning statutory interpretation is more balanced, with examples of the application of more narrow interpretive approaches alongside wider ones. Whilst he has been accused of being too deferential towards the executive,[144] Lord Sumption's actual voting record against the state is not too noteworthy in this respect, although he was still more likely than average to side with public bodies over individuals. Further, whilst he was hardly the Court's most ardent supporter of the underdog, he was a lot more moderate than some might expect in this respect, too.

Overall, then, in many ways Sumption's judicial record does reveal a degree of conservatism. But this mainly takes the form of a rejection of judicial activism,[145] and an endorsement of judicial restraint (particularly, but not exclusively, in public law cases) rather than a rejection of a liberal approach in favour of a conservative one per se. He also shows some preference for an institutional position.

[138] See eg J Sumption, 'You cannot imprison an entire population' *The Spectator* (17 May 2020).

[139] J Sumption, 'Judicial and Political Decision-Making: The Uncertain Boundary' (2011) 16(4) *Judicial Review* 301, 304.

[140] Sumption (n 137); Lord Sumption, 'The Limits of Law' (27th Sultan Azlan Shah Lecture, Kuala Lumpur, 20 November 2013) and see generally N Barber, R Ekins and P Yowell (eds), *Lord Sumption and the Limits of Law* (Hart Publishing, 2016).

[141] Lord Sumption himself has suggested that there is a significant difference between his own views, expressed in lectures and in extracurricular activities, and the way he judges: J Sumption, 'A Response' in Barber, Ekins and Yowell (ibid) 213.

[142] See eg his speech, disagreeing with the more radical view of the three judges in the plurality in *Privacy International* (n 122) and *Arorangi Timberland Ltd v Cook Islands National Superannuation Fund* [2016] UKPC 32; [2017] 1 WLR 99 at [101].

[143] His speech in *R (Lord Carlile) v Secretary of State for the Home Department* [2014] UKSC 60; [2015] 1 AC 945 perhaps typifies his approach, where he suggested that in some circumstances when applying the Human Rights Act, the Court should forego its usual scrutiny of executive actions, and should defer to the executive unless the view is not in effect a 'tenable' one. Whilst in the majority in that case, he was not joined by any of his colleagues in this respect.

[144] Which may – or may not – conflict with his libertarian ideals, see S Sedley, 'Judicial politics' (2012) 34(4) *London Review of Books* 15, 15–16.

[145] Lee is right in saying that Lord Sumption 'exhibits caution in the development of the law': J Lee, 'The Judicial Individuality of Lord Sumption' (2017) 40(2) *UNSWLJ* 862, 886.

It is unsurprising, then, that Sumption's brand of 'legal conservatism' has been positively endorsed by Lord Brown, as the two adopted a fairly similar approach to their work.[146] The legal conservatism which Sumption expressed in his judgments may have an analogue with the ideological viewpoints he has expressed both before and after his time on the Court, but they are not synonymous with one another. His legal approach is no more improperly ideological than any other judge's. Whilst he was certainly a very different judge to someone like Lord Kerr, if Sumption's judicial output is to be described as conservative, it must certainly be 'with a small c' rather than with a capital one.[147]

N. Lord Reed

Unlike some of his predecessors, Lord Reed only wrote when it was necessary to do so. When it *was* necessary, however, he would write at great length and with considerable authority.[148] His voting record is not straightforward and it is fairly difficult to pin down any particular preferences which manifest across the board. He did not appear, overall, to vote in a way which disclosed strong sympathies for or against either the state, nor for or against socio-economic underdogs. He took a balanced approach to precedent and whilst he was not particularly likely to vote in favour of finding an ECHR breach, he *was* comparably more comfortable with finding a breach of rights sourced from the common law or international law. He was less likely than his colleagues to recognise a breach of tort, uphold a devolution challenge, adopt a pro-immigration position or (especially) uphold a contract, whilst he was more likely to impose criminal liability and find a breach of EU rights.

Interestingly, some of Lord Reed's preferences were more pronounced when he delivered a lead judgment or a substantive addition of his own. For example, whilst his approach to statutory interpretation was moderate overall, he was much more likely to adopt a wider, more purposive approach when he delivered a lead judgment. Similarly, whilst his record does not appear ideologically-driven in general, he was more likely to exhibit a conservative or restrained attitude in those cases where he felt strongly enough about a point to issue a dissent or where he was to deliver the lead judgment himself.

As such, Lord Reed appears to have been a fairly moderate judge during the Court's first decade, but came into his own, as a more activist but politically conservative figure, in cases in which he held a particularly strong view.

[146] Lord Brown (n 88) 192.

[147] He has been described as such, without objection from Sumption: Political Thinking with Nick Robinson, 'The Jonathan Sumption One' (*BBC Radio 4*, 29 May 2020), available at www.bbc.co.uk/sounds/play/p08fjy9j.

[148] Paterson describes him as a particularly persuasive judge and good at convincing his colleagues to his point of view: n 25, 206–207.

In 2019, one conservative commentator praised him for being 'keenly aware of his responsibility … to avoid the temptation to subvert law in an attempt to do justice' and for holding what he considered to be a 'traditional understanding of the judicial function'.[149] Around the same time, in a radio interview, Lord Reed himself suggested that whilst he rejected the idea that UKSC judges had overstepped their mark or had otherwise become too powerful, he nonetheless considered himself to be more 'restrained' than some of his colleagues, especially in areas of controversy.[150] This self-evaluation is probably accurate: his judicial record reveals a moderate preference for judicial restraint and a conservative approach, but only really in the hardest cases.

In early 2020 (and therefore taking place *outside* the dates relevant to the dataset used in this work) Lord Reed took over from Lady Hale to become the Court's fourth President. Since then, a number of commentators have suggested that, under his premiership, the Court's output has become notably more conservative (whether or not this change is believed to be due to the influence of Lord Reed himself, or any number of other factors, is not always clear). Obviously, the jurisprudence of the 'Reed Court' falls outside the parameters of the dataset. However, the nature of the Court's more recent output, and the potential influence of Lord Reed as President, is explored in the next chapter.

O. Lord Carnwath

Lord Carnwath was another judge whose judicial preferences seemed to conform to a model of moderation and balance rather than ideological extremes. He did, however, have a relatively high dissent rate of around 9 per cent, and was more comfortable than some of his colleagues when it came to dissenting alone.[151] He exhibited a tendency for finding tax liability and was likely to recognise the Court's jurisdiction, but was not likely to recognise and uphold the validity of contracts. He also tended to vote in favour of granting winning parties comparatively generous remedies. It is hard to identify more general, cross-cutting preferences from his records. He showed something of an inclination towards applying a narrow approach to statutory interpretation, but not a strong one. He showed no particular loyalty towards or against the state, and had a balanced approach towards precedent.

[149] R Ekins, 'What the most recent appointments mean for the future of the Supreme Court' (*ConservativeHome*, 26 July 2019) conservativehome.com/2019/07/26/richard-ekins-what-the-most-recent-nominations-mean-for-the-future-of-the-supreme-court/. In addition, Lord Neuberger considered Lord Reed to sit at the 'opposite end … of the spectrum' to Lord Kerr (A Paterson, 'Presidency and the Supreme Court: Lord Neuberger's Legacy', UCL Judicial Institute, 2 December 2019, 48). Given Lord Kerr's profile, above, this suggests that Neuberger sees Reed as a reserved, conservative figure.

[150] Lord Reed, *BBC Law in Action* (29 January 2019).

[151] This is in spite of the fact that, according to Lord Hope, Carnwath was very keen to convince others to sign up to his views 'behind the scenes': Hope (n 37) 176.

Like his colleague Lord Wilson, Lord Carnwath could go either way in cases involving the ECHR; he, too, would vote in quite different directions, sometimes endorsing quite an expansive view of human rights under the Convention, and at other times being much more conservative. He seemed to approach each Convention issue on its own facts rather than relying on any more general judicial philosophy in this context. True to form, he 'balances out' as a moderate when it comes to the ECHR. However, despite his veneration of the common law in high-profile cases such as *Privacy International*,[152] he was actually particularly unlikely to side with parties alleging a breach of human rights outside the framework of the ECHR, including in cases when so-called common law rights are invoked. Overall, despite being described by one commentator as falling on the 'activist end of the spectrum',[153] an analysis of Carnwath's voting records suggests that he generally took a moderate-to-conservative approach overall (with the important caveat that this *general* approach was departed from in a number of significant outlier cases). As with a number of his colleagues, it is particularly difficult to ascribe a particular label to Lord Carnwath when it comes to diagnosing judicial ideology.

P. Lord Neuberger

Lord Neuberger took over as the Court's President following the retirement of Lord Phillips in 2012, leading the Court in formal as well as more informal ways.[154] He was a 'workaholic'[155] who sat on a huge number of cases during his time on the Court, by far the highest rate per year of any judge in the dataset, and had a greater output (in paragraphs) than any other judge in the dataset, despite sitting for less than half the duration of some of his contemporaries. He produced many lead judgments, and authored the longest lead of any judge in the dataset (all the more remarkable considering that he clearly took on considerable extra work during this time, as evidenced by the long list of extrajudicial speeches on the Court's website bearing his name). He was good at convincing other judges to come to his point of view, and, in the spirit of building consensus and enhancing the Court's image and reputation, encouraged compromise amongst his

[152] *Privacy International* (n 122).

[153] Rozenberg, (n 80) 153. In a lecture, Lord Carnwath himself noted that he had been called a 'judicial activist' by James Delingpole of Breitbart News because of his academic interest in environmental law: Lord Carnwath, 'Climate Change and the Courts' (Oxford Centre for Islamic Studies, 26 November 2015) 3.

[154] The definitive work on judicial leadership on the UKSC is Hunter and Rackley (n 83). Judicial 'leadership' can be conceptualised in various ways, see eg E Ryder and S Hardy, *Judicial Leadership* (OUP, 2019) see especially ch 3 and ch 5; M Tushnet, 'Judicial Leadership' in J Kane, H Patapan and P Hart, *Dispersed Democratic Leadership: Origins, Dynamics and Implications* (OUP, 2009) 153–55.

[155] Paterson (n 71) 125; A Paterson 'Presidency and the Supreme Court: Lord Neuberger's Legacy' (UCL Judicial Institute, 2 December 2019) 2.

colleagues and showed flexibility with his own viewpoints and positions.[156] As such, his dissent rate was very low (around 2 per cent).

In terms of the content of his judgments, Lord Neuberger tended to prioritise certainty and continuity over developing the case law.[157] He was relatively reluctant to find tortious liability or uphold contractual claims. He was somewhat less likely than some of his colleagues to find in favour of human rights claims, but not strongly. When it came to matters of statutory interpretation, he took a moderate stance, employing different canons of construction across different cases and showing no real preference for any particular approach overall. In terms of parties, however, his records disclose a tendency to side with the state against the citizen, as well as a tendency to side with the comparatively powerful party against the underdog.

As such, according to this analysis, Lord Neuberger showed a notable, and perhaps surprising, degree of political conservatism and institutional deference (although neither were extreme, and this characterisation must be understood as being relative to the position of his somewhat more adventurous colleagues). In terms of activism, he was a moderate. Whilst he certainly presents a more cautious profile than the Court's other Presidents (Cahill-O'Callaghan's work, for example, shows he placed a high value on conformity, at least to a greater extent than other Court Presidents)[158] this should not be mistaken for anything approaching reticence. Although Lord Neuberger sat in lots of cases, as a President he strived to forge consensus and usually found himself in the majority faction when the Court split. Therefore, even more so than other judges, his relative positioning should be considered in light of his particular institutional position and specific goals.[159] Further, whilst he was generally quite reserved, he could sometimes adopt positions which were more innovative – even radical[160] – when necessary.

Q. Lord Hughes

During the five years Lord Hughes spent on the Court, he spoke infrequently, very rarely adding concurrences or vanity judgments, and rarely dissented. However,

[156] ibid 41–47.

[157] Empirical studies have identified a correlation between a high workload and the adoption of conservative or restrained behaviour: M Giles, J Strayhorn and T Peppers, 'Policymaking under constraint: Decision Modes in the US Courts of Appeals (2015) 36(2) *Justice System Journal* 95; C Engell and K Weinshall, 'Manna from Heaven for Judges: Judges' Reaction to a Quasi-Random Reduction in Caseload' (2020) 17(4) *Journal of Empirical Legal Studies* 722.

[158] Cahill-O'Callaghan (n 29) 145–46.

[159] See Paterson (n 155).

[160] His majority judgment in *Evans* (n 121) is something of a bête noire for sceptics of judicial power: R Ekins and C Forsyth, *Judging the Public Interest: the Rule of Law vs the Rule of Courts* (Judicial Power Project, 2015).

this should not be taken to suggest that he was a passive judge or that he did not have any strong preferences of his own. On those occasions in which he did author a dissent, his views were strongly and passionately communicated, and he was one of the few judges who seemed comfortable with dissenting on his own should the need arise. It might be inferred, then, that much like his colleague Lord Wilson, he was generally content to sign up to the views of his colleagues, but would feel compelled to stake his own claim powerfully and clearly when they adopted a position he found particularly troublesome.

Despite his reluctance to formally dissent, he showed consistently strong preferences across various categories. For example, he was very likely to cast his vote in favour of the state, and against the relative underdog, in relevant cases. He also consistently voted to uphold and follow contested precedent. His views on human rights were similarly conservative, particularly in relation to the ECHR, where he was the most unlikely of all judges examined to adopt a pro-rights position in salient cases. He leaned towards a narrow approach to statutory interpretation, although this was less absolute than his other preferences.

It is not surprising, then, to find that in terms of his voting record, Lord Hughes emerges as both the most conservative judge in terms of politics and the most restrained judge in terms of activism. He also seems to have held an institutional disposition, although this was not as strong as that of some of the other judges. Although other scholars have claimed that he has no distinctive judicial voice,[161] Hughes's records actually seem to indicate that, at least on those occasions in which he felt it important enough to speak out, he was in fact the Court's most reliably conservative figure.

R. Lord Toulson

Although Lord Toulson sat on the Court as a full-time judge for just three years, he had a 'disproportionate'[162] impact on the law (and his colleagues) during that time, delivering the lead judgment in a number of high-profile cases[163] and issuing some particularly influential dissents.[164] He was happy to dissent on his own when necessary – he was, in fact, the only judge in the dataset to author more solo dissents than group ones.

[161] Hunter and Rackley (n 83) 213.

[162] Statement of Lord Neuberger, 'Lord Toulson RIP' (28 June 2017), www.jcpc.uk/news/lord-toulson-rip.html.

[163] See eg his lead in *R v Jogee* [2016] UKSC 8; [2017] AC 387; *Michael v Chief Constable of South Wales Police* [2015] UKSC 2; [2015] 1 AC 1732.

[164] Most notable, perhaps, was *PJS v News Group Newspapers* [2016] UKSC 26; [2016] 1 AC 1081 which saw Toulson praised excessively in the press: J Rozenberg, 'The celebrity threesome case risks undermining the law' *The Guardian* (19 May 2016); D Barrett, 'Celebrity threesome injunction: Top judges rule identities of 'PJS' and 'YMA' must remain secret' *The Telegraph* (19 May 2016).

He held quite a middle-ground position in terms of his likelihood to side with the state overall, as indeed he did with regard to most subject areas. He did, however, stand out in some respects: he would usually take a fairly expansive approach towards the scope of the Court's jurisdiction, he was the least likely of all judges to find criminal liability and he showed sympathy towards the socio-economic underdog in relevant cases. He was also more comfortable with developing the law than some of his colleagues, although often this was done in a fairly modest way. He was responsible for a number of significant private law developments during his time on the court, including *Patel v Mirza*[165] (reformulation of defence of illegality in tort cases) and *Willers v Joyce*[166] (extension of tort of malicious prosecution to cover civil as well as criminal proceedings); McBride suggests that such cases demonstrate an 'altogether more swashbuckling' attitude towards the development of the common law, at least in the private law sphere, than that adopted by his colleagues.[167]

Overall, whilst Toulson's record is quite moderate in a political sense, he was (at least compared to his colleagues) more of an anti-institutional figure as well as a notably more activist judge. Prior to becoming a judge, Toulson sat as Chairman of the Law Commission, and in many ways it is easy to see how Toulson's profile reflects this: an independent-minded thought leader conscious about the need to make change where necessary, and unlikely to rely on notions of tradition and deference for the sake of it, but nonetheless respectful of the limited ambit of his own role, preferring solutions which are pragmatic where possible.

S. Lord Hodge

In sharp contrast to his predecessor (Lord Hope), Lord Hodge was much more reluctant to contribute something of his own to written judgments, and tended to add his own comments only when he considered that he had something particularly important to say.[168] He did, however, speak more frequently in judgments involving appeals from Scottish courts; he contributed something of his own around half of such cases.

Lord Hodge would generally side with the state against the citizen (especially when the Court was split on this issue) and would generally side with more powerful parties against socio-economic underdogs. Similarly, he was fairly unlikely to side with parties claiming that their human rights had been breached

[165] *Patel v Mirza* [2016] UKSC 42; [2017] AC 467.

[166] *Willers v Joyce (No 1)* [2016] UKSC 43; [2016] 3 WLR 477.

[167] N McBride, *The Humanity of Private Law, Part II* (Hart Publishing, 2020). McBride expressly compares Lord Toulson's approach to the more 'incremental' approach preferred by Lord Reed although he rightly notes that applying these labels without qualification can be 'over-simplistic': 181–82.

[168] This is another example of a judge which Hunter and Rackley described as having no 'distinctive voice': n 83, 213.

(he did not vote to issue any declarations of incompatibility under section 4 HRA during his time on the Court, for example). In terms of precedent, he was something of a moderate, but was comfortable with adopting wider, more purposive canons of statutory interpretation and granted comparatively generous remedies to successful parties.

Lord Hodge therefore seems to be one of the Court's broadly more conservative figures, whilst adopting, albeit less consistently, a restrained and institutional approach to his decision-making. Revealingly, he once stated that he was 'generally averse to developing the … law other than by the application of general principles'[169] which feels like a good encapsulation of his cautious approach. He would tend to side with the more conservative option available to the court but would rarely lead the charge to push the law in a radically more conservative direction himself, especially if he detected little appetite for this from his colleagues. He was a judge with his own preferences, but also a clear understanding that the Court operates as a collegiate organ, whereby his own preferences must sometimes give way to the need to achieve practical solutions. That attitude likely contributed to his promotion to the position of Deputy President in 2020.

T. More Recent Appointments

There are a number of judges who were appointed to the Court towards the end of the period covered by the dataset. The contributions of these judges formed a significant part of the court's output during more recent years, but the lack of robust data in relation to each judge's *individual* output, certainly compared to that of their predecessors, made it fairly difficult to draw any particularly robust or illuminating conclusions about their judicial attitudes and behaviour. Nevertheless, the following observations may be noted, with the caveat that they are based on an assessment of very limited records (and that, for judges who continued to sit after 2020, their preferences may have become more pronounced, or may have changed over time):

- Lady Black was appointed to the Court in October 2017.[170] Her records disclose a preference for a narrow, rather than purposive, approach to statutory interpretation, and a tendency to vote in favour of finding a breach of the ECHR. She also seemed much more likely than her (modern) contemporaries to author long concurrences.

[169] *Zurich Insurance v International Energy Group* [2015] UKSC 33; [2016] AC 509 at [102]. Note, however, that this restraint is not applied dogmatically: whilst judges are to 'decide cases, when he or she can, using existing legal principles', the lack of 'fixed boundaries' in this respect mean that when a more activist approach is called for, judges should pay heed to 'wisdom, humanity and common sense': Lord Hodge, 'The scope of judicial decision-making in the common law tradition' (Max Planck Institute for Comparative and International Private Law, 28 October 2019) 10–11.

[170] She retired from the Court in 2021.

- Lord Lloyd-Jones was appointed in October 2017.[171] He exhibited relatively moderate behaviour across the board, with slight conservative tendencies in some areas, and was more likely to side against socio-economic underdogs than others.
- Lord Briggs was appointed to in October 2017.[172] Notably, he seemed comfortable with dissenting from the offset, even if he was on his own. His dissents spanned a number of different subject areas, indicating a general confidence in approach. He tended to recognise or enlarge the jurisdiction for the Court fairly readily, and often showed something of a preference for a wider method of statutory interpretation.
- Lady Arden was appointed in October 2018.[173] She sat on few cases before the cut-off point of this dataset, but tended to author short, snappy lead judgments.[174] She was also more likely than others to issue concurrences.
- Lord Kitchin was appointed in October 2018.[175] During the examined period, he did not deliver a single concurrence or dissent[176] and his output revealed little about his personal preferences.
- Lord Sales was appointed in January 2019.[177] He sat on *very* few cases in the dataset, but seemed to show confidence and independence from the very start, delivering the lead judgment in a remarkable five out of the eight cases in which he was involved.

For completeness, it is worth mentioning that Lord Saville did not sit on many cases or author many leads during his brief time on the Court, due to his continued involvement in the bloated Bloody Sunday inquiry. As such, it is unsurprising that his contributions were very short, he authored only one real lead judgment and did not author a single dissent.

III. Conclusions

This chapter has sought to map the tricky relationship between legal and political attitudes, and has shown that it is all too easy to ascribe political labels to judicial behaviour in ways which are inaccurate and sometimes contradictory. At the same

[171] He retired in 2022 upon reaching mandatory retirement age, but was reappointed thereafter following a change of law. He remains on the Court as of December 2022.

[172] He remains on the Court as of December 2022.

[173] She retired from the Court in 2022.

[174] Ironically, in July 2020, Lady Arden delivered the lead judgment in *Lehtimäki v Cooper* [2020] UKSC 33; [2022] AC 155, which became the longest lead judgment in the UKSC, at 204 paragraphs. That judgment fell outside the ten-year period covered by the dataset in this study.

[175] He remains on the Court as of December 2022.

[176] As was noted in ch 3, as of December 2022, he had issued just one concurrence, and had indicated agreement with (but did not contribute substantively to) just one dissenting judgment.

[177] He remains on the Court as of December 2022.

time, there is an inevitable relationship between politics, howsoever defined, and law, and therefore an obvious relationship between legal behaviour and political behaviour. As such, an attempt has been made to translate the findings in earlier chapters very generally onto different scales, broadly correlating with political attitudes, activist tendencies and institutional independence. Readers are at liberty to disregard these definitions, which were (intentionally) defined *very* roughly and applied subject to the many caveats outlined throughout this chapter.

These labels, however imperfect, helped with the objective of collating the results set out in earlier chapters of this work, and forming composite profiles of the Court's individual judges. Some of these profiles are more developed than others – this is natural when some judges exhibit strong and consistent indicators of a certain kind of behaviour, whilst others exhibit tendencies which are more slight, nuanced or contradictory. Notably, some judges showed very little evidence of having strong and consistent preferences one way or the other (or, at least, preferences which manifested in such a way that they could be captured by the kind of content analysis undertaken in this work).

Notwithstanding these many limitations inherent in these judicial profiles, it is hoped that this chapter has nevertheless provided an interesting way of considering and explaining the voting records explored throughout this book. There is always a risk that the invocation of terms such as 'activist' and 'conservative' when describing judicial behaviour can lead to a misunderstanding about the judges and their actions. It is therefore worth repeating that despite arguing that judges, as individuals, will have their own preferences which will inevitably affect how they perform their role, *and* that we can describe some of these preferences using certain labels, this does not mean that the judges have acted improperly, or that they have been turned into politicians. Whilst judges such as Lord Sumption and Lord Hughes are very different judges to Lady Hale and Lord Kerr (and whilst the former pairing might reasonably be described as *conservative* and the latter two *liberal*), all four operated within the legitimate area of discretion afforded to them, as was explained in chapter one. These issues are further developed in chapter eleven, but for present purposes let it be said that nothing in this chapter should cast any doubt on the legitimacy of the judges on the UKSC.

As has been acknowledged, the work presented in this chapter is based on a dataset which covers only a specified temporal range, its outer limit broadly coinciding with the end of Lady Hale's premiership. Since then, of course, the Court has continued to work under its new President, Lord Reed, and has been producing a steady stream of judgments which are ripe for examination. Whilst an exhaustive quantitative overview of this recent output is impractical if not impossible, the following chapter considers some *general* trends in the Court's output since 2020, and tries to highlight some of the more interesting or notable contributions from some of its individual judges. It should offer valuable context for understanding and contextualising the findings presented in this chapter, as well as a starting point for considering judicial behaviour on the UKSC going forward.

10

The Supreme Court Since 2020: A More Conservative Court?

The dataset used in this book runs from the day the Supreme Court opened its doors on 1 October 2009 to the end of its final term of its tenth year. It covered the Presidencies of Lords Phillips, Neuberger and Hale. In January 2020, Lady Hale retired from the Court and was replaced with Lord Reed (Lord Hodge replaced Lady Hale as the Court's Deputy President). Further, within the year, three further judges retired: Lords Carnwath, Lord Wilson and Kerr. The four resulting vacancies were filled by Lords Hamblen, Leggatt, Burrows and Stephens, meaning that 2020 saw a significant changing of the guard when it came to judicial personnel.

A number of legal commentators have since argued that, starting from around this point, the Court has adopted a more conservative, or certainly a more restrained, position towards many issues. Perhaps most notably, in a blistering essay in the *London Review of Books*, Conor Gearty attacked the Court's new-found 'commitment to formalism' and what he considered to be an overly-deferential approach to public laws issues.[1] Elsewhere Adam Tomkins noted the 'conservative turn'[2] in the Court's more recent jurisprudence; Jonathan Jones suggested that there is evidence of the Court's newer judges holding a 'conservative constitutionalist view'[3] and Brice Dickson has identified 'a more restrained approach' in the Court's judgments compared to 'just a few years' prior.[4] Of course, not all evaluations are so critical. Richard Ekins of the Judicial Power Project has noted with approval the Court's recent 'more disciplined approach'[5] which he saw as 'pushing back against [the] judicial activism' espoused by earlier incarnations of the Court.[6] Former Chancellor Robert Buckland has praised the Court's more 'sensible' approach, one in which the judges, in his view, exercised an 'appropriate

[1] C Gearty, 'In the shallow end' (2022) 44(2) *London Review of Books* (27 January 2022).

[2] A Tomkins, 'Why did the Tories retreat from taking on the Supreme Court judges?' *The Herald* (11 August 2021).

[3] A Dean, 'The government wanted to rein in the Supreme Court. Now it may not need to.' (*Prospect*, 16 October 2021).

[4] B Dickson, 'Judgement Day for the Supreme Court' (*New Law Journal*, 28 January 2022) 17.

[5] R Ekins, 'The Government's judicial review legislation is welcome, but could go even further' (*ConservativeHome*, 22 July 2021) conservativehome.com/2021/07/22/richard-ekins-the-governments-judicial-review-legislation-is-welcome-but-could-go-even-further/.

[6] R Ekins, 'Under Lord Reed, the Supreme Court itself is pushing back against judicial activism' (*ConservativeHome*, 17 December 2021) conservativehome.com/2021/12/17/richard-ekins-under-lord-reed-the-supreme-court-itself-is-pushing-back-against-judicial-activism/.

degree of constraint'.[7] Many more examples could be noted, with some favourable towards the Court's direction of travel and others much less enthusiastic.[8]

It is not just academics who have pronounced upon these matters. Those who have likewise acknowledged the Court's move towards a more restrained jurisprudence include former Supreme Court judges Lord Brown,[9] Lord Sumption[10] and Lady Hale.[11] Parliamentarians have also taken note: a 2022 Report by the All-Party Parliamentary Group on Democracy and the Constitution alleged that the Court's recent judgments show a trend towards restraint and deference, and create the impression of a Court which is 'more favourable to the executive'[12] than it was before.

In this chapter, I will assess some of the evidence for these claims.[13] The section below considers the Court's output between 2020 and 2022 and assesses it for evidence of conservatism (which I defined in the last chapter as exhibiting a tendency to side with the state and against the underdog, and a reluctance to pro-immigration and pro-human rights outcomes) and judicial restraint (which I defined in the last chapter, roughly, as exhibiting a tendency to interpret provisions narrowly, follow authorities, and adopt a narrow view of the court's role and jurisdiction). Although there is at present insufficient data to inform any strong empirical observations about the individual judges on the Court, some of the Court's more prolific post-2020 judges are noted. Overall, I suggest that the Court has more recently adopted a position which is generally conservative in nature but is *not* characterised strongly by judicial restraint across the board.

I. A Conservative Approach

It is useful to begin with an examination of the Court's attitude towards the legislature. This is easiest to diagnose through looking at the small number of areas in which courts are empowered to evaluate the substance of primary legislation, for example under the Human Rights Act (HRA). Illustrative in this regard is the

[7] R Buckland, 'Lecture on the ECHR' (personal website, 28 February 2022) at www.robertbuckland.co.uk/news/lecture-echr. See also R Buckland, 'Judges have become more restrained since ruling against prorogation of Parliament' *The Telegraph* (17 July 2021).

[8] See eg A Horne, 'Has the UK Supreme Court Reformed Itself?' (*Prospect*, August 5 2021); G Tan, 'Children's Rights and the Influence of Lord Sales in the UKSC's Political Constitutionalist Turn' (2022) 26(1) *Edinburgh Law Review* 93, N Langen 'Under Lord Reed, the Supreme Court has Retreated into itself' (*The Justice Gap*, 27 July 2021).

[9] In an interview with Dean (n 3) Lord Brown noted that, in his view, there had been 'some measure of retrenchment' in the Court's recent jurisprudence.

[10] 'Letters' 44(3) *London Review of Books*, 10 February 2022.

[11] Double Jeopardy Podcast, 'Judicial Independence and its enemies' (Episode 15, 17 November 2022).

[12] APPG on Democracy and the Constitution, 'An Independent Judiciary – Challenges since 2016' (8 June 2022) 49, available at www.icdr.co.uk/judicial-independence-inquiry (last accessed 31 July 2023).

[13] The substance of this chapter draws on research undertaken for an article, the finished version of which will be published as L Graham, 'Has the Supreme Court become more restrained in public law cases?' (forthcoming, *Modern Law Review*).

SC case,[14] involving a challenge to legislation which limited the availability of child tax credits to a family's first two children in most circumstances. The question for the Court was whether treating larger families differently from smaller ones for welfare purposes could be justified. The Court ruled that in answering such a question, where a balance had already been struck by the legislature, only a 'rational connection' between the policy and the aim behind it was needed for it to be considered proportionate by the Court: there was 'no basis, consistent with the separation of powers' upon which the Court could apply a more intense review standard.[15] The Court seemed to go beyond its usual deferential position by framing the question of proportionality as something inappropriate for judicial determination: since the issue 'boils down to how generous social security benefits should be',[16] the question of whether discrimination could be justified became an issue ill-suited to judges, as it '*can only be* determined … through a political process'.[17] There was 'no basis … on which the courts could properly overturn Parliament's judgment that the measure was … appropriate'.[18]

The Court has adopted a similar approach in other cases. Where political issues appeared before it, especially if those issues had already been addressed by the legislature,[19] the Court would often bow out entirely, in order to 'respect the boundaries between legality and the political process' and to mitigate 'a risk of undue interference by the courts in the sphere of political choices'.[20] To do otherwise would '[e]nable […] those who had lost the political debate'[21] (often, apparently, 'campaigning organisations which lobbied unsuccessfully' against the law under challenge at the legislative stage)[22] to inappropriately 'continue their campaign'[23] in the courts. The Court has also adopted a wide definition of what constitutes a 'political' issue, therefore bringing a case into the prohibited zone. Not only are welfare-related issues inherently political, but so are 'measures of economic or social strategy' in general,[24] cases involving 'competing interests'[25] and issues involving subjects likely to generate controversy.[26]

Taken together, the breadth of the Court's understanding of what constitutes a political issue (which human rights claim would *not* involve a consideration

[14] *R (SC) v Secretary of State for Work and Pensions* [2021] UKSC 26; [2022] AC 223.

[15] ibid [209].

[16] House of Lords Constitution Committee, Annual evidence session with the President and Deputy President of the Supreme Court, 6 April 2022, Response to Lord Falconer, Q22.

[17] *SC* (n 14) at [208]. Emphasis mine.

[18] ibid [209]. Lord Reed recently confirmed this interpretation: 'We said how much the taxpayer should be expected to contribute to the upkeep of other people's children is not a matter for decision by courts […] that ultimately is not a justiciable issue, and that is what we said.': House of Lords Constitution Committee (n 16), Response to Lord Falconer, Q22.

[19] *SC* (n 14) at [203]; *R (Z) v Hackney LBC* [2020] UKSC 40; [2020] 1 WLR 4327 at [107].

[20] *SC* (n 14) at [162].

[21] *Re Attorney-General's Reference (Safe Access Zones)* [2022] UKSC 32; [2023] AC 505 at [156].

[22] *SC* (n 14) at [162].

[23] ibid [162].

[24] *Z* (n 19) at [108].

[25] ibid [107].

[26] *SC* (n 14) at [180], [207].

of competing interests, or involve subject-matter which might be controversial in the eyes of some voters?) alongside the acutely deferential approach adopted when reviewing these issues means that review of legislative choices under the HRA is significantly limited in practice; that the HRA and other laws empower courts to determine *legal questions* (which might sometimes *require* the courts to 'align the law with the values of opponents of reform') does not seem to matter should politically controversial subjects be engaged.

The Court's anxiety to stay away from anything political makes sense in light of the fairly expansive conception of sovereignty it adopted in the *UNCRC Bill Reference* case.[27] In the course of its judgment, it described both section 3 of the HRA[28] (permitting an expansive rights-consistent interpretation of statutory provisions) and the European Communities Act 1972[29] (permitting both an expansive interpretation and potential disapplication of statutory provisions which conflict with EU law) as effecting a 'qualification' of sovereignty. More unusually, section 4 of the HRA was similarly described as a limit upon sovereignty, because whilst declarations of incompatibility made under this provision have no direct legal effect, the resulting political pressure to respond to them limits the freedom of the legislature in practice.[30] A similarly expansive understanding of how far Parliament's exclusive jurisdiction lies can be seen in the Court's judgment holding that the Scottish Parliament's Bill providing for a referendum on Scottish independence fell outside its legal competence[31] on the basis that such a referendum, whatever its outcome, would have no direct legal effects, but would have significant political impact on Westminster.[32] Both cases saw a clear 'departure from orthodoxy'[33] from the Court in its application of 'a thicker conception of parliamentary sovereignty' than that which it had employed previously.[34] Separately, sovereignty was also invoked by the Court in order to limit the development of the common law,[35] as a justification for limiting both the temporal scope of the HRA[36] and the effect of section 2 of the same Act[37] and as a reason

[27] *Re United Nations Convention on the Rights of the Child (Incorporation) (Scotland) Bill* [2021] UKSC 42; [2021] 1 WLR 5106.

[28] ibid [28], [84].

[29] ibid [40].

[30] ibid [50]. Commentators have rightly noted that the Court here seemingly departs from its earlier, more orthodox views on this provision without real acknowledgment: M Elliott and N Kilford, 'The Supreme Court's defence on unqualified lawmaking power: parliamentary sovereignty, devolution and the Scotland Act 1998' (2022) 81(1) *CLJ* 4, 6.

[31] *Re Scottish Independence Referendum Bill* [2022] UKSC 31; [2022] 1 WLR 5435.

[32] ibid [79] and [81].

[33] Elliott and Kilford (n 30) 7.

[34] G Cowie, 'The power to make bills for Scotland: the Treaty Incorporation Bills Reference' [2022] *PL* 189, 199.

[35] *R (Elgizouli) v Secretary of State for the Home Department* [2020] UKSC 10; [2021] AC 937 at [232]: 'it is Parliamentary legislation rather than the common law which has created and delimits the right to life'.

[36] *Re McQuillan* [2021] UKSC 55; [2022] 2 WLR 49 at [155]–[156], [158], [163]–[167]. See also *Re Dalton* [2023] UKSC 36.

[37] *R (Elan-Cane) v Secretary of State for the Home Department* [2021] UKSC 56; [2023] AC 559 at [90] and [108]: To interpret the HRA as permitting domestic courts to find a breach of Convention rights

for adopting light-touch review of secondary legislation.[38] Taking these cases together, it seems that over the last few years the Court has adopted a particularly muscular conception of parliamentary sovereignty, no longer some background constitutional principle but in some cases almost a distinct legal tool in and of itself.

The court's attitude towards the executive during this recent period is even more striking. The Court was disproportionately likely to side with the state during this time (public authorities won 62 per cent of the 84 applicable cases between 2020 and 2022);[39] and its case law, by and large,[40] moved the law in a more conservative direction in this respect, permitting the executive greater discretion and subjecting it to a lower standard of scrutiny overall. A particularly deferential approach was applied, for example: when reviewing the exclusion of trafficking victims from a compensation scheme, describing it as a 'social welfare policy'[41] involving the allocation of 'finite public resources';[42] when reviewing the rule requiring binary determination of gender on passports, a question involving 'sensitive moral and ethical issues';[43] when reviewing the government's compliance with its prior environmental commitments, because the statutory duties in question were framed broadly and invited the decision-maker to draw upon their expertise;[44] when reviewing the deprivation of a claimant's citizenship, because the discretionary nature of the decision was 'incapable of objectively verifiable assessment'[45] and one which the Court was unsuited to review on both 'institutional and constitutional'[46] grounds: the Court had neither the expertise nor the democratic legitimacy of the Home Secretary.[47] The Court also showed a particular reluctance to review the executive when it came to reviewing both the application and lawfulness of policies.[48] It seems that, overall, the Court's approach to the executive might well be described as a conservative one.

in circumstances where the Strasbourg Court has ruled that the issue falls within the domestic authorities' margin of appreciation would, said the Court, constitute an 'encroachment upon Parliamentary sovereignty'.

[38] *A v Criminal Injuries Compensation Authority* [2021] UKSC 27; [2021] 1 WLR 3746 at [84].

[39] The numbers can be broken down further; 32 cases involved central government departments, which won in 63% of cases. The Court was kind to local authorities, which won 85% of the 13 relevant cases they were involved in, as well as members of the Scottish and Northern Irish executive, which were involved in such 8 cases, winning 81% of them. Tax authorities, on the other hand, were less successful overall, with HMRC winning 39% of the 15 relevant cases it found itself involved in.

[40] Although certainly not exclusively: see *R (Palestine Solidarity Campaign) v Secretary of State for Housing, Communities and Local Government* [2020] UKSC 16; [2020] 1 WLR 1774; *R (Majera) v Secretary of State for the Home Department* [2021] UKSC 46; [2022] AC 461 at [1], [29]–[31], [44]–[45], [56]; *Craig v HM Advocate* [2022] UKSC 6; [2022] 1 WLR 1270 at [44], [46], [53].

[41] *A* (n 38) at [83].

[42] ibid [90].

[43] *Elan-Cane* (n 37) at [61].

[44] *R (Friends of the Earth) v Heathrow Airport Ltd* [2020] UKSC 52; [2021] 2 All ER 967 at [144].

[45] *R (Begum) v Special Immigration Appeals Commission* [2021] UKSC 7; [2021] AC 765 at [70].

[46] ibid [109]. See similar language in *Elgizouli* (n 35) at [179].

[47] *Begum* (n 45) at [70], [62] and [134].

[48] *R (A) v Secretary of State for the Home Department* [2021] UKSC 37; [2021] 1 WLR 3921 at [3], [39], [40] (policies are different in nature from laws, and subject to a lower degree of judicial

Conservatism was also evident in the Court's human rights judgments. On a purely numerical basis, the Court handed down 34 cases involving some kind of human rights claim between 2020 and 2022. The 'success rate'[49] in those cases was just 29.4 per cent.[50] This is significantly lower than the comparable rates of previous years; prior to 2020 the average annual success rate before the UKSC was 41 per cent, and in 2019, Lady Hale's last year as President of the Court, the success rate jumped to 60 per cent.[51] The likelihood of the UKSC finding a breach of human rights in a given case roughly halved once Lady Hale retired and Lord Reed took over as President.

In terms of the HRA, since 2020, the Court has issued no declarations of incompatibility in relation to primary legislation under section 4, has struck down no secondary legislation under the Act and has almost always rejected attempts to invoke its interpretive powers under section 3.[52] Its case law reveals a similarly conservative attitude; the Court has adopted a restrained approach to the temporal scope of the Act;[53] has applied great restraint to the assessment of proportionality;[54] has been very reluctant to import a proportionality requirement into domestic frameworks;[55] has adopted a fairly permissive approach to the requirement that any action which interferes with a Convention right must be sufficiently 'prescribed by law';[56] and has narrowed the circumstances under which it might impugn general measures which might breach the rights of parties some of the time, but not necessarily in every case in which the HRA applies.[57]

Of course, there are other sources of human rights protection beyond the ECHR. But these avenues disclose a similar pattern of reticence; between 2020 and 2022, there were, for example, no cases in which claims based on rights derived

oversight); *Begum* (n 45) at [123]–[124] (application of policies should generally not be policed by courts); *Advocate General for Scotland v KE Entertainments* [2020] UKSC 28, [2020] 4 All ER 441 at [57]–[60] (policy only capable of providing guidance rather than rigid directions which could be relied upon); *Friends of the Earth* (n 44) (statutory obligations limiting discretion over treatment of policies construed narrowly); *R (BF) v Secretary of State for the Home Department* [2021] UKSC 38; [2021] 1 WLR 3967 at [49] and [52] (limited grounds under which a policy can be challenged).

[49] As with the approach adopted in previous chapters, here the coding was binary; cases involving (only) successful human rights claims were marked as 1, whilst failures were marked as 0. Mixed results – for example, where two distinct human rights breach allegations are made, and one succeeds but not the other, were marked as 0.5.

[50] If just ECHR cases are included, this rises to 34.5%.

[51] Graham (n 13).

[52] *Z* (n 19) at [111]; *General Dynamics UK v Libya* [2021] UKSC 22; [2022] AC 318 at [99] *cf* the dissent in that case at [243]. See also the similar reluctance to adopt a conforming interpretation under EU law in *Google v Lloyd* [2021] UKSC 50; [2022] AC 1217 at [120]. A potential exception of *Ziegler*, where the relevance of that provision was 'common ground' between the parties: *DPP v Ziegler* [2021] UKSC 23; [2022] AC 408 at [16].

[53] *McQuillan* (n 36).

[54] *SC* (n 14) at [162].

[55] See eg *Z* (n 19) at [96]–[110] and *Re Abortion Services Bill* (n 21) at [29].

[56] *Re T* [2021] UKSC 35; [2022] AC 723 at [91], [152]; *A* (n 48) at [50]–[52]. Compare eg *R (T) v Chief Constable of Greater Manchester* [2014] UKSC 35; [2015] AC 49.

[57] *Abortion Services Bill* (n 21) at [12]–[19]. See generally S Stark, 'Section 4 of the Human Rights Act 1998: Still Standing or Standing Still?' (UK Constitutional Law Association Blog, 16 November 2022).

from EU law succeeded, but multiple cases where these claims failed.[58] Much the same can be said about common law rights; the Court has been reluctant to add any rights to the existing canon[59] and has interpreted those rights it has recognised narrowly,[60] emphasising that it is important to keep the class of common law rights 'within narrow bounds'[61] primarily to preserve legal certainty.[62] The Court has likewise been reluctant to recognise, much less enforce, human rights sourced in international law, with a rigid conception of dualism ousting almost any influence at the domestic level.[63] Not only was any possibility of a direct invocation of international law rights expressly disavowed,[64] but the Court was also reluctant to recognise international human rights law as an influence on interpretation of statutory provisions or upon the development of the common law.[65] As such, the presence of international human rights law in the UKSC's judgments has almost vanished since 2020, unless those frameworks were expressly and voluntarily incorporated into (for example) arbitration agreements which fell to be interpreted by the Court.[66]

The Court's approach to human rights claims confirms the conservative trends sketched out above: the scope of many rights is being narrowed, the impact of the court's tools is being softened, and the Court is clearly being particularly careful to ensure that it does not usurp the functions of the legislature and the executive. Whether this is justified in the context of specific statutory duties to protect human rights remains an open question.

[58] *Z* (n 19) at [62]–[65]; *Robinson v Secretary of State for the Home Department* [2020] UKSC 53; [2022] AC 659; *Lloyd* (n 52) at [128]; *Fratila v Secretary of State for Work and Pensions* [2021] UKSC 53; [2022] 3 All ER 1045.

[59] *Elgizouli* (n 35) at [141] (Lord Kerr); see also Lord Reed at [169]; *R (Project for the Registration of Children as British Citizens) v Secretary of State for the Home Department* [2022] UKSC 3; [2023] AC 255; *R (Coughlan) v Minister for the Cabinet Office* [2022] UKSC 11; [2022] 1 WLR 2389.

[60] See L Morón, 'Presumptions of Legislative Intent in R (Coughlan) v Minister for the Cabinet Office' (2023) 86(3) *MLR* 801 at 802: the case law 'threatens to erode the principle of legality'; *Begum* (n 45) at [88], [94], [102], [110], [135]; *General Dynamics* (n 52) at [85] cf the dissenting view at [242]–[243] cf *R (Haworth) v HMRC* [2021] UKSC 25; [2021] 1 WLR 3521 at [59].

[61] *PRCBC* (n 59) at [43].

[62] ibid [29].

[63] See eg *SC* (n 14) at [78] and R Ekins, 'Convention rights, child tax credits and the constitution' (2022) 138 LQR 551 at 553 ('the decision vindicates constitutional dualism').

[64] See eg *SC* (n 14) at [76]–[78].

[65] L Graham, 'The supreme court's recent approach to unincorporated human rights treaties' (2024) 1 EHRLR 49 and see in particular *PRCBC* (n 59) at [56]; *A* (n 38) at [33]; *R (AB) v Secretary of State for Justice* [2021] UKSC 28; [2022] AC 487 at [64]; In *Re Independence Referendum Bill* (n 31) at [87] the Court did at least recognise a 'strong presumption' that national legislation should be interpreted so as to avoid a breach of international law, even with regards to unincorporated treaties, if the statute's meaning is 'not clear on its face'.

[66] An emphasis on dualism could also be detected in the *Friends of the Earth* case, which concerned a statutory duty to consider certain relevant policies. The Court held that the ratification of agreements in international law, such as the Paris Agreement, did not constitute such a policy for the purposes of domestic law, on the basis that '[r]atification is an act on the international plane', and any obligations flowing from this 'are not part of UK law and give rise to no legal rights or obligations in domestic law': *Friends of the Earth* (n 44) at [108].

II. Activism and Restraint

What about the Court's approach to developing the law, and its level of judicial activism? First, there is, within the Court's case law, a real retreat from the use of public policy considerations in judicial reasoning, at least in respect of the extent to which it will actively consider public policy arguments as part of its own reasoning.[67] For example, in *Flyde Farms*, the Court interpreted and applied a statutory provision relating to time limits for planning applications.[68] It acknowledged that there were multiple tenable interpretations of the statute, but that it would be inappropriate for policy considerations to play any role in determining which is to be preferred: it was 'not a case where the court can choose between rival interpretations on the basis that one of them serves the court's own perception of promoting efficient administration and proportionate or timely litigation better than the other.'[69] Similarly, in *Adelekun*, the Court was required to construe the applicable Qualified One-way Costs Shifting rules, and in doing so confirmed that it was 'not necessary or appropriate'[70] to consider any of the 'adverse policy consequences' which may follow their preferred interpretation, notwithstanding the 'great emphasis' placed on this factor by both parties;[71] the Court limited itself to being guided exclusively by the relevant 'language'[72] and as such it did not matter whether, as some of the parties claimed, the outcome would be 'counter-intuitive', 'unfair' or 'anomalous'[73] as a result. Whilst it cannot be said that policy never plays a part in its more recent judgments,[74] there is, I think, a clear reluctance on the part of most judges to engage with public policy questions, at least explicitly. Legal rules and established frameworks are seemingly to be preferred to the invocation of vague public policy concerns, which risks veering into political territory and is thus unsuitable for the Court to determine.

[67] There is a related phenomenon, largely affecting private law cases, where the court has shown a real reluctance to endorse any role for public policy in the formulation of legal tests: *see Various Claimants v WM Morrison Supermarkets* [2020] UKSC 12; [2020] AC 989; *Manchester Building Society v Grant Thornton UK* [2021] UKSC 20; [2022] AC 783 at [5], *Khan v Meadows* [2021] UKSC 21; [2022] AC 852 at [59]. Note the similarities to other cases handed down by Lord Reed prior to 2020: *Robinson v Chief Constable of West Yorkshire* [2018] UKSC 4; [2018] AC 736; *Poole BC v GN* [2019] UKSC 25; [2020] AC 780; on which, see J Morgan, 'Nonfeasance and the end of policy? Reflections on the revolution in public authority liability' (2019) 35(1) *Professional Negligence* 32.

[68] Town and Country Planning Act 1990, s 61N.

[69] *R (Flyde Coast Farms) v Flyde BC* [2021] UKSC 18; [2021] 1 WLR 2794 at [43].

[70] *Ho v Adelekun* [2021] UKSC 43; [2021] 1 WLR 5132 at [31].

[71] ibid [30].

[72] ibid [32], [41], [42].

[73] ibid [44]–[45].

[74] The Court did rely heavily on policy in some private law cases handed down during the relevant period, including *Whitting Hospital NHS Trust v XX* [2020] UKSC 14; [2021] AC 275 when considering whether the costs of overseas surrogacy ought to form part of an award in negligence (at [53]). The case was argued in the middle of 2019, and the three members of the majority (Lady Hale, Lord Kerr, Lord Wilson) soon retired. Lords Carnwath and Reed strongly dissented, and were openly sceptical about the majority's reliance on policy considerations: see [63]–[67]. See also *Stoffel and Co v Grondona* [2020] UKSC 42; [2021] AC 540 and *Henderson v Dorset Healthcare University NHS Foundation Trust* [2020] UKSC 43; [2021] AC 563.

Further, in some cases,[75] the Court indicated a strong preference for the adoption of bright-line rules over discretionary powers and multi-factorial principles. For example, in *Zabolotnyi* the Court saw was little room for the exercise of discretion to admit fresh evidence outside the tight rules set out in the relevant statute,[76] and a majority of judges in *Pathan* adhered to a rigid and somewhat artificial distinction between procedural and substantive fairness (with only the former being enforceable by the Court), severely limiting the remedy available to the claimant against a failure to inform him of changes to his visa sponsorship.[77] The Court has otherwise taken a particular interest in explaining or otherwise reformulating legal problems as resolvable through a series of steps, rules or questions.[78]

On the other hand, certainty did not always win the day and on occasion, the Court readily applied a more flexible approach in the interests of achieving justice. This approach is most evident in the private law cases, which, for example, saw the Court reject a rigid separation of the notions of 'advice' and 'information' which had taken root in the case law, in favour of a more flexible approach based on a spectrum.[79] The most stark example of the Court placing emphasis on a flexible approach which ensured that justice was done came in *T*, where it was unwilling to let considerations of certainty prevent it from exercising its discretion to authorise unregistered placements.[80] In a remarkably powerful statement underlining the importance of the Court's role, Lady Black said that 'it is unthinkable that the … Court, with its long-established role in protecting children, should have no means to keep … unfortunate children (and others who may be at risk from them) safe from extreme harm, in some cases death.'[81] In that case, the Court was adamant that justice demanded flexibility rather than adherence to rigid rules. Therefore, whilst the Court sometimes relies more heavily upon the

[75] This section considers public law cases; for instances of certainty trumping fairness in private law cases see eg *Sevilleja v Marex* [2020] UKSC 31; [2021] AC at [167] (rigid rules in relation to reflective loss endorsed even if this risked causing some degree of injustice in edge cases); *Alexander Devine Children's Cancer Trust v Housing Solutions Ltd* [2020] UKSC 45; [2020] 1 WLR 4783 at [42]–[47] (behaviour of parties an irrelevant factor when it comes to modifying a covenant, despite arguments of unfairness); *AIC Ltd v Federal Airports Authority of Nigeria* [2022] UKSC 16; [2022] 1 WLR 3223 (a discretion for varying an order before it is formally sealed technically recognised but would not be exercised in practice owing to importance of finality).

[76] *Zabolotnyi v Hungary* [2021] UKSC 14; [2021] 1 WLR 2569 at [57]–[58].

[77] *R (Pathan) v Secretary of State for the Home Department* [2020] UKSC 41; [2020] 1 WLR 4506.

[78] See eg *MBS* (n 67) at [6]; *Khan* (n 67) at [28] (an attempt to frame the determination of negligence liability as a six-step sequence) *A* (n 48) at [46]–[47] (setting out three circumstances where policies can be challenged).

[79] *MBS* (n 67) at [18], [22], [90]–[92], [195]–[197]; *Khan* (n 67) at [41] and [71] and note also in those cases the principle set out in *South Australia Asset Management Co v York Montague Ltd* [1997] AC 1 being treated as one legal consideration amongst many (*Khan*, [36]; *MBS*, [106]), and a 'cross check' (*Khan*, [71]; *MBS*, [23], [192]) rather than a rigid rule applicable in every case. See likewise *Guest v Guest* [2022] UKSC 27; [2022] 3 WLR 911 at [79], [80], [82] (*cf* the dissenting judges at [162]–[166] and [181]) and *Pakistan International Airline Corp v Times Travel* [2021] UKSC 40; [2023] AC 101 (*cf* Lord Burrows at [93]).

[80] *T* (n 56).

[81] *T* (n 56) at [141].

idea of certainty over fairness or vice-versa, neither value has seemingly taken priority overall. Whilst the Court's fairly consistent resistance to the use of public policy factors suggests the adoption of a more restrained approach, the court's preference for certainty over justice in some cases, but justice over certainty in others, suggests an attitude which is neither strongly activist nor restrained. The Court's preferred approach differs depending on what is needed in each case.[82]

Another potential marker of restrained behaviour may be a tendency to uphold existing decisions, and a reluctance to re-open and intervene in disputes which have already been determined by a judicial body, in order to respect the values of finality and certainty. 140 of the 146 cases handed down by the Court during the examined period were appeals from lower courts. Overall, appeals were allowed in 43.6 per cent of cases. This figure is somewhat low, but well within the range of the Court's 40–55 per cent success rate in any given year. Numbers, as ever, only tell a partial story; more helpful perhaps is that the Court has set out guidance as to the standards to be applied when considering appeals in various contexts. On the one hand, the Court has repeatedly emphasised that the court or tribunal determining issues at first instance should be considered to have 'primary responsibility'[83] for determining the facts and the law and has often exercised a fair degree of deference to that court.[84] The Court has also emphasised the distinct role to be played by the Court of Appeal and has outlined a number of situations in which its determinations will not be disturbed on appeal.[85] That said, these standards merely emphasise the inherent limitations of the appellate role, and the Court has not strayed from correcting the first instance court where errors were clearly made, either at first instance[86] or at the lower appellate level.[87]

[82] As Lord Sales has suggested in an extra-judicial speech, different cases will call for different degrees of rigidity and flexibility: Lord Sales, 'Default Rules in the Common Law: Substantive Rules and Precedent' (International Workshop on Default Rules in Private Law, 24 March 2023) 1.

[83] *Cardtronics UK v Sykes* [2020] UKSC 21; [2020] 1 WLR 2184 at [4].

[84] *Shagang Shipping Co Ltd v HNA Group Co* [2020] UKSC 34; [2020] 1 WLR 3549 at [58]; *Re HW* [2022] UKSC 17; [2022] 1 WLR 3243 at [48]–[49]; *Cardtronics*, ibid [4]; *SC (Jamaica) v Secretary of State for the Home Department* [2022] UKSC 15; [2022] 1 WLR 3190 at [70]; *HA (Iraq) v Secretary of State for the Home Department* [2022] UKSC 22; [2022] 1 WLR 3784 at [72] and [110]; *Alexander Devine* (n 75) at [51]; *Begum* (n 45) at [104]; *Bloomberg v ZXC* [2022] UKSC 5; [2022] AC 1158 at [157]; *Hastings v Finsbury Orthopaedics Ltd* [2022] UKSC 19; [2023] 1 All ER 885 at [62].

[85] *R (Gourlay) v Parole Board* [2020] UKSC 50; [2020] 1 WLR 5344 at [24], [36], [49]; *CPRE Kent v Secretary of State for Communities and Local Government* [2021] UKSC 36; [2021] 1 WLR 4168 at [15]–[16]; *R v Maughan* [2022] UKSC 13; [2022] 1 WLR 2820 at [14].

[86] In *Serafin v Malkiewicz* [2020] UKSC 23; [2020] 1 WLR 2455 at [48] the Court criticised, in very strong terms, a trial judge for his 'barrage of hostility towards the claimant's case, and towards the claimant himself … in immoderate, ill-tempered and at times offensive language'. In *Mastercard v Merricks* [2020] UKSC 51; [2021] 3 All ER 285 at [63] the Court identified five errors of law in the reasoning of the tribunal, despite 'bearing well in mind that the CAT has unique expertise in making sophisticated economic analysis of a wide variety of data in competition cases, that it is an expert tribunal constituted for that purpose, with economists as well as lawyers on its panels of judges, and that it is the tribunal to which Parliament has entrusted both the exclusive jurisdiction over collective proceedings and, in particular, the conduct of the task of certification, with wide discretionary power for that purpose'.

[87] *Begum* (n 45) esp at [108]–[111] and [132]–[136]; *Ziegler* (n 52) at [53], [113]; *SC Jamaica* (n 84) at [98], [102], [108], [114]; *Okpabi v Royal Dutch Shell* [2021] UKSC 3; [2021] 1 WLR 1294 at [102].

In a number of judgments handed down in this period, the Court grappled with the deceptively tricky question of what the proper standard to be applied by an appellate court ought to be when considering a lower court's evaluation of proportionality. In some cases, such as *Z*,[88] *HW*[89] and *Ziegler*[90] the Court applied a fairly restrained approach, directing appellate courts to give considerable weight to the decisions of lower courts (each in slightly different circumstances). The most recent authority on the issue, however, might indicate something of a change in direction on this issue: in the *Abortion Services (Safe Access Zones) Bill Reference*[91] the Court unanimously rejected the narrower approach endorsed by the majority in *Ziegler* to appeals by way of case stated[92] and suggested that in all appellate cases (case stated or otherwise) the reviewing court has a duty to ensure for itself that statutory rights, including those in the HRA, are protected.[93] When considering a lower court's determination of proportionality (at least when it comes to the compatibility of a general measure),[94] the Court should adopt an 'interventionist' approach,[95] requiring it to 'carry out its own assessment' and 'not accord any deference to the assessment of proportionality by the courts below'.[96] Whether this aligns the current law with the view of the minority in *Ziegler* or compels a yet more exacting standard of review is somewhat ambiguous, but it is clear that the narrow approach to proportionality review which seemed to command majority support until very recently is no longer good law.

The case law therefore reveals a mixed picture when it comes to the prevailing attitude towards lower courts. There is evidence of restraint, but this is not apparent across the board. If the Court is therefore to be described as restrained, this is not necessarily because of any consistently deferential attitude it holds towards lower courts.

The Court's use of its legal tools may also evidence some kind of restrained approach. Some commentators have argued the Court is increasingly likely to apply a formalistic, deductive approach to statutory interpretation[97] However,

[88] *Z* (n 19) at [74] and see also Lady Arden at [119]–[120].
[89] *HW* (n 84) at [48].
[90] *Ziegler* (n 52) at [29] and see also [42], [44], [54], [99], [106].
[91] *Re Abortion Services Bill* (n 21).
[92] ibid [33].
[93] ibid [32].
[94] One reading of the Court's reasoning suggests that a different standard might be applicable in the context of appeals against proportionality assessments relating to a specific decision or measure, although it was noted that the more interventionist approach has been adopted in the past in cases 'concerned with rules or policies in which the facts of the individual case were of greater significance' too: ibid [31].
[95] ibid [33].
[96] ibid [31].
[97] J Hayes, 'Discrimination by legal design? UK Supreme Court in Mencap v Tomlinson-Blake finds care workers are not protected by minimum wage law for sleep-in shifts' (2022) 51(3) *Industrial Law Journal* 696, 698–99; J Bell and E Fisher, 'The Heathrow Case in the Supreme Court: Climate Change Legislation and Administrative Adjudication' (2023) 86(1) *MLR* 226.

there is little evidence of the Court applying a particularly reserved or restrictive approach to the interpretation of statutes across the board. Rather, it has often repeated the classic formulation of its task in this respect: to interpret the wording of a provision, in light of its context and purpose.[98]

It is true that some recent judicial statements might be interpreted as endorsing something of a narrow(er) approach, emphasising that the starting point for the Court, and ultimately the most important influence for a judge conducting statutory interpretation, should always be the specific wording of a statute,[99] and there are certainly some examples of the courts adopting a narrow approach in practice.[100] But there are, by contrast, many other cases in which the Court highlighted the importance of adopting a construction of a statute which brings about its underlying purpose, rather than placing an undue focus on the wording used.[101] It is 'always necessary', according to the Court in *Flyde Farms*, to determine and attempt to give effect to the statute's purpose, 'even where particular words used in a statute appear at first sight to have an apparently clear and unambiguous meaning.'[102] In addition, the Court has sanctioned departing from the natural meaning of words where it is necessary to produce a 'sensible … comprehensible' result[103] and where doing so would better promote access to justice in practice.[104]

Clearly, the Court therefore does not employ some one-size-fits-all approach to statutory interpretation. The preferred approach will depend on the specific statute being interpreted in each case. There may be some evidence that the Court is indicating a preference for a more straightforward – perhaps *restrained*? – approach to statutory interpretation. But this is the case, the signal has not yet been followed consistently. Sometimes a much more holistic, purposive interpretation is adopted, with judges acknowledging expressly that they are departing from a statute's literal meaning. For now, it cannot be said that the Court's approach to statutory interpretation is restrained overall.

A similar conclusion applies to the Court's recent approach to issues relating to jurisdiction – there are many cases in which it construed its own jurisdiction

[98] *R (Highbury Poultry Farm Produce) v Telford Magistrates' Court* [2020] UKSC 39; [2020] 1 WLR 4309 at [37], [53]; *R (KBR) v Director of the Serious Fraud Office* [2021] UKSC 2; [2022] AC 519 at [27]; *Kostal UK v Dunkley* [2021] UKSC 47; [2022] All ER 607 at [109], *R v Luckhurst* [2022] UKSC 23; [2022] 1 WLR 3818 at [42].

[99] *FirstPort Property Services v Settlers Court RTM Co Ltd* [2022] UKSC 1; [2022] 1 WLR 519 at [53] *PRCBC* (n 59) at [29]. See also *Coughlan* (n 59) at [13] and [17].

[100] See eg *R v Copeland* [2020] UKSC 8; [2021] AC 815 at [33], [36]; *Kostal* (n 98) at [30]–[33], [41]; see also *KBR* (n 98) at [28]; *Test Claimants in the Franked Investments Income Group Litigation v HMRC (No 1)* [2020] UKSC 47; [2022] AC 1 at [218]–[219].

[101] *Hurstwood Properties v Rossendale BC* [2021] UKSC 16; [2022] AC 690 at [9]; *Matthew v Sedman* [2021] UKSC 19; [2022] AC 299 at [40]; *Rittson-Thomas v Oxfordshire CC* [2021] UKSC 13; [2022] AC 129 at [33]; *Royal Mail Group v Efobi* [2021] UKSC 33; [2021] 1 WLR 3863 at [29]–[34]; *Basfar v Wong* [2022] UKSC 20; [2023] AC 33 at [34], [64]–[65], [67].

[102] *Flyde* (n 69) at [6].

[103] *TW Logistics Ltd v Essex CC* [2021] UKSC 4; [2021] AC 1050 at [81]. See also *Rittson-Thomas* (n 101) at [29] and [31].

[104] *Haworth* (n 60) at [59]–[61].

widely,[105] or where it enlarged the remit of courts in general.[106] Yet there are a number of instances where the Court narrowed the scope of its jurisdiction or refused to recognise any jurisdiction at all.[107] Perhaps the most notable of these was *Begum*, concerning the routes available to challenge a decision to deprive an individual of their citizenship; whilst acknowledging that an affected party is entitled by legislation to challenge a deprivation decision by means of a full appeal rather than mere review, the Court nonetheless interpreted the required intensity of oversight to be applied in these appeals so narrowly that it seemed indistinguishable from a mere review in practice.[108] The Court therefore endorsed a significantly narrower conception of the applicable judicial role than that which had been adopted by the lower courts[109] and that which had been set out in previous case law.[110]

The Court was more likely to find that it lacked jurisdiction to determine an issue when the matter had been covered separately by some statutory framework,[111] but even in such a case the Court would often find that its inherent jurisdiction remained active alongside, or in addition to, the relevant statutory controls.[112] *Begum* also suggests that where questions relating the Court's jurisdiction overlap with questions about the exercise of public power, the Court's preference for enlarging its jurisdiction gave way to its tendency to defer to the executive. Nevertheless, this does not detract from the position that, in general, the Court has adopted a mixed approach to questions of jurisdiction, and its case law could not really be said to epitomise judicial restraint in this respect.

[105] *Test Claimants in the Franked Investments Income Group Litigation v HMRC (No 2)* [2021] UKSC 31; [2021] 1 WLR 4354 at [79]–[80]; *Re Scottish Independence Referendum Bill* (n 31) at [13]–[54]; *Attorney General v Crosland* [2021] UKSC 58; [2022] 2 All ER 401.

[106] *Children's Investment Fund Foundation v Attorney General* [2020] UKSC 33; [2022] AC 155; *Unwired Planet International v Huawei Technologies* [2020] UKSC 37; [2021] 1 All ER 1141; *Villiers v Villiers* [2020] UKSC 30; [2021] AC 838; *Okpabi* (n 87); *FS Cairo (Nile Plaza) LLC v Lady Brownlie* [2021] UKSC 45; [2022] AC 995.

[107] *Re AG for Northern Ireland's Reference of Devolution Issues* [2020] UKSC 2; [2020] NI 820; *Re McGuinness* [2020] UKSC 6; [2021] AC 392; *Aspen Underwriting v Credit Europe Bank NV* [2020] UKSC 11; [2021] AC 493.

[108] *Begum* (n 45) at [65], [68], [69], [118].

[109] *Begum v Special Immigration Appeals Commission* [2020] EWCA Civ 918 at [29].

[110] *Wallie v Secretary of State for the Home Department* [2022] UKUT 17 (IAC) at [37] ('narrower than the Upper Tribunal and Court of Appeal [had] previously thought'). There remains some ambiguity as to whether the approach in *Begum* is restricted to the specific provisions in that case or whether it applies to other, similar provisions: *Laci v Secretary of State for the Home Department* [2021] EWCA Civ 769; [2021] 4 WLR 86 at [40]; *P3 v Secretary of State for the Home Department* [2012] EWCA Civ 1642; [2022] 1 WLR 2869 at [114]–[115]; *U3 v Secretary of State for the Home Department* [2023] EWCA Civ 811.

[111] *Flyde Farms* (n 69) (statutory limits on planning reviews usurp scope of judicial review); *General Dynamics* (n 52) at [76], [81] (rules as to treatment of arbitration documents covered entirely by statute).

[112] *Anwar v Advocate General for Scotland* [2021] UKSC 44; 2021 SLT 1453 at [37]–[39] (statute has not ousted Scottish courts' power relating to diligence on the dependence of the action); *T* (n 56) at [115]–[121], [141] (Court's power to authorise childrens' placements not usurped by provisions of Children Act 1989); *Maughan* (n 85) at [43]–[44] (courts able to consider factors beyond those set out in statute in exercise of their sentencing jurisdiction).

When it came to precedent, we see something of a difference between what the Court emphasised in its reasoning, and what it claimed to be doing, and what it did in practice. Sometimes, the Court expressly considered whether to depart from its earlier case law, and it did so on four occasions during this period.[113] Perhaps unsurprisingly, the Court was much more likely to refuse an invitation to depart from its earlier position than to accede to it[114] primarily on the basis of legal certainty.[115] Indeed, in some cases, the Court refused to depart from an earlier authority on this basis despite harbouring serious reservations about its reasoning and overall correctness.[116] Otherwise, besides the obvious reason that the earlier case was correctly decided, the Court refused to depart from an earlier authority when such a course of action had not been properly argued and was unnecessary to determine the case at hand[117] and where it considered that the problems with the authority were valid, but at the time of the case hypothetical.[118]

So far, so restrained. However, on a number of occasions, the Court departed from earlier authorities without expressly acknowledging that it has done so. In 2022, the All-Party Parliamentary Group on Democracy and the Constitution issued a Report which identified at least seven cases handed down between 2020 and 2021 which, according to the authors, involved some unacknowledged departure from a previous UKSC position.[119] Some of the examples provided in the Report are more convincing than others, and are noted below. But the authors are certainly correct in suggesting that there is more to the Court's approach to following its previous decisions than is perhaps suggested. Indeed, I suggest that the Court has employed at least four different methods in order to engineer a departure from its previous case law without acknowledging this expressly.

[113] *Franked Investment 1* (n 100) (departing from *Deutsche Morgan Grenfell Group v IRC* [2006] UKHL 49; [2007] 1 AC 558); *AM (Zimbabwe) v Secretary of State for the Home Department* [2020] UKSC 17; [2021] AC 633 (departing from *N v Secretary of State for the Home Department* [2005] UKHL 31; [2005] 2 AC 296); *Sevilleja* (n 75) (departing from *Johnson v Gore Wood* [2002] 2 AC 1); *Peninsula Securities v Dunnes Stores* [2020] UKSC 36; [2021] AC 1014 (departing from *Esso Petroleum Co Ltd v Harper's Garage* Ltd [1968] AC 269).

[114] *BTI 2014 LLC v Sequana SA* [2022] UKSC 25; [2022] 3 WLR 709 (following *MacDonald v Carnbrow Estates* [2019] UKSC 57; 2019 SLT 1469); *Henderson* (n 74) (following *Gray v Thames Trains Ltd* [2009] UKHL 33; [2009] 1 AC 1339); *Franked Investment 1* (n 100) (following *Kleinwort Benson v Glasgow CC* [1999] 2 AC 349); *Secretary of State for Health v Servier Laboratories* [2021] UKSC 24; [2022] AC 959 (following *OBG Ltd v Allan* [2007] UKHL 21; [2008] 1 AC 1); *CPS v Aquila Advisory Ltd* [2021] UKSC 49; [2021] 1 WLR 5666 (following *Bilta v Nazir* [2015] UKSC 23; [2016] AC 1). In *Sevilleja* (n 75) the minority of the Court advocated departing from authority which recognised the reflective loss principle; the majority, although developing the law to some extent, refused to do so. Further, the Court seemingly made a special effort to emphasise the correctness of earlier decisions in cases such as *McGuinness* (n 107) at [45], *HMRC v Parry* [2020] UKSC 35; [2020] 1 WLR 3692 at [72], [99] and *Guest* (n 79) at [52] and [71].

[115] *Henderson* (n 74) at [87]; (see also *MBS* (n 67) at [178]). In *Franked Investment 1* (n 100) Lord Reed criticised his colleagues for what he saw as a 'readiness to overturn centuries of authority' in unjust enrichment cases: [239]. See also Lord Reed's dissenting judgment in the Privy Council case of *Broad Idea v Convoy Collateral* [2021] UKPC 24; [2023] AC 389.

[116] *Franked Investment 1* (n 100) at [148]–[161].

[117] *HMRC v NCL Investments Ltd* [2022] UKSC 9; [2022] 1 WLR 1829 at [47].

[118] *Servier Laboratories* (n 114) at [83]–[84].

[119] APPG Report (n 12).

First, the Court has sometimes avoided explicit overruling by denying that there is any difference between its (in truth distinctive) stated position and that which is found in the earlier case law, essentially leading to a kind of departure by stealth.[120] In various judgments, the Court has modified the law on vicarious liability,[121] the so-called *SAAMCO* principle;[122] and (arguably) the retrospective application of the HRA[123] but in each case the Court sought to frame its rulings in terms of continuity rather than change. Second, and similarly, the Court has acknowledged that *some* degree of development has taken place, but has downplayed the extent to which the Court moved the law in a new direction: in such cases the new position is described as merely 'clarifying'[124] or 'modif[ying]'[125] the earlier law, or presenting it in a 'more fruitful' way[126] rather than departing from it. Third, the Court has sometimes adopted an interpretation of the earlier case law which artificially brought it in line with with the Court's preferred position.[127] In this case, any alternative interpretation of that earlier case law was to be disavowed as a misinterpretation or a misreading of the true position.[128] Fourth, the Court has at times accepted that there is a difference between its current position and passages in an earlier authority, but has denied, sometimes unconvincingly, that those passages constitute binding precedent. The Court has relegated troublesome passages to obiter dicta[129] or per incuriam statements,[130] and has

[120] In *Elan-Cane* (n 37) the Court arguably ignored or underemphasised some important cases which may have been harder to reconcile with its preferred approach: see L Graham, 'Taking Strasbourg Jurisprudence into Account' (2022) 2 *EHRLR* 163 at 167–68 and APPG Report (n 12) 43.

[121] *Morrisons* (n 67). Giliker argues that the Court's reasoning 'disguises a potentially radical judgment in sheep's clothing: P Giliker, 'Can the Supreme Court halt the ongoing expansion of vicarious liability? Barclays and Morrison in the UK Supreme Court' (2021) 37(2) *PN* 55, 64–67 and see J Lee, 'The Supreme Court, Vicarious Liability and the Grand Old Duke of York' (2020) 136 *LQR* 553, 556–58, calling *Morrisons* a 'revision' of the previous law.

[122] *MBS* (n 67), *Khan* (n 67), considering *SAAMCO* (n 79). Commentators have suggested that the two UKSC cases cannot be 'reconciled neatly' with *SAAMCO* and are 'a … departure' from it: J Blow, 'The scope of duty principle revisited by the Supreme Court in a wrongful birth case' (2021) 37(4) *PN* 187, 192–93.

[123] *McQuillan* (n 36). The Court noted that it had not invited by parties to depart from any of its earlier case law: [144] and see the tenor of continuity at [168]. Compare *Re McCaughey* [2011] UKSC 20; [2012] 1 AC 725 (see especially at [62] and [135]) and *Re Finucane* [2019] UKSC 7; [2019] 3 All ER 191). The *McQuillan* Court did express 'reservations' about *Finucane* (see [144]) but did not depart from it. The APPG Report (n 12) suggested that the Court in *McQuillan* 'departed from' *Finucane* in practice: 44.

[124] *Khan* (n 67) at [28]; *MBS* (n 67) at [6]. cf Lord Burrows in *Khan* at [78] and *MBS* at [212] and see D Nolan and J Plunkett, 'Keeping Negligence Simple' (2022) 138 *LQR* 175, 178.

[125] *SC* (n 14) at [158].

[126] ibid [161].

[127] See *A* (n 48) at [62], see also [68] and [76]: this case did not involve departing from Supreme Court authority, but rather a significant body of authority from lower courts. In order to do so, many cases which, on their face, clearly conflicted with the Court's new approach were reconstrued, sometimes artificially, as being ultimately consistent with it.

[128] *HA* (n 84) at [31] and [40]; *Morrisons* (n 67) at [29].

[129] *SC* (n 14) at [86], [88], [93] and [96]; *Elan-Cane* (n 37) at [72]–[73] and [103]; *Sevilleja* (n 75) at [143] and *A* (n 48) at [56].

[130] *SC* (n 14) at [91]; *Elan-Cane* (n 37) at [72].

undermined precedents by presenting them as inconsistent with even earlier case law.[131]

The UKSC has used all four methods to depart from case law, as evidenced in the cases set out above.[132] The point of this exegesis is not to chastise the Court for its creative approach to its treatment of authorities – that is a practically inevitable feature of stare decisis which is neither new nor necessarily illegitimate.[133] Rather, it is to show that, despite employing the language of restraint, the Court has not really applied a restrained approach to precedent in practice. Again, if the Reed Court is to be described as restrained, this should not be taken to apply to its approach to following earlier decisions.

III. Conclusions

What, then, is to be made of the Court's more recent output? I suggest that the case law reveals certain trends and tendencies on the part of the judges, and that certain discrete directions of travel can be identified. Overall, the admittedly tentative overview of the case law reveals some evidence for a conservative approach, but not necessarily for a restrained approach.

Does this mean that the current crop of judges is both conservative and activist? Not necessarily. As this work has acknowledged throughout, judicial preferences have a significant influence on the content of the Court's output, but this is neither the singular nor necessarily the primary influence. Judicial reasoning, and judicial politics more widely, are, to state the obvious, very complicated. And yet, there must be some merit to the idea that the court's *conservative but activist* output is attributable, in part, to the *conservative but activist* tendencies of the judges constituting it. As has been shown in chapter nine, not all judges hold these kind of preferences – it is difficult, for example, to disagree with Lady Hale's suggestion that the outcome of a number of recent cases would not have been unanimous if Lord Kerr had been a member of the sitting panel.[134] This intuition is perhaps confirmed when looking at who the 'repeat players' are in the more high-profile judgments which featuring heavily in this chapter. Two judges emerge as particularly prominent – Lord Reed and

[131] *Elan-Cane* (n 37) at [81], [82] and [101]; *SC* (n 14) at [80], [85].

[132] A further notable case where many of these techniques were invoked is the *Re Abortion Services Bill* (n 21) esp. at [18]–[19] (assessment of ECHR compatibility where a provision may breach rights in some but not all cases) [30] (appellate review standards); [30], [33], [66] (proportionality as a question of law and fact).

[133] See generally F Emmert, 'Stare Decisis: A Universally Misunderstood Idea' (2002) 6(2) *Legisprudence* 207, 221–24; R Summers and S Eng, 'Departing from Precedent' in N MacCormick, R Summers and A Goodhart (eds), *Interpreting Precedents* (Routledge, 1997).

[134] Lady Hale, 'Women and Children First' in B Dickson and C McCormick (eds), *The Judicial Mind: A Festschrift for Lord Kerr of Tonaghmore* (Hart Publishing, 2021) 46, fn 70.

Lord Sales.[135] Although Lord Reed seemed to adopt a fairly balanced position overall prior to 2020, it has already been noted (see chapter nine) that he would often a more conservative position in his lead and dissenting judgments. Perhaps his elevation to President, which may have encouraged him to take the lead on big controversial and constitutional cases, allowed him an opportunity to manifest his preferences more directly? As for Lord Sales, his appointment to the Court was so close to the end of the cut-off point for the empirical dataset used in this work that we had very little evidence to work from. However, from what we do know (see in particular chapter three) it is clear that Sales was very happy to sit on lots of cases, and quickly handed down a number of lead judgments in those cases. He emerges as a prolific and confident judgment writer. It would therefore not be too surprising to see him emerge as a thought-leader in this new era of the Court. Time will tell.

For now, this is little more than speculation. Perhaps some future edition of this work will look more closely at the records and attitudes of the Court's more recent appointments, and pinpoint the cause of the conservatism and activism we find in the case law. In the meantime, this chapter simply seeks to raise attention to this intriguing possible change in direction. It highlights, just as the rest of this work tries to, the intrinsic (yet imprecise) relationship between judicial appointments, judicial attitudes, judicial reasoning and judicial outcomes. It repeats, once again: *it matters who our judges are.*

[135] See eg *SC* (n 14), *Independence Referendum* (n 31), *A* (n 38) and *Begum* (n 45) and see further Tan (n 8).

11

Implications and Conclusions

This book owes a great debt to the long-prevailing myth of Herculean judicial neutrality. The idea that a judge will be absolutely impartial, and completely detached from any possible preferences, is so often framed as something possible, normatively desirable, or even required, in a given legal system, including the UK's. Judges, once human, must become *super*-human when their robes and wigs are donned. Any personal attitudes, preferences or ideologies must be left at the courtroom door.

Nobody can seriously believe that this is possible. Indeed, once probed, most will readily admit that the idea is naïve. Yet it is easy to see why the myth endures, and why it is so attractive. The idea, however questionable, generates a useful story, one which may be needed to serve an essential purpose. Would the adoption of a more realistic view of judges, of the kind evidenced and advocated for in this book, undermine the judicial function? Is absolute judicial neutrality too essential a fiction to discard?

I. The Problem

Perhaps the idea that judges are uniquely independent and absolutely neutral is necessary to justify their constitutional authority, grant them reverence, and separate them from politicians and other decision-makers.[1] Supposing there is *some* truth to the argument presented in this book, therefore, has the supposed authority of the judiciary been undermined? Are the judges' determinations unfair and, ultimately, illegitimate?

Some may well think so. Indeed, some allege that since judges essentially just decide cases according to their own whims[2] and abuse their position to conduct 'politics by other means',[3] this fatally undermines the case for judicial power. But

[1] K Bybee, *All Judges Are Political Except When They Are Not* (Stanford, 2010) *cf* M Hailbronner, 'Rethinking the Rise of the German Constitutional Court: From Anti-Nazism to Value Formalism' (2014) 12(3) *International Journal of Constitutional Law* 626, 642–49.

[2] D Nicol, 'Supreme Court Against the People' (UK Constitutional Law Blog, 25 September 2019).

[3] R Ekins, 'Protecting the Constitution: How and why Parliament should limit judicial power' (Judicial Power Project, 2019), 12. See also D Campbell, 'Decency, disobedience and democracy in immigration law' [2018] *PL* 413.

is there any real alternative to this? We could try to erase preferences and their influence from the judges' mind. Presumably, this might be achieved through judicial training and raising awareness of potential bias, empowering judges to manage their own preferences.[4] Whilst some judges have indicated that such a cleansing is possible,[5] it is hard to believe that the types of preferences examined in this thesis – a sympathy for the state, or a preference for purposive interpretation of statutes, for example – can be either properly identified and, more importantly, effectively neutralised through some kind of training. Griffith put it this way: 'Judges in the United Kingdom cannot be politically neutral because they are placed in positions where they are required to make political choices'.[6] *Some* political decision-making is in some sense intrinsic to the judicial role.

If preferences cannot be eliminated, should the power of the judges wielding them be limited instead? Certainly, the groups like the Judicial Power Project think so,[7] and there is a logic, however unsophisticated, to the idea that we can satisfactorily reduce the influence of judicial partiality in the judicial decision-making process by simply removing those judicial decision-making processes in the first place. Of course, greatly reducing the scope of judicial power and discretion comes with its own problems, too obvious to detail here.[8] Further, Griffith has intriguingly suggested that such a plan may be counterproductive because judges tend to increase their 'activist' tendencies when their powers are limited, as 'an attempt to gain what status they have lost'.[9]

If the influence of judicial preferences cannot be eliminated without severely curtailing the role of judges more generally, could the specific preferences which affect the development and application of the law instead be controlled? We might imagine, for example, that some possible mechanism could be implemented to ensure that there is a fair spread of judicial *types* on the Court, or that a fair range of different preferences are represented on a panel. This would make it so that a number of different preferences and ideologies necessarily come to affect the decision-making process, helping to ensure that one philosophy does not come to dominate the Court, or to try and ensure, as Cardozo put it, that 'the eccentricities of judges balance one another'.[10] But the problems with such a proposal are obvious: even presuming that preferences could somehow be identified in advance (no small task), not only does this present difficulties regarding panel selection

[4] Retired judge Nicholas Webb suggested a more radical solution: removing 'political' subjects such as criminology from the law school curriculum altogether: *The Telegraph*, Letters, 3 January 2020.

[5] Lord Bingham believed that judges can 'alert themselves to, and … neutralize … any extraneous considerations which might bias their judgments': T Bingham, *The Rule of Law* (Penguin, 2011) 93; Lady Hale believed that with effort, 'most people' can 'suppress' personal inclinations: 'Safeguarding London's Standing in International Dispute Resolution' (*Prospect Webinars*, 6 October 2020).

[6] J Griffith, *Politics of the Judiciary*, 5th edn (Fontana Press, 1997) 336.

[7] See judicialpowerproject.org.uk/.

[8] P Craig, 'Judicial Power, The Judicial Power Project and the UK' (2017) 36 *University of Queensland Law Journal* 355.

[9] Griffith (n 6) 335.

[10] B Cardozo, *The Nature of the Judicial Process* (Yale University Press, 1921) 177.

(ie which judges from an available range would sit on particular cases) but the range of different preferences held by judges would render a fair balance almost impossible to achieve in practice as judges do not sit on a neat axis: a judge's approach to one legal question may be very different from their approach to another. These ideas are too impractical to take seriously.

Another option, of course, would be to recognise that judicial preferences exist, and pursue the idea that they ought to be controlled, but to leave the question of which kinds of judges should exert influence to politicians, enhancing, in a crude way, democratic legitimacy. In Germany, for example, it used to be the case that each of the main political parties would appoint 50 per cent of judges to the Federal Constitutional Court.[11] In such a system, politicians might not only consider a candidate's credentials and expertise, but might also want to appoint someone with a history of a particular kind of judicial thinking. But many are sceptical of political involvement in judicial appointments[12] believing, very fairly, that this would inevitably compromise the principles of independence and accountability. There are obvious practical issues with this route, too: which parties should fill vacancies? How long should politically-appointed judges sit? Is the level of scrutiny in the UK political process sufficient to ensure that any appointments would be suitably qualified?

II. A Reconsideration?

It seems, then, that an easy solution to combat the 'problem' of judicial preferences is hard to find. Before throwing our hands in the air and giving up, we might want to consider whether this problem, if indeed it *is* a problem, is really as significant as might be assumed. We should take stock: is the presence of judicial preferences and the reality of judicial decision-making really so fatal to the legitimacy of what our judges do? If not, should we really mourn the loss of our idea of judicial impeccability?

Eric Voeten points out that even if the influence of preferences is 'normatively undesirable', their influence is 'modest' in many contexts.[13] Indeed, whilst this thesis has shown that the influence of preferences may be greater than some believe (or perhaps, would *like to believe*), this does not mean that such preferences

[11] G Lübbe-Wolff, 'Why is the German Federal Constitutional Court a Deliberative Court?' in B Häcker and W Ernst (eds), *Collective Judging in Comparative Perspective* (Intersentia, 2020) 169–70. The position is changing due to the cessation of two-party dominance in German politics.

[12] Lady Hale admitted that she is 'extremely relieved' that judicial appointments in the UK are not made via political selection, adding 'we all want it to stay that way': Emma Barnett Show (*BBC Radio 5*, 11 June 2019). *cf* K Ewing, 'A Theory of Democratic Adjudication: Towards a Representative, Accountable and Independent Judiciary' (2000) 38 *Alberta Law Review* 708; G Gee, 'Rethinking the Lord Chancellor's role in judicial appointments' (2017) 20(1) *Legal Ethics* 4.

[13] E Voeten, 'Politics, Behaviour and Institutional Design' in J Christoffersen and M Madsen (eds), *The European Court of Human Rights: Between Law and Politics* (OUP, 2011).

are the only driving force behind judicial-decision making, nor even the main one. Many who instinctively recoil at the idea of internal preferences affecting judicial decision-making presume that these interrupting influences are inherently political (sometimes with a 'capital-P') when this is often not the case. Whilst some of the US-based literature conflates the language of 'judicial preferences' with 'judicial politics', and it should be acknowledged there is certainly considerable overlap between the two concepts, they remain distinct. As has been shown, many preferences held by judges are purely legal in nature.[14] Some judges adhere to precedent more firmly than others, and some prefer a broad, purposive approach to statutory interpretation over a more formal and literal one. But this is not the sort of political behaviour certain critics tend to have in mind.[15] Even when it comes to those preferences that correlate strongly with a certain ideology (this thesis has, after all, employed 'left' and 'right' labels in chapter ten), ideology does not always equate to partisanship.[16] Judicial politics may, and often will, connote something different from 'ordinary' politics.[17] Even if it is thought that judges sometimes act in a 'political' manner, this should not be understood as judges acting in line with a political party, or for advancing their own political agendas. To presume as such is to adopt too narrow a definition of 'political'.

Judges all act within a permissible constitutional boundary. This includes those with a tendency to uphold disputed contracts where possible, a lack of confidence overturning lower court decisions, a scepticism towards human rights claims, and so on. Lord Reed has suggested that all UKSC judges operate 'within a band' (of preferences and positions) but that each judge, including those with more distinctive or outsider preferences always adopts a view within a range of reasonable positions.[18] It is also worth noting that much of the 'seepage' of personal preferences is not down to some conspiracy on the part of the judges themselves but 'rooted … in unconscious assumptions'.[19] Nothing in this thesis suggests that judges are acting in anything but good faith. There is no reason to doubt judges like Gerard Hogan, who argues that even if 'psychology and pragmatism means that judges cannot always be neutral, then they should nonetheless strive to be so.'[20]

Finally, the importance of judicial independence should not be forgotten. This book has argued that judges will have preferences by virtue of being human. These

[14] See in particular ch 8. *cf* W Farnsworth, 'Signatures and Ideology: The Case of the Supreme Court's Criminal Docket' (2005) 104 *Michigan Law Review* 67, 71–73.

[15] It is accepted that there may be an overlap between legal and political decision-making: see ch 9, s I.

[16] B Tamanaha, 'The Several Meanings of Politics in Judicial Politics Studies: Why Ideological Influence is not Partisanship' (2012) 61(4) *Emory Law Journal* 759.

[17] M Rosenfeld, 'Judicial Politics versus Ordinary Politics' in C Landfried (ed), *Judicial Power: How Constitutional Courts Affect Political Transformations* (CUP, 2019).

[18] Law in Action (*BBC Radio 4*, 26 February 2019) per Lord Reed.

[19] Griffith (n 6) 340.

[20] G Hogan, 'Should Judges Be Neutral?' (2021) 72 *NILQ* 63, 90.

preferences are more likely to be exhibited if judges are free to do as they wish, otherwise they might be stymied by outside influence. If judges are not uniform in their actions (and they are not), and do not always follow the line of the state or some other powerful actor (and they do not) and often disagree with one another (and they do), this is very strong evidence that *judicial independence is working well.* In one sense, the greater the independence of the judiciary, the more likely it will be that judicial preferences can be identified.[21]

Independence is, of course, only one requirement of a healthy judicial system. Should it necessarily trump considerations such as authority, accountability or transparency and so forth? This question does not necessarily require some black and white answer. It is not necessarily helpful to see courts as *neutral* or *not*; *independent* or *not*; *authoritative* or *not.* As Castillo-Ortiz has correctly noted,[22] most courts only exhibit each these features to a certain extent in any case (although the question of *to what extent?* is an important one). The question should instead be: are the judges *neutral enough*? Are they *independent enough*? Are they *authoritative enough*?

Even if we accept the above – that the influence of personal preferences is likely to be both conditional and modest; that political influence is unlikely to be partisan; that greater scope for the influence of internal preferences may evidence or even strengthen judicial independence – some serious problems potentially remain. Below I set out the four most important issues which, I think, need to be taken seriously in light of the overall arguments I have presented in this book. I present no straightforward, tidy solutions to these problems, but I do suggest that solutions to them are very much possible. Ultimately, it is my belief that whilst abandoning the myth of absolute judicial neutrality in favour of a more realistic approach carries inevitable risks, these are neither insurmountable nor intolerable. Overall there is a strong case for embracing reality over fiction.

III. Four Final Issues

A. Issue 1: Accountability

The first issue relates to accountability. If we allow judges to act in accordance with *certain* preferences, what is to stop them from acting in accordance with *illegitimate* preferences? We might feel comfortable with a judge being slightly more sceptical of the state than their colleague; we may be less comfortable with

[21] D Woodhouse, 'The constitutional and political implications of a United Kingdom Supreme Court' (2004) 24 *Legal Studies* 134, 140–41; 143–45.

[22] P Castillo-Ortiz, 'The Dilemmas of Constitutional Courts and the case for a New Design of Kelsenian Institutions' (2020) 39 *Law and Philosophy* 617, 626.

a judge refusing to find liability against the political party they donate to.[23] What can be done to prevent this?

Before determining how UKSC judges *should* be held accountable, we need to consider how UKSC are currently held accountable. Perhaps surprisingly, it can be difficult to answer such a seemingly fundamental question. There are many different theories of judicial accountability in the literature.[24] Most agree, however, that holding senior judges accountable in the UK is something of a challenge (especially when considering how this can be reconciled with independence).[25] There are, of course, some formal measures in place, such as registering financial interests, and regular audits, which can help identify any overt conflicts of interest.[26] But this would not necessarily prevent a judge from acting on potentially illegitimate preferences.

One major source of accountability seems to be the judges themselves. Judges act with 'self-discipline'[27] in order to maintain their authority and legitimacy. Rackley has identified the 'operative effects' of the neutrality paradigm[28] which, even if recognised as artificial, continue to discourage expressly ideological behaviour.[29] Judges must, of course, explain their reasoning. Whilst judges may of course dress up illegitimate aims in acceptable legal language,[30] the requirement to publish reasons which are scrutinised by other judges, the public and academics, goes some way to discourage improper actions.[31] Further, a hypothetical judge considering whether to act in a clearly partisan manner would have to consider the negative impact on how they are perceived and the effect on the public image of

[23] That is not to say, of course, that everyone will be comfortable with judges acting on the preferences identified in earlier chapters. The distinction between legitimate and illegitimate preferences is far from clear-cut.

[24] The clearest overview is provided in A Le Sueur, 'Developing mechanisms for judicial accountability in the UK' (2004) 24 *Legal Studies* 73. See more generally E Delaney, Searching for Constitutional Meaning in Institutional Design: the Debate over Judicial Appointments in the United Kingdom' (2016) 14(3) *International Journal of Constitutional Law* 752 and R Hazell, 'Judicial Independence and accountability in the UK have both emerged stronger as a result of the Constitutional Reform Act' [2015] *Public Law* 198.

[25] A Paterson, *Final Judgment: The Last Law Lords and the Supreme Court* (Hart Publishing, 2013) 306–11.

[26] Le Sueur (n 24) 81–85.

[27] M Volcansek, 'Judicialisation of Politics or Politicization of the Courts in New Democracies?' in Landfried (n 17) 76–77.

[28] E Rackley, 'When Hercules met the happy prince: re-imagining the judge' (2005) 12 *Texas Wesleyan Law Review* 213, 220.

[29] A Paterson, *The Law Lords* (Palgrave Macmillan, 1982) 102–109, 132–46, 170–76; E Thomas, *The Judicial Process* (CUP, 2005) 244, 246–48, 250–51; F Morrison, *Courts and the Political Process in England* (Sage, 1973) 28–29.

[30] R Kirkham, 'JR55, judicial strategy and the limits of textual reasoning' [2017] *PL* 46, 55: 'at least in hard cases, the judge will often have conflicting case law to make use of and a choice of legal rules to apply which provides them with sufficient opportunity to disguise underlying preferences'.

[31] Lord Phillips, 'Judicial Independence' (Commonwealth Law Conference, 12 September 2007) 13–14; J Beatson, 'Judicial Independence and Accountability' (Nottingham Trent University, 16 April 2008) 13–15.

the court;[32] there may be backlash, including formal repercussions.[33] Judges tend to believe in the merits of the court they sit upon, and care about preserving its image.[34] But even on a more selfish level, if a judge leaned too heavily on improper considerations, to the extent that it was noticed by others, the likely consequences would limit that same judge's ability to exhibit these preferences in the future.

Ultimately, accountability is intertwined with authority,[35] which is considered below. Judges police their own actions so that their judgments remain authoritative and acceptable. As Shapiro puts it, courts thrive when they act 'with sufficient prudence or strategic sense not to offend majoritarianism too deeply'.[36] There may be significant weaknesses in this accountability structure, but the influences of personal preferences on judicial decision-making are far from incompatible with it.

B. Issue 2: Authority

How do judges maintain authority if their neutrality has been questioned? Lord Neuberger suggested that in order to be seen as authoritative, 'justice has always to be detached, almost Olympian'.[37] Lord Phillips argued that citizens must see judges as impervious to 'influences, pressures or inducements' to have any confidence in them.[38] Similarly, Lord Reed said this:

> it is inevitable that the Supreme Court will have to act as an arbiter when political solutions cannot be found. The court's success in performing that role depends on public and political confidence in the court's complete impartiality: something which both the court and the political institutions involved have a responsibility to maintain and support[39]

Academics have noted that judges must pay lip service to this idea of absolute neutrality even if they do not believe in it themselves.[40] Such performances

[32] J Ura, 'Backlash and Legitimation: Macro Political Responses to Supreme Court Decisions' (2014) 58 *American Journal of Political Science* 110.

[33] Volcansek (n 27) 75.

[34] And are acutely aware of threats to it: A Mark and M Zilis, 'Blurring Institutional Boundaries: Judges' Perceptions of Threats to Judicial Independence' (2018) 6(2) *Journal of Law and Courts* 333.

[35] Judicial power only comes when there is an acceptance of a court and its authority; see *Planned Parenthood v Casey*, 505 US 833 (1992): 'The Court's power lies … in its legitimacy, a product of substance and perception that shows itself in the people's acceptance of the Judiciary as fit to determine what the Nation's law means and to declare what it demands.'

[36] M Shapiro, 'Judicial Power and Democracy' in Landfried (n 17) 35.

[37] D Neuberger and P Riddell, *The Power of Judges* (Haus Curiosities, 2018) 22.

[38] Lord Phillips (n 31) 2.

[39] Lord Reed, 'Scotland's Devolved Settlement and the Role of Courts' (Inaugural Dover House Lecture, 27 February 2019).

[40] T Maroney, 'The Persistent Cultural Script of Judicial Dispassion' (2011) 99 *California Law Review* 629; K Mack and S Anleu, 'Performing Impartiality: Judicial Demeanor and Legitimacy' (2010) 35(1)

represent 'an institutional agreement that combines judicial exceptionalism with fostered ignorance'.[41] Even if there is 'widespread recognition of the truth' judges must continue to *talk the talk*.[42]

But is authority *really* dependent on absolute neutrality? Linda Mulcahy recognises the premium we place on the concept, saying that neutrality has 'become something of a grundnorm for lawyers and society more generally'.[43] It is true that if the public perceive judges as neutral, this bolsters their confidence in them. But this is not to say that *absolute* neutrality, at least in terms of being completely impervious to internal preferences, is a necessary prerequisite for public confidence, or that it is the only aspect of the judicial role which inspires public confidence. Indeed, studies in other jurisdictions have shown that even those who believe that judges are influenced by explicit political considerations can maintain trust in them if other factors are present.[44]

Similarly, studies have shown that judiciaries attract wider support if their judgments are considered principled[45] or are simply seen to have been decided correctly.[46] Judges who are considered to be truly independent also garner support, even if they are not considered completely neutral.[47] It has also been argued that the character of the judge is more important than their neutrality: they ought to be patient and fair, and exhibit common sense.[48] It has also been found that those with a greater understanding of law and the role of the judiciary are more likely to endorse judicial decisions, even if it is accepted that the judges writing them are not entirely neutral.[49] Indeed, an understanding that judges are not entirely neutral may, paradoxically, improve public trust, with transparency about decision-making considered just as important as neutrality.[50]

Law and Social Inquiry 137; R Hunter, S Anleu and K Mack, 'Judging in lower courts: conventional, procedural, therapeutic and feminist approaches' (2016) 12(3) *International Journal of Law in Context* 337, 340–42.

[41] G Edmond and K Martire, 'Just Cognition: Scientific Research on Bias and Some Implications for Legal Procedure and Decision-Making' (2019) 82(4) *MLR* 633, 654.

[42] D Klein, 'Law in Judicial Decision-Making' in L Epstein and S Lindquist, *Oxford Handbook of US Judicial Behaviour* (OUP, 2017) 237.

[43] L Mulcahy, 'The Possibilities and Desirability of Mediator Neutrality: Towards an Ethic of Partiality' (2001) 10(4) *Social & Legal Studies* 506.

[44] J Gibson and G Caldeira, *Citizens, Courts and Confirmations: Positivity Theory and the Judgments of the American People* (Princeton, 2009); M Hall, 'Judicial Impact' in Epstein and Lindquist (n 42).

[45] S Benesh, 'Understanding Public Confidence in American Courts' (2006) 68(3) *Journal of Politics* 697; J Gibson and M Nelson, 'The Legitimacy of the US Supreme Court: Conventional Wisdoms and Challenges Thereto' (2014) 10 *Annual Review of Law and Social Science* 201; M Kumm, 'On the Representativeness of Constitutional Courts' in Landfried (n 17).

[46] B Bartels and C Johnson, 'On the ideological foundations of Supreme Court legitimacy and the American Public' (2013) 57(1) *American Journal of Political Science* 184.

[47] H Bentsen, 'Dissent, Legitimacy and Public Support for Court Decisions: Evidence from a Survey-Based Experiment' (2019) 53(2) *Law and Society Review* 588.

[48] J Dyson, *A Judge's Journey* (Hart Publishing, 2019) 198.

[49] J Gibson and G Caldeira, 'Has Legal Realism Damaged the Legitimacy of the US Supreme Court?' (2011) 47(2) *Law and Society Review* 195.

[50] Woodhouse (n 21) 143; Le Sueur (n 24) 89–92.

All of the above leads to a kind of judicial diplomacy where judges work hard to ensure their decisions are principled, authentic, transparent, fair and clear.[51] The presence of these factors seems to imbue judges with authority and legitimacy. *Absolute* neutrality is, seemingly, not essential in this regard. It is just one factor amongst many which increases public confidence in the judiciary. This public confidence, rather than the specific factors which lead to it, is what guarantees judges their authority.

C. Issue 3: Lawyers

A separate issue concerns the impact a more widespread understanding of judicial preferences may have on the lawyers appearing before judges. One fear is that lawyers who are privy to the preferences of the judges before them can, in one sense, hijack a hearing, winning a judge over by accommodating their preferences rather than convincing them with legal argument. Writing in 2000, JAG Griffith wrote:

> We have now reached the stage in the evolution of the judicial system when knowledge and understanding of the political philosophy of individual judges are directly relevant[52]

He further stated that 'lawyers … will need to know as much as they can about the general sympathies and antipathies of individual judges'[53] in order to win their case. Paterson has a more reserved view, saying that whilst lawyers once had 'very limited potential' to 'tailor their arguments to the individual traits of the judges sitting on a particular panel', this scope has been further constrained by the tendency for shorter oral hearings in the UKSC.[54]

Is it true that barristers care about the judge before them? Some have certainly suggested that this is the case.[55] At least one barrister acknowledged, when interviewed by Bondy and Sunkin, some degree of predictability in this respect: 'you often know that if you get a certain judge you are going to win or lose'.[56] The identity of the judge dealing with a case might certainly, therefore, affect litigation strategy, at least in the context of the High Court, where applications are usually dealt with

[51] G Davies, 'The Rise of Judicial Diplomacy in the UK: aims and challenges' (2020) 40(1) *Legal Studies* 77.

[52] J Griffith, 'The Brave New World of Sir John Laws' (2000) 63(2) *MLR* 159, 160.

[53] ibid 159.

[54] Paterson (n 25) 39.

[55] Jolyon Maugham QC complained on Twitter that Good Law Project was refused by a judge with 'a reputation for being very Government minded' (@GoodLawProject, 26 March, 6:52 am); he later characterised his comment as typical of one which public lawyers 'say to clients all the time' (26 March, 3:47 pm).

[56] V Bondy and M Sunkin, 'Accessing Judicial Review' [2008] *PL* 647, 663. Other solicitors interviewed by the authors used more explicit political terms, with one describing a judge as 'a big leftie' (664).

by a single judge.[57] Perhaps as a result of this, certain commercial websites are now promoting the use of AI and data analysis tools to help practitioners 'know their judge'[58] so they can tailor their arguments accordingly.

In response to this problem, three important points should be considered. First, the argument that barristers might tailor their arguments before the judge sitting in their case likely has more purchase in lower courts, where cases are heard by smaller numbers of judges; as the UKSC generally sits in a panel of five or more judges, 'tailoring' in this way would be more difficult to achieve.[59]

Second, as this work has shown, there are some very serious limitations when it comes to 'predicting' the behaviour of judges. Some specific judicial tendencies are easy enough to identify (some of the time); however, these tendencies do not decide cases. Knowledge of judicial preferences may provide some light steer as to which arguments are likely to be receptive; they do not provide anything like the clairvoyance required to inform a solid litigation strategy.

Third, and perhaps most convincingly, it is clear from the above examples that barristers *already* know who the judges are, and are *already* taking into account their intuitions about judicial preferences, even when they are told time and time again that judges are completely neutral in their disposition. This knowledge may be private, it may even be denied, but it is certainly there. Admitting the truth about judicial behaviour will not change anything; empirical data is no match for experience. If lawyers are already tailoring their arguments, consciously and unconsciously, to curry favour with the judges hearing them, then this will continue whether we like it or not. It does not provide a good reason to cease drawing attention to an accurate description of the judicial role.

D. Issue 4: Panel Selection

So far, it has been argued that the UK legal system can accommodate, however imperfectly, a more realistic understanding of judicial behaviour. Problems relating to a possible lack of accountability, a dilution of authority, or a shift in the way lawyers work, may not be insurmountable after all. However, one issue in which serious problems arise, and with respect to which a positive case for change will be made, relates to panel selection.

[57] It is known in law firms that some judges are 'more minded' to grant relief than others and this affects litigation strategy: Z Nabi, 'The Dynamics of Judicial Review Litigation' (Judicial Review Trends and Forecasts, Public Law Project Annual Conference 2020).

[58] Thomson Reuters, 'The Importance of Knowing Your Judge' (11 November 2020) legal.thomsonreuters.com/blog/the-importance-of-knowing-your-judge/.

[59] However, this 'tailoring' technique was apparently successful before the Court of Appeal on at least one occasion: counsel in one case chose to focus on common law speech protections rather than the ECHR because they knew Lord Judge would be more receptive to the former, according to one legal blogger: A Richards, 'Twitter joke and Lord Judge-made law – without the ECHR bits' (personal website, 9 December 2013) alrich.wordpress.com/2013/12/09/lord-judge-lecture-echr-human-rights-act/.

In the UKSC, the full roster of judges almost never sits together on a single case; rather, they sit in panels of five or more judges at a time. If the argument presented in this book is in any way accurate, and individual UKSC judges have different predilections from one another which affect the way they decide cases, *who sits matters*. More precisely, the choice of which five judges out of the roster of 12 sit on a given case matters (or, at minimum, *could* matter). This will not affect all decisions, perhaps not even most decisions. But there will be occasions where some judges sitting on the Court might lean more heavily in one direction or another, and their presence or absence on a given case may well influence the outcome (especially as UKSC decisions are decided by majority vote).

Lord Neuberger has admitted that the use of panels means that there 'can be a perception on the part of some observers, that, if the panel had consisted of different Justices, the result would have been different.'[60] Commentators have argued that this is not just a perception, but a reality: Dickson has argued that 'the outcome of an appeal … can sometimes depend on which judges are sitting';[61] Blom-Cooper and Drewry claimed that 'a decision in a particular case might depend on the permutation of [judges] selected to sit'[62] and Arvind and Stirton have wondered whether 'the entire direction of the development of the common law in certain areas could … be determined by the circumstances of the selection of a panel of the Supreme Court.'[63]

How are panels currently[64] formulated? Whilst the process is somewhat opaque, it seems that the job primarily falls to the Court Registrar,[65] with some input from the President and Deputy President.[66] The judges determining permission to appeal in a given case also sometimes contribute to this decision.[67] Factors likely to be taken into account include a judge's availability, interest, expertise and workload.[68] An attempt is also made to ensure that

[60] Lord Neuberger, 'Tweaking the Curial Veil' (Blackstone Lecture 2014, 15 November 2014) at para 47.

[61] B Dickson, 'Close Calls in the House of Lords' in J Lee (ed), *From House of Lords to Supreme Court: Judges, Jurists and the Process of Judging* (Hart Publishing, 2011) 302.

[62] L Blom-Cooper and D Drewry, *Final Appeal: A Study of the House of Lords in its Judicial Capacity* (OUP, 1972) 402 and see also at 262, fn 3: 'it is hard to believe that [*McEldowney v Forde*] would have gone the same way if Lord Reid presided rather than Lord Hudson.'

[63] TT Arvind and L Stirton, 'Legal ideology, legal doctrine and the UK's top judges' [2016] *PL* 418, 430–31.

[64] Pre-UKSC, Lord Dyson confessed that it was a 'mystery' how panels were allocated (n 48, 130). Dawn Oliver points to the influence of the Lord Chancellor and senior clerks in this respect: D Oliver, 'The Lord Chancellor as the Head of the Judiciary' in L Blom-Cooper, B Dickson and G Drewry (eds), *The Judicial House of Lords: 1876–2009* (OUP, 2009).

[65] Paterson (n 25) 72.

[66] Lord Reed, 'Collective Judging in the UK Supreme Court' in Häcker and Ernst (n 11) 26.

[67] PTA panels 'give directions as to … the composition of the court' (ibid 25, fn 11) and 'advise on the number of members of the Court who should sit' (ibid 26).

[68] See eg Paterson (n 25) 72. However, Lord Reed has stated that the Court registrar tries to specifically include on each panel at least one member of the court who is *not* an expert in the field in order to bring a fresh perspective to each case: Reed (n 66) 27.

judges from Scotland and Northern Ireland sit on cases involving their respective jurisdictions.[69]

This practice seems sensible enough, although considering the importance of impartiality and independence, it is a surprisingly informal affair. It leaves open the possibility that a judge or administrator might 'tweak' a certain panel to make a certain outcome more likely. Suggesting as much is close to heretical.[70] But judges have admitted that this has happened in the past, when the Lord Chancellor sat on the Court,[71] and studies suggest that there is some evidence of this happening in other jurisdictions, too.[72] The Lord Chancellor, of course, no longer has the power to influence panel selection, but senior judges still retain the power to influence panel composition. Indeed, some have been quite open about this practice. Lord Neuberger admitted he had on occasion modified panels, although his changes were 'slight', and, in any case, never employed to manufacture a certain result.[73] Lord Reed said something similar, and also limited himself to tweaking only so as to accommodate a lack of availability.[74]

It might be said that the possibility that certain judges might stack panels in their favour is so remote, and that it would require the imputation such bad faith on the part of the judiciary, that it does not justify any real concern. That would indeed be convincing enough, were it not for some disconcerting evidence provided – perhaps somewhat inadvertently – by Lord Hope in his published diaries suggesting that intentional panel fixing may well have occurred in recent times.[75] There, for example, he admitted that he considered removing Lord Kerr from a draft panel because of his apparent tendency to take a particular (minority) view on matters relating to devolution and human rights.[76] Whilst he ultimately decided that this was not a 'proper course for [him] to take', the fact that such an opportunity was open to him and, at one point, was a serious enough possibility to note in his diaries, remains of great concern.

Unfortunately, this was not an isolated incident. Hope also alleges that Lord Judge once petitioned the sitting President, Lord Phillips, to ensure that he sat on a panel in an important case relating to compensation for miscarriages of justice.

[69] See Lord Reed, 'The Supreme Court and Scotland: The First Ten Years' (UK Supreme Court Ten-Year Anniversary Lecture Series, 19 November 2019).

[70] Commentators have balked at such a prospect: R Cornes, 'Gains (and dangers of losses) in translation – the leadership function in the United Kingdom's Supreme Court, parameters and prospects' [2011] *PL* 509, 518.

[71] Lady Hale, 'Should the Law Lords have Left the House of Lords?' (Michael Ryle Lecture 2018, 14 November 2018) 11.

[72] L Hausegger and S Haynie, 'Judicial Decisionmaking and the Use of Panels in the Canadian Supreme Court and the South African Appellate Division' (2003) 37(3) *Law and Society Review* 635; Y Givata and I Rosenberg, 'How Would Judges Compose Judicial Panels? Theory and Evidence from the Supreme Court of Israel' (2020) 17(2) *Empirical Legal Studies* 317.

[73] Neuberger (n 60) paras 45–46.

[74] Reed (n 69) 27–28.

[75] L Graham, 'Lessons from Lord Hope's Diaries: Judicial Ideology and Panel Selection' (UK Constitutional Law Association Blog, 18 June 2020).

[76] D Hope, *UK Supreme Court 2009–2015: Lord Hope's Diaries* (Avizandum, 2019) 118.

It is not clear whether this was done after the draft panel was drawn up, or whether Judge was included in the original draft panel. According to Hope, Judge made the plea, not (only) because of his criminal law expertise, but because he was ideologically committed to a position on the law which he feared his fellow judges may depart from.[77] In the end, the case was decided 5–4, with Lord Judge's position winning a bare majority. Without Judge's petitioning (and Lord Phillips' agreement), the decision may very well have been a different one.

The most worrisome example, however, comes from an entry[78] which suggested that this kind of petitioning had occurred with respect to Privy Council cases concerning the use of the death penalty in Commonwealth jurisdictions. It seems that Lord Hoffmann, who had consistently upheld the constitutionality of the penalty in previous cases, had pushed for the inclusion of Edward Zacca (the former Chief Justice of Jamaica) on the panel hearing the case in place of Lady Hale. According to Lord Hope, his reasons for doing so were clear: Zacca, who had previously defended the practice and was considered likely to uphold the Jamaican regime, would be more likely to agree with Lord Hoffmann than the more predictably liberal Lady Hale. In the end, Hoffmann's plea was effective. Hale was replaced by Zacca, and the Board decided that the death penalty was constitutional in both Barbados and Trinidad and Tobago.[79] Each decision was decided bare majority of 5–4, with Zacca voting alongside Hoffmann in the majority. There is a very strong case that the change in the panel composition directly affected the outcome in these cases. Whilst it should be stressed that Hope's account of Hoffmann's behaviour is neither official nor verified, if it is at all accurate, it paints a fairly damning picture of how the flexibility and informality of the panel selection procedure can be subject to serious abuse. In the situation as Hope describes it, Lord Hoffmann could certainly be accused of engaging in a kind of judicial 'gerrymandering', a practice all the more remarkable when considering that these Privy Council cases are some of the very few which can be said to involve a literal matter of life or death. Remarkably enough, Lord Hope was not at all critical of Hoffmann's actions in his account of the affair. He voted with Hoffmann and Zacca in both cases.

The prospect of 'stacking' panels therefore seems to be less theoretical than we might hope. Whilst it is not suggested that any of the Court's current judges have engaged in this practice, and even if we trust judges not to do this in future, there is little to prevent panel selections from being subconsciously or subliminally affected by the way the selector thinks a judge may vote. In any case, enacting further safeguards in this respect can help reduce the *appearance* of bias and bolster confidence in the system.

[77] ibid 219.

[78] D Hope, *House of Lords 1996–2009: Lord Hope's Diaries* (Avizandum, 2018) 213.

[79] *Boyce v The Queen* [2004] UKPC 32; [2005] 1 AC 400; *Matthew v Trinidad and Tobago* [2004] UKPC 33; [2005] AC 433.

There are two proposed solutions to this problem. The first, and less radical solution, would be to put into effect a system of random allocation, in a similar manner to panel selection in Grand Chamber cases before the European Court of Human Rights. This could be qualified in certain ways, such as by requiring judges to sit on a certain minimum number of cases, or by requiring that at least one judge from a relevant jurisdiction sits in appropriate cases, but would otherwise remove leeway for judges to unfairly meddle in panel selection.[80] The constitution of panels may well still make a difference to outcomes, and imbalanced constitutions may fall together arbitrarily, but this proposal would at least eliminate the particular problem of intentional judicial interference.

A more radical solution would be to require the Court to sit en banc. There are, of course, significant downsides to this: it is likely that fewer cases would be heard,[81] judgments may take longer to produce (especially if there are many divisions), and the practice may eat up time in which judges may have other engagements (including important outreach and education activities). For such reasons, some academics have expressly considered, and rejected, the idea that this practice should be implemented.[82]

Yet, the judges *have* sat en banc (or something very close to it) on two occasions: first, to hear *Miller I* (on whether the Prime Minister can personally exercise the power to trigger the relevant Treaty article to begin the process of leaving the European Union) in 2016,[83] and secondly to hear *Miller II* (on the lawfulness of Prime Minister's prorogation of Parliament) in 2019.[84] It was clear at the time, and has since been acknowledged expressly, that these panels were set up 'so that no-one could say that the result would have been different had the panel been different'.[85] This special, quite revealing, approach was justified by the particular importance attached both cases. But could the same not be said for other controversial cases? Why else would the Court set up a panel of seven, or nine judges? And even in seemingly straightforward cases, involving a unanimous panel of five judges, could it always be said that the other seven might not have come to a very different view? Tantalisingly, this very prospect has been raised by a number of judges.[86]

[80] See also P Vandamme and D Bello Hutt, 'Selecting constitutional judges randomly' (2020) *Swiss Political Science Review* (online, doi:10.1111/spsr.12416).

[81] *cf* Edwards, 'Collegial Decision-Making in the US Courts of Appeals' in Häcker and Ernst (n 11) 62.

[82] J Lee, 'Against All Odds: Numbers Sitting in the UK Supreme Court and Really, Really Important Cases' in P Daly (ed), *Apex Courts and the Common Law* (Toronto, 2019) 96, 119.

[83] *R (Miller) v Secretary of State for Exiting the European* Union [2017] UKSC 5; [2018] AC 61.

[84] *R (Miller) v Prime Minister* [2019] UKSC 41; [2020] AC 373.

[85] Lady Hale, 'Judges, Power and Accountability: Constitutional Implications of Judicial Selection' (Constitutional Law Summer School, Belfast, 11 August 2017) 18.

[86] Usually in the context of justifying adherence to precedent, but the point is more generally applicable: see *Re Dalton* [2023] UKSC 36 at [47] *Lewis v AG of Jamaica* [2001] 2 AC 50 at [90] (Lord Hoffmann).

Further, opposition to the idea of en banc sittings is not universal. Lady Hale seemed somewhat receptive to the idea, admitting that if 'all or most of the top judges in the country have given the case their best shot then perhaps it is the best that can be done.'[87] Darbyshire expressly viewed larger panels as a safeguard against arbitrariness: 'they should sit in sevens or nines as often as possible'.[88] Other advocates of *en banc* sittings – at least in theory – include Brice Dickson[89] as well judges like Richard Buxton[90] and Lord Brown.[91]

En banc sittings would remove from the minds of observers any possibility that a case might have gone a different way if a different panel had been sitting. Whilst it would be too far to say that their implementation is urgently necessary, or that this would provide the only solution to the problems relating to panel selection, I submit that their use should at least be seriously considered, at least in some cases,[92] for the reasons set out above.

IV. Conclusions

This book has argued that there is ample evidence that the personal preferences and legal and political ideologies of judges affect decision-making on the UK Supreme Court. Those who still believe in the idea of a Herculean judge, or that there is no space for UK judges to exert their values, should look to chapter one for a rebuttal. Those who seek evidence of these judicial preferences on the UKSC should look to chapters two to eight. Those who are interested in how a particular judge tends to vote, and what can be inferred from this, can find many judicial profiles in chapter nine. Those interested in the future of the Court should consult chapter ten. Those worried about what all of this might mean for the role of judges in the UK should look to chapter eleven.

The claims made in this book should not be stretched too far. The judges on the UKSC do not necessarily behave like judges on the US Supreme Court, for example. Whilst Segal and Spaeth's suggestion that 'a single personnel change [in the Court's roster] may fundamentally alter the course of … law'[93] is true in the US context, its application to the UKSC remains doubtful (although the lack of concrete evidence for this does not mean that it could never be true). It should be borne in mind what this work shows, and what it does not show. It is submitted that judges are neither superhuman nor complete partisans. They are not entirely

[87] Lady Hale (n 71) 11.
[88] P Darbyshire, *Sitting in Judgment* (Hart Publishing, 2011) 151.
[89] Dickson (n 61) 302.
[90] R Buxton, 'Sitting en banc in the New Supreme Court' (2009)125 *LQR* 288.
[91] S Brown, 'In praise of dissenting judgments' (*Prospect*, 28 May 2020). An anonymous UKSC judge said likewise in an interview with Penny Darbyshire: n 88, 169.
[92] Although the question of which cases, and who decides this, presents another problem.
[93] E Segal and H Spaeth, *The Supreme Court and the Attitudinal Model Revisited* (CUP, 2002) 26.

neutral, but neither are they total ideologues. Some mythical, external thing we call 'the law' may not exclusively determine the outcome of cases, but neither are judges entirely free to act as they please. What can be said is that the preferences of judges play a part in judicial decision-making; in some contexts, perhaps quite a significant part.

There is a superficially convincing argument that the idea of absolute neutrality – or as Baird and Gangl put it, the 'myth of legality'[94] – is a kind of essential lie, but this final chapter has tried to argue that we can, in fact, do without this myth – or at least adopt a variation of it which is more attuned with reality. Abandoning Olympia not a fatal prospect – the maintenance of authority, the safeguard of accountability, the and the actions of lawyers can all be accommodated for. There are, further, some practical solutions which can be adopted to combat remote but important concerns relating to panel selection. We should take all of this seriously, but doing so requires the adoption of a more nuanced discourse when it comes to the identity and ideology of judges and the judicial role more generally. Judicial politics and party-politics are different creatures. Judges with preferences do not become politicians. We can acknowledge the individuality of judges without distorting the truth, however enticing.

We should, of course, continue to expect judges to act in good faith. Nothing in this book should be taken to suggest that UKSC judges have ever done otherwise, even those who directly acknowledge the influence of their own personal preferences in their decision-making. And nothing in this thesis should be taken to suggest that judges should henceforth behave in any fundamentally different way. Burton's definition of 'good faith judging' is a good one and all UKSC judges should be held to it: a judge is acting properly whenever they act faithfully to what they honestly believe to be the correct (or, in appropriate situations, the best) position of the law, notwithstanding that an absolutely objectively correct answer to legal questions cannot be reached by messy, value-laden, experienced, minds.[95]

Further, the benefits of acknowledging the reality of the situation should not be ignored. There is power in understanding the truth: on one view, 'the more we know … the better off we are'.[96] Opening up our traditional understandings of the position of the judge to scrutiny may make space for at least the possibility of different, perhaps better, modes of judging.[97] It may also help the cause for a more diverse, and a more representative judiciary. If preferences and biases colour the development of the law, it makes sense for us to try and ensure that as many different perspectives, rather than a single viewpoint, are considered. This is not only so

[94] V Baird and A Gangl, 'Shattering the myth of legality: The impact of the media's framing of Supreme Court procedures on perceptions of fairness' (2006) 27 *Political Psychology* 597.

[95] S Burton, *Judging in Good Faith* (CUP, 1992).

[96] R Hyland, 'Should Judges Tell Us What They Think?' in Häcker and Ernst (n 11) 325.

[97] Hunter, Anleu and Mack (n 40) 346–51 and see further R Moorhead, 'The Passive Arbiter: Litigants in Person and the Challenge to Neutrality' (2007) 16(3) *Social and Legal Studies* 405.

that 'something greater [can] be forged out of ... the attrition of diverse minds'[98] but so that, to at least some extent, the law takes different perspectives and viewpoints into account; as Lord Neuberger acknowledged, 'the broader the variety of judicial views, the more likely it is that the law will reflect the totality of different outlooks'.[99] As Malleson put it,

> If we accept that judges cannot come to a case without conceptions and that some degree of bias is unavoidable, then it is more acceptable if there is a wider range of different types of bias across the judiciary as a whole.[100]

Once it is acknowledged that judges inevitably engage their preferences when judging, the importance of diversity snowballs. The more diverse the court, the more ideas are on the table, which expands the kinds of arguments and ideas which might have purchase, which only increases the need for diversity.[101]

Most fundamentally, however, our objections to abandoning a particular myth can do nothing to erase the falsehood behind it or make that myth a reality. Judges, including those sitting in the UKSC, *are not* the caricatures some presume them to be, and they do, and will continue to, act on their preferences. We should acknowledge this, especially since, as this final chapter has argued, we can manage just as well without the fig leaf, whilst maintaining faith in our judges. As Griffith himself noted, although a judge 'cannot be said to act neutrally ... [they] may still be the person best suited to make [a] particular decision'.[102]

This book has sought to shine a light of the humanity of our judiciary. This is important because ultimately, as one eminent judge once observed, 'the Bench makes no claim to be more than human'.[103] We would do well to remember this.

[98] Law in Action (n 18).

[99] Neuberger (n 60) paras 50–51. Elsewhere, he said: '[w]hen deciding cases it is important for judges to bring to the table ... as many different views as possible, as many different experiences as possible. And that is only achievable when you have a properly diverse Judiciary': Neuberger and Riddell (n 37) 24.

[100] K Malleson, 'Safeguarding Judicial Impartiality' (2002) 22 *Legal Studies* 53.

[101] See similarly: E Rackley, 'Judicial diversity, the woman judge, and fairy tale endings' (2007) 27(1) *Legal Studies* 74; N Fielding, 'Judges and Their Work' (2011) 20(1) *Social & Legal Studies* 97, 100–102.

[102] Griffith (n 6) 57.

[103] R Megarry, *Miscellany-at-Law* (Stevens & Sons, 1955) 3.

BIBLIOGRAPHY

Judicial Speeches

Lady Hale 'Judges, Power and Accountability: Constitutional Implications of Judicial Selection' (Constitutional Law Summer School, Belfast, 11 August 2017).

Lady Hale, 'Appointments to the Supreme Court' (University of Birmingham, 6 November 2015).

Lady Hale, 'Judgment Writing in the Supreme Court' (UK Supreme Court First Anniversary Seminar, 30 September 2010).

Lady Hale, 'Lessons from our first ten years' (UK Supreme Court Ten-Year Anniversary Lecture Series, 12 December 2019).

Lady Hale, 'Principle and pragmatism in developing private law' (Cambridge Freshfields Lecture, 7 March 2019).

Lady Hale, 'Principle and Pragmatism in Public Law (Sir David Williams Lecture 2019).

Lady Hale, 'Safeguarding London's Standing in International Dispute Resolution' (Prospect Webinars, 6 October 2020).

Lady Hale, 'Should the Law Lords have Left the House of Lords?' (Michael Ryle Lecture 2018, 14 November 2018).

Lady Hale, 'The Supreme Court', (BBC Radio 4, *BBC Law in Action*, 26 February 2019).

Lady Hale, 'Valedictory for Lord Sumption' (UK Supreme Court, 12 December 2018).

Lady Hale, 'Women in the Judiciary' (The Law Society, 27 June 2014).

Lord Carnwath, 'Climate Change and the Courts' (Oxford Centre for Islamic Studies, 26 November 2015).

Lord Dyson, 'Criticising Judges: Fair Game or Off-Limits?' (Third Annual Bailii Lecture, 27 November 2014).

Lord Dyson, 'The Shifting Sands of Statutory Interpretation', (Statute Law Society, 9 October 2010).

Lord Hodge, 'The scope of judicial decision-making in the common law tradition' (Max Planck Institute for Comparative and International Private Law, 28 October 2019).

Lord Kerr, 'Dissenting judgments – self-indulgence or self-sacrifice?' (The Birkinhead Lecture, 8 October 2012).

Lord Kerr, 'The Impact of the Supreme Court on the law of Northern Ireland' (UK Supreme Court Ten-Year Anniversary Lecture Series, 4 December 2019).

Lord Kerr, 'The UK Supreme Court – the modest underworker of Strasbourg?' (Clifford Chance Lecture, 25 January 2012).

Lord Mance, 'Should law be certain?' The Oxford Shrieval Lecture, 11 October 2011).

Lord Neuberger, 'Judges and Policy: a delicate balance' (Institute for Government, 18 June 2013).

Lord Neuberger, 'Judgment and Judgments – the Art of Forming and Writing Judicial Decisions' (Denning Society Lecture, 30 November 2017).

Lord Neuberger, 'Judicial Impartiality: Essential or Impossible?' (Clare College Cambridge, 12 March 2018).

Lord Neuberger, 'No judgment – no justice' (First Annual Bailii Lecture, 20 November 2012).

Lord Neuberger, 'The Role of the Judge: Umpire in a Contest, Seeker of the Truth or Something in Between?' (Singapore Panel on Judicial Ethics and Dilemmas on the Bench, 19 August 2016).

Lord Neuberger, 'The Role of the Supreme Court Seven Years on: Lessons Learnt' (Bar Council Law Reform Lecture, 21 November 2016).

Lord Neuberger, 'Tweaking the Curial Veil' (Blackstone Lecture 2014, 15 November 2014).

Lord Neuberger, 'UK Supreme Court decisions on private and commercial law' (Centre for Commercial Law Studies Conference, 4 December 2015).
Lord Phillips, 'Judicial Independence' (Commonwealth Law Conference, 12 September 2007).
Lord Reed, 'Scotland's Devolved Settlement and the Role of Courts' (Inaugural Dover House Lecture, 27 February 2019).
Lord Reed, 'The Supreme Court and Scotland: The First Ten Years' (UK Supreme Court Ten-Year Anniversary Lecture Series, 19 November 2019).
Lord Reed, 'The Supreme Court Ten Years On' (Bentham Association Lecture, 6 March 2019).
Lord Reed, 'Tribute for Lord Kerr' (UK Supreme Court, 30 September 2020).
Lord Reed, 'Tribute for Lord Wilson' (UK Supreme Court, 30 September 2020).
Lord Sales 'Proportionality and Appellate Courts' (ALBA Annual Lecture, 10 November 2020).
Lord Sales, 'Default Rules in the Common Law: Substantive Rules and Precedent' (International Workshop on Default Rules in Private Law, 24 March 2023).
Lord Sumption, 'A Question of Taste: The Supreme Court and the Interpretation of Contracts' (Harris Society Annual Lecture, 8 May 2017).
Lord Sumption, 'The Limits of Law' (27th Sultan Azlan Shah Lecture, Kuala Lumpur, 20 November 2013).
Lord Walker, 'The Indefinite Article 8' (Thomas More Lecture, Lincoln's Inn, 9 November 2011).
Lord Wilson, 'Our Human Rights: A Joint Effort?' (Howard J Trienens Lecture, 25 September 2018).

Journals and Books

Adams, E, 'Judicial discretion and the declaration of incompatibility: constitutional considerations in controversial cases' [2021] *PL* 311.
Adams, J and Brownsword, R, 'The Ideologies of Contract' (1987) 7(2) *Legal Studies* 205.
Alaire, B and Green, A, *Commitment and Cooperation on High Courts* (OUP, 2017).
Aletras, N et al, 'Predicting judicial decisions of the European Court of Human Rights: a Natural Language Processing perspective' (2016) *PeerJ Computer Science* 2:e93.
Amaral-Garcia, S and Garoupa, N, 'Judicial Behavior and Devolution at the Privy Council' (2017) 13(3) *Review of Law and Economics*, online, DOI: doi.org/10.1515/rle-2015-0013.
APPG on Democracy and the Constitution, 'An Independent Judiciary – Challenges since 2016', 8 June 2022.
Appleby, G and Lynch, A (eds), *The Judge, the Judiciary and the Court: Individual, Collegial and Institutional Judicial Dynamics in Australia* (CUP, 2021).
Arguelhes, D and Hartmann, I, 'Timing Control without Docket Control: How Individual Justices Shape the Brazilian Supreme Court's Agenda' (2017) 5(1) *Journal of Law and Courts* 105.
Arvind, TT and Stirton, L, 'Legal ideology, legal doctrine and the UK's top judges' [2016] *PL* 418.
Atiyah, P 'Judicial-Legislative Relations in Britain' in Katzmann (ed), *Judges and Legislators: Towards Institutional Comity* (Brookings, 1988).
Atkins, B, 'Party Capability Theory as an Explanation for Intervention: Behavior in the English Court of Appeal' (1991) 35 *American Journal of Political Science* 881.
Aydin-Cakir, C, 'What do we know about the Middle Eastern Constitutional Courts?' in N Garoupa, R Gill and B Tiede (eds), *High Courts in Global Perspective: Evidence, Methodologies, and Findings* (UVA Press, 2021).
Bailey, M and Maltzman, F, *The Constrained Court: Law, Politics, and the Decisions Justices Make* (Princeton, 2011).
Baird, V and Gangl, A, 'Shattering the myth of legality: The impact of the media's framing of Supreme Court procedures on perceptions of fairness' (2006) 27 *Political Psychology* 597.
Balcombe, J, 'Judicial Decisions and Social Attitudes' (1993) 84 *Proceedings of the British Academy* 209.
Bandes, S, 'Empathetic Judging and the Rule of Law' (2009) *Cardozo Law Review De Novo* 133.

Barber, N, Ekins, R and Yowell, P (eds), *Lord Sumption and the Limits of Law* (Hart Publishing, 2016).
Barmes, L and Malleson, K, 'Lifting the Judicial Identity Blackout' (2018) 38(2) *Legal Studies* 357, 367–68.
Barrett D, 'Celebrity threesome injunction: Top judges rule identities of "PJS" and "YMA" must remain secret' *The Telegraph* (19 May 2016).
Bartels, B and Johnson, C, 'On the ideological foundations of Supreme Court legitimacy and the American Public' (2013) 57(1) *American Journal of Political Science* 184.
Barry, B, *How Judges Judge: Empirical Insights into Judicial Decision-Making* (Routledge, 2021).
Baum, L, 'Motivation and Judicial Behaviour: Expanding the Scope of Enquiry' in D Klein and G Mitchell (eds), *The Psychology of Judicial Decision Making* (OUP, 2010).
Baum, L, *The Puzzle of Judicial Behaviour* (Michigan, 1997).
BBC News, 'Kwasi Kwarteng criticised for biased judges comment' (12 September 2019) www.bbc.co.uk/news/uk-politics-49670901.
Beatson, J, 'Judicial Independence and Accountability' (Nottingham Trent University, 16 April 2008).
Bell, J and Fisher, E, 'The Heathrow Case in the Supreme Court: Climate Change Legislation and Administrative Adjudication' (2023) 86(1) *MLR* 226.
Bell, J, *Policy Arguments in Judicial Decisions* (OUP, 1983).
Belleau, M and Johnson, R, 'Judging gender: difference and dissent at the Supreme Court of Canada' (2008) 15(1) *International Journal of the Legal Profession* 57.
Benesh, S, 'The Use of Observational Data to Study Law and the Judiciary' in L Epstein and S Lindquist, *The Oxford Handbook of US Judicial Behavior* (OUP, 2017).
Benesh, S, 'Understanding Public Confidence in American Courts' (2006) 68(3) *Journal of Politics* 697.
Bentsen, H, 'Dissent, Legitimacy and Public Support for Court Decisions: Evidence from a Survey-Based Experiment' (2019) 53(2) *Law and Society Review* 588.
Berns, W, 'Law and Behavioral Science' in HW Baade, *Jurimetrics* (Basic Book, 1963).
Bingham, T, *The Rule of Law* (Penguin, 2011).
Black, R and Boyd, C, 'US Supreme Court Agenda Setting and the Role of Litigant Status' (2012) 28(2) *Journal of Law, Economics and Organization* 286.
Black R et al, 'Emotions, Oral Arguments and Supreme Court Decision Making' (2011) 73(2) *The Journal of Politics* 572.
Blackwell, M, 'Indeterminacy, Disagreement and the Human Rights Act: An Empirical Study of Litigation in the UK House of Lords and Supreme Court 1997–2017' (2020) 83(2) *MLR* 285.
Blom-Cooper, L and Drewry, G, *Final Appeal: A Study of the House of Lords in its Judicial Capacity* (OUP, 1972).
Blom-Cooper, L, '1966 and All That: the Story of the Practice Statement' in L Blom-Cooper, B Dickson and G Drewry (eds), *The Judicial House of Lords* (OUP, 2009).
Blow, J, 'The scope of duty principle revisited by the Supreme Court in a wrongful birth case' (2021) 37(4) *PN* 187.
Bondy, V and Sunkin, M, 'Accessing Judicial Review' [2008] *PL* 647.
Bondy, V, Platt, L and Sunkin, M, *The Value and Effects of Judicial Review: The Nature of Claims, their Outcomes and Consequences* (Public Law Project, 2015).
Bontrager, S, Barrick, K and Stupi, E, 'Gender and Sentencing: A Meta-Analysis of Contemporary Research' (2013) 16 *Journal of Gender Race and* Justice 349.
Boyd, C, 'Representation on the Courts? The Effects of Trial Judges' Sex and Race' (2016) 69 *Political Research Quarterly* 788.
Boyd, C and Rutkowski, A, 'Judicial Behaviour in Disability Cases: Do Judge Sex and Race Matter?' (2020) 8(4) *Politics Groups and Identities* 834.
Braverman, S, 'People we elect must take back control from people we don't. Who include the judges' (*ConservativeHome*, 30 January 2020) conservativehome.com/2020/01/27/suella-braverman-people-we-elect-must-take-back-control-from-people-we-dont-who-include-the-judges/.
Bridges, L, Meszaros, G and Sunkin, M, *Judicial Review in Perspective*, 2nd edn (Cavendish, 1995).
Brown, S, 'Dissenting Judgments' in A Burrows, D Johnston and R Zimmerman (eds), *Judge and Jurist: Essays in Memory of Lord Rodger of Earlsferry* (OUP, 2013).

Brown, S, *Playing off the Roof* (Marble Hall, 2020).

Brudney, J and Distlear, C, 'Canons of Construction and the Elusive Quest for Neutral Reasoning' (2005) 58(1) *Vanderbilt Law Review* 1.

Buckland, R, 'Judges have become more restrained since ruling against prorogation of Parliament' *The Telegraph* (17 July 2021).

Buckland, R, 'Lecture on the ECHR' (personal website, 28 February 2022) at www.robertbuckland.co.uk/news/lecture-echr.

Burnett, I, 'Lord Chief Justice: why accusations that judges have gone soft are unfounded' (*Prospect*, 22 January 2021).

Burrows, A, 'Numbers Sitting in the Supreme Court' (2013) 129 *LQR* 305.

Burrows, A, *Thinking About Statutes* (CUP, 2018).

Burrows, J, 'The Changing Approach to the Interpretation of Statutes' (2002) 33(3) *Victoria University of Wellington Law Review* 981.

Burton, S, *Judging in Good Faith* (CUP, 1992).

Buxton, R, 'Sitting en banc in the New Supreme Court' (2009)125 *LQR* 288.

Bybee, K, *All Judges Are Political Except When They Are Not* (Stanford, 2010).

Hanretty, C, 'Haves and Have-Nots Before the Law Lords' (2014) 62 *Political Science* 686.

Cahill-O'Callaghan, R, 'Lord Kerr's Dissents: Jewels in the Crown of the Supreme Court' in B Dickson and C McCormick (eds), *The Judicial Mind: A Festschrift for Lord Kerr of Tonaghmore* (Hart Publishing, 2021).

Cahill-O'Callaghan, R, *Values in the Supreme Court* (Hart Publishing, 2020).

Campbell, D, 'Decency, disobedience and democracy in immigration law' [2018] *PL* 413.

Cardozo, B, *The Nature of the Judicial Process* (Yale University Press, 1921).

Carroll, R and Tiede, L, 'Judicial Behaviour on the Chilean Constitutional Court' (2011) 8 *Journal of Empirical Legal Studies* 856.

Carty, H, 'Precedent and the Court of Appeal: Lord Denning's views explored' (1981) 1(1) *Legal Studies* 68.

Castillo-Ortiz, P, 'The Dilemmas of Constitutional Courts and the case for a New Design of Kelsenian Institutions' (2020) 39 *Law and Philosophy* 617.

Chandrachud, A, 'An Empirical Study of the Supreme Court's Composition' (2011) 46 *Economic and Political Weekly* 71.

Chandrachud, C, 'Reconfiguring the discourse on political responses to declarations of incompatibility' [2014] *Public Law* 624.

Coons, J and Espinoza, R, 'An Examination of Aversive Heterosexism in the Courtroom: Effects of Defendants' Sexual Orientation and Attractiveness, and Juror Gender on Legal Decision making' (2017) 5 *Psychology of Sexual Orientation and Gender Diversity* 36.

Coontz, P, 'Gender and judicial decisions: Do female judges decide cases differently than male judges?' (2000) 18 *Gender Issues* 59.

Cornes, R, 'Gains (and dangers of losses) in translation – the leadership function in the United Kingdom's Supreme Court, parameters and prospects' [2011] *PL* 509.

Cowie, G, 'The power to make bills for Scotland: the Treaty Incorporation Bills Reference' [2022] *PL* 189.

Cox, L, 'Supporting and Inspiring Women Judges' in R Hunter and E Rackley (eds), *Justice for Everyone: the Jurisprudence and Legal Lives of Brenda Hale* (CUP, 2022).

Craig, P, 'Judicial Power, The Judicial Power Project and the UK' (2017) 36 *University of Queensland Law Journal* 355.

Cross, F and Lindquist, S, 'The Decisional Significance of the Chief Justice' (2006) 154 *Pennsylvania Law Review* 1665.

Cross, R and Harris, J, *Precedent in English Law*, 4th edn (Clarendon, 1991).

Crowe, J, 'Not-So-Easy Cases' (2019) 40(1) *Statute Law Review* 75.

Cumberland Lodge, 'A Conversation with Baroness Hale' (16 March 2020), available at www.cumberlandlodge.ac.uk/whats-on/conversation-baroness-hale.

Daily Mail, 'Ex-barmaid with a spider brooch who spun legal web that snared PM' (24 September 2019).

Daily Mail, 'judges who will rule on Brexit impact' (7 November 2016).

Daily Mail, 'Shout at your spouse and risk losing your home: it's just the same as domestic violence, warns woman judge' (27 January 2011).

Daly, P, 'Appellate standard of review in public law cases' [2021] *PL* 334.

Darbyshire, P, *Sitting in* Judgment (Hart Publishing, 2011).

Dean, A, 'The government wanted to rein in the Supreme Court. Now it may not need to.' (*Prospect*, 16 October 2021).

Delaney, E, Searching for Constitutional Meaning in Institutional Design: the Debate over Judicial Appointments in the United Kingdom' (2016) 14(3) *International Journal of Constitutional Law* 752.

Desposato, S, Ingram, M and Lannes, O, 'Power, Composition, and Decision Making: The Behavioral Consequences of Institutional Reform on Brazil's Supremo Tribunal Federal' (2014) 31 *Journal of Law, Economics and Organization* 534.

Dickson, B and McCormick, C, 'The Development of Lord Kerr's Judicial Mind' in B Dickson and C McCormick (eds), *The Judicial Mind: A Festschrift for Lord Kerr of Tonaghmore* (Hart Publishing, 2021).

Dickson, B and McCormick, C, 'Northern Ireland Dimensions to the First Decade of the United Kingdom Supreme Court' (2020) 83 *MLR* 1133.

Dickson, B, 'Activism and Restraint within the UK Supreme Court' (2015) 21(1) *European Journal of Current Legal Issues*.

Dickson, B, 'Apex Courts and the Development of the Common Law' in P Daly (ed), *Apex Courts and the Common Law* (Toronto, 2019).

Dickson, B, 'Close Calls in the House of Lords' in J Lee (ed), *From House of Lords to Supreme Court: Judges, Jurists and the Process of Judging* (Hart Publishing, 2011).

Dickson, B, 'Judgement Day for the Supreme Court' (*New Law Journal*, 28 January 2022).

Dickson, B, 'Lord Kerr and Articles 2 and 3 of the ECHR' in B Dickson and C McCormick (eds), *The Judicial Mind: A Festschrift for Lord Kerr of Tonaghmore* (Hart Publishing, 2021).

Dickson, B, 'The processing of appeals in the House of Lords' (2007) 123 *LQR* 571.

Dickson, B, 'UK Supreme Court Justices and Human Rights in the 2015–16 Legal Year' (2016) 7 *UK Supreme Court Yearbook* 214.

Dickson, B, *Human Rights and the United Kingdom Supreme Court* (OUP, 2013).

Double Jeopardy Podcast, 'Judicial Indpendence and its enemies' (Episode 15, 17 November 2022).

Dressel, B, 'Courts and Constitutional Politics in Southeast Asia' in M Bünte and B Dressel (eds), *Constitutions and Politics in Southeast Asia* (Routledge, 2017).

Dresselm B, 'The Politics of Judicial Review in Asia' in D Law, H Lau and A Schwartz (eds), *The Oxford Handbook of Asian Constitutional Law* (OUP, 2023).

Dressel, B and Inoue, T, 'Informal networks and judicial decisions: Insights from the Supreme Court of the Philippines, 1986–2015' (2018) 39(5) *International Political Science Review* 616.

Dressel, B, Inoue, T and Bonoan, C, 'Justices and Political Loyalties: An Empirical Investigation of the Supreme Court of the Philippines, 1987–2020' (2023) *forthcoming*, Law and Social Inquiry.

Drewry, G, 'Judges and Political Inquiries: Harnessing a Myth' (1975) 23 *Political Studies* 49.

Dudley, R and Ducat, C, 'The Burger Court and Economic Liberalism' (1986) 38(2) *Western Political Quarterly*, 236.

Duxbury, N, *Jurists and Judges: An Essay on Influence* (Bloomsbury, 2001).

Duxbury, N, *The Nature and Authority of Precedent* (CUP, 2011).

Dworkin, R, 'Stare decisis in the House of Lords' (1962) 25(2) *MLR* 163.

Dyevre, A 'Unifying the Field of Comparative Judicial Politics: Towards a General Theory of Judicial Behaviour' (2010) 2(2) *European Political Science* Review 297.

Dyson, J, 'Some Reflections on Lord Rodger's Contribution to the Development of the Common Law' in A Burrows, D Johnston and R Zimmerman (eds), *Judge and Jurist: Essays in Memory of Lord Rodger of Earlsferry* (OUP, 2013).

Dyson, J, *A Judge's Journey* (Hart Publishing, 2019).
Dyson, J, *Justice: Continuity and Change* (Hart Publishing, 2018).
Dyzenhaus, D, 'The Snake Charmers' (*Verfassungsblog*, 7 March 2022).
Edmond, G and Martire, K, 'Just Cognition: Scientific Research on Bias and some Implications for Legal Procedure and Decision-Making' (2019) 82(4) *MLR* 633.
Eisenberg, T et al, 'Does the Judge Matter? Exploiting Random Assignment on a Court of Last Resort to Assess Judge and Case Selection Effects' (2012) 9 *Journal of Empirical Legal Studies* 246.
Eisenberg, T, Fisher, T and Rosen-Zvi, I, 'Israel's Supreme Court Appellate Jurisdiction: An Empirical Study' (2011) 96 *Cornell Law Review* 693.
Ekins, R and Forsyth, C, *Judging the Public Interest: the Rule of Law vs the Rule of Courts* (Judicial Power Project, 2015).
Ekins, R, 'Convention rights, child tax credits and the constitution' (2022) 138 *LQR* 551.
Ekins, R, 'In memory of Lord Brown' *The Spectator* (10 July 2023).
Ekins, R, 'Protecting the Constitution: How and why Parliament should limit judicial power' (Judicial Power Project, 2019).
Ekins, R, 'The Government's judicial review legislation is welcome, but could go even further' (*ConservativeHome*, 22 July 2021) conservativehome.com/2021/07/22/richard-ekins-the-governments-judicial-review-legislation-is-welcome-but-could-go-even-further/.
Ekins, R, 'Under Lord Reed, the Supreme Court itself is pushing back against judicial activism' (ConservativeHome, 17 December 2021) conservativehome.com/2021/12/17/richard-ekins-under-lord-reed-the-supreme-court-itself-is-pushing-back-against-judicial-activism/.
Ekins, R, 'What the most recent appointments mean for the future of the Supreme Court' (ConservativeHome, 26 July 2019) conservativehome.com/2019/07/26/richard-ekins-what-the-most-recent-nominations-mean-for-the-future-of-the-supreme-court/.
Elgie, R, McAuley, A and O'Malley, E, 'The (Not-so-Surprising) Non-Partisanship of the Irish Supreme Court' (2018) 33 *Irish Political Studies* 88.
Elliott, M and Hughes, K, 'The Nature and Role of Common Law Constitutional Rights' in M Elliott and K Hughes (eds), *Common Law Constitutional Rights* (OUP, 2020).
Elliott, M and Kilford, N, 'The Supreme Court's defence on unqualified lawmaking power: parliamentary sovereignty, devolution and the Scotland Act 1998' (2022) 81(1) *CLJ* 4.
Elliott, M, 'Beyond the European Convention: Human Rights and the Common Law' (2015) 68 *Current Legal Problems* 85.
Emmert, F, 'Stare Decisis: A Universally Misunderstood Idea' (2002) 6(2) *Legisprudence* 207.
Engell, C and Weinshall, K, 'Manna from Heaven for Judges: Judges' Reaction to a Quasi-Random Reduction in Caseload' (2020) 17(4) *Journal of Empirical Legal Studies* 722.
Epstein, L and Knight, J, *The Choices Judges Make* (CQ Press, 1998).
Epstein, L, 'Courts and Interest Groups' in J Gates and C Johnson, *The American Courts: A Critical Assessment* (CQ Press, 1991).
Epstein, L, Landes, W and Posner, R, 'Why (and when) Judges Dissent: A Theoretical and Empirical Analysis' (2011) 3(1) *Journal of Legal Analysis* 101.
Epstein, L, Landes, W and Posner, R, *The Behavior of Federal Judges: A Theoretical and Empirical Study of Rational Choice* (Harvard, 2013).
Epstein, L, Parker, C and Segal, J, 'Do Justices Defend the Speech They Hate? An Analysis of In-Group Bias on the US Supreme Court' (2018) 6(2) *Journal of Law and Courts* 237.
Eskridge, W and Baer, L, 'The continuum of deference: Supreme Court treatment of agency statutory interpretations from Chevron to Hamdan' (2008) 96(4) *Georgetown Law Journal* 1083.
Etherton, T, 'Liberty, the archetype and diversity: a philosophy of judging' [2010] *PL* 727.
Ewing, K and Gearty, C, *The Struggle for Civil Liberties, Political Freedom and the Rule of Law in Britain 1914–1945* (OUP, 2000).
Ewing, K, 'A Theory of Democratic Adjudication: Towards a Representative, Accountable and Independent Judiciary' (2000) 38 *Alberta Law Review* 708.

Farnsworth, W, 'Signatures and Ideology: The Case of the Supreme Court's Criminal Docket' (2005) 104 *Michigan Law Review* 67.
Federico, V, 'Going Against the Grain? The Growing but Uneven Role of Courts in Framing Principled Migration Law' (ECPR General Conference, 25 August 2020).
Feldman, D, 'Human Rights' in L Blom-Cooper, B Dickson and G Drewry (eds), *The Judicial House of Lords 1876–2009* (OUP, 2009).
Feldman, D, 'Orthodox Principles and Unconventional Outcomes in Public Law' in R Hunter and E Rackley (eds), *Justice for Everyone: the Jurisprudence and Legal Lives of Brenda Hale* (CUP, 2022).
Fielding, N, 'Judges and Their Work' (2011) 20(1) *Social & Legal Studies* 97.
Financial Times, 'British Institutions: The Supreme Court' (19 April 2013).
Fischman, J and Law, D, 'What is judicial ideology and how should we measure it?' (2009) 29 *Washington University Journal of Law and Policy* 133.
Flango, V and Ducat, C, 'Toward an Integration of Public Law and Judicial Behavior' (1977) 39(1) *The Journal of Politics* 41.
Flemming, R and Krutz, G, 'Selecting Appeals for Judicial Review in Canada: A Replication and Multivariate Test of American Hypotheses' (2002) *Journal of Politics* 64(1) 232.
Galanter, M, 'Why the Haves Come Out Ahead: Speculations on the Limits of Social Change' (1974) 9 *Law and Society Review* 95.
Garoupa, N et al, 'Political Influence and Career Judges: An Empirical Analysis of Administrative Review by the Spanish Supreme Court' (2012) 9 *Empirical Legal Studies* 795.
Gaus, G, 'Ideological dominance through confusion: liberalism in the twentieth century' in M Freeden (ed), *Reassessing Political Ideologies: The Durability of Dissent* (Routledge, 2001).
Gatmayan, D and Magno, C, 'A review of appointments and nominations to the Philippine supreme court' (2018) *Asian Journal of Comparative Law* 61.
Gearey, A, Morrison, W and Jago, R, *The Politics of the Common Law*, 2nd edn (Routledge, 2013).
Gearty, C, 'In the shallow end' (2022) 44(2) *London Review of Books* (27 January 2022).
Gee, G et al, *The Politics of Judicial Independence in the UK's Changing Constitution* (CUP, 2015).
Gee, G, 'Rethinking the Lord Chancellor's role in judicial appointments' (2017) 20(1) *Legal Ethics* 4.
George, T and Epstein, L, 'On the Nature of Supreme Court Decision Making' (1992) 86(2) *American Political Science Review* 323.
George, T and Weaver, T, 'The Role of Personal Attributes and Social Backgrounds on Judging' in L Epstein and S Lindquist, *The Oxford Handbook of US Judicial Behaviour* (OUP, 2017).
Gerring, J, 'Ideology: A Definitional Analysis' (1997) 50(4) *Political Research Quarterly* 957.
Gibson, J and Caldeira, G, 'Has Legal Realism Damaged the Legitimacy of the US Supreme Court?' (2011) 47(2) *Law and Society Review* 195.
Gibson, J and Caldeira, G, *Citizens, Courts and Confirmations: Positivity Theory and the Judgments of the American People* (Princeton, 2009).
Gibson, J and Nelson, M, 'The Legitimacy of the US Supreme Court: Conventional Wisdoms and Challenges Thereto' (2014) 10 *Annual Review of Law and Social Science* 201.
Gibson, J, 'The Role Concept in Judicial Research' (1981) *Law and Policy Quarterly* 291.
Giles, M, Strayhorn, J and Peppers, T, 'Policymaking under constraint: Decision Modes in the US Courts of Appeals (2015) 36(2) *Justice System Journal* 95.
Giliker, P, 'Can the Supreme Court halt the ongoing expansion of vicarious liability? Barclays and Morrison in the UK Supreme Court' (2021) 37(2) *PN* 55.
Gill, N et al, 'The Limits of Procedural Discretion: Unequal Treatment and Vulnerability in Britain's Asylum Appeals' (2018) 27(1) *Social & Legal Studies* 49.
Gilligan, C, *In a Different Voice* (Harvard, 1982).
Gillman, H, 'What's law got to do with it? Judicial behaviouralists test the legal model of judicial decision making' (2001) 26 *Law and Social Inquiry* 465.
Givata, Y and Rosenberg, I, 'How Would Judges Compose Judicial Panels? Theory and Evidence from the Supreme Court of Israel' (2020) 17(2) *Empirical Legal Studies* 317.
Goodhart, A, 'Determining the Ratio Decidendi of a Case' (1930) *Yale Law Journal* 161.

Goodhart, A, 'The Ratio Decidendi of a Case' (1959) 22(2) *MLR* 117.
Goodman, J et al, 'Money, Sex, and Death: Gender Bias in Wrongful Death Damage Awards' (1991) 25 *Law and Society Review* 263.
Goudkamp, J and Katsampouka, E, 'An Empirical Study of Punitive Damages' (2018) 38 *Oxford Journal of Legal Studies* 90.
Graham, L, 'Has the Supreme Court become more restrained in public law cases?' (forthcoming, *Modern Law Review*).
Graham, L, 'Lady Justices and Dissent on the Court of Appeal of England and Wales' (UK Constitutional Law Association Blog, 15 November 2018).
Graham, L, 'Lessons from Lord Hope's Diaries' (UK Administrative Law Association Blog, 18 June 2020).
Graham, L, 'Taking Strasbourg Jurisprudence into Account' (2022) 2 *EHRLR* 163.
Graham, L, 'The Modern Mirror Principle' [2021] *Public Law* 523.
Graham, L, 'The supreme court's recent approach to unincorporated human rights treaties' (2024) 1 *EHRLR* 49.
Griffith. J, *Politics of the Judiciary*, 5th edn (Fontana Press, 1997).
Griffith, J, 'The Brave New World of Sir John Laws' (2000) 63(2) *MLR* 159.
Hagle, T, 'Freshman Effects for Supreme Court Justices' (1993) *American Journal of Political* Science 1142.
Hailbronner, M, 'Rethinking the Rise of the German Constitutional Court: From Anti-Nazism to Value Formalism' (2014) 12(3) *International Journal of Constitutional Law* 626.
Hale, B, 'Lord Rodger's Mental Health Law' in A Burrows, D Johnston and R Zimmerman (eds), *Judge and Jurist: Essays in Memory of Lord Rodger of Earlsferry* (OUP, 2013).
Hale, B, 'Women and Children First' in B Dickson and C McCormick (eds), *The Judicial Mind: A Festschrift for Lord Kerr of Tonaghmore* (Hart Publishing, 2021).
Hale, B, *Spider Woman: A Life* (Vintage, 2021).
Hale, B, The Emma Barnett Show (*BBC Radio 5*, 11 June 2019).
Hall, M, 'Judicial Impact' in L Epstein and S Lindquist, *Oxford Handbook of US Judicial Behaviour* (OUP, 2017).
Hanretty, C, 'The celebrity judges of the UKSC?' (Medium, 19 February 2016) available at medium.com/@chrishanretty/the-celebrity-judges-of-the-uksc-7ab33eacb7bf.
Hanretty, C, *A Court of Specialists* (OUP, 2020).
Harlow, C and Rawlings, R, *Law and Administration*, 3rd edn (CUP, 2009).
Hausegger, L and Haynie, S, 'Judicial Decisionmaking and the Use of Panels in the Canadian Supreme Court and the South African Appellate Division' (2003) 37(3) *Law and Society Review* 635.
Hayes, J, 'Discrimination by legal design? UK Supreme Court in Mencap v Tomlinson-Blake finds care workers are not protected by minimum wage law for sleep-in shifts' (2022) 51(3) *Industrial Law Journal* 696.
Haynie, S, 'Paradise Lost: Politicisation of the Philippines supreme court in the post Marcos era' (1998) 22(4) *Asian Studies Review* 459.
Hazell, R, 'Judicial Independence and accountability in the UK have both emerged stronger as a result of the Constitutional Reform Act' [2015] *Public Law* 198.
Hickman, T, 'Bill of Rights Reform and the Case for Going Beyond the Declaration of Incompatibility Model' [2015] *NZLR* 35.
HM Courts and Tribunals, 'The structure of the courts', available at: www.judiciary.uk/wp-content/uploads/2021/07/courts-structure-0715.pdf.
Ho, D and Morse, M, 'New Measurement Technologies: A Review and Application to Nuremberg and Justice Jackson' in L Epstein and S Lindquist, *The Oxford Handbook of US Judicial Behaviour* (OUP, 2017).
Hodder-Williams, R, 'Six Notions of "Political" and the United States Supreme Court' (1992) 22 *British Journal of Political Science* 1.
Hoffmann, L, 'Language and Lawyers' (2018) 134 *Law Quarterly Review* 553.

Hogan, G, 'Should Judges Be Neutral?' (2021) 72 *NILQ* 63.

Holmes, J and Rovet, E, 'The Ontario Court of Appeal: Some Observations on Judicial Behaviour' (1969) 7(1) *Osgoode Hall Law Journal* 31.

Hope, D, *House of Lords 1996–2009: Lord Hope's Diaries* (Avizandum, 2018).

Hope, D, *UK Supreme Court 2009–2015: Lord Hope's Diaries* (Avizandum, 2019).

Horne, A, 'Has the UK Supreme Court Reformed Itself?' (*Prospect*, 5 August 2021).

Hume, D, *Enquiries Concerning the Human Understanding and Concerning the Principles of Morals*, 2nd edn (reprod. Selby-Begge, 1892).

Hunter, R and Rackley, E, 'Feminist Judgments on the UK Supreme Court' (2020) 32(1) *Canadian Journal of Women and the Law* 85.

Hunter, R and Rackley, E, 'Judicial Leadership on the UK Supreme Court' 38(2) *Legal Studies* 191.

Hunter, R and Rackley, E, 'Lady Hale: A Feminist Towering Judge' in R Abeyratne and I Porat, *Towering Judges: A Comparative Study of Constitutional Judges* (CUP, 2021).

Hunter, R, 'More than Just a Different Face? Judicial Diversity and Decision-making' (2015) 68 *Current Legal Problems* 119.

Hunter, R, Anleu, S and Mack, K, 'Judging in lower courts: conventional, procedural, therapeutic and feminist approaches' (2016) 12(3) *International Journal of Law in Context* 337.

Hunter, R, McGlynn, C and Rackley, E (eds), *Feminist Judgments: From Theory to Practice* (Hart Publishing, 2010).

Hutchinson, A, 'Judges and Politics: An Essay from Canada' (2004) 24 *Legal Studies* 275.

Hutt, D, 'Measuring judicial and popular deliberation: a critical comparison' (2018) 16(4) *IJCL* 1121.

Hyland, R, 'Should Judges Tell Us What They Think?' in E Häcker and W Ernst (eds), *Collective Judging in Comparative Perspective* (Intersentia, 2020).

Iaryczower, M and Katz, G, 'More than Politics: Ability and Ideology in the British Appellate Committee' (2016) 32(1) *Journal of Law, Economics and Organizations* 61.

Johnson, S and Songer, D, 'Judge gender and the voting behavior of justices on two North American Supreme Courts' (2009) 30(3) *Justice System Journal* 265.

Johnson, S, Songer, D and Jilani, N, 'Judge gender, critical mass, and decision making in the appellate courts of Canada' (2011) 32(3) *Journal of Women, Politics & Policy* 237.

Johnson, T, Wahlbeck, P and Spriggs, J, 'The Influence of Oral Arguments on the US Supreme Court' (2006) 100 *American Political Science Review* 99.

Joseph, K and Sumption, J, *Equality* (John Murray, 1979).

Jost, J, Federico, C and Napier, J, 'Political Ideology: Its Structure, Functions and Elective Affinities' (2009) 60 *Annual Review of Psychology* 307.

Judicial Power Project, *50 Problematic Cases*, available at judicialpowerproject.org.uk/50-problematic-cases/.

JUSTICE, 'Increasing Judicial Diversity', April 2017, at justice.org.uk/wp-content/uploads/2017/04/JUSTICE-Increasing-judicial-diversity-report-2017-web.pdf.

Kavanagh, A, *Constitutional Review Under the UK Human Rights Act* (CUP, 2009).

Kennedy, D, 'The Political Significance of the Structure of the Law School Curriculum' (1983) 14 *Seton Hall Law Review* 1.

Kirby, M, 'A Darwinian Reflection on Judicial Values' in J Lee (ed), *From House of Lords to Supreme Court: Judges, Jurists and the Process of Judging* (Hart Publishing, 2011).

Kirkham, R and O'Loughlin, E, 'A Content Analysis of Judicial Decision-Making' in N Creutzfeldt, M Mason and K McConnachie, *Routledge Handbook of Socio-Legal Methods* (Routledge, 2020).

Kirkham, R, 'JR55, judicial strategy and the limits of textual reasoning' [2017] *PL* 46.

Klein, D, 'Law in Judicial Decision-Making' in L Epstein and S Lindquist, *Oxford Handbook of US Judicial Behaviour* (OUP, 2017).

Koopmans, T, *Courts and Political Institutions: A Comparative View* (CUP, 2003).

Kritzer, H and Silbey, S (eds), *Litigation: Do the 'Haves' Still Come Out Ahead?* (Stanford, 2003).

Kumm, M, 'On the Representativeness of Constitutional Courts' in C Landfried (ed), *Judicial Power: How Constitutional Courts Affect Political Transformations* (CUP, 2019).

Laleng, P, 'Winners and Losers in the Court of Appeal: An Empirical Study of Personal Injury Cases, 2002–16' (2018) *JPIL* 36.

Langen, N 'Under Lord Reed, the Supreme Court has Retreated into itself' (*The Justice Gap*, 27 July 2021).

Laponce, J, *Left and right: the topography of political perceptions* (Toronto, 1981).

Law in Action, 'The Supreme Court' (*BBC Radio 4*, 26 February 2019).

Le Sueur, A, 'Developing mechanisms for judicial accountability in the UK' (2004) 24 *Legal Studies* 73.

Lee, J, 'The Judicial Individuality of Lord Sumption' (2017) 31 *UNSW Law Journal* 862.

Lee, J, 'Against All Odds: Numbers Sitting in the UK Supreme Court and Really, Really Important Cases' in P Daly (ed), *Apex Courts and the Common Law* (Toronto, 2019).

Lee, J, 'Fides et ratio: Precedent in the early jurisprudence of the UK Supreme Court' (2015) 21(1) *European Journal of Current Legal Issues*.

Lee, J, 'Judging Reformers and Reforming Judges' (2019) 21 *European Journal of Law Reform* 15.

Lee, J, 'The Supreme Court, Vicarious Liability and the Grand Old Duke of York' (2020) 136 *LQR* 553.

Lee, S and Lee, J, 'Humility in the Supreme Court' (2015) 16(2) *King's LJ* 165.

Lee, S, *Judging Judges* (Faber & Faber, 1988).

Lewis, D, 'Empirical Studies of African High Courts: An Overview' in N Garoupa, R Gill and B Tiede (eds), *High Courts in Global Perspective: Evidence, Methodologies, and Findings* (UVA Press, 2021).

Lindquist, S and Cross, F, *Measuring Judicial Activism* (OUP, 2009).

Brown, S, 'In praise of dissenting judgments' (*Prospect*, 28 May 2020).

Loughlin, M, 'What would John Griffith have made of Jonathan Sumption's Reith Lectures?' (2019) 90(4) *Political Quarterly* 785.

Lübbe-Wolff, G, 'Why is the German Federal Constitutional Court a Deliberative Court?' in B Häcker and W Ernst (eds), *Collective Judging in Comparative Perspective* (Intersentia, 2020).

Mack, M and Anleu, S, 'Performing Impartiality: Judicial Demeanor and Legitimacy' (2010) 35(1) *Law and Social Inquiry* 137.

Macnair, M, 'Can Judges Be Trusted with the Common Law?' in R Ekins and G Gee, *Judicial Power and the Left* (Policy Exchange, 2018).

MacQueen, H, 'Alan Ferguson Rodger', *Biographical Memoirs of Fellows of the British Academy XII* (2013).

Malleson, K, 'Safeguarding Judicial Impartiality' (2002) 22 *Legal Studies* 53.

Malleson, K, *The New Judiciary: The Effects of Activism and Expansion* (Routledge, 1999).

Mallory, C and Tyrrell, H, 'Discretionary space and Declarations of Incompatibility' (2021) 32(3) *Kings Law Journal* 466.

Mark, A and Zilis, M, 'Blurring Institutional Boundaries: Judges' Perceptions of Threats to Judicial Independence' (2018) 6(2) *Journal of Law and Courts* 333.

Maroney, T, 'The Persistent Cultural Script of Judicial Dispassion' (2011) 99 *California Law Review* 629.

Martin, A, Quinn, K and Epstein, L, 'The Median Justice on the United States Supreme Court' (2004–05) 83 *North Carolina Law Review* 1275.

McBride, N, *The Humanity of Private Law, Part II* (Hart Publishing, 2020).

McCall, M and McCall, M, 'How far does the gender gap extend? Decision making on state supreme courts in Fourth Amendment cases, 1980–2000' (2007) 44(1) *Social Science Journal* 67.

McCormick, P, 'Party Capability Theory and Appellate Success in the Supreme Court of Canada, 1949–1992' (1993) 26(3) *Canadian Journal of Political Science* 523.

McFarlane, E, 'Consensus and Unanimity at the Supreme Court of Canada' (2010) 52 *Supreme Court Law Review* 379.

McLauchlan, D, 'Continuity, not change, in contract interpretation?' (2017) 133 *LQR* 546.

McLauchlan, D, 'The lingering confusion and uncertainty in the law of contract interpretation' (2015) *LMCLQ* 406.

McNeilly, K, 'Human Rights, Gender Equality and the Judge's Toolbox' in B Dickson and C McCormick (eds), *The Judicial Mind: A Festschrift for Lord Kerr of Tonaghmore* (Hart Publishing, 2021).

Mediano, A and Carrasco, D, 'Ideology beyond Partisanship: The Behavior of Judges on Freedom of Information Cases in Chile' (2019) 36 *Government Information Quarterly* 61.

Megarry, R, 'The Authority of the Central London and High Trees Case' (1948) *LQR* 29.
Megarry, R, *Miscellany-at-Law* (Stevens & Sons, 1955).
Ministry of Justice, 'Judicial Diversity Statistics 2019', www.judiciary.uk/wp-content/uploads/2019/07/Judicial-Diversity-Statistics-2019.pdf.
Mistry, H, 'A Performative Theory of Judicial Dissent' (2023) 86(3) *MLR* 729.
Monaghan, C, 'Returning to Bancoult: New Perspectives' [2022] *Judicial Review* 337.
Monteith, K et al, 'Racial Bias and the Bench' (Centre on the Dynamics of Ethnicity, University of Manchester, November 2022).
Montrose, J, 'The Ratio Decidendi of a Case' (1957) 20(6) *MLR* 587.
Moorhead, R, 'The Passive Arbiter: Litigants in Person and the Challenge to Neutrality' (2007) 16(3) *Social and Legal Studies* 405.
Moran, L, 'In Conversation with Lord Justice Etherton: judicial legitimacy, diversity and the representation of judicial authority' [2010] *PL* 662.
Morgan, J, 'Nonfeasance and the end of policy? Reflections on the revolution in public authority liability' (2019) 35(1) *Public Negligence* 32.
Morón, L, 'Presumptions of Legislative Intent in R (Coughlan) v Minister for the Cabinet Office' (2023) 86(3) *MLR* 801.
Morris, J, The Authority of the Central London and High Trees Case' (1948) *LQR* 28.
Morrison, F, *Courts and the Political Process in England* (Sage, 1973).
Moses, A, 'Hitting the Balls out of Court: Are Judges Stepping Over the Line?' (Creaney Memorial Lecture, 24 February 2014).
Mulcahy, L, 'The Possibilities and Desirability of Mediator Neutrality: Towards an Ethic of Partiality' (2001) 10(4) *Social & Legal Studies* 506.
Muro, S et al, 'Testing Representational Advantage in the Argentine Supreme Court' (2018) 6(1) *Journal of Law and Courts.*
Nabi, Z, 'The Dynamics of Judicial Review Litigation' (Judicial Review Trends and Forecasts, Public Law Project Annual Conference 2020).
Nagel, S, 'Testing Relationships between Judicial Characteristics and Judicial Decision-Making' (1962) 15(3) *Western Political Quarterly* 425.
Nelson, G, *Pathways to the US Supreme Court* (Macmillan, 2013).
Neuberger, D and Riddell, P, *The Power of Judges* (Haus Curiosities, 2018).
Neuberger, D, 'Judge not, that ye be not judged': Judging Judicial Decision-Making' (2016) 6 *UK Supreme Court Yearbook* 13.
Neuberger, D, 'Lord Toulson RIP' (28 June 2017), www.supremecourt.uk/news/lord-toulson-rip.html.
Neuberger, D, 'On the Bench with Brenda' in R Hunter and E Rackley (eds), *Justice for Everyone: the Jurisprudence and Legal Lives of Brenda Hale* (CUP, 2022).
Neuberger, D, BBC World News (*HardTALK*, 30 January 2018).
Nicol, D, 'Supreme Court Against the People' (UK Constitutional Law Blog, 25 September 2019).
Nolan, D and Plunkett, J, 'Keeping Negligence Simple' (2022) 138 *LQR* 175.
Oliver, D, 'The Lord Chancellor as the Head of the Judiciary' in L Blom-Cooper, B Dickson and G Drewry (eds), *The Judicial House of Lords: 1876–2009* (OUP, 2009).
Ostberg, C, Wetstein, E and Ducat, C, 'Attitudinal Dimensions of Supreme Court Decision Making in Canada: The Lamer Court, 1991–1995' (2002) 55(1) *Political Research Quarterly* 235.
Parikh, S, 'Empirical Studies of Judicial Behavior and Decision-Making on Indian Courts' in N Garoupa, R Gill and B Tiede (eds), *High Courts in Global Perspective: Evidence, Methodologies, and Findings* (UVA Press, 2021).
Paterson, A, 'Assessing Lady Hale's impact on the UK's final appeal courts' in R Hunter and E Rackley (eds), *Justice for Everyone: the Jurisprudence and Legal Lives of Brenda Hale* (CUP, 2022).
Paterson, A, 'Presidency and the Supreme Court: Lord Neuberger's Legacy' (UCL Judicial Institute, 2 December 2019).
Paterson, A, *Final Judgment: The Last Law Lords and the Supreme Court* (Hart Publishing, 2013).
Paterson, A, *The Law Lords* (Palgrave Macmillan, 1982).

Peck, S, 'A Behavioural Approach to the Judicial Process: Scalogram Analysis' (1967) 5(1) *Osgoode Hall Law Journal* 1.
Pellegrina, D, Escresa, L and Garoupa, N, 'Measuring Judicial Ideal Points in New Democracies: the case of the Philippines (2014) 1(1) *Asian Journal of Law and Society* 125.
Petrie, N, 'Indications of Inconsistency' (2019) 78 *CLJ* 612.
Phillips, N 'Terrorism and Human Rights' (2006) 2(2) *High Court Quarterly Review* 61.
Phillips, N, 'Strasbourg Has Spoken' in A Burrows, D Johnston and R Zimmerman (eds), *Judge and Jurist: Essays in Memory of Lord Rodger of Earlsferry* (OUP, 2013).
Pinello, D, *Gay Rights and American Law* (CUP, 2003).
Pinelo, D, 'Linking Party to Judicial Ideology in American Courts: A Meta-Analysis' (1999) 20 *Justice System Journal* 219.
Poole, T and Shah, S, 'The Law Lords and Human Rights' (2011) 74 *MLR* 79.
Pócza, K (ed), *Constitutional Review in Central and Eastern Europe* (Routledge, 2024).
Pócza, K (ed), *Constitutional Politics and the Judiciary: Decision-making in Central and Eastern Europe* (Routledge, 2019).
Posner, E, *How Judges Think* (Harvard, 2008).
Potter, M, 'Do the Media Influence the Judiciary?', Foundation for Law, Media and Society, www.fljs.org/sites/www.fljs.org/files/publications/Potter_PB.pdf.
Powell, F and Needleman, S, 'How Radical an Instrument is Section 3 of the Human Rights Act 1998?' (UK Constitutional Law Association Blog, 24 March 2021).
Pritchett, C, *Civil Liberties and the Vinson Court* (Chicago, 1954).
Rachlinski, J and Johnson, S, 'Does Unconscious Racial Bias Affect Trial Judges?' (2009) 84 *Notre Dame Law Review* 1195.
Rackley, E, 'Judicial diversity, the woman judge, and fairy tale endings' (2007) 27(1) *Legal Studies* 74.
Rackley, E, 'Representations of the (Woman) Judge: Hercules, the Little Mermaid and the Vain and Naked Emperor' 22(4) *Legal Studies* 602.
Rackley, E, 'When Hercules met the happy prince: re-imagining the judge' (2005) 12 *Texas Wesleyan Law Review* 213.
Ramseyer, J and Rasmusen, E, 'Why are Japanese judges so conservative in politically charged cases?' 95 *American Political Science Review* 331.
Reed, R, 'Collective Judging in the UK Supreme Court' in B Häcker and W Ernst, *Collective Judging in Comparative Perspective* (Intersentia, 2020).
Reed, R, 'Foreword' in B Dickson and C McCormick (eds), *The Judicial Mind: A Festschrift for Lord Kerr of Tonaghmore* (Hart Publishing, 2021) viii.
Reed, R, 'The Form and Language of Lord Rodger's Judgments' in A Burrows, D Johnston and R Zimmerman, *Judge and Jurist: Essays in Memory of Lord Rodger of Earlsferry* (OUP, 2013).
Richards, A, 'Twitter joke and Lord Judge-made law – without the ECHR bits' (personal website, 9 December 2013): alrich.wordpress.com/2013/12/09/lord-judge-lecture-echr-human-rights-act/.
Ritenhouse, D, 'What's Orientation Got to Do With It? The Best Interest of the Child Standard and Legal Bias against Gay and Lesbian Parents' (2011) 15 *Poverty* 309.
Robertson, D, 'Judicial Ideology in the House of Lords: A Jurimetric Analysis' (1982) 12(1) *British Journal of Political Science* 1.
Robertson, D, *Judicial Discretion in the House of Lords* (Clarendon, 1998).
Rodger, A, 'A time for everything under law: some reflections on retrospectivity' (2005) 121 *LQR* 57.
Rosenberg, G, 'Protecting Privilege: The Historic Role of the U.S. Supreme Court and the Great Progressive Misunderstanding' in R Ekins and G Gee, *Judicial Power and the Left* (Policy Exchange, 2018).
Rosenfeld, M, 'Judicial Politics versus Ordinary Politics' in C Landfried (ed), *Judicial Power: How Constitutional Courts Affect Political Transformations* (CUP, 2019).
Ross, A, *On Law and Justice* (California Press, 1959).
Roux, T, *The Politics of Principle: the First South African Constitutional Court, 1995–2005* (CUP, 2013).
Rozenberg, J, 'The celebrity threesome case risks undermining the law' *The Guardian* (19 May 2016).
Rozenberg, J, *Enemies of the People? How Judges Shape Society* (Bristol, 2020).

Ryan, S, 'The Challenges of Researching African High Court Opinions' 32(4) *Legal References Services Quarterly* 294.
Ryder, E and Hardy, S, *Judicial Leadership* (OUP, 2019).
Sales, P 'Modern Statutory Interpretation' (2017) 38(2) *SLR* 125.
Sales, P, 'Legalism in constitutional law: judging in democracy' [2018] *PL* 687.
Sales, P, 'Reflections on legal life', *Counsel*, April 2020.
Salzberger, E and Fenn, F, 'Judicial Independence: Some Evidence from the English Court of Appeal' (1999) 42(2) *Journal of Law and Economics* 831.
Schubert, G, 'Opinion Agreement Among High Court Justices in Australia' (1968) 4 *Australia and New Zealand Journal of Sociology* 2.
Schubert, G, 'Political Ideology on the High Court' (1968) 3(1) *Politics* 21.
Schubert, G, *Quantitative Analysis of Judicial Behaviour* (The Free Press, 1959).
Schubert, G, *The Judicial Mind: Attitudes and Ideologies of Supreme Court Justices* (Northwestern, 1965).
Schulz, U and Shaw, G (eds), *Gender and Judging* (Hart Publishing, 2013).
Schwartz, A, 'International Judges on Constitutional Courts: Cautionary Evidence from Post-Conflict Bosnia' (2019) 44(1) *and Social Enquiry* 1.
Sedley, S, 'Judicial politics' (2012) 34(4) *London Review of Books* 15.
Segal, A, Songer, D and Cameron, M, 'Decision Making on the US Courts of Appeals' in L Epstein, *Contemplating Courts* (CQ Press, 1995).
Segal, E and Spaeth, H, 'The Influence of Stare Decisis on the Votes of United States Supreme Court Justices' (1996) 40(4) *American Journal of Political Science* 971.
Segal, E and Spaeth, H, *The Supreme Court and the Attitudinal Model Revisited* (CUP, 2002).
Segal, S, Cover, A and Albert, D, 'Ideological Values and the Votes of U.S. Supreme Court Justices' (1989) 83(2) *American Political Science Review* 557.
Shapiro, M, 'Judicial Power and Democracy' in C Landfried (ed), *Judicial Power: How Constitutional Courts Affect Political Transformations* (CUP, 2019).
Sheehan, R, Mishler, W and Songer, D, 'Ideology, Status, and the Differential Success of Different Parties before the Supreme Court' (1992) 86 *American Political Science Review* 464.
Shetreet, S and McCormack, W, *The Culture of Judicial Independence in a Globalised World* (Brill, 2016).
Simpson, A, 'The Ratio Decidendi of a Case' (1958) 21(2) *MLR* 155.
Skiple, J et al, 'Supreme Court Justices' Economic Behaviour: A Multilevel Model Analysis' (2016) 13(1) *Scandinavian Political Studies* 73.
Smyth, R, 'Empirical Studies of Judicial Behavior and Decision-Making in Australian and New Zealand Courts' in N Garoupa, R Gill and B Tiede (eds), *High Courts in Global Perspective: Evidence, Methodologies, and Findings* (UVA Press, 2021).
Smyth, R, 'Explaining Voting Patterns on the Latham High Court 1935–50' (2002) 26 *Melbourne University Law Review* 8.
Songer, D and Lindquist, S, 'Not the Whole Story: The Impact of Justices' Values on Supreme Court Decision Making' (1996) 40(4) *American Journal of Political Science* 1049.
Songer, D and Sheehan, R 'Who Wins on Appeal? Upperdogs and Underdogs on the United States Courts of Appeals' (1992) 36 *American Journal of Political Science* 235.
Songer, D, Kuersten, A and Kaheny, E, 'Why the Haves Don't Always Come Out Ahead: Repeat Players Meet Amici Curiae for the Disadvantaged' (2000) 53(3) *Political Research Quarterly* 537.
Sotomayor, S, Talk at University of Houston (26 January 2018).
Spaeth, H, 'The Attitudinal Model' in Epstein L (ed) *Contemplating Courts* (CQ Press, 1995).
Sprague, J, *Voting Patterns of the United States Supreme Court: Cases in Federalism, 1889–1959* (Bobbs-Merrill, 1968).
Stanton, K, 'Comparative Law in the House of Lords and Supreme Court' (2013) 42 *Common Law World Review* 269.
Stanton, K, 'Use of Scholarship by the House of Lords in Tort Cases' in J Lee (ed) *From House of Lords to Supreme Court* (Hart Publishing, 2011).
Stark, S, 'Facing Facts: Judicial Approaches to Section 4 of the Human Rights Act 1998' (2017) *LQR* 631.

Stark, S, 'Section 4 of the Human Rights Act 1998: Still Standing or Standing Still?' (UK Constitutional Law Association Blog, 16 November 2022).
Steury, E and Frank, N, 'Gender Bias and Pretrial Release: More Pieces of the Puzzle' (1990) 18 *Journal of Criminal Justice* 417.
Stevens, R, 'Unpacking the Judges' (1993) 46 *CLP* 1.
Stevens, R, *Law and Politics: The House of Lords as a Judicial Body 1800–1976* (Weidenfeld and Nicolson, 1979).
Stevens, R, *The English Judges: Their Role in the Changing Constitution* (Hart Publishing, 2002) 36–37, 45, 141.
Stone, J, 'The Ratio of the Ratio Decidendi' (1959) 22(6) *MLR* 597.
Strother, L, 'Case Salience and the Influence of External Constraints on the Supreme Court' (2019) 7(1) *Journal of Law and Courts* 129.
Summers, R and Eng, S, 'Departing from Precedent' in N MacCormick, R Summers and A Goodhart (eds), *Interpreting Precedents* (Routledge, 1997).
Sumption, J, 'A Response' in N Barber, R Ekins and P Yowell (eds), *Lord Sumption and the Limits of Law* (Hart Publishing, 2016).
Sumption, J, 'Judicial and Political Decision-making: The Uncertain Boundary' 16(4) *Judicial Review* 301.
Sumption, J, 'Law's Expanding Empire' (Reith Lectures, 21 May 2019).
Sumption, J, 'You cannot imprison an entire population' *The Spectator* (17 May 2020).
Sumption, J, *Trials of the State* (Profile Books, 2019).
Sunstein, C, et al, *Are Judges Political?* (Brookings, 2006).
Sutton Trust, 'Elitist Britain 2019' (24 June 2019), available at: www.suttontrust.com/wp-content/uploads/2019/12/Elitist-Britain-2019.pdf.
Swadling, W, 'Legislating in Vain' in A Burrows, D Johnston and R Zimmerman, *Judge and Jurist: Essays in Memory of Lord Rodger of Earlsferry* (OUP, 2013).
Szmer, J, Songer, D and Bowie, J, 'Party Capability and the US Courts of Appeals: Understanding Why the "Haves" Win' (2016) 4(1) *Journal of Law and Courts* 65.
Tamanaha, B, 'The Several Meanings of Politics in Judicial Politics Studies: Why Ideological Influence is not Partisanship' (2012) 61(4) *Emory Law Journal* 759.
Tan, G, 'Children's Rights and the Influence of Lord Sales in the UKSC's Political Constitutionalist Turn' (2022) 26(1) *Edinburgh Law Review* 93.
Tate, N and Handberg, R, 'Time Binding Theory and Theory Building in Personal Attribute Models of Supreme Court Voting Behaviour 1916–1988' (1991) 35 *American Journal of Political Science* 460.
Tate, N and Haynie, S, 'Authoritarianism and Functions of Courts: A time series analysis of the Philippine supreme court' (1993) 27(4) *Law and Society Review* 707.
Tate, N and Sittiwong, P, 'Decision Making in the Canadian Supreme Court: Extending the Personal Attributes Model Across Nations' (1989) 51(4) *The Journal of Politics* 900.
The Express, 'Supreme Court justices expressed strident disbelief over Brexit vote, Tory peer claims' (27 September 2019).
The Guardian, 'How Lady Hale's spider brooch sent the web into a spin' (28 September 2019).
The Guardian, 'Jonathan Sumption: the brain of Britain' (6 August 2015).
The Guardian, 'Lady Hale: at least half of judiciary should be female' (24 March 2019).
The Guardian, 'Supreme court prorogation hearing: who are the judges?' (17 September 2019).
The Independent, 'Jonathan Sumption: Donnish but deadly' (15 October 2011).
The Spectator, 'Only the judiciary can save the Tories from themselves' (18 September 2019).
The Sun, 'Judges blew their hallowed status with the Supreme Court ruling and will now be fair game for public scrutiny' (24 September 2019).
The Sun, 'The day free speech drowned in a paddling pool of olive oil … outrage at gagging verdict' (20 May 2016).
The Daily Telegraph, 'Lord Sumption: I have observed that lockdown scepticism goes with high levels of education' (4 June 2021).
The Times, 'Rights: how the law lords line up' (25 July 1997).

The Times, 'Seven may be the general's lucky number' (18 January 1999).
Thomas, E, *The Judicial Process* (CUP, 2005).
Thompson, E, *Whigs and Hunters: The Origin of the Black Act* (Allen Lane, 1975).
Thomson Reuters, 'The Importance of Knowing Your Judge' (11 November 2020) legal.thomsonreuters.com/blog/the-importance-of-knowing-your-judge/.
Tomkins, A, 'Why did the Tories retreat from taking on the Supreme Court judges?' *The Herald* (11 August 2021).
Tushnet, M, 'Judicial Leadership' in J Kane, H Patapan and P Hart, *Dispersed Democratic Leadership: Origins, Dynamics and Implications* (OUP, 2009).
Tyree, A, 'The Geometry of Law' (1975) 8 *Victoria University of Wellington Law Review* 403, 419–20.
Tyrrell, H, *Human Rights in the UK and the Influence of Foreign Jurisprudence* (Hart Publishing, 2018).
UK Supreme Court Blog, Interview with Lord Toulson (28 July 2016) available at: ukscblog.com/interview-with-lord-toulson/.
Ulmer, S, 'Dissent Behaviour and the Social Background of Supreme Court Judges' (1970) 32 *Journal of Politics* 580.
Ulmer, S, 'The Analysis of Behavior Patterns on the United States Supreme Court' (1960) 22 *Journal of Politics* 629.
Ura, J, 'Backlash and Legitimation: Macro Political Responses to Supreme Court Decisions' (2014) 58 *American Journal of Political Science* 110.
Vandamme, P and Bello Hutt, D, 'Selecting constitutional judges randomly' (2020) *Swiss Political Science Review* (online, doi:10.1111/spsr.12416).
Vanberg, G, *Politics of Constitutional Review in Germany* (CUP, 2004).
Varuhas, J, 'The Principle of Legality' (2020) 79(3) *CLJ* 578.
Vidal, J and Leaver, C, 'Social Interactions and the Content of Legal Opinions' (2013) 29(1) *Journal of Law, Economics and Organization* 78.
Voeten, E, 'Politics, Behaviour and Institutional Design' in J Christoffersen and M Madsen (eds), *The European Court of Human Rights: Between Law and Politics* (OUP, 2011).
Volcansek, M, 'Judicialisation of Politics or Politicization of the Courts in New Democracies?' in C Landfried (ed), *Judicial Power: How Constitutional Courts Affect Political Transformations* (CUP, 2019).
Walker, R, 'Developing the Common Law: How far is too far?' (2013) 37(1) *Melbourne Law Review* 232.
Waltman, J and Holland, K, *The Political Role of Law Courts in Modern Democracies* (Palgrave Macmillan, 1988).
Weiden, D, 'Judicial Politicization, Ideology, and Activism at the High Courts of the United States, Canada, and Australia' (2011) 64(2) *Political Research Quarterly* 335.
West, R, Meserve, R and Stanovich, K, 'Cognitive sophistication does not attenuate the bias blind spot' (2012) 103 *Journal of Personality and Social Psychology* 506.
White, G, 'Unpacking the Idea of the Judicial Center' (2004–05) 83 *North Carolina Law Review* 1089, 1172.
Whitehouse, L, Bright, S and Dhami, M, 'Improving procedural fairness in housing possession cases' (2019) 38(3) *CJQ* 351.
Woodhouse, D, 'The constitutional and political implications of a United Kingdom Supreme Court' (2004) 24 *Legal Studies* 134.
Woolf, H et al, *De Smith's Judicial Review*, 8th edn (With 4th supplement, 2021).
Wright, R, 'Precedents' (1943) 8(2) *CLJ* 118.
Xin, H and Su, Y, 'Do the Haves Come Out Ahead in Shanghai Courts?' (2013) 10(1) *Journal of Empirical Legal Studies* 120.
YouGov, 'Left-wing vs right-wing: it's complicated', (14 August 2019), yougov.co.uk/topics/politics/articles-reports/2019/08/14/left-wing-vs-right-wing-its-complicated.
Young, A, *Parliamentary Sovereignty and the Human Rights Act* (Hart Publishing, 2009).

INDEX

Please see individual entries for individual judges for information on that judge

www.ingramcontent.com/pod-product-compliance
Ingram Content Group UK Ltd.
Pitfield, Milton Keynes, MK11 3LW, UK
UKHW020244290926
15470UKWH00002B/738

9 781509 97110